T5-AFM-389

The DEMOCRATIC and REPUBLICAN PARTIES
★ ★ ★ ★ in America ★ ★ ★ ★

This bibliography was conceived and compiled from the periodicals database of the American Bibliographical Center by editors at ABC-Clio Information Services.

Susan Kinnell, project coordinator

Lance Klass
Robert de V. Brunkow
Jeffery B. Serena
Suzanne Robitaille Ontiveros

Pamela R. Byrne
Gail Schlachter

The DEMOCRATIC and REPUBLICAN PARTIES
★ ★ ★ ★ in America ★ ★ ★ ★

a historical bibliography

ABC-Clio Information Services

Santa Barbara, California
Oxford, England

Library of Congress Cataloging in Publication Data
Main entry under title:

The Democratic and Republican Parties in America:
a historical bibliography.

    Includes index.
    1. Democratic Party (U.S.)–History–Bibliography.
2. Republican Party (U.S.)–History– Bibliography.
I. ABC-Clio Information Services.
Z7164.P8D45 1983 [JK2261] 016.324273 83-12230
ISBN 0-87436-364-0

Copyright © 1984 by ABC-Clio, Inc.

All rights reserved. No part of this publication may be
reproduced, stored in a retrieval system, or transmitted,
in any form or by any means, electronic, mechanical,
photo-copying, recording, or otherwise, without the prior
written permission of ABC-Clio, Inc.

ABC-Clio Information Services
2040 Alameda Padre Serra, Box 4397
Santa Barbara, California 93103

Clio Press Ltd.
55 St. Thomas Street
Oxford 0X1 1JG, England

Cover design and graphics by Lance Klass
Printed and bound in the United States of America

851133

LIBRARY
ALMA COLLEGE
ALMA, MICHIGAN

ABC-CLIO RESEARCH GUIDES

The ABC-Clio Research Guides are a new generation of annotated bibliographies that provide comprehensive control of the recent journal literature on high-interest topics in history and related social sciences. These publications are created by editor/historians and other subject specialists who examine every article entry in ABC-Clio Information Services' vast history database and select abstracts of all citations published during the past decade that relate to the particular topic of study.

Each entry selected from this database—the largest history database in the world—has been reedited to ensure consistency in treatment and completeness of coverage. The extensive subject profile index (ABC-SPIndex) accompanying each volume has also been reassessed, specifically in terms of the particular subject presented, to allow precise and rapid access to the entries.

The titles in this series are prepared to save researchers, students, and librarians the considerable time and expense usually associated with accessing materials manually or through online searching. ABC-Clio's Research Guides offer unmatched access to significant scholarly articles on the topics of most current interest to historians and social scientists.

ABC-CLIO RESEARCH GUIDES

Gail Schlachter, Editor
Pamela R. Byrne, Executive Editor

1.
World War II from an American Perspective
1982   LC 82-22823   ISBN 0-87436-035-8

5.
Corporate America
1983   LC 83-11232   ISBN 0-87436-362-4

2.
The Jewish Experience in America
1982   LC 82-24480   ISBN 0-87436-034-x

6.
Crime and Punishment in America
1983   LC 83-12248   ISBN 0-87436-363-2

3.
Nuclear America
1983   LC 83-12227   ISBN 0-87436-360-8

7.
The Democratic and Republican Parties
1983   LC 83-12230   ISBN 0-87436-364-0

4.
The Great Depression
1983   LC 83-12234   ISBN 0-87436-361-6

8.
The American Electorate
1983   LC 83-12229   ISBN 0-87436-372-1

CONTENTS

LIST OF ABBREVIATIONS

A.	Author-prepared Abstract	*Illus.*	Illustrated, Illustration
Acad.	Academy, Academie, Academia	*Inst.*	Institute, Institut-.
Agric.	Agriculture, Agricultural	*Int.*	International, Internacional,
AIA	Abstracts in Anthropology		Internationaal, Internationaux,
Akad.	Akademie		Internazionale
Am.	America, American	*J.*	Journal, Journal-prepared Abstract
Ann.	Annals, Annales, Annual, Annali	*Lib.*	Library, Libraries
Anthrop.	Anthropology, Anthropological	*Mag.*	Magazine
Arch.	Archives	*Mus.*	Museum, Musee, Museo
Archaeol.	Archaeology, Archaeological	*Nac.*	Nacional
Art.	Article	*Natl.*	National, Nationale
Assoc.	Association, Associate	*Naz.*	Nazionale
Biblio.	Bibliography, Bibliographical	*Phil.*	Philosophy, Philosophical
Biog.	Biography, Biographical	*Photo.*	Photograph
Bol.	Boletim, Boletin	*Pol.*	Politics, Political, Politique, Politico
Bull.	Bulletin	*Pr.*	Press
c.	century (in index)	*Pres.*	President
ca.	circa	*Pro.*	Proceedings
Can.	Canada, Canadian, Canadien	*Publ.*	Publishing, Publication
Cent.	Century	*Q.*	Quarterly
Coll.	College	*Rev.*	Review, Revue, Revista, Revised
Com.	Committee	*Riv.*	Rivista
Comm.	Commission	*Res.*	Research
Comp.	Compiler	*RSA*	Romanian Scientific Abstracts
DAI	Dissertation Abstracts	*S.*	Staff-prepared Abstract
	International	*Sci.*	Science, Scientific
Dept.	Department	*Secy.*	Secretary
Dir.	Director, Direktor	*Soc.*	Society, Societe, Sociedad,
Econ.	Economy, Econom-.		Societa
Ed.	Editor, Edition	*Sociol.*	Sociology, Sociological
Educ.	Education, Educational	*Tr.*	Transactions
Geneal.	Genealogy, Genealogical,	*Transl.*	Translator, Translation
	Genealogique	*U.*	University, Universi-.
Grad.	Graduate	*US*	United States
Hist.	History, Hist-.	*Vol.*	Volume
IHE	Indice Historico Espanol	*Y.*	Yearbook

INTRODUCTION

"If I could not go to heaven but with a party," wrote Thomas Jefferson, "I would not go there at all." Like the other Founding Fathers, Jefferson believed political parties to be pernicious organizations that institutionalized factionalism to the detriment of consensus and fostered private interest at the expense of the public good. Yet he and other leaders of the New Republic found that parties were a necessary aspect of the nation's political process. In time, parties came to be recognized as positive agencies that formulated and implemented public policy and guarded against the abuse of political authority by officeholders.

To a degree that would have scandalized the nation's architects, political parties have become a significant feature of American life. Indeed, surveys of American history are often periodized according to the fortunes of the various parties. Scholars have created a vast literature on party constituencies, political organizations, and the process of party formation, and the need for bibliographic control of this important body of scholarship is now manifest.

The 1,006 abstracts of articles presented in this volume were drawn from ABC-Clio Information Services' database—the largest history database in the world—which includes abstracts of scholarship from more than 2,000 journals in 42 languages, published in 90 countries.

The article abstracts were selected by the editors, who examined every abstract in the database for 1973-82. This careful selection process has provided thorough coverage of the modern periodical literature on the Democratic and Republican parties, as well as antecedent political organizations and third parties that influenced major-party development. The result far exceeds in breadth of coverage what is obtainable through either an online search of the database or even an intensive manual search using the database's subject index.

The abstracts are organized into five chapters. The variance in size of these chapters represents not editorial predisposition, but rather the amount of scholarship on each chapter's topic published in the journal literature during the decade covered by this volume. The first chapter includes a broad range of topics that do not necessarily fall into one of the time periods covered in the next four chapters.

Access to the article abstracts is provided by ABC-SPIndex—one of the most advanced and comprehensive indexing systems yet developed. ABC-SPIndex affords the user fast, analytical, and pinpoint access by linking together the key subject terms and the chronology of each abstract to form a composite index entry that furnishes a complete subject profile of the journal article. Each set of index terms is rotated so that the complete profile appears in the index under each subject term.

In this way, the number of access points is increased severalfold over conventional hierarchical indexes, and irrelevant materials can be eliminated early in the search process. The explanatory note at the beginning of the subject index provides more information about ABC-SPIndex.

The editors have taken great care to eliminate any inconsistencies that might have appeared in the subject index as a result of combining a decade of scholarship from the database. In addition, cross-references have been added to facilitate fast and accurate searching. This editorial effort insures easy access to the scholarly works summarized in this volume.

1

PARTY POLITICS IN AMERICA

1. Adamany, David W. THE SOURCES OF MONEY: AN OVERVIEW. *Ann. of the Am. Acad. of Pol. and Social Sci. 1976 425: 17-32.* The American system of raising campaign funds does not conform to democratic theory. Money itself has qualities which distinguish it from other kinds of political resources. Few Americans contribute; those that do are disproportionately drawn from the upper socioeconomic classes; and big givers and special interests dominate campaign financing. Equal citizen influence in politics is thwarted by these patterns. Although most individual and group contributions divide along the same class and policy lines as divide the two major parties, there are many switch-givers who seek advantages by giving to either party or both. Contributions tend to flow more readily to executive office candidates, to powerful congressional figures, to incumbents, to close districts, and perhaps to ideological candidates. Wealthy contenders also have an edge. These imbalances diminish vigorous competitive campaigning, which is necessary to alert citizens to their choices in democracy. Sweeping congressional reforms in 1971 and 1974 probably reduce the influence of big contributors and broaden citizen participation through the income tax check-off. But they do not address other failures of the campaign financing system, and they may create new imbalances and inequalities of their own.   J

2. Alvarez, David J. and True, Edmond J. CRITICAL ELECTIONS AND PARTISAN REALIGNMENT: AN URBAN TEST-CASE. *Polity 1973 5(4): 563-576.* Ward-by-ward voting behavior in Hartford, Connecticut, during 1896-1940 indicates that support for the Democrats came from established middle-class, Protestant sectors of society, rather than from realignment of pro-Democratic Party ethnic groups in 1928.

3. Argersinger, Peter H. RELIGIOUS POLITICS AND THE PARTY SYSTEM. *Rev. in Am. Hist. 1979 7(4): 547-552.* Review essay of Paul Kleppner's *The Third Electoral System, 1853-1892: Parties, Voters, and Political Cultures* (Chapel Hill: U. of North Carolina Pr., 1979).

4. Babu, B. Ramesh. NATURE AND FUNCTIONS OF POLITICAL PARTIES IN AMERICA: AN ANALYTICAL SURVEY. *Indian J. of Am. Studies [India] 1976 6(1-2): 1-17.* Discusses characteristics of American political parties and various calls for reform. Suggests that the greatest task facing American political parties today is the resolution of the conflict between the hopes of increasing numbers of independent voters calling for reform, and the large segments of people within the system opposed to reform. 27 notes.   L. V. Eid

5.   Bailey, Thomas A.   WAR-BENT DEMOCRATS?   *Soc. of the Hist. of Am. Foreign Relations Newsletter 1978 9(3): 25-27.* In statistics for ruling political parties in the 19th as well as the 20th century, the Republican Party and the Democratic Party are more equally represented in the tendency toward military hostilities; the components for war seldom are absent in world affairs.

6.   Bartley, Numan V.   VOTERS AND PARTY SYSTEMS: A REVIEW OF THE RECENT LITERATURE.   *Hist. Teacher 1975 8(3): 452-469.* Discusses recent interpretations of political behavior in America. The ordinary voter has been stable in his support for candidates of the major parties, yet party realignments have occurred regularly in American history, usually during periods of crisis as in the 1820's, 1850's, 1890's and 1930's. These realignments have been group processes which crystallized into stable voting patterns once the period of readjustment was over. Presents the possibility that a new realignment has been under way since 1968, characterized by mass awareness of political issues and ideological responses to them. Primary and secondary sources; illus., 27 notes.
P. W. Kennedy

7.   Beck, Paul Allen.   PARTISAN DEALIGNMENT IN THE POSTWAR SOUTH.   *Am. Pol. Sci. Rev. 1977 71(2): 477-496.* This study attempts to explain post-World War II southern electoral politics by examining the party identifications of southerners between 1952 and 1972. Pronounced decreases in Democratic loyalties and increases in Independent leanings appear during this period and constitute a dealignment of the southern electorate. While interregional population exchanges have diluted Democratic strength, their effects are almost counterbalanced by the mobilization of blacks into politics. Instead, the principal source of dealignment is the generational replacement of the native white electorate. Its youngest members, who entered the electorate after World War II, have come to favor political independence increasingly in recent years. This behavior seems partially attributable to a tendency for young native whites in particular to bring their partisan loyalties into line with their attitudes and party images on racial issues. Even so, there are clear signs that the racial question is losing its place as the major determinant of the region's politics. For the future, one can expect a continuation of dealignment politics and little chance of a partisan realignment.   J

8.   Benjamin, Gerald.   PATTERNS IN NEW YORK STATE POLITICS.   *Pro. of the Acad. of Pol. Sci. 1974 31(3): 31-44.* Examines the party system in the state of New York, with special emphasis on voting behavior within the Democratic Party and the Republican Party since World War II.   S

9.   Berry, Jeffrey M.   PUBLIC INTEREST VS. PARTY SYSTEM.   *Society 1980 17(4): 42-48.* Argues that the increasing popularity of public interest groups since the late 1960's poses a threat to an effective and viable party system of politics.

10.   Bigham, Barbara.   PISTOL PACKIN' POLITICIANS.   *Early Am. Life 1977 8(1): 36-38.* Discusses the custom of duelling practiced among American politicians during 1770's-1850's.

11. Bonetto, Gerald M. ALEXIS DE TOCQUEVILLE'S CONCEPT OF POLITICAL PARTIES. *Am. Studies 1981 22(2): 59-79.* Reviews criticisms of Tocqueville's discussion of parties and argues that his analysis was perceptive in a theoretical rather than a descriptive manner. Like many Europeans, Tocqueville agreed that parties were a dangerous and destructive force, but still found some good in them—thereby reflecting emerging American attitudes. Surveys Tocqueville's analysis of political parties and his categorization of party systems, in particular his distinctions between "great" and "small" parties. Tocqueville assumed that an age of democracy had emerged. Based largely on Tocqueville's writings and secondary sources; 22 notes. J. A. Andrew III

12. Brady, David W. and Murray, Richard W. THE AMERICAN PARTY SYSTEM IN PERSPECTIVE. *Current Hist. 1974 67(395): 1-4, 36.* Reviews history of the two-party system and claims it is a dynamic and uncertain element in the political structure. One of seven articles on the American two-party system. S

13. Brady, David W. CONGRESSIONAL PARTY REALIGNMENT AND TRANSFORMATIONS OF PUBLIC POLICY IN THREE REALIGNMENT ERAS. *Am. J. of Pol. Sci. 1982 26(2): 333-360.* This study focuses on the relationship between cross-cutting issues, electoral realignments, the U.S. House and public policy changes during the Civil War, 1890's and New Deal realignments. The results show that in each case the policy changes are voted through by a partisan "new" majority party. However, unlike other studies which focus on single realignments, the comparative approach allows us to distinguish important differences between realignments. The major difference is that the Civil War and 1890's realignments were more polarized than was the New Deal realignment, and the extent of party structuring of issue dimensions was greater. J

14. Brady, David W. and Bullock, Charles S., III. IS THERE A CONSERVATIVE COALITION IN THE HOUSE? *J. of Pol. 1980 42(2): 549-559.* The "Conservative Coalition" meets none of the process or organizational criteria for a coalition, but is based on the shared policy objectives of southern Democrats and Republicans. It emerged to fight federal support for organized labor (1937-44) and later opposed liberal legislation concerning civil liberties (1937-38, 1943-present), social welfare (1943-present), agricultural assistance (1943-48, 1951-52), and foreign policy (1957-present). It has been most successful when northern Democrats were few and lacked cohesion. 3 tables, 15 notes.

A. W. Novitsky

15. Brady, David W. and Althoff, Phillip. PARTY VOTING IN THE U.S. HOUSE OF REPRESENTATIVES, 1890-1910: ELEMENTS OF A RESPONSIBLE PARTY SYSTEM. *J. of Pol. 1974 36(3): 753-775.* Examines the relationships among sectionalism, industrialization, and centralized leadership in the House. Concludes that "the constituency bases of the legislative parties were polarized on both an agricultural-industrial continuum and on sectional lines, and that the evolution of the leadership structure centered power in a small group of leaders." Party voting took place at a high level on both procedural and substantive issues. Unlike the contemporary House, congressional parties of the 1890-1910 period "exhibited . . . important characteristics of a responsible party system." 7 tables, fig., 26 notes. A. R. Stoesen

16.   Bridges, Amy Beth.   ANOTHER LOOK AT PLUTOCRACY AND POLITICS IN ANTEBELLUM NEW YORK CITY.   *Pol. Sci. Q. 1982 97(1): 57-71.* While it is commonly thought that men of wealth abandoned their involvement in local politics in New York City, city politics in that period makes most sense when the political activity of those wealthy men is taken into account. Discusses the beginnings of class politics in the 1850's and describes the long struggle that began in those years between reformer and party boss.   Based on newspapers and secondary sources; 60 notes.   L. J. Klass

17.   Broh, C. Anthony.   UTILITY THEORY AND PARTISAN DECISION-MAKING: CUMULATIVE VOTING IN ILLINOIS.   *Social Sci. Q. 1974 55(1): 65-76.* "Three representatives are elected from each of Illinois' 59 districts in which each voter has three votes that may be distributed 3-0, 1 1/2-1 1/2, or 1-1-1 among the candidates. The author looks at the utility of a one-candidate, two-candidate or three-candidate partisan strategy at different levels of electoral support. Above 'critical points' of electoral support, the utility of partisan strategies varies with the number of nominees. Broh finds a resemblance of the utility theory predictions to the actual behavior of political parties in Illinois and makes a case for the use of utility theory to predict political behavior."   J

18.   Burnham, Walter Dean.   AMERICAN POLITICS IN THE 1980S. *Dissent 1980 27(2): 149-160.* Discusses the conservative revival of 1980, immediate pressures in foreign relations over Iran and Afghanistan, and Republican and Democratic party politics since 1932.

19.   Burstein, Paul.   PARTY BALANCE, REPLACEMENT OF LEGISLATORS, AND FEDERAL GOVERNMENT EXPENDITURES, 1941-1976. *Western Pol. Q. 1979 32(2): 203-208.* Considerable work has shown that political variables, such as change in the party balance, have little impact on political outputs in many circumstances, once social and economic variables have been taken into account. Critics of past work have argued that research would discover "political" effects if it were carefully designed. The work reported here was designed to enhance the probability that political effects would be discovered. Two questions were asked: Do changes in the party balance in Congress, or changes in party control of Congress or the presidency, lead to changes in federal government expenditures in highly aggregated functional areas such as health, agriculture, defense, etc.? Do changes in the rate at which legislators are replaced, regardless of party, lead to such changes in spending? Time series analysis of data for the period 1941-76 indicates that the answer to both questions is no.   J

20.   Burton, Agnes Rose.   POLITICAL PARTIES: EFFECT ON THE PRESIDENCY.   *Presidential Studies Q. 1981 11(2): 289-298.* Suggests that political parties are necessary for a republican form of government and that they act as a constraint on the president. Discusses the purpose of parties and their roles in the election process and in Congress to support this thesis. Considers possble infringements on party functions of the media and interest groups. Studies the relationship of the Jefferson and Eisenhower presidencies with political parties. Primary sources; 46 notes.   A. Drysdale

21. Busch, Ronald J. and Abravanel, Martin D. THE URBAN PARTY ORGANIZATION AS AN OPPORTUNITY STRUCTURE: RACE AND PARTY DIFFERENCES AMONG CLEVELAND WARD LEADERS. *Western Pol. Q. 1976 29(1): 59-85.* Viewing the political party as an opportunity structure, this study examines race and party differences among ward leaders in a major American city. When communications patterns, recruitment incentives, and retention incentives are examined, race and party differences in basic political orientations emerge. The findings suggest that Black ward leaders tend to be more constituency oriented while White ward leaders tend to be more leader oriented. Moreover, the party differences indicate that minority party durability may be influenced by incentives originating in other political jurisdictions. These findings further suggest that Black ward leaders, like their White ethnic predecessors, may use the party as a vehicle for upward mobility, especially when the opportunities in the private sector are limited. In addition to the party differences, so often identified in this genre of literature, then, race of the ward leader furthers our understanding of the incentives underlying partisan involvement in an urban setting.　　　　J

22. Ceaser, James W. POLITICAL PARTIES AND PRESIDENTIAL AMBITION. *J. of Pol. 1978 40(3): 708-739.* The recent decline in the role of parties during presidential elections is a direct result of decisions by party commissions and state legislatures to open the nomination process. Both the authors of *The Federalist Papers* and the originators of permanent party competition (notably Martin Van Buren) sought electoral processes which regulated candidate behavior. On the contrary, Populist and Progressive movements (and Woodrow Wilson) sought a system which would elevate a dynamic leader above his party. A balance between these positions maintained the mixed system of candidate-oriented primaries and organization-dominated selection procedures until the post-1968 Democratic Party reforms. Primary and secondary sources; 59 notes.

A. W. Novitsky

23. Christman, Roy B. PARTY REFORM LITERATURE: A REVIEW ESSAY. *Western Pol. Q. 1982 35(3): 442-448.* Reviews seven works on party reform in the Democratic and Republican parties. Both parties, though they have become weaker as institutions, have survived, partly because of party reforms. Nevertheless, both parties play a diminished role in campaigning, recruiting, influencing voting, and fund raising. The reforms are a necessary but inadequate response to the lack of influence of the parties.　　　　J. Powell

24. Cohen, Steven Martin and Kapsis, Robert E. RELIGION, ETHNICITY, AND PARTY AFFILIATION IN THE U.S.: EVIDENCE FROM POOLED ELECTORAL SURVEYS, 1968-72. *Social Forces 1977 56(2): 637-653.* By analyzing a white Christian subsample of pooled national survey data collected in 1968, 1970, and 1972 (subsample's n = 4,142), we try to determine whether ethnicity has a direct effect on party identification net of parental party identification. In so doing, we raise a number of subsidiary issues: (1) how best to measure ethnicity, (2) the need to distinguish between ethnically identified and ethnically assimilated respondents, and (3) possible regional variation in the impact of ethnicity. We find that religion alone (Protestant versus Catholic) is an adequate measure of ethnicity for this analysis, there being little intrareligious variation in party identification by national origin. Second, religion's effect is largely limited

to the ethnically identified. Third, its effect holds up when controlling for parental party identification and SES. Fourth, regional variation in the impact of religion is understood as largely flowing from regional variations in the distribution of Catholics.   J

25.   Cole, Cheryl L.   CHINESE EXCLUSION: THE CAPITALIST PER-SPECTIVE OF THE *SACRAMENTO UNION,* 1850-1882.   *California Hist. 1978 57(1): 8-31.* Traces the position of the *Sacramento Union* on the issue of Chinese exclusion. As a conservative Republican newspaper, the *Union* promoted construction of the transcontinental railroad and development of business enterprise in the state. It also defended the economic contributions of Chinese immigrants in their work on the railroad, their payment of the Foreign Miners Tax (which by 1870 accounted for half the state's total income), and their employment in occupations which did not compete with white workers, such as laundries and delta reclamation. The *Union* supported the anticipated trade with China. It condemned anti-Chinese agitation as the prejudiced view of Democratic Irish labor agitators. After a change in owners in 1875 and takeover by the Central Pacific Railroad, the *Union* came to support Chinese exclusion as a tactic of Republican political survival. The arguments centered, however, on the inability of the Chinese to assimilate culturally or socially, an argument that contributed to the congressional vote for the Chinese Exclusion Act (1882). The *Union* position 1850-80 contrasts with the more widely used San Francisco newspapers which were Democratic and opposed to Chinese immigration. Based on contemporary and secondary published works; illus., photos, 77 notes.   A. Hoffman

26.   Costain, Anne N.   AN ANALYSIS OF VOTING IN AMERICAN NA-TIONAL NOMINATING CONVENTIONS.   *Am. Pol. Q. 1978 6(1): 95-120.* Statistically analyzes the response of US political parties to an electoral imperative in their selection of presidential nominees. Discusses whether their choices are made in relation to a balance of issue orientation and electoral interests within the party. Applies the method to both Democratic and Republican conventions. Concludes: "1) There has been a significant increase in the frequency of ideological voting in the selection of presidential nominees; and 2) the major change has occurred in the Democratic party." 8 notes, ref.   R. V. Ritter

27.   Cummings, Scott.   A CRITICAL EXAMINATION OF THE POR-TRAYAL OF CATHOLIC IMMIGRANTS IN AMERICAN POLITICAL LIFE.   *Ethnicity 1979 6(3): 197-214.* The new ethnicity of Catholic minorities, expressed in aggressive political behavior, cannot be equated with conservatism. What is labeled incorrectly as reactionary politics on the part of Catholic ethnics is a part of the traditional antagonism between working-class ethnics and upper-middle-class Protestant reformers in the Democratic Party that has existed since the 1890's. The antielitist and antiprivilege sentiments of the Catholic ethnics were galvanized by the Populist Movement. Biblio.   S

28.   Deckard, Barbara and Stanley, John.   PARTY DECOMPOSITION AND REGION: THE HOUSE OF REPRESENTATIVES, 1945-1970.   *Western Pol. Q. 1974 27(2): 249-264.* According to the *Congressional Quarterly,* party unity scores and responses to issues selected by the *New Republic* to determine liberalism and party cohesiveness have declined since World War II, especially in the Republican Party, with increasing regional and ideological cleavages.

29. Dekay, Kenneth. THE DEMOCRATIC PARTY: CHALLENGE OR CONTRADICTION? *Texas Q. 1976 19(3): 191-201.* To succeed in the future, the Democratic Party must reject techniques employed by past heroes and realize that today's economy requires an end to subsidizing small farms and to minimum wage laws. The Democratic Party must recognize that automation will allow more people to live on a higher level with reduced human effort.

R. H. Tomlinson

30. Easterbrook, Gregg. THE REPUBLICAN SOUL. *Washington Monthly 1981 13(5-6): 13-24.* Discusses the Republican state of mind in 1981, especially as represented by Ronald Reagan, whose life is characterized as a kind of Norman Rockwellian idyll that romanticizes American life but ignores social problems and the poor; and traces Reagan's life from the Depression era in Illinois to his election as President.

31. Edwards, George C., III. PRESIDENTIAL ELECTORAL PERFORMANCE AS A SOURCE OF PRESIDENTIAL POWER. *Am. J. of Pol. Sci. 1978 22(1): 152-168.* One of the most fertile areas of research in American politics has been that focusing on the vote in presidential elections. Most studies in this area, however, take the presidential vote as the dependent variable. This research carries the analysis further and examines the influence of the presidential vote in a congressional constituency on the support of that constituency's congressman for the President's policies. Using the techniques of causal modeling and path analysis, this article tests for both the direct influence of the presidential vote on presidential support and for its indirect influence through its effect on the party which wins the seat in a congressional district while controlling for the effects of constituency party strength. The basic finding is that presidential electoral performance does influence presidential support, particularly in Democratic presidential years.						J

32. Elliott, Charles P. POLITICAL ATTITUDES OF POLITICAL PARTY COUNTY CHAIRMEN IN TEXAS. *Rocky Mountain Social Sci. J. 1974 11(2): 73-83.*

33. Everson, David H. THE DECLINE OF POLITICAL PARTIES. *Pro. of the Acad. of Pol. Sci. 1982 34(4): 49-60.* Discusses the decline in traditional party politics and the corresponding rise in the new technological politics or the influence of special interest groups, 1830-1982. Primary sources; 8 notes.

T. P. Richardson

34. Fee, Joan L. PARTY IDENTIFICATION AMONG AMERICAN CATHOLICS, 1972, 1973. *Ethnicity 1976 3(1): 53-69.* Examines the relationship between the Catholic Church and the Democratic Party, comparing social and vital statistics to determine culturally what type of Catholic is a Democrat and what the personal perceptions of Catholic Democrats are.

35. Fenton, John H. TURNOUT AND THE TWO-PARTY VOTE. *J. of Pol. 1979 41(1): 229-234.* Contrary to conventional wisdom, Democratic candidates for national office usually do not win elections when there are large turnouts, nor do Republican candidates win when the turnout is small. The relationship between size of victory and turnout is negative for both parties. Rather, turnout has been greatest in closely contested elections and least in

landslide victories of either party. There is little difference in the size of turnout when the victorious party is considered. Abnormal interest in an election due to candidates or issues tends to accompany and is necessary for a Republican victory. 2 tables, 2 fig., 5 notes.   A. W. Novitsky

36.   Field, Phyllis F.   REPUBLICANS AND BLACK SUFFRAGE IN NEW YORK STATE: THE GRASS ROOTS RESPONSE.   *Civil War Hist. 1975 21(2): 136-147.* A statistical analysis of rank and file Whig-Republican Party voting on three New York state referenda (1846, 1860, 1869) designed to expunge clauses discriminatory against Negro suffrage from the 1821 constitution. Party leaders favored equal suffrage on each occasion, but grass roots opposition was strong in 1846, moderate in 1860, and relatively weak by 1869. The growing party solidarity on the question reflected developments during Reconstruction, but also was marked by declining political effectiveness of the party in the state.
E. C. Murdock

37.   Fotheringham, Peter.   CHANGES IN THE AMERICAN PARTY SYS-TEM, 1948-72.   *Government and Opposition [Great Britain] 1973 8(2): 217-241.* Discusses organizational and administrative changes, emphasizing regional representation, primaries, and electoral reform.

38.   Freidel, Frank.   PARTY OR PRESIDENT? HISTORIANS VIEW TWENTIETH-CENTURY POLITICS.   *Prologue 1979 11(2): 107-119.* Surveys historians' works on the party system in American politics, written from 1888 to 1979. 39 notes.   J. Powell

39.   Freie, John F.   MINOR PARTIES IN REALIGNING ERAS.   *Am. Pol. Q. 1982 10(1): 47-63.* Treats the minor party as an independent variable in the realignment process and establishes an association between the strength of the minor party and the sharpness of the realignment. The research correlates the percentage of the Democratic vote in counties throughout the nation over three historical periods, 1884-1900, 1916-32, and 1960-76. In the first two eras the minor parties (the Populist Party in the election of 1892 and the Progressive Party in the election of 1924) were strongly associated with the sharpness of the realignment process. No realignment was uncovered for the third period, although there was evidence of electoral disaggregation. The relevance of the minor party, the American Independent Party, could not be determined.   J

40.   Gray, Virginia.   THE EFFECT OF PARTY COMPETITION ON STATE POLICY, A REFORMULATION: ORGANIZATIONAL SUR-VIVAL.   *Polity 1974 7(2): 248-263.* The theory that political party leaders attempt to promote the survival of their organizations accounts for state government policy differences during 1872-1968 between states with similar levels of political party competition and wealth.   S

41.   Greeley, Andrew M.   HOW CONSERVATIVE ARE AMERICAN CATHOLICS?   *Pol. Sci. Q. 1977 92(2): 199-218.* The conventional wisdom about Catholic ethnics is false. They have not been more racist, less likely to support civil liberties, more antagonistic toward the counter culture, stronger supporters of the Vietnam War, or heavier supporters of George Wallace than other Americans. Catholics are in fact less conservative than the average, and they have not abandoned the Democratic Party as they have become more

affluent and moved to the suburbs. Their conservative image may be based not on substantial issues, but rather on political style; Catholics are more likely to call their precinct captains than to join civic organizations. Based on NORC General Social Surveys, Gallup polls, voting records, and secondary sources; 9 tables, 5 figs., 13 notes. W. R. Hively

42. Guest, Avery M. CLASS CONSCIOUSNESS AND AMERICAN PO-LITICAL ATTITUDES. *Social Forces 1974 52(4): 496-510.* The arguments of Richard Centers and Philip Converse about the relationship of subjective class consciousness to political attitudes are reanalyzed with the use of longitudinal survey data from 1956 to 1968. Respondents may be split into four groups based on identification with the working class versus the middle class and on admitting awareness of social class membership as opposed to unawareness. Consistent with previous research, working-class identification is associated with collectivist views on the role of government and voting for the Democratic party. Awareness, however, contrary to previous research, increases the collectivist tendencies of both the working and middle classes. Furthermore, the effects of class identification and awareness on political attitudes show little change over time, although they do seem to have different effects on presidential voting in a Democratic as opposed to Republican victory. J

43. Guillory, Ferrel. SOUTHERN REPUBLICANS: NOT THAT THEY HATE WATERGATE LESS BUT LOVE THE SOUTHERN STRATEGY MORE. *Southern Voices 1974 1(1): 13-17.* Documents the growth of the Republican Party in the southern states since the 1940's. S

44. Hadley, Charles D. THE NATIONALIZATION OF AMERICAN POLITICS: CONGRESS, THE SUPREME COURT AND THE NATIONAL POLITICAL PARTIES. *J. of Social and Pol. Studies 1979 4(4): 359-380.* During the 1970's, reform was the dominant subject; Congress, the Supreme Court, and the political parties worked together in supportive roles to nationalize the political process.

45. Hain, Paul L. CONSTITUENCY CHARACTERISTICS, POLITICAL AMBITION AND ADVANCEMENT. *Am. Pol. Q. 1976 4(1): 47-62.* Explores the impact of the political party system and the political opportunity structure on the political ambitions and careers of 504 members of the California, New Jersey, Ohio, and Tennessee legislatures 1957-November 1970. An additional concern was the nature of political ambitions as these were expressed in confidential interviews. Interparty competition among constituents and the size of the constituency have about equal impact upon legislators' ambitions and careers. Progressive ambitions indicate the greatest commitment to a political career while discrete ambitions represent the least. Expressions of political ambition are generally predictive of subsequent political behavior. P. Travis

46. Havard, William C. INTRANSIGENCE TO TRANSITION: THIRTY YEARS OF SOUTHERN POLITICS. *Virginia Q. R. 1975 51(4): 497-521.* Argues that since World War II "political change of great magnitude" has occurred in the South as reflected in the "changing status of the black," "the demise of the one-party system," and the growth of "cosmopolitanism." O. H. Zabel

47.   Hochman, William R.   SHIFTING PERSPECTIVES IN THE ROLE OF
GOVERNMENT IN THE UNITED STATES.   *Kleio [Netherlands] 1976
17(12): 1112-1125.* Describes American attitudes toward government in the past
200 years. Discusses Thomas Jefferson's view of limited government and laissez-
faire based on the idea of 18th-century natural law; indicates successive modifica-
tions of this concept by Hamiltonians, Whigs, Republicans, Social Darwinists, the
consequences of industrialization, and the Progressive movement. Changes in
attitudes, influenced by a pragmatic approach to everyday problems, culminated
in a powerful government used as an instrument for promoting the welfare of all
Americans. Mentions problems relating to pragmatism and the lack of long-range
goals and cautions that "people can no longer regard pragmatic government as
a door to progress." Concludes that "the key to the future may be in the revitalization of the democratic political process after recent disillusion."
R. C. Alltmont

48.   Hofstetter, C. Richard.   INTER-PARTY COMPETITION AND ELEC-
TORAL TURNOUT: THE CASE OF INDIANA.   *Am. J. of Pol. Sci. 1973
17(2): 351-366.* "Based on data for Indiana counties from 1876 to 1968, this
correlational analysis demonstrates that inter-party competition increases voter
turnout, even after the effects of socio-economic and historical variables have
been controlled. Thus, it appears that competitive political situations induce civic
participation and may contribute to party responsiveness to citizens' demands."
J

49.   Hopper, Stanley D.   THE INSTITUTIONAL CONTEXT OF CROSS-
FILING.   *Social Sci. Hist. 1976 1(1): 1-19.* A review of political crossfiling in
California. The practice began in 1914 as progressives sought to establish themselves as distinct from the Republican Party from which they sprang. The decline
of the Progressives also caused a decline in crossfiling until 1939 and the end of
the one-party politics of the 1920's and 1930's. Crossfiling was thus more preva-
lent during periods of political competitiveness and in areas where one-party
dominance was weakest. Crossfiling gave incumbents a big edge in electoral races,
but it may have contributed to the weakness of political parties in California,
although surely it was not the only factor involved. Table, 2 fig., 41 notes.
V. L. Human

50.   Huston, James A.   POLITICS IN MID-TWENTIETH CENTURY
AMERICA.   *Current Hist. 1974 67(395): 20-23, 40-42.* Analyzes influences on
presidential nominations and elections 1920-48, including issues, personalities,
and historical forces. One of seven articles in this issue on the two-party system.
S

51.   Jackameit, William P.   THE EVOLUTION OF PUBLIC HIGHER EDU-
CATION GOVERNANCE IN WEST VIRGINIA: A STUDY OF POLITI-
CAL INFLUENCE UPON EDUCATIONAL POLICY.   *West Virginia Hist.
1975 36(2): 97-130.* Radical Republicans began West Virginia's higher education
system and Democrats extended it in the 1870's. When Republicans returned to
power in the 1890's they divided school regents and employees equally between
the parties and created new schools as well. By 1907 there were six separate
boards of regents which were then consolidated, but within 20 years a separate
board for the state University was re-created. When Democrats came to power

in the state after 1930 they fired some Republicans (including the president of Marshall College, causing a student strike) but failed in an attempt to oust the president of West Virginia University. After several false starts, a single Board of Regents for all colleges was created in 1969. Based on primary and secondary sources; 127 notes. J. H. Broussard

52. Johnson, Loch and McCormick, James M. THE DEMOCRATIC CONTROL OF INTERNATIONAL COMMITMENTS. *Presidential Studies Q. 1978 8(3): 275-283.* Assesses the impact of democratic controls on American postwar commitments abroad. Analyzes the number, substance, and legal bases of these agreements. Congress participated in 93% of all international commitments, but a significant number of sensitive military agreements were enacted as executive agreements or through departmental arrangements. Party loyalty and House-Senate jurisdictional disputes have prevented Congress from curtailing the use of executive agreements and it is unlikely that such action will be taken against a president from the Democratic Party. Table, 2 fig., 27 notes. S. C. Strom

53. Jones, Bryan D. PARTY AND BUREAUCRACY: THE INFLUENCE OF INTERMEDIARY GROUPS ON URBAN PUBLIC SERVICE DELIVERY. *Am. Pol. Sci. Rev. 1981 75(3): 688-700.* Using data on citizen complaints, agency outputs and service impacts in neighborhoods, this study of building code enforcement in Chicago finds that the party structure is efficacious at all stages of the service provision process, but that groups are not effective at any stage. J/S

54. Kehl, James A. THE DELEGATE CONVENTION: AGENT OF THE DEMOCRATIC PROCESS. *South Atlantic Q. 1973 72(1): 53-65.* Political conventions began in America as a mechanism for determining social consensus. Independence, the Revolution, and the Constitution depended upon conventions to determine national action. The Hartford Convention of 1814 and Calhoun's concept of nullification changed the convention into a method for protecting minority rights. The emergence of the Republican Party of 1856 from a series of conventions marked total acceptance of the format as a permanent instrument for handling social issues. Today pressure blocs promoting social reform work most effectively in local, state, and national conventions. W. L. Olbrich

55. Kelley, Robert Lloyd. IDEOLOGY AND POLITICAL CULTURE FROM JEFFERSON TO NIXON. *Am. Hist. Rev. 1977 82(3): 531-562.* A revolution has occurred in the way historians look at American politics. We no longer consider just economic influences, but cultural ones; ethnic identity, religious attitudes and memberships, styles of life; influences emotional as well as rational, cultural and ideological as well as economic and pragmatic. American politics begins in the British Isles, where the Anglican English served as the dominant host culture, the Scots, Irish, Welsh, and Dissenting English as the outgroups. Centuries of warfare and mutual hatred helped align peoples on either side in the two parties which formed in the United States: the Federalist-Whig-Republican line of descent being rooted in those of English (Yankee, New England) descent, aggressively moralistic in the older state-church tradition; the Jeffersonian Republican-Jacksonian Democratic line of descent being derived from a coalition of out-groups (Southern whites, Scotch-Irish, Dutch and Ger-

man in the Middle States) with the secularistic, libertarian and equalitarian groups who were anti-Yankee, and devoted to laissez-faire not only in economics (designed to prevent capitalists from getting undue privileges and power over others through use of government) but in cultural affairs as well. Article traces progression of this fundamental alignment through the five party systems to the 1970's, relating party ideologies to their cultural membership. [Includes comments by Geoffrey Blodgett, Ronald P. Formisano, and Willie Lee Rose].   A

56. Kenski, Henry C. THE IMPACT OF UNEMPLOYMENT ON PRESIDENTIAL POPULARITY FROM EISENHOWER TO NIXON. *Presidential Studies Q. 1977 7(2-3): 114-126.* Discusses the influence of unemployment on presidents' political popularity from Dwight D. Eisenhower through Richard M. Nixon (1953-74). Economic slump, not unemployment, has the greatest effect on presidential popularity. The rate of unemployment, though, does have a more negative effect on Republican administrations than on Democratic ones, and the change in the unemployment rate affects both Republican and Democratic presidencies. For unemployment to be politically devastating, it would need to reach double-digit figures in an absence of social welfare programs. Gallup polls, newspapers, and secondary sources; 3 tables, 65 notes.   R. D. Hurt

57. Knoke, David and Hout, Michael. SOCIAL AND DEMOGRAPHIC FACTORS IN AMERICAN POLITICAL PARTY AFFILIATION, 1952-72. *Am. Sociol. R. 1974 39(5): 700-713.* This analysis of changes in the party affiliations of American adults between 1952 and 1972 assesses the stability of the relationship between party and a set of causal variables and examines the extent to which the observed changes are attributable to changes in the electorate's demographic composition. We found that indicators of stratification position, race, region, religion, and political socialization have exerted a nearly constant causal influence on party throughout the twenty-year period. A model which assumed constant effects (equal regression slopes) across the six elections explained only 2% less of the variance in party than a model which allowed the slopes to vary across elections. Of the variables in the causal model, socialization —as indicated by father's party preference—has the largest effect on party affiliation. The addition to our model of the demographic variables, age and cohort, revealed that both factors influence individuals' party affiliations. Though age and cohort explain only a small portion of the variance in party, examination of the net differences in mean party affiliation between age groups and between cohorts showed that aging does produce a net shift away from the Democratic party and that the Depression has had lasting effects on the preferences of cohort members formulating their preferences at that time.   J

58. Kolbe, Richard L. CULTURE, POLITICAL PARTIES AND VOTING BEHAVIOR: SCHUYLKILL COUNTY. *Polity 1975 8(2): 241-268.* In Schuylkill County, Pennsylvania, the Republican party has dominated in the twentieth century, where the ethnic (Catholic majority) and economic (low income) composition of the population might lead to expectations of Democratic strength. The uniqueness of the particular experience is conveyed, along with implications from and for the literature of parties and elections. In explaining the paradox of Republican success (after a strong nineteenth-century tendency to division on ethnic lines) with a population whose economic interests might reasonably have led them to support Democrats, the individualistic culture of the

voters and the consonant laissez-faire ideology of the Republicans emerge as significant. One-party politics is the consequence, and the effect of an ineffective opposition is considered.

J

59. Kolson, Kenneth. PARTY, OPPOSITION AND POLITICAL DEVELOPMENT. *Rev. of Pol. 1978 40(2): 163-182.* Recent revisionist interpretations of the development of the American party system have tended to equate political parties with democracy. They do not realize that American party politics have not made much progress since the development of the two-party system. To call for an improvement in the two-party system to ensure better democracy is to fly in the face of history and to ask us to venerate a political "hack" such as Van Buren instead of nationalists such as "Washington, Adams, Jefferson, Hamilton, Madison et al." 93 notes.

L. E. Ziewacz

60. Kostroski, Warren. THE EFFECT OF THE NUMBER OF TERMS ON THE RE-ELECTION OF SENATORS 1920-1970. *J. of Pol. 1978 40(2): 488-497.* Analysis of senatorial reelection campaigns during 1920-70 indicates that the success rate rises 6% between first and second terms, and again between second and third terms, before leveling near 90% in subsequent efforts. Republicans have greater success in earlier bids. Democrats from safe states have the greatest longevity. Defeated veteran senators generally were past retirement age, and suffered declining support in their two immediately preceding contests before being soundly defeated. Primary and secondary sources; 4 tables, fig., 3 notes.

A. W. Novitsky

61. Ladd, Everett Carll, Jr. and Hadley, Charles D. PARTY DEFINITION AND PARTY DIFFERENTIATION. *Public Opinion Q. 1973 37(1): 21-34.* "Contrasts the 'issue profiles' that emerge when the two major political parties are defined according to differing criteria. Over a wide array of issues, and from 1948 to the present, the Democratic party as defined by behavioral criteria (voting support) has been more 'liberal' than its self-identified counterpart, while behavioral Republicans are persistently more 'conservative' than self-identified GOP partisans. Ladd and Hadley note that in periods distinguished by rapid social change and partisan realignment, the adequacy of self-perception for determining the definition of party membership is called into question."

J

62. Lamis, Alec Peter. THE DISRUPTION OF A SOLIDLY DEMOCRATIC STATE: CIVIL RIGHTS AND SOUTH CAROLINA ELECTORAL CHANGE, 1948-1972. *J. of Pol. Sci. 1977 5(1): 55-72.* Stresses differences among counties. The realignment has left the Democrats a decided minority in South Carolina. The civil rights issue was at the heart of the electoral change. The preoccupation with race dominated South Carolina voting for president. Based on the author's M.A. thesis, Vanderbilt University, 1975; 3 tables, 2 fig., 54 notes.

T. P. Richardson

63. Lenchner, Paul. PARTISAN CONFLICT IN THE SENATE AND THE REALIGNMENT PROCESS. *J. of Pol. 1979 41(2): 680-686.* Senate roll-call voting patterns during 1925-73 were examined for polar opposition between Democrats and Republicans, especially during periods of general partisan realignment. Polar conflict was generally absent, with major cleavages occurring on economic issues during the Truman and Kennedy administrations, and reflect-

ing New Deal patterns. Never did Senate realignment correspond to mass voting realignment, perhaps due to Senatorial six-year terms, the importance of incumbency, and the disaggregation of American electoral politics. 2 tables, 14 notes.

A. W. Novitsky

64. Lengle, James I.   DIVISIVE PRESIDENTIAL PRIMARIES AND PARTY ELECTORAL PROSPECTS, 1932-1976.   *Am. Pol. Q. 1980 8(3): 261-277.* Using two different units of analysis, this article examines the impact of divisive presidential primaries on party electoral prospects. First, an examination of state-level data from 1932 to 1976 shows that divisive presidential primaries hurt both parties' chances of winning those same states in the November general election. This effect is stronger for Democrats and remains even after controlling for incumbency and state party orientation. Second, an examination of survey data collected in 1972 and 1976 shows that supporters of losing contenders are likely to defect in general elections. Here again, the effect is present for both parties, but more pronounced for Democrats.   J

65. Leuchtenburg, William E.   THE LEGACY OF FDR.   *Wilson Q. 1982 6(2): 77-93.* Discusses the residual impact of Franklin D. Roosevelt's New Deal on three Democratic presidents: Harry S. Truman, John F. Kennedy, and Lyndon B. Johnson, with special attention to Johnson's Great Society legislation; 1933-68.

66. Levine, Arthur.   WHAT THE REPUBLICAN PARTY MEANS TO ME. *Washington Monthly 1975 7(3): 40-48.* Examines the present philosophy and image of the Republican Party.

67. Lindley, Lester G.   THE AMERICAN POLITICAL SYSTEM: 1840-1890.   *Current Hist. 1974 67(395): 9-12, 14, 38-40.* Rapid economic development, acceptance of the two-party system, and the evolution of methods for nominating and electing officeholders were the primary achievements of this period. One of seven articles on the American two-party system.   S

68. Mandelbaum, Michael and Schneider, William.   THE NEW INTERNATIONALISMS.   *Int. Security 1978 2(3): 81-98.* In the US, liberals (found most often in the Democratic Party) are antimilitarist and favor detente, while conservatives (generally found in the Republican Party) tend to be promilitarist and suspicious of detente, but these polarizations are usually obscured in presidential election campaigns (the 1976 campaign being a good example) so as not to evoke antagonism between the extreme wings of each party, while each candidate attempts to project a foreign policy based on morality, which may not be a very solid foundation for such matters.

69. McIver, John P.   UNEMPLOYMENT AND PARTISANSHIP: A SECOND OPINION.   *Am. Pol. Q. 1982 10(4): 439-451.* The Schlozman and Verba hypothesis that unemployment leads to abandonment of affiliation with the incumbent party is questioned in light of the Niemi critique of partisan recall data. The 1974-76 Center for Political Studies National Election Panel provides more appropriate data for testing the hypothesis. Support is not as strong as Schlozman and Verba's analysis would suggest. However, the panel data do lend some credence to the proposition that job loss will lead to erosion of political support for the incumbent party.   J/S

70. McMilen, Neil R. PERRY W. HOWARD, BOSS OF BLACK-AND-TAN REPUBLICANISM IN MISSISSIPPI, 1924-1960. *J. of Southern Hist. 1982 48(2): 205-224.* Long after most Southern "black-and-tan" party organizations were lost to "lily-white" Republican Party organizations and after Perry W. Howard had left Mississippi to reside in Washington, D.C., or elsewhere in the North, Howard wisely played the politics of race to survive politically. From the 1920's until just before his death in 1961, he remained the Republican national committeeman from Mississippi and a perennial black showpiece of the Republican Party. Based on the Warren Harding and Herbert Hoover Papers, NAACP records, materials stored at Federal Records centers, other manuscripts, periodicals, and printed primary sources; 80 notes. T. Schoonover

71. McNitt, Andrew D. A COMPARISON OF EXPLANATIONS OF COMPETITION FOR GUBERNATORIAL AND SENATORIAL NOMINATION: 1954-1974. *Western Pol. Q. 1982 35(2): 245-257.* A multiple regression analysis of all gubernatorial and senatorial nominations made in the United States between 1954 and 1974 finds that incumbency, average party vote, and to a lesser extent, office sought and the degree of party control over state level nominations are related to competition for nominations. The relationship between the degree of party control over state level nominations and competition for nominations, however, is not consistent with the view that party organization is becoming less effective during the late 20th century. Rather, party organization has consistently played only a role in controlling competition for nominations. J/S

72. Mladenka, Kenneth R. THE URBAN BUREAUCRACY AND THE CHICAGO POLITICAL MACHINE: WHO GETS WHAT AND THE LIMITS TO POLITICAL CONTROL. *Am. Pol. Sci. Rev. 1980 74(4): 991-998.* This study of Chicago found no evidence to suggest that the political machine uses vital public services to reward supporters and to punish enemies. With few exceptions, distribution patterns are a function of past decisions, population shifts, technological changes, and reliance upon technical-rational criteria and professional values. The urban bureaucracy is the major actor in the distributional process. Equity in the distribution of resources is accomplished according to formula and is increasingly a by-product of allegiance to professional standards. J/S

73. Moore, William V. GRASSROOTS POLITICS IN SOUTH CAROLINA: A COMPARATIVE ANALYSIS OF DEMOCRATIC AND REPUBLICAN COUNTY CHAIRMEN. *J. of Pol. Sci. 1978 6(1): 1-15.* Party chairmen in South Carolina have demographic backgrounds similar to their nonsouthern counterparts, but there are major differences; the ideological outlook continues to reflect the conservatism of the South. Based on data collected from Democratic and Republican county chairmen in 1975 and 1976; 9 tables, 23 notes. T. P. Richardson

74. Munk, Margaret. ORIGIN AND DEVELOPMENT OF THE PARTY FLOOR LEADERSHIP IN THE UNITED STATES SENATE. *Capitol Studies 1974 2(2): 23-41.*

75.   Namenwirth, J. Zvi.   WHEELS OF TIME AND THE INTERDEPEN-
DENCE OF VALUE CHANGE IN AMERICA.   *J. of Interdisciplinary Hist.
1973 3(4): 649-683.* The history of value change is basically cyclical. Content
analysis of Republican and Democratic platforms from 1844 to 1964 suggests a
variety of trends in different value categories. In combination these trends describe much of the variation in value concerns, although long- and short-term
dynamics are not equally important in the determination of value change. 8
tables, 5 figs., 38 notes.   R. Howell

76.   Natchez, Peter B.   AMERICAN POLITICS AFTER ROOSEVELT:
1948-1964.   *Current Hist. 1974 67(395): 24-29, 37-38.* Analyzes elections
1948-64 and such issues as corruption, campaign finance, public welfare, and
government structure in relation to New Deal policies. One of seven articles in
this issue on the two-party system.   S

77.   Nelson, Garrison.   PARTISAN PATTERNS OF HOUSE LEADER-
SHIP CHANGE, 1789-1977.   *Am. Pol. Sci. Rev. 1977 71(3): 918-939.* This
study of 364 leadership selections in the U.S. House from 1789 through 1977
discovered that Democrats have a higher proportion of appointed leaders than
Republicans; their leaders move between posts in an ordered succession; their
appointed leaders are often "removed from above" by their elected ones; and their
leaders are subjected to infrequent and unsuccessful caucus challenges. Republicans rely upon election to choose their leaders; their leaders' rate of interposi-
tional mobility is very low; their appointed leaders were never removed by their
elected ones; and their leaders face the contests at the same rate as the Democrats
do, but the incidence of successful challenges is much greater. They are "removed
from below." Majority vs. minority status had little statistically significant impact
upon leadership contests and what variation appeared indicated that challenges
were more frequent in the majority party where the stakes are higher and the
rewards are greater than in the minority. Regardless of electoral consequences,
however, Republican leaders are more vulnerable to caucus defeat than Democratic ones, which lends further support to the contention that party identity is
more important than party status.   J

78.   Norpoth, Helmut and Rusk, Jerrold G.   PARTISAN DEALIGNMENT
IN THE AMERICAN ELECTORATE: ITEMIZING THE DEDUCTIONS
SINCE 1964.   *Am. Pol. Sci. Rev. 1982 76(3): 522-537.* The proportion of
Americans identifying with a political party declined from approximately 75%
to 63% between 1964 and 1976. The changing age composition of the electorate,
the entry of new voters into the electorate, the party desertion among voters
already in the electorate, and the suppression of age gains in partisanship explain
close to 100% of the aggregate decline, with the single largest contribution made
by entry of new voters. Nevertheless, the decline occurred throughout all age
cohorts and suggest the potency of dealigning period forces. These forces simply
had their strongest effect on those voters with predictably the least resistance, the
youngest cohorts.   J/S

79.   Orbell, John M. and Fougere, Geoffrey.   INTRA-PARTY CONFLICT
AND THE DECAY OF IDEOLOGY.   *J. of Pol. 1973 35(2): 439-458.* Examines the view that party platforms tend to be nonideological documents which lie
between liberalism and conservatism, with the consequence that activists at the

extreme ends are driven out, while the party seeks the votes of the majority. Additional research has demonstrated the impossibility of locating voters on a liberal-conservative scale; and that platforms are unread by most voters. Nevertheless, the process of seeking "ideological consistency" takes place as party leaders attempt to eliminate conflict within a party. They may do this by "issue decomposition" or by the exclusion of issue-oriented activists. In the latter case party leaders must assume that the preferences of activists are a significant factor affecting the party's image. Under certain conditions a policy which seeks the most votes will exclude the most activists. Fig., 2 tables, appendix.

A. R. Stoesen

80. Pernacciaro, Samuel J. and VanDerSlik, Jack R. AMBITION THEORY AND PRESIDENTIAL ASPIRATIONS: HOW THE SENATORS VOTE. *J. of Pol. Sci. 1976 4(1): 52-65.* Identifies senators who are presidential aspirants of the 91st Congress (1969-70), and studies their roll-call voting records. Focuses on whether there is more homogeneity in the voting of aspirant senators than in the voting of the nonaspirant. Comparison of the variance of scores of "All Democrats" and nonsouthern Democrats shows that presidential aspirants vote with similarity on policy positions, whereas nonaspirants vote in behalf of parochial interests. Aspirants seek to satisfy or reflect the consensus perceived in the national electorate of their own party. 2 tables, 14 notes, appendix.

T. P. Richardson

81. Petrocik, John R. VOTER TURNOUT AND ELECTORAL OSCILLATION. *Am. Pol. Q. 1981 9(2): 161-180.* Nonvoters have many characteristics which mark them as Democratic voters, but there is no reason to believe that high turnout elections, especially at the presidential level, would benefit Democratic candidates. The lower levels of involvement and commitment which characterize chronic nonvoters and peripheral voters would simply promote greater interelection oscillation if these voters began to turn out.

J/S

82. Pomper, Gerald M. NEW RULES AND NEW GAMES IN PRESIDENTIAL NOMINATIONS. *J. of Pol. 1979 41(3): 784-805.* Rule changes provide an important explanation of the surprising features of the 1976 major party conventions, especially the victory of Jimmy Carter and the strong performance of Ronald Reagan. Primaries or preference polls were involved in the selection of 76.9% of the Democrats and 71.5% of the Republicans. Since 1952, politics has become more open with electronic journalism; federal matching funds financed marginal candidates; and the role of conventions shifted from the site of bargaining among state parties to the formal expression of the preferences of an activist electorate. Delegate apportionment has favored the conservative south and southwest for the Republicans and the industrial northeast for the Democrats. 4 tables, 19 notes.

A. W. Novitsky

83. Press, Charles. PARTISAN REALIGNMENT IN THE SOUTH. *Am. Pol. Q. 1976 4(3): 379-382.* Review article prompted by Numan V. Bartley and Hugh D. Graham's *Southern Politics and the Second Reconstruction* (Baltimore: Johns Hopkins University Press, 1976), and Louis M. Seagull's *Southern Republicanism* (New York: Schenkman Publishing Co., 1975). Both works follow a V. O. Key tradition and share the unifying theme of the southern arena of partisan realignment and of the emergence of a new majority coalition. The

spotlight focuses on the emergence of southern Republicanism and genuine two-party competition as early as the revolt of the Texas Regulars in 1944. Both books divide the South into deep and rim southern states. Seagull presents a state-by-state analysis, while Bartley and Graham present their data in terms of six stages of postwar historical development.   P. Travis

84. Prindle, David F. VOTER TURNOUT, CRITICAL ELECTIONS, AND THE NEW DEAL REALIGNMENT. *Social Sci. Hist. 1979 3(2): 144-170.* Empirically tests "critical election" theory, using quantitative analysis of material from Wisconsin, Pennsylvania, and the city of Pittsburgh, during the New Deal era. Democratic Party mobilization or increasing voter turnout was more important than party switching or voter realignment. No single election or sharply defined time period stands out as critical. Covers 1912-40. Based on local election returns, census data, voter registration lists, and other primary materials; 11 tables, 9 graphs.   L. K. Blaser

85. Protess, David L. and Gitelson, Alan R. POLITICAL STABILITY AND URBAN REFORM CLUB ACTIVISM. *Polity 1978 10(4): 524-541.* Few political constructs have evoked more widespread discussion and application than James Q. Wilson's concept of the "Amateur Democrat." Using a sample of reform club activists in Chicago, the authors critically examine the validity of the concept itself as well as the means by which Chicago's reform club movement has managed to maintain and enhance its organizational interests in an environment of increasingly entrenched machine politics. They find that Wilson's criteria are in need of modification. As for organizational motivations and development, they conclude that the best explanation for people's joining reform clubs can be provided in terms of the "logic of utility."   J

86. Robinson, Pearl T. WHITHER THE FUTURE OF BLACKS IN THE REPUBLICAN PARTY? *Pol. Sci. Q. 1982 97(2): 207-231.* Reviews policies of Republican and Democratic administrations that courted the black vote in the United States, since 1937. Special attention is given to post-1976 probes between black leaders and Republican leaders, and to Republican National Committee leader Richard Brock's efforts to make his party more attractive to black voters in 1980, by changing the party's image. Blacks also sought to negotiate with the Republicans in order to get the Democrats to take them seriously. 4 tables, 63 notes.   J. Powell

87. Rojek, Dean G. THE PROTESTANT ETHIC AND POLITICAL PREFERENCE. *Social Forces 1973 52(2): 168-177.* In a series of articles, Benton Johnson has investigated the effects of ascetic Protestantism on political party preference. His findings indicate that among laymen exposed to fundamentalist teachings, religious involvement would vary directly with Republican party preference. However, among laymen exposed to liberal teachings, religious involvement would vary inversely with Republican identification. This present study shows that church involvement and political party identification are not significantly related. A refinement of Johnson's liberal-fundamentalist dichotomy and his church interaction index again resulted in non-significant findings. Finally, a weighted least-squares procedure was employed yielding a set of linear estimation equations that again showed no significant effect. Results such as these should make the social scientist wary of the dangers associated with the measurement of religion and the contemporary relevance of Weber's Protestant ethic.
                                    J

88. Royster, Vermont. AMERICAN POLITICS: 1932-1972. *Am. Scholar 1973 42(2): 205-214.* Richard M. Nixon's presidential landslide in 1972 amid Democratic congressional gains can only be explained by the steady erosion of Democratic Party power since 1936. Harry S. Truman's minority of the popular vote made 1948 an historic election. Kennedy also was a minority president. The Johnson victory was not seen as a durable resurgence of the Democratic Party. Nixon in 1968 won with only 43.4 percent of the popular vote. "The Republican failure to build a solid national majority has been a major factor in midcentury American politics, right up to the election of 1972 . . . there is no proof that the nation is ready yet to award to either party that sought-for mandate to govern."
E. P. Stickney

89. Sackett, S. J. A NEW POLITICAL ALIGNMENT. *Colorado Q. 1975 23(3): 317-326.* Suggests a realignment of parties with Democrats and Republicans virtually interchangeable, conservatives in the American Independent Party, and liberals in a newly created third party. S

90. Sanford, D. Gregory. REPUBLICAN VERMONT: AN ERODING TRADITION. *Vermont Hist. 1980 48(4): 197-224.*
Hand, Samuel B. THE MECHANISMS OF CONTROL: THE MOUNTAIN RULE, *pp. 198-201.* This rule limited factional fragmentation of the Republican majority by expecting gubernatorial, senatorial, and (during 1880-1930) congressional candidates to be equally from western and eastern Vermont.
Bryan, Frank. CHARTING THE EROSION, *pp. 201-209.* The Democratic Party broke through in 1952 by gaining 20% and holding it in later years, with generally larger votes in off-year elections than in presidential years. Quantitative analysis shows that Democratic gains were from active organization and leadership and from the divisive effect of hard-fought Republican primaries. Party cohesion has generally declined, but was greatest during 1964-70.
—. THE NOT SO TACITURN YANKEES: THE AUDIENCE RESPONDS, *pp. 210-224.* Most of the participants in this discussion of Vermont state politics were Vermont politicians. T. D. S. Bassett

91. Shade, William G. AMERICAN POLITICAL DEVELOPMENT: 1789-1840. *Current Hist. 1974 67(395): 5-8, 40.* This period (1789-1840) witnessed the rise of the two-party system and the acceptance of the spoils system as part of the normal political process. One of seven articles on the American two-party system. S

92. Shaffer, Stephen D. THE POLICY BIASES OF POLITICAL ACTIVISTS. *Am. Pol. Q. 1980 8(1): 15-33.* The nature of policy differences between political strata are examined with survey data from 1952 to 1976. In identifying policy biases, one must consider the interaction between issue area, time period, and partisan grouping. Prior to 1966, a conservative bias on domestic economic issues existed among the more active, due to the conservative bias of the higher SES and hyperactivity among conservative Republicans. After 1966, no consistent bias on domestic economic issues existed among the more active, due to hyperactivity among liberal Democrats as well as conservative Republicans. After 1966 a definite liberal bias existed among activists on black rights and social-

cultural issues, because of the greater liberalism of the more educated, and hyperactivity among Democratic liberals. Foreign affairs patterns are more complex, though there is usually an internationalist bias among activists, due to the greater internationalism of the more educated. 5 tables, fig., 3 notes.   J

93. Shienbaum, Kim Ezra. IDEOLOGY VS. RHETORIC IN AMERICAN POLITICS. *Midwest Q. 1979 21(1): 21-32.* First published in *Midwest Quarterly* in 1975. The homogeneity of American ideology as seen in its political environment has limited the possibility of meaningful political change. Therefore, "this nation is only able to respond to crisis in symbolic terms—with rhetoric, not substantive action." An examination of the Jeffersonian revolution of 1800, the Jacksonian revolution of 1828, the New Nationalism, the New Freedom, the New Deal, Kennedy's New Frontier, Johnson's Great Society and Nixon's New American revolution reveals no radical change commensurate with the rhetoric. The symbolism of rhetoric took the place of action. Selective bibliography.
R. V. Ritter

94. Styskal, Richard A. and Sullivan, Harold J. INTERGENERATIONAL CONTINUITY AND CONGRUENCE ON POLITICAL VALUES. *Western Pol. Q. 1975 28(3): 516-527.* Examination of party identification, image of party, and issue orientation among college students and parents traditionally loyal to the Democratic party indicates that although parental influence on choice of party exists, television and other mass media substantially contribute to this decision. Furthermore, variations were found in the images of the parties held by two generations. This, together with the findings of little or no parental influence on issues, suggests caution in linking widespread parent-child agreement on party identification to the successful transmission of political values.   J

95. Sundquist, James L. WHITHER THE AMERICAN PARTY SYSTEM? *Pol. Sci. Q. 1973 88(4): 559-581.* "Offers . . . explanation of the shifts in the basic strength of the Democratic and Republican parties over the past 40 years. Looking ahead he anticipates not an inevitable disintegration of the party system, but a reversal of the current trend toward political independence and a rebirth and reinforcement of party loyalties along lines of cleavage resembling those of the New Deal era."   J

96. Swain, Martha H. THE LION AND THE FOX: THE RELATIONSHIP OF PRESIDENT FRANKLIN D. ROOSEVELT AND SENATOR PAT HARRISON. *J. of Mississippi Hist. 1976 38(4): 333-359.* Describes the development (1928-37), cooling (1937-39), and renewal (1938-41) of the political friendship of Franklin D. Roosevelt and Mississippi Democratic Senator Pat Harrison, chairman of the powerful Committee on Finance. Harrison's problems with Roosevelt stemmed partly from policy disagreements, especially on taxation, and partly from the President's personality and methods. "In dealing with another master strategist . . . FDR often met his match." Based on primary sources, especially newspapers and the papers of Harrison and Roosevelt; 67 notes.
J. W. Hillje

97. Tatalovich, Raymond. RESEARCH NOTE: THE EMERGING SOCIO-ECONOMIC CLEAVAGE OF MISSISSIPPI REPUBLICANISM. *J. of Pol. Sci. 1978 5(2): 109-113.* Republican presidential contenders' voter support in

Mississippi was related to economic rather than racial factors. When Republican presidential contenders obtained extraordinary voter support in Mississippi, their upper socioeconomic cleavage was either weakened or undermined. In these instances, the marked shift to the Republican Party may be related to the status anxieties of the white mass who live among the blacks, rather than to the economic "class" interests of the middle-class white community. Based on the study of 10 presidential elections; 2 tables, 7 notes. T. P. Richardson

98. Terekhov, V. I. KONTSEPTSIIA ISKLIUCHITEL'NOSTI PAR-TIINO-POLITICHESKOI SISTEMY SOEDINENNYKH SHTATOV V RABOTAKH A. TOKVILIA, DZH. BRAISA I M. OSTROGORSKOGO [The conception of the exceptionalism of the party and political system of the United States in the work of A. Tocqueville, J. Bryce, and M. Ostrogorski]. *Vestnik Moskovskogo U. Seriia 8: Istoriia [USSR] 1981 (5): 30-44.* Tocqueville saw the United States as exceptional in its political development; the party system guaranteed the avoidance of tyranny of the majority. After World War I, this interpretation became the basis of American conservatism. Bryce saw the parties as divided on issues of federal versus local power and freedom versus restraint by the government. Ostrogorski criticized the parties as organizations which would become increasingly incapable of deciding national issues. He believed that England's government was more ideal and thought that America's exceptional character had disappeared. 74 notes. Russian. D. Balmuth

99. Todd, John R. and Ellis, Kay Dickenson. ANALYZING FACTIONAL PATTERNS IN STATE POLITICS: TEXAS, 1944-1972. *Social Sci. Q. 1974 55(3): 718-731.* Explores the patterns, alignments, and coalitions of political factions. S

100. Tufte, Edward R. POLITICAL PARTIES, SOCIAL CLASS AND ECONOMIC POLICY PREFERENCES. *Government and Opposition [Great Britain] 1979 14(1): 18-36.* Studies economic factors (income, income equalization through taxes, inflation, unemployment, etc.) in the United States and 10 other industrialized countries from 1936 to 1976 and concludes that the single most important determinant of variations in macroeconomic performance from one industrialized democracy to another is the location on the left-right spectrum of the governing political party, this party being very much responsible for major macroeconomic outcomes, e.g., unemployment rates, inflation rates, income equalization, and the size and rate of expansion of the government budget.

101. Walton, Hanes, Jr. and Sanford, Delacy W. BLACK GOVERNORS AND GUBERNATORIAL CANDIDATES IN U.S.A.: 1868-1972. *Pol. Sci. Rev. [India] 1980 19(3): 312-328.* Surveys the attempts of Negroes to obtain the position of governor and lieutenant governor. There were two black governors and six black lieutenant governors in the 1870's, but since then no black has held these political offices, although they have run for the positions more than 36 times in 14 different states. Due to declining Republican backing after the 1870's, blacks increasingly looked to new political parties or tried to form their own to field candidates. 2 tables, 37 notes. D. H. Watson

102. Walton, Hanes, Jr. and Gray, C. Vernon.   BLACK POLITICS AT THE NATIONAL REPUBLICAN AND DEMOCRATIC CONVENTIONS 1868-1972. *Phylon 1975 36(3): 269-278.* Contrary to popular, and some scholarly opinion, black influence at the national conventions has been at times considerable. Reviews past and contemporary attempts by blacks to influence Republican and Democratic Convention proceedings. Finds that from 1868 to 1936, blacks, being mainly Republican, determined several Republican presidential nominations. After 1936, shifting their allegiance to the Democratic Party, they began to influence that party. In 1964 and 1968 black voters overwhelmingly supported the Democratic Party. 26 notes.   R. V. Ritter

103. Ward, James F. TOWARD A SIXTH PARTY SYSTEM? PARTISANSHIP AND POLITICAL DEVELOPMENT. *Western Pol. Q. 1973 26(3): 385-413.* Discusses the weaknesses of Walter Dean Burnham's theory of political change and critical elections, according to which the decline of the American party system has been underway since 1896.   S

104. Wattenberg, Martin P. FROM PARTIES TO CANDIDATES: EXAMINING THE ROLE OF THE MEDIA. *Public Opinion Q. 1982 46(2): 216-227.* Examines the relationship between campaign media expenditures and the saliency of attitudes about parties and candidates. A negative relationship is found between media spending and party saliency. In contrast, a strong positive correlation exists between media expenditures and candidate saliency. These relationships are accentuated when the party organizations in the congressional district are weak and where political action committees contribute a large proportion of total campaign expenses.   J/S

105. Wheeler, Harvey. DEMOCRATS AND THEIR FUTURE. *Center Mag. 1973 6(2): 65-69.*

106. Wiggins, Charles W. ARE SOUTHERN PARTY LEADERS REALLY DIFFERENT? *J. of Pol. 1973 35(2): 487-492.* Tests V. O. Key, Jr.'s argument that under the one-party system, southern parties and party leaders did little other than handle routine matters. Power tended to reside in unofficial leaders, while elected officials immersed themselves in national affairs. Party organization frequently acted as a clearing house for intraparty differences. Today this pattern remains essentially the same, except that leaders are more concerned with promoting a favorable party image—an activity induced by the developing two-party system in the South. 3 tables, 6 notes.   A. R. Stoesen

107. Wildavsky, Aaron. THE THREE-PARTY SYSTEM: 1980 AND AFTER. *Public Interest 1981 (64): 47-57.* Three parties compete for control in the United States. The party of government consists of those who foster expanding government's role. The party of opposition seeks to increase the size and power of the private sector and reduce the size of government. The party of responsibility is reactive and consists of members of both the Republican and Democratic parties who promote stability. Presidential administrations may be seen as representatives of any of these parties. Secondary sources.   J. M. Herrick

108. Williams, E. Russ, Jr. JOHN RAY: FORGOTTEN SCALAWAG. *Louisiana Studies 1974 13(3): 241-262.* Studies the political career of John Ray over five decades of Louisiana politics, in which he faithfully supported his

Republican Party. His scalawaggery destroyed his reputation in Louisiana and marred his record of public involvement. "Ray's accomplishment . . . seem seem inconsequential when compared to his efforts to equalize the black minority with its white counterpart. His efforts for the blacks would have made him a lasting reputation in a later century, but in his lifetime it sealed his infamy." Having supported the party least attuned to the majority, he has been almost forgotten. 92 notes.

R. V. Ritter

109. Wilson, James Q.   REAGAN AND THE REPUBLICAN REVIVAL. *Commentary 1980 70(4): 25-32.* Compares the rise of Ronald Reagan and the New Republicans to the 1896 election and William Jennings Bryan's similar appeal to the Democratic Party, an election that resulted in a major realignment of the political parties; events of the 1960's and 1970's may signal the Fourth Great Awakening, because the First Great Awakening (1730-60), the Second Great Awakening (1800-30), and the Third Great Awakening (1890-1920) were all preceded by religious and cultural upheavals similar to those of the 1960's and 1970's.

110. Wrong, Dennis H.   THE RHYTHM OF DEMOCRATIC POLITICS. *Dissent 1974 21(1): 46-55.* Discusses the theory that American politics alternate between periods of protest by the Left and retrenchment by the Right.   S

111. Zipp, John F.; Landerman, Richard; and Luebke, Paul.   POLITICAL PARTIES AND POLITICAL PARTICIPATION: A REEXAMINATION OF THE STANDARD SOCIOECONOMIC MODEL.   *Social Forces 1982 60(4): 1140-1153.* Examines conventional explanations as to why many lower status persons in the United States are less inclined than others to participate in politics. Such explanations ignore characteristics of US political institutions—especially the programs and recruitment strategies employed by the major political parties —that are important sources of lower status political disinterest and nonpartici- pation. Examination of political party recruitment patterns on voting and cam- paign activity shows that voter contact by a political party or candidate increases the likelihood of voting and campaign activity, although it made no difference which party made the overture; voter contact by the two major parties did not reduce the greater likelihood that high status citizens would participate more in politics; and the impact of contact was the same across social status and political party lines.

J/S

112. —.   [AGE AND PARTISANSHIP].   *Am. J. of Pol. Sci. 1979 23(1): 78-100.*
Abramson, Paul R.   DEVELOPING PARTY IDENTIFICATION: A FUR- THER EXAMINATION OF LIFE-CYCLE, GENERATIONAL, AND PERIOD EFFECTS, *pp. 78-96.* Party loyalty does not increase with age. While Philip E. Converse's research has buttressed this hypothesis, his meth- odology needs refinement.   14 notes, biblio.
Converse, Philip E.   REJOINDER TO ABRAMSON, *pp. 97-100.*   S

113. —.   POLITICAL PARTIES AND DECENTRALIZATION.   *Publius 1976 6(4): 33-59.*
Gilligan, John J.   TOWARD CONSENSUS AND COORDINATION: PRIN- CIPLES OF REFORM IN AMERICA, *pp. 35-48.* The function of politi-

cal parties is to consolidate individual and group political preferences, develop a solid party policy, and extend party membership and influence to all levels of government.

Sundquist, James.   TWO MODELS OF PARTY ORGANIZATION: UN-RECONCILED,   *pp. 49-52.* Gilligan presented two separate models for political reform and governmental functioning which were not and cannot be reconciled.

Petri, Thomas E.   POLITICAL REALISM AND POLITICAL PARTIES, *pp. 53-56.* Gilligan's recommendations for political party reform would overdiversify the power of political parties.

Gilligan, John J.   A RESPONSE TO PETRI AND SUNQUIST,   *pp. 57-59.*

2

THE EMERGING TWO-PARTY SYSTEM
(1789-1860)

114. Adams, William H. THE LOUISIANA WHIGS. *Louisiana Hist. 1974 15(3): 213-228.* Discontent over the destruction of the Bank of the United States, the Compromise Tariff of 1832, and the Maysville Road Bill, all supported by Andrew Jackson, drove dissident Louisianans into forming the Louisiana Whig Party, soon to be an integral part of the national Republican Party.

115. Alberts, Robert C. THE NOTORIOUS AFFAIR OF MRS. REYNOLDS. *Am. Heritage 1973 24(2): 8-11, 89-93.* Alexander Hamilton's alleged adultery in 1791 with Maria Lewis Reynolds led to blackmail, which in turn led to a quarrel, a near duel, an incident in Federalist and Anti-Federalist politics, and charges of dishonesty against Hamilton, the secretary of the treasury. In 1971 Julian Boyd reexamined the Hamilton-Reynolds incident and called for a reassessment of Hamilton's character and of his services to the early republic. Illus.
D. L. Smith

116. Albin, Ray R. EDWARD D. BAKER AND CALIFORNIA'S FIRST REPUBLICAN CAMPAIGN. *California History 1981 60(3): 280-289.* Describes the contribution of Colonel Edward D. Baker to the Republican Party's first presidential campaign in 1856. Baker, a former Whig, found the new Republican Party's views opposing the extension of slavery and favoring a transcontinental railroad to his liking. An accomplished orator, Baker traveled to numerous towns on behalf of the party, often winning over hostile audiences. Although the Republicans came in third behind the Democrats and Know-Nothings on election day, the party felt it had done very well and laid plans for a better showing in 1860. The Know-Nothings, however, declined as Republican fortunes rose. 5 illus., 43 notes.
A. Hoffman

117. Ambacher, Bruce. GEORGE M. DALLAS AND THE BANK WAR. *Pennsylvania Hist. 1975 42(2): 117-135.* In 1832 Senator George M. Dallas of Pennsylvania backed efforts to pass legislation rechartering the Second Bank of the United States. Though long associated with the bank, Dallas had secretly opposed it for several years. His support of efforts to recharter the bank was necessary because many of his Democratic supporters and the legislature backed the bank. When President Andrew Jackson's veto was upheld, Dallas urged his followers to drop the recharter effort and support Jackson. Though his efforts

brought about Democratic unity in the elections of 1832, Dallas knew that unity would soon evaporate and that there would be strong opposition in the legislature to his reelection. Senator Dallas chose to announce his intention not to seek reelection while the Democrats were still united and enjoying the election victories of 1832. Based on the Dallas, Biddle, and Gilpin papers; illus., 76 notes.

D. C. Swift

118.   Ambacher, Bruce.   GEORGE M. DALLAS, CUBA, AND THE ELECTION OF 1856.   *Pennsylvania Mag. of Hist. and Biog. 1973 97(3): 318-332.* By appointing George M. Dallas the American Minister to Great Britain, President Franklin Pierce silenced an influential critic of the administration's Cuban policy. Pierce's action also had the effect of removing Dallas, a potential presidential contender, from competing against him in his unsuccessful quest for the Democratic nomination in 1856. Primary and secondary sources; 47 notes.

E. W. Carp

119.   Anderson, David L.   ANSON BURLINGAME: REFORMER AND DIPLOMAT.   *Civil War Hist. 1979 25(4): 293-308.* Anson Burlingame skyrocketed from Michigan frontiersman to Massachusetts Free-Soil stalwart and state senator. As US Representative from 1854, he wielded wide, effective Republican leadership. For that support, President Lincoln appointed him minister to China. Burlingame's personality, oratory, optimism, sensitivity, and boldness in furthering democracy helped him accomplish more than his more gifted rivals. These talents also caused him to grasp China's need for cooperative support in internal and external (diplomatic) reform and to carry through soundly and brilliantly. Proof was his appointment as first imperial envoy to the West, 1867-69. Based on family papers, State Department China Dispatches, and other sources; 56 notes.   R. E. Stack

120.   Anderson, Grant K.   THE POLITICS OF LAND IN DAKOTA TERRITORY: EARLY SKIRMISHES, 1857-1861.   *South Dakota Hist. 1979 9(3): 210-232.* The agitation for the creation of Dakota Territory between 1857 and 1861 came from speculators rather than settlers. The Democrats who controlled the Minnesota Territorial legislature formed the Dakota Land Company in 1857 in an attempt to gain economic and political control of the unsettled area west of Minnesota. The company failed to secure control through its political connections with the Democratic administration in Washington, D.C., and the use of propaganda to attract settlers. The reasons for the company's failure were counter-lobbying by rival speculators and the growing strength of the newly created Republican Party. Primary sources; 3 illus., photo, 2 maps.

P. L. McLaughlin

121.   Ashworth, John.   THE JACKSONIAN AS LEVELLER.   *J. of Am. Studies [Great Britain] 1980 14(3): 407-421.* Ever present in Jacksonianism was a particularistic view of equality, here described as "levelling," which Democrats refined and articulated from 1836 to 1846. Jacksonian social theory advocated equal opportunity, and, though human differences rendered the outcomes among people unequal, the societal resultant of levelling approximated true equality of conditions. Levelling, Jacksonians believed, proceeded when government allowed individual self-interest to assert itself and, in turn, members of society achieved substantial equality of wealth. These ideas particularly shaped Jacksonian era

decisions on westward expansion, tariffs, immigration, and Democratic views on moral and religious questions. Primary and contemporary newspaper sources; 28 notes.

H. T. Lovin

122.   Austin, Aleine.   VERMONT POLITICS IN THE 1780'S: THE EMERGENCE OF RIVAL LEADERSHIP.   *Vermont Hist. 1974 42(2): 140-154.* "The 1780's laid the foundations for further party divisions; social and ideological differences between leaders of the Revolutionary Era and college trained lawyers resulted in conflict over such issues as debtor relief and return of loyalist property." 53 notes.

E. P. Stickney

123.   Babu, B. Ramesh.   THE EPHEMERAL AND THE ETERNAL IN *THE FEDERALIST. Indian J. of Am. Studies [India] 1979 9(1): 3-14.* Explores the enduring political themes found in the 85 essays of Alexander Hamilton, James Madison, and John Jay published as *The Federalist.* Such themes include: union and liberty, the federal system of government, the separation of powers, the system of checks and balances, and elections. In all this, the single overriding concern was the freedom of the individual. The complex system of government was proposed to secure the blessings of liberty. In the mixture of the ephemeral and the eternal found in *The Federalist,* the latter outweighs the former. 17 notes.

L. V. Eid

124.   Baggett, James A.   THE CONSTITUTIONAL UNION PARTY IN TEXAS.   *Southwestern Hist. Q. 1979 82(3): 233-264.* Analyzes factors in the formation of the Constitutional Union Party from former Whig elements and from the American Party. The Party in Texas was composed primarily of Texas Whigs, voting along traditional lines. Examines the political developments which led to the withdrawal of Sam Houston as a candidate and the support of the Texas party for John Bell. Analyzes the causes of the failure of the Unionists in Texas. Includes tables on voting in 1860 for the Unionists, in certain counties, as compared to those counties' vote for Whigs in 1852 and for the American Party in 1856, as well as a table giving biographical data on Unionists. 4 tables, 42 notes.

L. B. Atkinson

125.   Baldasty, Gerald J.   THE BOSTON PRESS AND POLITICS IN JACKSONIAN AMERICA.   *Journalism Hist. 1980 7(3-4): 104-108.* The two-party system arrived with the Jacksonian Democrats and the National Republicans (later the Whigs), leadership of such Boston, Massachusetts newspaper editors as David Henshaw, J. K. Simpson and Nathaniel Greene of the *Boston Statesman,* Nathan Hale of the *National Republican Daily Advertiser* and *Boston Patriot,* Charles G. Greene of the *Boston Morning Post* and *Statesman,* and Benjamin F. Hallett of the *Boston Advocate.*

126.   Baldasty, Gerald J.   POLITICAL STALEMATE IN ESSEX COUNTY: CALEB CUSHING'S RACE FOR CONGRESS, 1830-1832.   *Essex Inst. Hist. Collections 1981 117(1): 54-70.* Caleb Cushing was the central figure in the congressional stalemate in North Essex District, 1830-32. The electors finally found a majority candidate after 12 separate elections and Cushing's withdrawal from the race. Three principal factors exacerbated the stalemate and thwarted Cushing's attempts to become a congressman: divisions within the National Republican (later Whig) Party, charges that Cushing had engaged in unethical

or unacceptable campaign practices, and the persuasive power wielded by the political newspapers in the campaign. Primary sources; 62 notes.

R. S. Sliwoski

127.   Baldwin, Carolyn W.   THE DAWN OF THE REPUBLICAN PARTY IN NEW HAMPSHIRE: IMPRESSIONS FROM THE JOURNAL OF BENJAMIN GERRISH, JR., OF DOVER, JANUARY TO MARCH, 1859. *Hist. New Hampshire 1975 30(1): 20-32.* The 1859 journal of Benjamin Gerrish, Jr., of Dover, New Hampshire, provides a record of social and political events and attitudes in New Hampshire on the eve of the American Civil War. Gerrish disdainfully but vividly describes Democratic Party rallies and their Irish immigrant participants while recording Republican activities enthusiastically but respectfully. He also comments on church services, demonstrations by traveling salesmen, such popular activities as concerts and lyceums, and gatherings in his store. 5 illus., 14 notes.

D. F. Chard

128.   Banning, Lance.   JEFFERSONIAN IDEOLOGY AND THE FRENCH REVOLUTION: A QUESTION OF LIBERTICIDE AT HOME. *Studies in Burke and His Time 1976 17(1): 5-26.* Events of the French Revolution were interpreted in America in terms of the domestic struggle between Federalists and Republicans. Republicans viewed the Revolution as a fight against executive tyranny and the destruction of liberty and believed themselves to be engaged in the same struggle against the Federalists. Primary sources; 61 notes.

H. T. Blethen

129.   Banning, Lance.   REPUBLICAN IDEOLOGY AND THE TRIUMPH OF THE CONSTITUTION, 1789 TO 1793. *William and Mary Q. 1974 31(2): 167-188.* Antifederalists thought the Constitution would endanger Republican government, yet they acceded to the Constitution. The Republican party of the 1790's Americanized English opposition thought, and with the Federalists found a meeting ground in classical constitutionalism. Analyzes historiography on the ratification of the Constitution and Republican ideology. Comments on the origin of political parties in America. Based on correspondence of period and secondary sources; 45 notes.

H. M. Ward

130.   Bartley, Numan V.   THE SOUTH AND SECTIONALISM IN AMERICAN POLITICS. *J. of Pol. 1976 38(3): 239-257.* Studies the impact of southern sectionalism on American politics. History and southern blacks have molded the group identity of southern whites. The attempted second party system of the Whigs collapsed quickly in the 1850's. Despite many occasions since then, when divisive issues have temporarily cut deeply into the Democrat's solid South, there is no likelihood that "the Americanization of Dixie" implies the coming of viable two-party politics in the South or a decline of political sectionalism. 33 notes.

R. V. Ritter

131.   Bassett, T. D. Seymour.   VERMONT POLITICS AND THE PRESS IN THE 1840'S. *Vermont Hist. 1979 47(3): 196-213.* Whigs dominated Vermont politics from the breakup of the Antimasonic Party in 1836 until 1853. Nearly all Vermonters opposed slavery, but few fugitives came through the state. Abolitionists increased their votes to 14%, 1845-47, and coalition building was the main sport as the Free Soil Party attracted more Democrats than Whigs, 1848-52.

With more than two parties in elections, many seats in the Assembly went unfilled because no candidate could win a majority. Lawyers, editors, and businessmen provided party machinery and "the needful" financing. The "Mountain Rule," that east and west sides of the State deserved an equal share of important offices, applied to US senators and governors by the 1840's. There was no sure political ladder and few lieutenant governors became governor. Towns with over 2,500 population were the residences of two-thirds of all major officeholders. Political methods have remained much the same since the 1840's, allowing for changes in scale and technology. The long-lived and profitable weekly newspapers were party organs in populous places, boosting local business and reflecting village society. 32 notes.

A

132. Baum, Dale. KNOW-NOTHINGISM AND THE REPUBLICAN MAJORITY IN MASSACHUSETTS: THE POLITICAL REALIGNMENT OF THE 1850'S. *J. of Am. Hist. 1978 64(4): 959-986.* During the 1850's in Massachusetts, nativism and antislavery were distinct as political forces. The success of the Republican Party in Massachusetts after 1855 did not depend significantly upon attracting former Know-Nothing voters. Even though the Native American Party enjoyed a brief and phenomenal success in the state, it still represented only a temporary stop for many voters searching for a true antislavery party. The Know-Nothing Party played a minor role in the transition from a Whig to a Republican Party in Massachusetts politics. Uses ecological regression to trace voters' transitions and alignments during the 1850's. 25 tables, 53 notes.

T. P. Linkfield

133. Baumann, Roland M. JOHN SWANWICK: SPOKESMAN FOR "MERCHANT-REPUBLICANISM" IN PHILADELPHIA, 1790-1798. *Pennsylvania Mag. of Hist. and Biog. 1973 97(2): 131-182.* Detailed biographical sketch of Democratic-Republican John Swanwick (1759-98) reveals that Philadelphia Republicans were supported by new entrepreneurial groups ("merchant-Republicans") as well as by persons with little or no property. These "merchant-Republicans" clashed with their Federalist counterparts over policy issues, "demanding greater protection of trade from foreign shippers, freer banking facilities, cheaper marine insurance, and a foreign policy that was immune from foreign domination." As spokesman at the national level for these "merchant-Republicans," Swanwick often was at odds with Jefferson on foreign and domestic issues. Swanwick's disagreements with Jefferson's policies sometimes reshaped Jefferson's thinking and are significant for revealing the strands of Democratic-Republicanism in the early National Period. Based on primary and secondary sources; 238 notes.

E. W. Carp

134. Baumann, Roland M. PHILADELPHIA'S MANUFACTURERS AND THE EXCISE TAXES OF 1794: THE FORGING OF THE JEFFERSONIAN COALITION. *Pennsylvania Mag. of Hist. and Biog. 1982 106(1): 3-40.* Manufacturers in Philadelphia, Pennsylvania, unhappy with the Hamiltonian tariff and the 1794 excise tax, moved from Federalism to the Democratic Republicans in an urban revolt more significant than the more famous agrarian insurrection. Based on manufacturers' MSS, Historical Society of Pennsylvania; published sources, official records; 4 tables, 135 notes.

T. H. Wendel

135. Becker, Ronald L. A BIBLIOGRAPHY RELATING TO THE BROAD SEAL WAR IN NEW JERSEY, 1838-40. *J. of the Rutgers U. Lib. 1982 44(1): 35-51.* The Broad Seal War was the result of a contested election between the Whig and Democratic parties for the six New Jersey seats in the US House of Representatives in 1838. This bibliography attempts to bring together all published sources dealing with the controversy. The argument is well-known by name to researchers of 19th-century American history but there has been little research based on many of the documents listed. Illus., biblio.

R. Van Benthuysen

136. Belohlavek, John M. THE DEMOCRACY IN A DILEMMA: GEORGE M. DALLAS, PENNSYLVANIA, AND THE ELECTION OF 1844. *Pennsylvania Hist. 1974 41(4): 391-411.* Discusses the events leading to the Democratic nomination of former Senator George M. Dallas for the vice-presidency in 1844 and the role Dallas played in formulating party strategy during the campaign. Based on the Polk and Dallas papers; illus., 26 notes.

D. C. Swift

137. Bloom, Jo Tice. THE CONGRESSIONAL DELEGATES FROM THE NORTHWEST TERRITORY. *Old Northwest 1977 3(1): 3-21.* Relates the services of the three Congressional territorial delegates from the Northwest Territory, William Henry Harrison (1773-1841), William McMillan (1764-1804), and Paul Fearing (1762-1822), who served between 1799 and Ohio's admission into the Union in 1803. Harrison, the superior, was responsible for two laws, the Harrison Land Law of 1800 which aided small farmers, and the law establishing the Ohio-Indiana boundry. He then became governor of Indiana Territory. McMillan and Fearing reflected Federalist strength at home but lacked influence in the Republican House after 1801. Based on Congressional documents, the St. Clair Papers, and secondary works; 68 notes.

J

138. Blue, Frederick J. CHASE AND THE GOVERNORSHIP: A STEPPING STONE TO THE PRESIDENCY. *Ohio Hist. 1981 90(3): 197-220.* Discusses the career of Salmon P. Chase during 1850-73, particularly his election as governor of Ohio in 1855 and his unrelenting bid to capture the Republican nomination for the presidency. As Ohio's governor, Chase managed to maintain a national prominence by subordinating state issues to national ones. Although he was a leader in the formation of the antislavery party, he ultimately failed to secure the presidential nomination because his stands on sectional issues, his obvious personal ambition, his past partisan record, and his inability to establish a smoothly functioning political machine alienated the moderates and conservatives within the Republican Party. Based on the Salmon P. Chase Papers at the Library of Congress, the Ohio Historical Society and the Historical Society of Pennsylvania, various archival collections of Harvard University and the Massachusetts Historical Society; photo, 74 notes.   L. A. Russell

139. Bochin, Hal W. CALEB B. SMITH'S OPPOSITION TO THE MEXICAN WAR. *Indiana Mag. of Hist. 1973 69(2): 95-114.* Moderate Whigs such as Caleb Blood Smith (1808-64) opposed Polk's war but supported the soldiers in the field. Smith was a recent appointee to the House Foreign Affairs Committee, and his importance to his party was growing. He presented antiwar resolutions to the House and delivered some of the House's strongest speeches against

the president and the war. He added nothing new to the debate; he merely selected and repeated the facts most damaging to the administration. Smith supported the Wilmot Proviso, yet called the issue of slavery in new territories a "distracting question." And though anxious to see an anti-Taylor, antiwar Whig nominated in 1848, Smith supported Taylor once that war favorite was nominated. Smith expected to be named Postmaster General, but was disappointed. Smith adopted positions which enjoyed the most popular support; he shifted with popular changes of mind. Based on primary sources; illus., 82 notes.   N. E. Tutorow

140.   Bochin, Hal W.   TOM CORWIN'S SPEECH AGAINST THE MEXI-CAN WAR: COURAGEOUS BUT MISUNDERSTOOD.   *Ohio Hist. 1981 90(1): 33-53.* Discusses Thomas Corwin's eloquent and emotional appeal delivered to the US Senate on 11 February 1847. Corwin's words allied him to the growing antiwar faction in the House of Representatives. Although he was attempting to unify the Whig Party stand he was misunderstood and served to further alienate the various intraparty factions. For a while the most praised and reviled speech against the Mexican War, Corwin's address formed the core of an important issue in the 1848 presidential election. Based on the archives of the Ohio Historical Society, the Indiana State Historical Society, the Indiana State Library, and the Library of Congress, the *Congressional Globe,* and other primary sources; photo, fig., 82 notes.   L. A. Russell

141.   Bourke, Paul F.   THE PLURALIST READING OF JAMES MADI-SON'S TENTH FEDERALIST.   *Perspectives in Am. Hist. 1975 9: 271-295.* In his 10th *Federalist*, James Madison exhibited a modern understanding of the character of political groupings and their inherent machinations. Many modern pluralists have cited the 10th *Federalist* as evidence of Madison's early perception of political expression, but the author believes this lifts Madison out of historical perspective. Calls for a reexamination of the accuracy of pluralists' views. 28 notes.   W. A. Wiegand

142.   Bowden, Mary Weatherspoon.   COCKLOFTS AND SLANG-WHAN-GERS: THE HISTORICAL SOURCES OF WASHINGTON IRVING'S *SAL-MAGUNDI.   New York Hist. 1980 61(2): 133-160.* The characters in *Salmagundi,* a periodical published by Washington Irving, his brother William, and Anthony Evergreen in 1807, were caricatures of such New York notables as Robert Fulton, DeWitt Clinton, Aaron Burr, Morgan Lewis, and the Livingston family. By caricaturing the Livingstons as the Cocklofts and Governor Morgan Lewis as Launcelot Langstaff, the Salmagundians ridiculed New York Federalist politics. Robert Fulton, caricatured as Will Wizard, is ridiculed for his steamboat, and Aaron Burr is portrayed as a pathetic "little man in black." Based on *Salmagundi,* contemporary newspapers, Washington Irving's letters, and secondary sources; 12 illus., 37 notes.   R. N. Lokken

143.   Boyd, Steven R.   ANTIFEDERALISTS AND THE ACCEPTANCE OF THE CONSTITUTION: PENNSYLVANIA, 1787-1792.   *Publius 1979 9(2): 123-137.* Pennsylvanian Antifederalists prepared the way for their own defeat by participating in the ratification process according to the rules established by the Federalists. They participated in the ratification convention and ran for offices in the federal election. Rather than reject outright the concept of the Constitution, they proposed revisions and a second constitutional convention;

consequently, they legitimized the concept of the federal government to the voters. 42 notes.   S

144. Boyett, Gene W.   A LETTER FROM ARCHIBALD YELL TO HENRY A. WISE, JULY 12, 1841.   *Arkansas Hist. Q. 1973 32(4): 337-341.* Yell hoped President Tyler would support states' rights Whigs by vetoing Clay's national bank bill.   S

145. Boyett, Gene W.   QUANTITATIVE DIFFERENCES BETWEEN THE ARKANSAS WHIG AND DEMOCRATIC PARTIES, 1836-1850. *Arkansas Hist. Q. 1975 34(3): 214-226.* The progressive historians' view that upper socio-economic classes supported Whigs and lower classes supported Jacksonian Democrats holds more truth in Arkansas than it does in states like New York and Michigan. The revisionists' theories of ethno-cultural differences among voters cannot be profitably applied in Arkansas because of the relative homogeneity of the population. Minor political and religious factors may have influenced voters, but class interests proved most important. Based on newspaper accounts, published documents, and secondary works; 3 tables, 25 notes.
T. L. Savitt

146. Bozeman, Theodore Dwight.   NEW (WHIG) LIGHT ON THE AMERICAN GREAT AWAKENINGS.   *Rev. in Am. Hist. 1979 7(3): 313-318.* Review article prompted by William C. McLoughlin's *Revivals, Awakenings, and Reform: An Essay on Religion and Social Change in America, 1607-1977* (Chicago: U. of Chicago Pr., 1978); applauds the author's theory of revitalization, but criticizes it for its liberal prejudices and Whig interpretation of history.

147. Breiseth, Christopher N.   LINCOLN, DOUGLAS, AND SPRINGFIELD IN THE 1858 CAMPAIGN.   Davis, Cullom; Strozier, Charles B.; Veach, Rebecca Monroe; and Ward, Geoffrey C., ed. *The Public and the Private Lincoln: Contemporary Perspectives* (Carbondale: So. Illinois U. Pr., 1979): 101-120. Abraham Lincoln and Stephen A. Douglas did not debate in Springfield, but the town and central Illinois were crucial for the election of the state legislature and selection of US senators. Of the local newspapers, the *Illinois State Journal* supported Lincoln while the *Illinois State Register* supported Douglas. The *Journal* had trouble explaining Lincoln's position on Negro equality while the *Register* harped on Negrophobia and the fear that Lincoln's hostility to slavery meant abolitionism and ultimately civil war. The *Register* was instrumental in swinging central Illinois behind the Democrats. 61 notes.   S

148. Briceland, Alan V.   THE PHILADELPHIA AURORA, THE NEW ENGLAND ILLUMINATI, AND THE ELECTION OF 1800.   *Pennsylvania Mag. of Hist. and Biog. 1976 100(1): 3-36.* During the election of 1800, Thomas Jefferson and the Republicans were accused by the high Federalist clergy of being agents of the Order of Illuminati, a European anti-Christian sect which through control of the societies of Freemasonry was blamed for overthrowing Church and state in revolutionary France. Writing in the *Aurora*, 1798-1800, Episcopal clergyman John C. Ogden (d. 1800) helped counteract this Federalist propaganda by portraying New England, the birthplace and main support of Jefferson's opponent, John Adams, as dominated by an intolerant clerical-political aristoc-

racy. Turning the tables on the Federalist clergy, Ogden began in 1799 to freely refer to to the Federalist clergy as the New England Illuminati, imputing to their antimasonry a desire to destroy religious liberty in America. Thus, in the minds of the *Aurora* readers Jefferson was associated with freedom of religion while Adams was tarred with the brush of religious bigotry. Based on primary and secondary sources; 117 notes.

E. W. Carp

149. Broussard, James H. THE NORTH CAROLINA FEDERALISTS, 1800-1816. *North Carolina Hist. Rev. 1978 55(1): 18-41.* Federalism in North Carolina differed from the usual pattern in other states. It had greater strength in North Carolina for the entire period 1800-16 than in any other southern state, and had less of a strictly sectional distribution than in Virginia and South Carolina. The North Carolina Federalists suffered little from malapportionment, gerrymandering, or partisan election laws, but the party did fail to capitalize on several issues which would have gained it some popularity among the electorate. Instead of rallying around the popular side of such controversies as judicial reform, legislators' pay, and taxation, the Federalists remained disorganized and unfocused. Based on family papers, legislative records, and contemporary newspaper reports; 10 illus., 2 tables, 64 notes.

T. L. Savitt

150. Broussard, James H. PARTY AND PARTISANSHIP IN AMERICAN LEGISLATURES: THE SOUTH ATLANTIC STATES, 1800-1812. *J. of Southern Hist. 1977 43(1): 39-58.* Very little work has been done to analyze or describe the workings of state legislatures during the era of the first party system, 1789-1820. Analysis of the legislatures of Virginia and both Carolinas reveals the lack of party affiliation, the lack of a party clash over the speakership, the casual allocation of committee seats, the moderate degree of party cohesion and the irregular use of the caucus. These factors indicate that party played a very modest role in legislative decisionmaking in the South Atlantic states. Based on archival and printed primary and secondary materials; 4 tables, appendix, 21 notes.

T. D. Schoonover

151. Broussard, James H. REGIONAL PRIDE AND REPUBLICAN POLITICS, THE FATAL WEAKNESS OF SOUTHERN FEDERALISM, 1800-1815. *South Atlantic Q. 1974 73(1): 23-33.* Consciousness of sectional interests caused southern voters to shun Federalist candidates and to be strongly Republican. Both presidential and congressional elections showed feeble Federalist resurgence from time to time, in contrast with strong Federalist revivals in some New England and Middle Atlantic states. The national Federalists were all commercial or professional northerners, not planters, and the votes of southern Federalists in Washington could only strengthen a party of commercial and financial men whose position ran counter to southern regional interests. 30 notes.

E. P. Stickney

152. Brown, Jeffrey P. SAMUEL HUNTINGTON: A CONNECTICUT ARISTOCRAT ON THE OHIO FRONTIER. *Ohio Hist. 1980 89(4): 420-438.* Discusses the career of Samuel Huntington, Jr. (1765-1817), especially the years after his move to the Ohio frontier. Born to one of Connecticut's most prominent families, he moved to frontier Ohio, became one of the leading figures in Great Lakes politics, and headed the coalition of conservative Republicans and Federalists that broke the liberal Republican hold in the state. An aristocratic leader in

a democratic society, Huntington illustrates the ease with which a prominent easterner could win high office in the sparsely settled West. Based on the archives of the Western Reserve Historical Society, the Ohio Historical society, and the State Library of Ohio; illus., 68 notes.   L. A. Russell

153. Brown, Thomas. THE SOUTHERN WHIGS AND ECONOMIC DEVELOPMENT. *Southern Studies 1981 20(1): 20-38.* In 1828, southerners who opposed the policies of Andrew Jackson became known as Whigs and vigorously opposed the nationalistic economic policies espoused by northern Whigs. By 1841, however, the southern Whigs had become supporters of economic nationalism. The change resulted from their primary feelings as members of a national party with national policies for the good of the entire country. They wanted to liberate the United States from economic subservience to Great Britain and supported the Tariff of 1842 as fundamental to American prosperity, which in turn supported American morals, religion, and law. By 1852 they reverted to local views and opposition. Based on the *Congressional Globe* (1841-52), newspaper accounts, and other primary sources; 47 notes.   J. J. Buschen

154. Brown, Thomas. SOUTHERN WHIGS AND THE POLITICS OF STATESMANSHIP, 1833-1841. *J. of Southern Hist. 1980 46(3): 361-380.* The old two-party South has been neglected and isolated as an area not deemed worthy of serious attention. The nagging question remains: Why did Southerners divide their loyalty between Democrats and Whigs when under attack as a region in the 1830's and 1840's? Clay's program of economic nationalism and concern for the general welfare allowed Southern Whigs to appear in an alluring combination as disinterested men of principle, party regulars, and statesmen. Based on the *Congressional Globe* and other printed primary and secondary sources; 46 notes.   T. D. Schoonover

155. Brown, Walter L. ROWING AGAINST THE STREAM: THE COURSE OF ALBERT PIKE FROM NATIONAL WHIG TO SECESSIONIST. *Arkansas Hist. Q. 1980 39(3): 230-246.* Arkansas lawyer Albert Pike's (1810-91) political loyalties changed from National Whig to Know-Nothing to Breckinridge Democrat to Secessionist during the 1850's and early 1860's. Based on newspapers, Pike's writings, and other primary sources; 45 notes.   G. R. Schroeder

156. Buel, Richard, Jr. THE DEMISE OF ANTIFEDERALISM. *Rev. in Am. Hist. 1980 8(3): 334-338.* Review essay of Steven R. Boyd's *The Politics of Opposition: Antifederalists and the Acceptance of the Constitution* (Millwood, N.Y.: KTO Pr., 1979) and John E. O'Connor's *William Paterson: Lawyer and Statesman, 1745-1806* (New Brunswick, N.J.: Rutgers U. Pr., 1979).

157. Bulkley, Robert D., Jr. A DEMOCRAT AND SLAVERY: ROBERT RANTOUL, JR. *Essex Inst. Hist. Collections 1974 110(3): 216-238.* Rantoul, a Massachusetts Democrat, evolved during his political career from a limited position to radical involvement in the abolition movement.   S

158. Burr, Nelson R. UNITED STATES SENATOR JAMES DIXON: 1814-1873, EPISCOPALIAN ANTI-SLAVERY STATESMAN. *Hist. Mag. of the Protestant Episcopal Church 1981 50(1): 29-72.* James Dixon of Connecticut served in the House of Representatives, 1845-49 and the Senate, 1857-69. His

religious upbringing—raised a Calvinist, he converted to Episcopalianism—influenced his politics. Opposed to slavery, he campaigned diligently for Lincoln in Connecticut, labored to get Gideon Welles in Lincoln's cabinet, and supported Johnson's policy of reconciliation in reconstruction. A very influential statesman, he contributed to both the Whig and the Republican Parties. Based on numerous collections of Dixon's papers in the Connecticut Historical Society, Connecticut State Library, the Library of Congress and New York Historical Society; 184 notes.

H. M. Parker, Jr.

159. Cain, Marvin R. RETURN TO REPUBLICANISM: A REAPPRAISAL OF HUGH SWINTON LEGARÉ AND THE TYLER PRESIDENCY. *South Carolina Hist. Mag. 1978 79(4): 264-280.* Despite the difficulty of forming a political coalition after the death of William H. Harrison, the Tyler administration, depending on the expertise of Attorney General Hugh Swinton Legaré, was able to revitalize republicanism and begin a movement to break the polarization between the Congress and the presidency, 1841-43.

160. Campbell, Leon G. THE POLITICS OF PREPARATION: A COMPARISON OF THE POLITICAL THOUGHT OF ALEXANDER HAMILTON AND JUAN BAUTISTA ALBERDI. *R. Interamericana R. [Puerto Rico] 1974 4(1): 85-95.* The careers of Hamilton (1755-1804) in the United States and Alberdi (1814-86) in Argentina are very much alike. Both men laid the philosophical groundwork for the constitutions of their countries. Secondary sources; 4 notes, biblio.

J. Lewis

161. Cardinal, Eric J. ANTISLAVERY SENTIMENT AND POLITICAL TRANSFORMATION IN THE 1850'S: PORTAGE COUNTY, OHIO. *Old Northwest 1975 1(3): 223-238.* Proposes that the slavery expansion issue became the overriding political issue in Portage County, Ohio, in the 1850's, by noting the previous failure of attempts to fuse local opposition to the national Democrats on other issues. Editor and Free Soil party leader Lyman W. Hall failed to fuse the Free Soilers and the Prohibitionists in 1853 and lost votes when he tried to fuse Republicans and Know-Nothings in 1855. Hall's striking 1856 victory in Portage County for Frémont was the result of his merger of all forces opposed to the Kansas-Nebraska Act (US, 1854). Based on Ohio newspapers, county histories, and secondary works; 38 notes.

162. Carriere, Marcus. POLITICAL LEADERSHIP OF THE LOUISIANA KNOW-NOTHING PARTY. *Louisiana Hist. 1980 21(2): 183-195.* Analysis of the age, wealth, and occupation of Louisiana's political leaders in the 1850's indicates that the American or Know-Nothing Party in this state differed significantly from its counterparts elsewhere. In Louisiana, the American Party was not exclusively the party of lawyers, businessmen, and older wealthy planters. Only in areas that lacked large concentrations of slaves did older wealth support the Americans. Moreover, Democrats and Americans in Louisiana were in many ways more similar than different. Based on 1860 US Census records; 7 tables, 44 notes.

D. B. Touchstone

163. Carson, Clarence B. THE FOUNDING OF THE AMERICAN REPUBLIC. *Freeman 1972 22(5): 273-283, (6): 341-354, (7): 419-433, (8): 471-485, (9): 550-561, (10): 616-627, (11): 684-699, (12): 734-736, 1973 23(1):*

31-44, (2): 85-98, (3): 165-182, (4): 195-206. Continued from a previous article (see abstract 10:103). Part X. A unique document, the American Declaration of Independence from Great Britain was a carefully rationalized justification of majority revolution; but its most enduring and essential message was its affirmation of what constitutes a good and proper government. 3 notes. Part XI. Traces civilian and military difficulties encountered by Americans in their struggle for independence, from the declaration of war to Valley Forge. 10 notes. Part XII. The most serious obstacle to the patriot war effort of the Revolution was inflation, the product of deficit financing and issuance of fiat money by the American governments. 38 notes. Part XIII. Considers ingredients of victory for the patriot cause: the war in the South which culminated in the glory of Yorktown; the happy, however inadequate, solution to the necessity for federated government, limited by the first written constitution of the United States; the double achievement of victory and empire negotiated at Paris; and the successful disbandment of the Army and the return of George Washington to Virginia without a crown. 14 notes. Part XIV. Changes in America after the Revolutionary War were directed toward freeing the individual citizen. 21 notes. Part XV. The impotence of the state and federal governments contributed to the series of domestic and international crises between 1782 and 1787 that in turn led to the call for a constitutional convention. 19 notes. Part XVI. Reviews the background of the participants and the issues at Philadelphia in 1787 at the Constitutional Convention. 29 notes. Part XVII. Examines the unique applications of political philosophy discussed and adopted by the Constitutional Convention: federal system, republican form of government, separation and balance of powers, limited government, and transformation of empire (state making). 19 notes. Part XVIII. The passage of the Bill of Rights was essential to the ratification of the U.S. Constitution, because without amendment there was no check against a consolidated government and no guarantee of individual freedom. 6 notes. Part XIX. Discusses the founding fathers' problems in making the federal government a reality in 1789. 15 notes. Part XX. Reviews the Washington administrations with particular emphasis on the unified program of Hamilton, which is defended, and the development of political parties. 15 notes. Part XXI. Concludes series with praise for the American revolutionaries, because they always kept their ideal in sight— "ordered liberty." From the author's *Rebirth of Liberty: The Founding of the American Republic, 1760-1800* (New Rochelle, N.Y.: Arlington House, 1973).

D. A. Yanchisin

164.   Castel, Albert.   **JIM LANE OF KANSAS.**   *Civil War Times Illus. 1973 12(1): 22-29.* Kansas state politics involving U.S. Senator James Henry Lane and the Free State Party.   S

165.   Cayton, Andrew R. L.   **THE FRAGMENTATION OF A "GREAT FAMILY": THE PANIC OF 1819 AND THE RISE OF THE MIDDLING INTEREST IN BOSTON, 1818-1822.**   *J. of the Early Republic 1982 2(2): 143-167.* In Boston, as the sizable post-Panic of 1819 business depression deepened, outdated Federalist notions of community, order, and deference were on the wane. During 1820-22, a coalition of tradesmen and mechanics, described as a "Middling Interest" that advocated majority rule and individualism, replaced Federalist organicism. Federalist control was weakened by the defeat of the Federalist Board of Selectmen over the issue of sales at auction in 1820, by the

growing power of the dissident Middling Interest in Boston as evidenced by the close vote in the Suffolk County congressional election of 1820, by the institution of ward voting for municipal contests, and by direct election of the mayor in the wards. The Middling Interest did not put an end to class structure or force an overt change in political personalities; however, this bloc did serve to accommodate new ideas, mediate conflicting interests, and promulgate majority rule. Primary and secondary sources; 52 notes.   G. A. Glovins

166. Collins, B. W.   ECONOMIC ISSUES IN OHIO'S POLITICS DURING THE RECESSION OF 1857-1858. *Ohio Hist. 1980 89(1): 46-64.* Discusses the interaction between local, state, and federal issues, as influenced by economics in Ohio. In the 1857-58 elections the Democrats suffered only mild losses because they were able to appeal to economic issues. However, after the elections the Republicans were able to turn public opinion to their advantage through the same economic issues. Primary sources; 59 notes.   J. Powell

167. Collins, Bruce.   THE IDEOLOGY OF THE ANTE-BELLUM NORTHERN DEMOCRATS. *J. of Am. Studies [Great Britain] 1977 11(1): 103-121.* Accounts for the popularity and substantial political support that Democrats enjoyed in the North for 15 years prior to the Civil War. Despite the Democratic Party's southern fire-eater and slaveowner elements, its ideologies provided ideas and helped build an image for Democrats that pleased many northern voters. Northern Democrats espoused states' rights, opposed banks, criticized corporate practices, and preached the ideals of a free society. They called for rapid territorial expansion of the United States, saying that in territorial expansion lay a means for "thwarting the pretensions of the Slave Power." Secondary sources; 51 notes.   H. T. Lovin

168. Collins, Bruce W.   THE DEMOCRATS' ELECTORAL FORTUNES DURING THE LECOMPTON CRISIS. *Civil War Hist. 1978 24(4): 314-331.* President James Buchanan exasperated and soured northern Democrats by his pro-slavery actions, but he did not destroy party popular support. Stephen A. Douglas fought for the 1860 presidential nomination because he believed that a less extreme prosouthern policy could keep a political coalition and assure his electoral victory. All that he had to do was to isolate the southern extremists. Modern historians have misread congressional party strength and politics. Published primary and secondary sources; 55 notes.   R. E. Stack

169. Conniff, James.   ON THE OBSOLESCENCE OF THE GENERAL WILL: ROUSSEAU, MADISON, AND THE EVOLUTION OF REPUBLICAN POLITICAL THOUGHT. *Western Pol. Q. 1975 28(1): 32-58.* James Madison revolutionized the political theory of the Republican form of government in *Federalist* #10. Republican theory before Madison's formulation was based on classical examples and on the idea that society could achieve an objective good. In addition it was thought that a Republic must have a homogeneous population and possess a small land area. The author shows how Jean Jacques Rousseau fitted into this pattern. The varied population and great expanse of the United States made it difficult for the Federalists to defend the new Constitution. Madison's solution was to reject the idea of the government enacting the general will and to maintain that its job was to balance competing interests. In that case the stronger the central government was and the greater was the size of the

country, the smaller the chance that any social group could gain unacceptable levels of power. Based on published works including the *Federalist Papers*, 116 notes.   G. B. McKinney

170.   Crackel, Theodore J.   JEFFERSON, POLITICS, AND THE ARMY: AN EXAMINATION OF THE MILITARY PEACE ESTABLISHMENT ACT OF 1802.   *J. of the Early Republic 1982 2(1): 21-38.* Investigates Thomas Jefferson's military policies in light of the Military Peace Establishment Act (US, 1802). Closer scrutiny reveals that the act proposed economies in army size with actually negligible financial expenditures. The true thrust of the act was to purge the army officer corps of its most vocal Federalist support and replace it with men of Republican sympathies. The act reinstated the rank of colonel in order to dilute the strength of the senior officers; it jettisoned key Federalist officers in the internal administration and control network, and transferred responsibilities to newly created civilian positions filled with Republicans. The act restructured the artillery corps and infantry companies to accommodate the appointment of junior grade Republican officers. Finally, it authorized the creation of West Point for the purpose of educating and training a Republican officer corps.   Primary and secondary sources; 2 plates, table, 37 notes.   G. A. Glovins

171.   Crosby, Richard W.   THE NEW YORK STATE RATIFYING CON-VENTION: ON FEDERALISM.   *Polity 1976 9(1): 97-116.* Discusses issues in forms of government in debates between Federalists and anti-Federalists over ratification of the proposed Constitution at the New York State Ratifying Con-vention in 1788.

172.   Curtis, James C.   IN THE SHADOW OF OLD HICKORY: THE PO-LITICAL TRAVAIL OF MARTIN VAN BUREN.   *J. of the Early Republic 1981 1(3): 249-267.* Ironically, the administration of Martin Van Buren, Andrew Jackson's second vice-president, is usually dismissed as a continuation of Jack-sonian policies. A new breed of party politician, Van Buren valued party over personal loyalty, and preferred to seek party goals through cooperation rather than confrontation with Congress. Ill at ease with Jackson's presidential style, Van Buren acted during his own administration to build party unity and rededi-cate the Democratic Party to states' rights. The Panic of 1837, however, led him to reject ineffectively controlled state banks for the federally managed subtreasury system. Accused of executive excess, portrayed as a lover of power, Van Buren misjudged the popular appeal of the Whig Party Log Cabin Campaign of 1840, losing to the other hero of the War of 1812, William Henry Harrison.   Based on Van Buren and Jackson papers and secondary literature; 40 notes.
                                                                              C. B. Schulz

173.   Dahl, Curtis.   THE CLERGYMAN, THE HUSSY, AND OLD HICK-ORY: EZRA STILES ELY AND THE PEGGY EATON AFFAIR.   *J. of Presbyterian Hist. 1974 52(2): 137-155.* The Peggy Eaton affair had considerable effect on the Democratic Party, the presidency of Andrew Jackson, and the ambitions of prominent politicians. Explains the role of the Presbyterian clergy-man the Reverend Dr. Ezra Stiles Ely in the scandal. 64 notes.   D. L. Smith

174. Danbom, David B. THE YOUNG AMERICA MOVEMENT. *J. of the Illinois State Hist. Soc. 1974 67(3): 294-306.* Young America was a loose coalition of young Democrats from the newer states in the early 1850's whose most important members were George Sanders of Kentucky and Stephen A. Douglas. Although both supported expansionism and intervention on the side of foreign republican movements, domestically they were Jeffersonian-Jacksonians. The movement's decline by 1856 was due to unsuccessful challenges to "old fogy" leaders, Douglas' failure to win the presidential nomination in 1852, an inability to deal with the slavery issue, and rising isolationism and disenchantment with reform in America. Primary and secondary sources; 2 illus., 30 notes.

L. Woolfe

175. Dearmont, Nelson S. FEDERALIST ATTITUDES TOWARD GOVERNMENTAL SECRECY IN THE AGE OF JEFFERSON. *Historian 1975 37(2): 222-240.* Shows that the issue of secrecy in government is a bedrock question dating not merely from the Nixon and other recent administrations, but back to the early years of the Constitution when controversies over foreign policy (Jefferson's embargo, acquisition of West Florida, war with Britain in 1812), parliamentary practice (voting the previous question), and the increasing use of closed congressional sessions led to popular suspicion of governmental power, and debate of the doctrine that publicity is essential to republicanism. Although traditionally associated with advocacy of aristocratic principles, the Federalists took the affirmative in this debate in part, perhaps, because they learned the importance of publicity to an out-of-office party during Jefferson's administration. Annals of Congress, 1789-1824; 57 notes.

N. W. Moen

176. Di Nunzio, Mario R. IDEOLOGY AND PARTY LOYALTY: THE POLITICAL CONVERSION OF LYMAN TRUMBULL. *Lincoln Herald 1977 79(3): 95-103.* Lyman Trumbull, whose political idol was Andrew Jackson, was typical of a number of Democrats who became Republicans during the late 1850's due to the controversy over the extension of slavery into the territories. His conversion was a slow, agonizing process, but his unwillingness to support Douglas and the Kansas-Nebraska Bill finally drove Trumbull into the newly formed Illinois Republican Party in 1856. For Trumbull, the extension of slavery overshadowed all other issues. He remained an effective Republican Senator until 1872, when he left the party over the issue of increased centralization of national power at the expense of local and states rights. Photo, 53 notes.

T. P. Linkfield

177. Di Nunzio, Mario R. and Galkowski, Jan T. POLITICAL LOYALTY IN RHODE ISLAND—A COMPUTER STUDY OF THE 1850'S. *Rhode Island Hist. 1977 36(3): 93-95.* Whig leaders shifted their allegience to nativist and antislavery parties, though most conservatives were unwilling to support radical Republicans in the 1860-61 gubernatorial elections. Democratic leaders remained loyal to their party. Based on published documents. newspapers, and secondary accounts; table, 8 notes.

P. J. Coleman

178. Dubovitskii, G. A. DEMOKRATICHESKAIA PARTIIA I POLITICHESKAIA BOR'BA V S.SH.A. V PERIOD PREZIDENTSTVA M. VANBIURENA (1836-1840) [SIC] [The Democratic Party and political struggle in the U.S.A. in the presidency of M. Van Buren]. *Vestnik Moskovskogo U., Seriia*

8: Istoriia [USSR] 1979 (3): 43-57. The depression of 1837-43 occurred during Martin Van Buren's presidency. The Democrats took over some of the ideas of the "locofocos" and proposed a variety of policies. Democrats favored an independent federal treasury, hard money, a reduced role for the government in the economy, and a liberal policy for the sale of public lands to encourage settlement; they opposed tariffs. The Southern plantation owners liked the Democratic emphasis on a weak central government. John C. Calhoun tried to get the party to take a pro-slavery position but this struggle over slavery took place after Van Buren. During his presidency, the Southerners were happy with the Democratic emphasis on economic policy and a weak central government. 62 notes. (See abstract 179).   D. Balmuth

179.   Dubovitskii, G. A.   THE DEMOCRATIC PARTY AND THE POLITICAL STRUGGLE IN THE UNITED STATES DURING THE PRESIDENCY OF M. VAN BUREN (1836-1840) [SIC]. *Soviet Studies in Hist. 1980 19(1): 61-86.* Translation of an article that first appeared in *Vestnik Moskovskogo Universiteta, Seriia 8. Istoriia* 1979. 62 notes.   S

180.   Duffy, John Joseph.   BROADSIDE ILLUSTRATIONS OF THE JEFFERSONIAN-FEDERALIST   CONFLICT   IN   VERMONT,   1809-1816. *Vermont Hist. 1981 49(4): 209-222.* Vermont prospered from the Champlain-Richelieu trade until Jefferson's 1807 embargo against trade with Great Britain was extended to prohibit inland trade with Canada. Federalists, especially large landowners and traders hurt by the embargo, distributed propaganda in broadsides hinting secession to join Canada and renew the vital trade. The poorer Jeffersonians, in counter broadsides, called violent resistance to revenue officers treason, pictured Britain as a devouring serpent, and capitalized on the patriotism aroused by the 1814 victories at Plattsburgh. 7 illus., biblio.
                                                                              T. D. S. Bassett

181.   Erler, Edward J.   THE PROBLEM OF THE PUBLIC GOOD IN *THE FEDERALIST*.   *Polity 1981 13(4): 649-667.* James Madison insisted in *The Federalist* (1787-88) that the public good derives not from virtue but from the diversity and rivalry of private interests. Yet by 1792 Madison had argued the necessity of a political party as the permanent representative of republican virtue. The author traces these changes and argues that it is doubtful if American political practices ever conformed to *The Federalist* position.   J/S

182.   Ethridge, Harrison M.   THE JORDAN HATCHER AFFAIR OF 1852: COLD JUSTICE AND WARM COMPASSION.   *Virginia Mag. of Hist. and Biog. 1976 84(4): 446-463.* When Governor Joseph Johnson commuted the death sentence of slave Jordan Hatcher to sale and transportation, the action precipitated a controversy with racial, political, and sectional overtones. A mob protest against Johnson at first produced a reaction in favor of the dignity of the office of governor. But during the next few months the affair was used by Johnson's fellow westerners to demand removal of the capital from Richmond, by Whigs to try to portray Democrat Johnson as an abolitionist, and by both parties to try to limit the governor's commutation powers. Based on several collections in the Virginia State Library, newspaper accounts, and published state records; 86 notes.   R. F. Oaks

183. Eulau, Heinz. POLARITY IN REPRESENTATIONAL FEDERA-LISM: A NEGLECTED THEME OF POLITICAL THEORY. *Publius 1973 3(2): 153-171.* Discusses the principle of administrative polarity in representational governmental bodies from 1787 to the 20th century, emphasizing the political theory of the *Federalist Papers*.

184. Fischer, Roger A. THE REPUBLICAN PRESIDENTIAL CAM-PAIGNS OF 1856 AND 1860: ANALYSIS THROUGH ARTIFACTS. *Civil War Hist. 1981 27(2): 123-137.* Historians, arguing from various printed documents, have claimed that the 1856 Republican Party campaign (John C. Frémont, presidential candidate) was a single-issue, ideological campaign while Abraham Lincoln's in 1860 was a multi-issue one and more personality-oriented. These descriptions are corroborated by the analysis of banners, buttons, and other artifacts from the two campaigns. Based on campaign artifacts and secondary sources; 37 notes.
G. R. Schroeder

185. Fisher, John E. THE DILEMMA OF A STATES' RIGHTS WHIG: THE CONGRESSIONAL CAREER OF R. M. T. HUNTER, 1837-1841. *Virginia Mag. of Hist. and Biog. 1973 81(4): 387-404.* Previous historians have misinterpreted the reasons which led R. M. T. Hunter to switch from the Whigs to the Democrats in the late 1830's. Rather than following the lead of John C. Calhoun, Hunter reluctantly changed parties after unsuccessful attempts to op-pose the positions of the Henry Clay faction on states' rights and the sub-treasury. Hunter first tried to maintain political independence, a position which led to his election as Speaker of the House, but eventually political realities forced him to join the party closest to his views. Based on newspapers and the Hunter-Garnett Papers at the University of Virginia; 38 notes.
R. F. Oaks

186. Folsom, Burton W., II. PARTY FORMATION AND DEVELOP-MENT IN JACKSONIAN AMERICA: THE OLD SOUTH. *J. of Am. Studies [Great Britain] 1973 7(3): 217-229.* Analyzes interpretations of Richard P. McCormick, especially those in his *The Second American Party System: Party Formation in the Jacksonian Era* (Chapel Hill: U. of North Carolina Press, 1966). McCormick focuses on institutional factors that engendered the party system, but Folsom challenges the "views of economic and sectional determinists" and em-phasizes other key forces in Jacksonian America. Based on secondary sources; 35 notes.
H. T. Lovin

187. Folsom, Burton W., II. THE POLITICS OF ELITES: PROMINENCE AND PARTY IN DAVIDSON COUNTY, TENNESSEE, 1835-1861. *J. of Southern Hist. 1973 39(3): 359-378.* Examines the prominent men of Davidson County, Tennessee, during 1835-61 in terms of political attitudes, affiliation, education, occupation, interrelations, religion, ethnic background, and Unionist sentiment. No clear socio-economic differences appear between Whig and Demo-cratic party members. Secondary sources; 45 notes.
N. J. Street

188. Formisano, Ronald P. DEFERENTIAL-PARTICIPANT POLITICS: THE EARLY REPUBLIC'S POLITICAL CULTURE, 1789-1840. *Am. Pol. Sci. Rev. 1974 68(2): 473-487.* The concepts of "party" and "party system" may be obscuring the nature of early national political culture. The presence of a modern party ethos before the 1830's seems to be taken for granted, as are

assumptions regarding the alleged benefits of party. Historians have not yet demonstrated, however, the many dimensions of institutionalized party behavior. Focus is recommended on three observable elements of party (after Sorauf): as organization, in office, in the electorate. Studies of party self-consciousness developing over the entire 1789-1840 period are necessary in various political units. Evidence is inconclusive, but weighs on balance against a first party system of Federalists and Republicans (1790's-1820's). While relatively stable elite coalitions and even mass cleavage patterns perhaps developed as staggered intervals in different arenas, especially during the war crisis period 1809-1816, the norms of party did not take root and pervade the polity. The era to the 1820's was transitional, a deferential-participant phase of mixed political culture roughly comparable to England's after 1832. Theories relating party to democratization, national integration, and political development, should be reconsidered.   J

189.   Fox, Stephen C.   THE BANK WARS, THE IDEA OF "PARTY," AND THE DIVISION OF THE ELECTORATE IN JACKSONIAN OHIO. *Ohio Hist. 1979 88(3): 253-276.* Describes the ambivalence of antebellum Americans regarding the use and trustworthiness of political parties, as illustrated by an analysis of voter response in Ohio to the organization and issues presented by the Democrats and Whigs. Could a two-party system, in doing away with the political caucus, really protect the rights of majorities and of minorities at the same time? Many voters distrusted national, strictly disciplined party regularity such as that demanded by the Democrats. There were social, religious and economic sources to account for pro- or anti-partyism. The Bank issue was political as well as economic and served only to renew the latent tension in regard to organized partisanship. 2 tables, 55 notes, ref.   H. F. Thomson

190.   Fox, Stephen C.   POLITICIANS, ISSUES, AND VOTER PREFERENCE IN JACKSONIAN OHIO: A CRITIQUE OF AN INTERPRETATION.   *Ohio Hist. 1977 86(3): 155-170.* Critiques two recent studies on political activity in Ohio during the Jacksonian era—James R. Sharp's *The Jacksonians versus the Banks: Politics in the State after the Panic of 1837* (N. Y., 1970) and Donald J. Ratcliffe's "The Role of Voters and Issues in Party Formation: Ohio, 1824" (see abstract 292). Both Sharp and Ratcliffe make narrow assumptions about the roots of political behavior and their methodologies are careless and unsophisticated. Discusses voters, economic issues, and party organization. Based on archival and secondary sources; illus., 2 tables, 28 notes.   N. Summers

191.   Friedman, Jean E. and Shade, William G.   JAMES M. PORTER: A CONSERVATIVE DEMOCRAT IN THE JACKSONIAN ERA.   *Pennsylvania Hist. 1975 42(3): 189-204.* James M. Porter, brother of Pennsylvania Governor David Porter, served briefly in 1843 as President John Tyler's Secretary of War until the Senate refused to confirm his appointment. Though not an important political figure, this Pennsylvania Democrat provides a case study of a politician, wed to traditional political values, who rejected the new political culture which was characterized by highly disciplined parties. James Porter supported the economic nationalism of Henry Clay and voted for him in the 1824 presidential election. In 1828 Porter supported John Quincy Adams for president. Porter joined the Democratic Party in large measure because he objected to the anti-Masonic and moralistic tone of the Pennsylvania Whigs. His brief tenure as a cabinet officer grew out of Tyler's efforts to forge a link with the David Porter faction of Pennsylvania Democrats. Illus., 50 notes.   D. C. Swift

192. Fritz, Harry W. THE WAR HAWKS OF 1812: PARTY LEADER-
SHIP IN THE TWELFTH CONGRESS. *Capitol Studies 1977 5(1): 25-42.* The
War Hawks of the 12th Congress constituted the leadership of the Republicans
(in the majority at the time), and Congress had the upper hand in dealing with
the President in the declaration of war with Great Britain in 1812.

193. Gienapp, William E. THE CRIME AGAINST SUMNER: THE CAN-
ING OF CHARLES SUMNER AND THE RISE OF THE REPUBLICAN
PARTY. *Civil War Hist. 1979 25(3): 218-245.* South Carolina Democratic
Congressman Preston S. Brooks's caning of Massachusetts Republican Senator
Charles Sumner on the Senate floor on 22 May 1856, after Sumner had made
scathing personal attacks on Brooks's relative, South Carolina Democratic Senator Andrew P. Butler, created even more support for the fledgling Republican
Party than did the repeal of the Missouri Compromise and the troubles in the
Kansas Territory. Describes the instant, rampant, and deep-seated indignation in
the North, protest meetings, Republican themes, the destruction of Millard Fillmore's chances in the 1856 election, and John Frémont's good showing in that
election. The caning caused such political and sectional animosity that it "was
a major landmark on the road to civil war." 97 notes.   S

194. Gilley, B. H. TENNESSEE WHIGS AND THE MEXICAN WAR.
Tennessee Hist. Q. 1981 40(1): 46-67. Despite the state's long association with
Texas and the large number of Tennesseans who volunteered for service, the state
parties argued bitterly over the war. Whigs not only accused President James K.
Polk of starting the war but also claimed that he suppressed news and played
politics with military appointments. Thus, the president's home state witnessed
much the same division of opinion as other states, including much opposition to
the acquisition of territory. Nevertheless, Polk was not greatly influenced and
continued on his expansionist course. Based on contemporary newspapers, congressional records, and Polk's diary; 80 notes.   C. L. Grant

195. Ginsberg, Judah B. BARNBURNERS, FREE SOILERS, AND THE
NEW YORK REPUBLICAN PARTY. *New York Hist. 1976 57(4): 475-500.*
Opposition to the Kansas-Nebraska Act and repeal of the Missouri Compromise
Line of 1820 led New York antislavery Democrats to secede from the party and
to join the new Republican Party by 1856. Suggests that ex-Democrats played a
key role in Republican election victories in New York State in 1856 and 1860.
3 illus., 4 tables, 52 notes.   R. N. Lokken

196. Goladay, Dennis. JOHN NICHOLAS: VIRGINIA CONGRESSMAN,
NEW YORK QUID. *New York Hist. 1979 60(1): 5-28.* John Nicholas (1764-
1819) was a Virginia Republican leader in the House of Representatives during
1793-1801, before he and other Virginians settled in the Finger Lakes region of
New York after 1801. In Genesee county he was active in farming, business,
and woolen manufacturing. Returning to Republican Party politics, he served in
local offices and, during 1805-09, in the state senate where he was associated with
the Quid faction of the party. Loyal to the Republican Party nationally, he was
too uncomfortable with the factionalism of New York Republicans to remain in
state office after 1809. 4 illus., 46 notes.   R. N. Lokken

197. Goldfield, David R.   MARKETING A CANDIDATE: HENRY A. WISE AND THE ART OF MASS POLITICS.   *Virginia Cavalcade 1976 26(1): 30-37.* With an enlarged franchise and a new provision in the state constitution for the popular election of the governor, Henry A. Wise, in 1854, a staunch Democrat, initiated and won the first campaign taken to the "people."

198. Goodman, Paul.   PERSPECTIVES ON THE PRESIDENCY AND THE PARTIES IN THE 1790'S.   *Rev. in Am. Hist. 1975 3(1): 71-76.* Review article prompted by Rudolph M. Bell's *Party and Faction in American Politics: The House of Representatives, 1789-1801* (Westport, Conn.: Greenwood Pr., 1973) and Forrest McDonald's *The Presidency of George Washington* (Lawrence: U. Pr. of Kansas, 1974).

199. Grant, C. L.   SENATOR BENJAMIN HAWKINS: FEDERALIST OR REPUBLICAN?   *J. of the Early Republic 1981 1(3): 233-247.* Benjamin Hawkins, first senator from North Carolina during 1790-95, usually has been classified as a Federalist because of his friendship with George Washington, his opposition to radical economic demands, his support of excise taxes, and his identification with the Federalist faction in North Carolina. A nationalist and a diligent senator who was at his best in committee assignments, Hawkins is more correctly viewed as an independent whose friendship with Thomas Jefferson, James Madison, and James Monroe increasingly led him to vote with the Jeffersonian faction for a permanent capital on the Potomac and against a national bank and the appointment of John Jay to England in 1794. Hawkins admired France and hated Great Britain, positions consistent with the views of his North Carolina constituents. Based on contemporary correspondence and *Annals of Congress;* 42 notes.

C. B. Schulz

200. Gudelunas, William, Jr.   NATIVISM AND THE DEMISE OF SCHUYLKILL COUNTY WHIGGERY: ANTI-SLAVERY OR ANTI-CATHOLICISM.   *Pennsylvania Hist. 1978 45(3): 225-236.* The Schuylkill County, Pennsylvania, Whigs disintegrated in 1853-54 because they were not the strong anti-Catholic and prohibitionist force that potential supporters wanted. The Kansas-Nebraska Act was not an important factor in the demise of the party in this farming and mining county. Benjamin Bannan, editor of the *Pottsville Miners' Journal,* played a major role in bringing about a coalition of prohibitionist and anti-Catholic forces. Uses quantitative methods based on newspapers and other primary and secondary sources; photo, 3 tables, 48 notes.

D. C. Swift

201. Hackett, D. L. A.   SLAVERY, ETHNICITY, AND SUGAR: AN ANALYSIS OF VOTING BEHAVIOUR IN LOUISIANA, 1828-1844.   *Louisiana Studies 1974 13(2): 73-118.* Analyzes voting behavior in Louisiana by parishes, examining the votes given to the National Republicans/Whigs and Democrats in the presidential elections, and the Creole/Whigs and American/-Democrats in the gubernatorial elections. These votes are examined in relation to the possible influence of ethnicity, nativity, slavery, sugar, cotton, wealth, and population change on voting patterns. Concludes that ethnicity and sugar production were the variables showing the greatest impact on voting behavior. Slavery is much less significant. Thus it appears that ethnocultural conflict, not class conflict, was more important in influencing voting behavior. 53 tables, 9 notes.

R. V. Ritter

202. Hackett, Derek L. A. "VOTE EARLY! BEWARE OF FRAUD!" A NOTE ON VOTER TURNOUT IN PRESIDENTIAL AND GUBER-NATORIAL ELECTIONS IN LOUISIANA, 1828-1844. *Louisiana Studies 1975 14(2): 179-188.* Examines the estimates of voter eligibility and turnout in Louisiana during the Age of Jackson by Richard McCormick, Joseph Tregle, Perry Howard, and Emmett Asseff. Discovers wide differences in the estimates of these writers. Points out the errors in the studies, gives new estimates, and depicts avenues for future research. Primary sources and secondary sources; table, 28 notes.
B. A. Glasrud

203. Hackett, Derek. THE DAYS OF THIS REPUBLIC WILL BE NUM-BERED: ABOLITION, SLAVERY, AND THE PRESIDENTIAL ELEC-TION OF 1836. *Louisiana Studies 1976 15(2): 131-160.* The presidential campaign of 1836 between Democratic candidate Martin Van Buren (1782-1862) and Whig candidate Hugh Lawson White (1773-1840) is significant because it marks the breakup of the dominant Democratic Party and inaugurates a national two-party system. In Louisiana, as an example, this situation came about for ideological reasons, especially the fear that a northerner such as Van Buren would be unable or unwilling to defend slavery. Newspapers in Louisiana during the campaign are filled with articles about fears of slave uprisings such as the "Mur-rell Conspiracy" of 1835 and attempts at abolition. Articles, letters to the editor, and editorials on these themes dominate in discussions of the election. Based on letters and papers in Louisiana State U. Library, Louisiana legislative records, Louisiana newspaper accounts, and secondary sources; table, 90 notes.
J. Buschen

204. Hake, Herbert V. THE POLITICAL FIRECRACKER: SAMUEL J. KIRKWOOD. *Palimpsest 1975 56(1): 2-14.* Samuel J. Kirkwood's political career was unique in the annals of Iowa history. A miller and farmer by trade, he helped organize the Republican Party in Iowa in 1856, and by 1859 had been elected governor. Declining appointment as Minister to Denmark, he was twice elected US Senator and in 1881 became Secretary of the Interior. Despite having held such prestigious federal positions, he took greatest pride in having been "War Governor" of Iowa. 2 illus., 6 photos, note.
D. W. Johnson

205. Hall, Kermit L. ANDREW JACKSON AND THE JUDICIARY: THE MICHIGAN TERRITORIAL JUDICIARY AS A TEST CASE, 1828-1832. *Michigan Hist. 1975 59(3): 131-151.* Local partisan demands, community pres-sure, and concern for judicial integrity guided Andrew Jackson's appointments to the Michigan bench, but national political priorities played a more important role. The President's willingness to subordinate local interests to national party development when making territorial court appointments indicates that substan-tial factional cohesion had developed by the early 1830's. But Jackson acted not merely out of political expediency, for he refused to remove opposition jurists summarily, preferring instead to make appointments only as terms expired. Based on primary and secondary sources; 3 illus., 70 notes.
D. W. Johnson

206. Hall, Kermit L. SOCIAL BACKGROUNDS AND JUDICIAL RE-CRUITMENT: A NINETEENTH CENTURY PERSPECTIVE ON THE LOWER FEDERAL JUDICIARY. *Western Pol. Q. 1976 29(2): 243-257.* Studies of the recruitment and backgrounds of federal lower court judges have

focused on the twentieth century. A longitudinal perspective raises questions about the impact of professionalization, the legitimacy of the judiciary in democratic government, and the relationship of party systems to the recruitment process. During the Second American Party System (1829-61), 101 men occupied positions in the federal lower judiciary. These judges exhibited greater diversity in social origins, education, preparation for the bench, and political activity than mid-twentieth-century district court judges. They were more active in seeking elected political office, but they attained levels of judicial and prosecutorial experience comparable to twentieth-century judges. These differences seem to parallel characteristics of the two-party systems of the eras. Attempts to professionalize the judiciary have not increased judicial experience, but have resulted in the recruitment of judges with little exposure to the democratic process of elected government.

J

207.   Harmond, Richard.   EBENEZER SAGE OF SAG HARBOR: AN OLD REPUBLICAN IN YOUNG AMERICA, 1812-1834.   *New-York Hist. Soc. Q. 1973 57(4): 309-325.* The "second Party System" saw 1) parties accepted as a part of society and 2) the political process become more democratic. The reaction of Ebenezer Sage shows what happened to the northern Old Republicans during this change. Sage, a three-term representative from Long Island, lived long enough to see the Jacksonians triumph; yet he remained basically true to the early Jeffersonian Republican principles. A study of such Old Republicans helps to indicate the vast differences between them and their Jacksonian successors. Contemporary correspondence and secondary sources; 4 illus., 39 notes.

C. L. Grant

208.   Harrison, Lowell.   THE PRESIDENT WITHOUT A PARTY.   *Am. Hist. Illus. 1981 16(1): 12-21.* Originally a Democrat, John Tyler joined the amorphous Whig Party that formed in the 1830's, was elected vice president on the Whig ticket in 1840, and became the first vice president to succeed to the presidency (when William Henry Harrison died); when policy differences with other Whigs expelled him from the party, Tyler was forced to govern without party support.

209.   Harrold, Stanley C., Jr.   FORGING AN ANTISLAVERY INSTRUMENT: GAMALIEL BAILEY AND THE FOUNDATION OF THE OHIO LIBERTY PARTY.   *Old Northwest 1976 2(4): 371-387.* Gamaliel Bailey (ca. 1808-59) refused to form an independent abolitionist party in Ohio in the 1830's because it could not influence the policies of the major parties, could not attract votes, and would alienate public opinion on constitutional grounds. Instead he formed a Liberty Party to be the political arm of the antislavery movement and to pressure either the Whigs or the Democrats into opposing slavery. Salmon P. Chase (1808-73) became the Ohio leader of the new party, and the conceptual groundwork for the Republican Party of the 1850's was established. Based on the Library of Congress' Chase Papers, newspapers, and secondary works; 54 notes.

J

210.   Hatzenbuehler, Ronald L. and Ivie, Robert L.   JUSTIFYING THE WAR OF 1812: TOWARD A MODEL OF CONGRESSIONAL BEHAVIOR IN EARLY WAR CRISES.   *Social Sci. Hist. 1980 4(4): 453-478.* This study analyzes congressional voting, party cohesion, and especially the rhetoric of

congressional debate in three crisis situations (1798, 1808, and 1812) in an attempt to isolate key factors responsible for the decision to go to war in 1812. The findings are then used to suggest a general model for understanding the declaration of war and the role of congressional partisanship in the decision. Based on *Annals of Congress* and secondary sources; 8 tables, 2 notes, biblio.

L. K. Blaser

211. Hatzenbuehler, Ronald L. THE WAR HAWKS AND THE QUESTION OF CONGRESSIONAL LEADERSHIP IN 1812. *Pacific Hist. Rev. 1976 45(1): 1-22.* Scale analyses of foreign policy roll calls in the Twelfth Congress isolate eight congressmen as war hawks. They were extremists who differed from their Republican Party colleagues in their support for an expanded navy and for reorganization of state militias. The eight war hawks were not the leaders of the war movement. The leaders were Speaker of the House Henry Clay, the House Foreign Affairs Committee, Secretary of State James Monroe, and President James Madison. They led a broad Republican consensus on the issues of troops, taxes, embargo, and war itself. Based on *Annals of Congress,* manuscripts in the Library of Congress, National Archives, Buffalo and Erie Historical Society, New York State Library, and published document collections; 6 tables, 55 notes.

W. K. Hobson

212. Hickey, Donald R. FEDERALIST DEFENSE POLICY IN THE AGE OF JEFFERSON, 1801-1812. *Military Affairs 1981 45(2): 63-70.* The traditional view of the Federalists is that after 1801 they had few capable leaders and no credible policies. A review of their speeches and votes in Congress and of their newspapers suggests that this view is unwarranted. The Federalists continued to advocate a pro-British foreign policy to take advantage of vital British trade, and military and naval preparedness. Primary sources; 45 notes. A. M. Osur

213. Hickey, Donald R. FEDERALIST PARTY UNITY AND THE WAR OF 1812. *J. of Am. Studies [Great Britain] 1978 12(1): 23-39.* Federalists more unitedly opposed the War of 1812 than has been supposed. Before the war Southern and western Federalists shared with New Englanders a distaste for conflict with Great Britain. Federalists in Congress voted unitedly against the declaration of war in 1812, and thereafter on key measures before Congress, such as financing and troops. At least 90% of the Federalists voted against the legislation. Similarly Federalists remained united, except at the beginning, in support of the Treaty of Ghent which ended the war. Based on archival material, newspapers, and secondary sources; 49 notes. H. T. Lovin

214. Hickey, Donald R. THE FEDERALISTS AND THE COMING OF WAR, 1811-1812. *Indiana Mag. of Hist. 1979 75(1): 70-81.* Discusses the role of the Federalist party in the origins of the War of 1812. The Federalist opposition to full-scale war with Great Britain was not simply the result of partisan politics, but was founded on policy concerns. Based on the successes of limited naval war against the French in 1798, the Federalists believed that a carefully limited naval war was the best way to defend US commerce. 37 notes. J. Moore

215. Hoadley, John F. THE EMERGENCE OF POLITICAL PARTIES IN CONGRESS, 1789-1803. *Am. Pol. Sci. Rev. 1980 74(3): 757-779.* Although the political leaders who wrote the Constitution did not hold the idea of party in high

regard, these same individuals (according to many historians) became the founders of a new party system within the first decade of the new government. This article considers the question (on which no consensus exists) of whether parties did develop. The analysis focuses upon one aspect of party development, namely, the agreement among members of Congress in their roll-call voting records. Spatial analysis (multidimensional scaling) permits a visual picture of the increased clustering of congressmen into two party blocs from 1789 to 1803, especially after the Jay Treaty debate in 1796. This very clear trend supports the idea that politics was moving away from a sectional basis to one founded more clearly on partisan grounds.   J

216.   Hoelscher, Robert J.   THADDEUS STEVENS AS A LANCASTER POLITICIAN, 1842-1868.   *J. of the Lancaster County Hist. Soc. 1974 78(4): 157-213.* Chronicles Thaddeus Stevens' political career in Lancaster, Pennsylvania, 1842-68, concentrating on his impact on local politics and his relations with constituents and political parties; touches on his community standing, personal relationships, activities as a philanthropist, and career in law.

217.   Holder, Ray.   THE BROWN-WINANS CANVASS FOR CONGRESS, 1849.   *J. of Mississippi Hist. 1978 40(4): 353-373.* William Winans's defeat by the incumbent, Albert Gallatin Brown, for representative of the Fourth Congressional District in 1849 tolled the death knell for Mississippi Whiggery. Brown's triumph marked the rise of Democratic Party domination of state politics for the next century. Because of the significance of the election and the canvass which preceded it, analyzes the tactics as well as the issues stressed by each candidate. Both men and their supporters expressed their positions on slavery, abolitionism, sectionalism, and secessionism. Particularly noteworthy were Winans's attitudes toward the authority of Congress to regulate the expansion of slavery into the territories.   M. S. Legan

218.   Holt, Michael F.   THE POLITICS OF IMPATIENCE: THE ORIGINS OF KNOW NOTHINGISM.   *J. of Am. Hist. 1973 60(2): 309-331.* The Know-Nothing Party was the fastest growing political force in many parts of the United States, 1853-56, probably contributing to the disintegration of the Whig Party as much as did the slavery issue. Know-nothingism fed on a surge of anti-Catholic sentiment among workers and the middle class in several eastern and midwestern states. These supporters were bewildered by rapid economic and social change and opposed political manipulators and the convention system. Voters previously identified with the traditional parties were impatient at their failure to take stands, especially on the issues of temperance and public schools. When the Know-Nothing Party nominated Millard Fillmore, many of its supporters turned to the Republicans who adopted the style and some issues of Know-Nothingism. 76 notes.   K. B. West

219.   Horowitz, Robert F.   JAMES M. ASHLEY AND THE PRESIDENTIAL ELECTION OF 1856.   *Ohio Hist. 1974 83(1): 4-16.* James M. Ashley aimed to create a national machine favoring Salmon P. Chase's candidacy. Though Chase established a power base by becoming governor, his Free Soil/Know-Nothing ties made him unelectable. Ashley played a major role in bringing about a national convention with a party platform in line with Chase's views. Primary and secondary sources; 2 illus., 74 notes.   S. S. Sprague

220. Howard, Victor B. JOHN BROWN'S RAID AT HARPERS FERRY AND THE SECTIONAL CRISIS IN NORTH CAROLINA. *North Carolina Hist. Rev. 1978 55(4): 396-420.* John Brown's Harpers Ferry raid greatly frightened North Carolinians owing to its proximity of their state. During 1840-57 North Carolinians engaged in sporadic activities such as intercepting antislavery mail and harrassing known abolitionists. Publication of *The Impending Crisis* by fellow state resident Hinton Rowan Helper embarrassed North Carolinians and caused an intensification of these antiabolitionist efforts. John Brown's raid brought home the threat of a change of status for blacks. Reaction was especially strong in the Piedmont, though suspicion and harrassment of blacks and antislavery whites was present throughout the state. In addition, Democrats used the raid to discredit Whigs. Contemporary newspaper accounts, unpublished correspondence, published state and local records and personal papers, and secondary sources; 8 illus., map, 88 notes.
T. L. Savitt

221. Howe, Daniel Walker. VIRTUE AND COMMERCE IN JEFFERSONIAN AMERICA. *Rev. in Am. Hist. 1981 9(3): 347-353.* Review essay of Drew McCoy's *The Elusive Republic: Political Economy in Jeffersonian America* (1980) and Robert E. Shalhope's *John Taylor of Caroline: Pastoral Republican* (1980), which focus on the debate between the Jeffersonians and the Hamiltonians regarding government and commerce.

222. Hutson, James H. COUNTRY, COURT, AND CONSTITUTION: ANTIFEDERALISM AND THE HISTORIANS. *William and Mary Q. 1981 38(3): 337-368.* Surveys treatment of the antifederalists by historians. Emphasis is placed on the Progressive historians, who, following Frederick Jackson Turner's 1893 thesis, portrayed the antifederalists as democrats. Antifederalism was strongest among inland farmers and frontiersmen. The Progressive interpretation of antifederalism as a democratic movement has been challenged since the 1950's, beginning with Merrill Jensen's two works on the Confederation period, stressing radical versus conservative struggle for rule. Cecelia M. Kenyon led the way for the consensus theory. Subsequent historiography on the antifederalists, by both the new revisionists and neo-Progressives, is analyzed. With the Progressive and consensus schools now finding common ground, the best interpretation is that of "country" versus "court." Based on writings on the adoption of the Constitution; 143 notes.
H. M. Ward

223. Igarashi, T. PENNSYLVANIA KYOWAHA NO SEIJISHIDO (1)— AMERICA GASHUKOKU RENPOTAISEI KEISEIKATEI NOIKOUK— [The political leadership of the Pennsylvania Republicans (1): a study of the evolution of federalism in the United States]. *Kokkagakkai Zasshi [Japan] 1976 89(3-4): 34-92.* Investigates the factors that contributed to the operation of the federal system after the Constitution was promulgated; article to be continued.

224. Ilisevich, Robert D. CLASS STRUCTURE AND POLITICS IN CRAWFORD COUNTY, 1800-1840. *Western Pennsylvania Hist. Mag. 1980 63(2): 95-119.* Examines the concentration of wealth and the stratification of society and their relationship to politics in Crawford County, Pennsylvania, which was divided into rich Federalists and poor Antifederalists.

225.   Jackson, Harvey.   BUTTON GWINNETT: WHIG TO EXCESS OR SCOUNDREL?   *Am. Hist. Illus. 1981 16(5): 18-24.* Biography of Button Gwinnett (d. 1777), Georgia signer of the Declaration of Independence, a businessman and politician who "personified both the constructive and the destructive forces unleashed in the colonial struggle for independence"; 1765-77.

226.   Jeffrey, Thomas E.   "FREE SUFFRAGE" REVISITED: PARTY POLITICS AND CONSTITUTIONAL REFORM IN ANTEBELLUM NORTH CAROLINA.   *North Carolina Hist. Rev. 1982 59(1): 24-48.* Contrary to most historians' statements, the possibility that free suffrage, or the 50-acre freehold requirement allowing one to vote for state senators, might be repealed was not key to the 1848-50 rise of Democrats over Whigs. Traditional interpretations assert that David S. Reid, the Democratic gubernatorial nominee, and William W. Holden, editor of the Raleigh *North Carolina Standard,* represented a new generation of progressive reform Democrats that enticed the electorate from Whigs who opposed free suffrage. Actually, reform issues split the precarious alliance between eastern and western Whigs. Holden also used his newspaper to misrepresent Whig attitudes toward free suffrage in the 1848 and 1850 elections. Based on North Carolina newspaper editorials and reports, and on private papers of key figures of the period; 9 illus., 4 maps, table, 56 notes.   T. L. Savitt

227.   Jeffrey, Thomas E.   INTERNAL IMPROVEMENTS AND POLITICAL PARTIES IN ANTEBELLUM NORTH CAROLINA, 1836-1860.   *North Carolina Hist. Rev. 1978 55(2): 111-156.* Political party affiliations played a small role in the general support North Carolina legislators gave to internal improvements during 1836-60. Sectionalism was much more important in determining votes, especially in the west, than was membership in the Whig or Democratic Party. Year-by-year analyses of state legislature party affiliations and voting behaviors on every internal improvements bill demonstrate how difficult it was for multisectional parties to address a sectional issue like internal improvements. Legislative records, private papers, and newspapers; 18 illus., 5 maps, 4 tables, 94 notes.   T. L. Savitt

228.   Jeffrey, Thomas E.   "THUNDER FROM THE MOUNTAINS": THOMAS LANIER CLINGMAN AND THE END OF WHIG SUPREMACY IN NORTH CAROLINA.   *North Carolina Hist. Rev. 1979 56(4): 366-395.* In explaining the end of Whig supremacy in North Carolina by 1852, historians have traditionally pointed both to the popularity of the free suffrage issue and to the disaffection of states' rights Whigs such as Thomas Lanier Clingman (1812-97) with the antislavery sentiments of northern Whigs. Western North Carolina registered the greatest shift in Whig support between 1840 and 1860, from 72% to 50%. Clingman's defection to the Democratic Party in the mid-1850's contributed to that loss, but not because antislavery was the main issue. His senatorial aspirations caused him to intone Democratic rhetoric, while his Whig constituents liked his stand on western rights issues and state political reform. Based on family papers, newspaper accounts, and local government documents; 11 illus., table, 82 notes.   T. L. Savitt

229.   Johannsen, Robert W.   THE LINCOLN-DOUGLAS CAMPAIGN OF 1858: BACKGROUND AND PERSPECTIVE.   *J. of the Illinois State Hist. Soc. 1980 73(4): 242-262.* Discusses the events leading up to the election of

Stephen A. Douglas as US senator from Illinois in 1858. At this time factions in the United States were deeply divided over the slavery question, and the campaign between Abraham Lincoln and Douglas assumed an important role as they were symbolic of the anti- and proslavery positons. Douglas won the election, but the victory for the Democrats only heightened the division over the slavery question. Primary sources; 58 notes.

J. Powell

230. Johnson, Dick. ALONG THE TWISTED ROAD TO CIVIL WAR: HISTORIANS AND THE "APPEAL OF THE INDEPENDENT DEMO-CRATS." *Old Northwest 1978 4(2): 119-141.* A bibliographical essay relating the opinions of 10 eminent historians from James Ford Rhodes (1848-1927) to David Potter (1910-71) regarding the 1854 "Appeal of the Independent Democrats in Congress to the People of the United States" by Salmon P. Chase (1808-73) and others, against the pending Kansas-Nebraska Act (US, 1854). Modern opinion holds that Stephen A. Douglas (1813-61), failing to control the forces he spoke for, earned southern support because Chase accused Douglas of deserving it. Wishing to form an antislavery party in Ohio, Chase intended to destroy Democratic Party unity at least in Ohio. Secondary works; 40 notes.

J. N. Dickinson

231. Johnson, Dick. THE ROLE OF SALMON P. CHASE IN THE FOR-MATION OF THE REPUBLICAN PARTY. *Old Northwest 1977 3(1): 23-38.* Salmon P. Chase's (1808-1873) role in the Republican Party's formation in 1855, neglected by modern historians, was indispensable. His was the only significant 1855 Republican victory in which he united diverse Ohio factions thus creating a model for other state organizations. He established a national Republican communication network; and as an avowed radical, he attracted conservatives trying to modify the movement when it appeared that the Republicans might succeed. Thus Nathaniel Banks (1816-1894) and Francis Blair, Sr. (1791-1876) launched the drive that made John C. Frémont (1813-1890) the 1856 presidential nominee. Based on the Historical Society of Pennsylvania's Chase Papers and secondary works; 34 notes.

J

232. Johnson, Reinhard O. THE LIBERTY PARTY IN VERMONT, 1840-1848: THE FORGOTTEN ABOLITIONISTS. *Vermont Hist. 1979 47(4): 258-275.* The Liberty Party won 319 votes for Birney in 1840, and soon replaced the Vermont Antislavery Society as the state abolitionist organization. Drawing first from the Whig Party and then from the Democrats, it prepared the base for the Free Soil Party of 1848-54 to "become the dominant element in Vermont state politics." Its weekly *Green Mountain Freeman,* edited by Joseph Poland, had the largest circulation of any Vermont newspaper in 1847. Based mainly on the abolitionist press; 55 notes.

T. D. S. Bassett

233. Johnson, Reinhard O. THE LIBERTY PARTY IN NEW HAMP-SHIRE, 1840-1848: ANTISLAVERY POLITICS IN THE GRANITE STATE. *Hist. New Hampshire 1978 33(2): 123-166.* The Liberty Party, founded by aboli-tionists at Albany, N.Y., in 1840, became the main conduit of antislavery senti-ments during the 1840's, and was a basis for many state Free Soil parties, as in New Hampshire. Although the New Hampshire party lacked strong leadership and an effective press, and drifted from election to election, it did attract unhappy Whigs and Democrats before merging with the Independent Democrats in 1846. 76 notes.

D. F. Chard

234.   Johnson, Reinhard O.   THE LIBERTY PARTY IN MAINE, 1840-1848: THE POLITICS OF ANTISLAVERY REFORM.   *Maine Hist. Soc. Q. 1980 19(3): 135-176.* Traces the origins and development of the antislavery Liberty Party in Maine politics in the 1840's. The groups involved in the state's abolition movement in the 1830's, at first reluctant to engage directly in politics, provided the strong leaders, such as Samuel Fessenden (1784-1869) and Austin Willey (1806-96), and the religious and moral convictions that characterized the party. It had a major impact on Maine politics until it merged into the Free Soil movement in the late 1840's. Based on newspapers and Willey's *History of the Antislavery Cause in State and Nation* (1886); 2 illus., 2 charts, 88 notes.
C. A. Watson

235.   Jones, Thomas B.   HENRY CLAY AND CONTINENTAL EXPANSION, 1820-1844.   *Register of the Kentucky Hist. Soc. 1975 73(3): 241-262.* Analyzes Henry Clay's role in the process of American expansion during 1812-44. Hemispheric dominance represented Clay's most ambitious plans, but the Missouri Compromise crisis challenged this position. Clay pressed for expansion along with his American System, slavery diffusion, and the colonization of free blacks. As Clay's domestic political fortunes ebbed, he opposed territorial expansion into Texas because of his fears of disunion, paying the price for this opposition in the 1844 presidential election. Primary and secondary sources; 54 notes.
J. F. Paul

236.   Jordan, Daniel P., ed.   PARTISAN POLITICS IN TERRITORIAL MISSISSIPPI: A STAUNCH REPUBLICAN'S DIRECT REPORT, 1807.   *J. of Mississsippi Hist. 1979 41(3): 231-240.* In 1807 Walter Leake, a Jeffersonian Republican who had recently emigrated to the Mississippi Territory from Virginia, wrote a letter to Wilson Cary Nichols of Albemarle County, Virginia, a chief lieutenant of President Jefferson. Leake's letter gives a surprisingly candid analysis of the partisan factionalism present in the Territory. He evaluates the territorial administration of Governor Robert Williams, and details specific controversies which centered on Seth Lewis, Colonel Ferdinand L. Claiborne, Colonel Aaron Burr, and Thomas Hill Williams. Developing a political base in his adopted state, Leake went on to serve as Territorial Judge, member of the first Constitutional Convention in 1817, as one of the two first United States Senators from the new state, State Supreme Court Justice, and the first two-term governor of Mississippi.
M. S. Legan

237.   Kaminski, John P.   POLITICAL SACRIFICE AND DEMISE: JOHN COLLINS AND JONATHAN J. HAZARD, 1786-1790.   *Rhode Island Hist. 1976 35(3): 91-98.* Analyzes the Rhode Island struggle to ratify the Constitution of the United States. The Antifederalists devised a strategy to secure ratification at little political cost to their party's popularity. John Collins and Jonathan J. Hazard were made scapegoats. Based on manuscripts, newspapers, and secondary sources.
P. J. Coleman

238.   Kamphoefner, Walter D.   ST. LOUIS GERMANS AND THE REPUBLICAN PARTY, 1848-1860.   *Mid-America 1975 57(2): 69-88.* German-American voting behavior, statistically analyzed, indicates that the Republican Party drew from Free Soil Democrats where Whig nativists were separate or subordinate. The influential Free Soil *Anzeiger des Westens*, edited by Forty-Eighter

Heinrich Boernstein, reflected the interaction of European ideology with American society. Its anticlericalism did not hurt its cause. Based on published sources, newspapers, and secondary works; 5 tables, 41 notes. T. H. Wendel

239. Kaplan, Lawrence S. TOWARD ISOLATIONISM: THE JEFFERSONIAN REPUBLICANS AND THE FRANCO-AMERICAN ALLIANCE OF 1778. *Hist. Reflections [Canada] 1976 3(1): 69-81.* Isolationism has frequently attracted American historians. Although the existence of a generalized fear of European exploitation among contemporaries has been noted by American scholars, credit for perceiving the dangers of the French influence has often been attributed to the Federalist party which rallied against the French Revolution and Napoleonic imperialism. Jeffersonians had an affinity for French ideas and culture which predated the American Revolution. The isolationist spirit in Jefferson's Inaugural Address, however, should be taken seriously. The French Alliance of 1778 came to fruition reluctantly, with few American illusions about the nature of the partnership. P. Travis

240. Kautz, Craig L. BENEFICIAL POLITICS: JOHN SLIDELL AND THE CUBAN BILL OF 1859. *Louisiana Studies 1974 13(2): 119-129.* The political divisions within the Democratic Party at the time of James Buchanan's assumption of the presidency in 1857 were exacerbated by the feud between Buchanan and Senator Stephen A. Douglas of Illinois and Senator John Slidell's (D.-Louisiana) hand-in-glove relationship with Buchanan. Traces the adroit political maneuvering that developed in relation to a bill introduced by Slidell to appropriate $30 million to facilitate acquisition of Cuba. The president had used Slidell's position on the Foreign Relations Committee as a weapon against Douglas. By 1860 they had weakened Douglas's influence in the Democratic Party; they had taken away his patronage, removed him from the chairmanship of the Committee on Territories, and reduced his leverage in the party. He still, however, remained a strong candidate for the Democratic nomination. 46 notes. R. V. Ritter

241. Kraut, Alan M. THE FORGOTTEN REFORMERS: A PROFILE OF THIRD PARTY ABOLITIONISTS IN ANTEBELLUM NEW YORK. Perry, Lewis and Fellman, Michael, ed. *Antislavery Reconsidered: New Perspectives on the Abolitionists* (Baton Rouge: Louisiana State U. Pr., 1979): 119-145. The Liberty Party, devoted exclusively to the abolition of slavery, was organized 1 April 1840 at Albany, New York, by such prominent abolitionists as Myron Holley, Gerrit Smith, Joshua Leavit, and William Goodell. Farmers, craftsmen, and professionals made up the bulk of the membership in this political party that, before its dissolution in 1848, played an important role in consolidating antislavery sentiment in early 19th-century New York. Based on poll listings from Smithfield, New York, a list of subscribers to a New York Liberal newspaper, and other primary sources; 10 tables, 43 notes. S

242. Kraut, Alan M. and Field, Phyllis F. POLITICS VERSUS PRINCIPLES: THE PARTISAN RESPONSE TO "BIBLE POLITICS" IN NEW YORK STATE. *Civil War Hist. 1979 25(2): 101-118.* To examine the sources of the strength of the US two-party system, investigates the response of the Democratic and Whig parties to the third-party morality-based political challenge of the abolitionist Liberty Party in New York, 1840-47. By 1845, the Liberty

Party had become strong enough to affect the outcome of elections, so the major parties forced a referendum over a proposal to remove or modify a stiff property qualification that limited Negro suffrage. Racism prevailed, the measure was soundly defeated, and the Liberty Party soon lost strength. It underwent a schism in 1847 and folded in 1848. 5 tables, 55 notes.   S

243.   Kremm, Thomas W.   THE OLD ORDER TREMBLES: THE FORMA-TION OF THE REPUBLICAN PARTY IN OHIO.   *Cincinnati Hist. Soc. Bull. 1978 36(3): 193-212.* The demise of the Whig Party and the growth in popularity of the Republican Party was due to anti-Catholicism, hostility toward Ohio's political system, and opposition to slavery extension, 1850's.

244.   Kushner, Howard I.   VISIONS OF THE NORTHWEST COAST: GWIN AND SEWARD IN THE 1850'S.   *Western Hist. Q. 1973 4(3): 295-306.* Some historians maintain that expanionism nearly disappeared from American thought after 1848. Others argue that expansionism was doomed because neither Democrats nor Northern Whigs would support the annexation of possible slave areas such as Mexico and Cuba. That both parties were looking to commercial and territorial expansion in the Pacific Northwest, plans eventually frustrated by the outbreak of the Civil War, has been overlooked. Political opposites William McKendree Gwin and William Henry Seward cooperated in efforts for American expansion. Gwin was a Mississippi plantation-owner and a leading Democratic senator from California. He was incarcerated during the Civil War by the Union government for alleged sympathies toward the South. Senator Seward, a leading Whig (later a Republican) and abolitionist, was a prime candidate for the Republican presidential nominations in 1856 and 1860. Their dreams were as expansive as any of the manifest destiny extremists of the 1840's. They collaborated closely in getting government support for a transcontinental railroad, the China trade, and Pacific whaling and trading projects. As early as 1854 Gwin attempted the purchase of Alaska which was achieved in 1867 by Secretary of State Seward. 34 notes.   D. L. Smith

245.   Kutolowski, Kathleen Smith.   THE JANUS FACE OF NEW YORK'S LOCAL PARTIES: GENESEE COUNTY, 1821-1827.   *New York Hist. 1978 59(2): 145-172.* This case study of local politics in Genesee County, New York, 1821-27, tests the concept of differential-participant politics at the grass roots. Despite their egalitarian political rhetoric, Bucktail faction and Clintonian faction leaders functioned in a deferential, community-leader elite political culture, and were antiparty in campaign rhetoric. During 1821-27 local political leadership was oligarchic rather than democratic, but there was a combination of party-oriented, participant politics with elements of deferential, traditional politics. The appearance of anti-Masonry resulted in the development of a new Bucktail-Democratic hierarchy consisting of a coalition of Bucktails, ex-Clintonians, and new recruits. 7 illus., 60 notes.   R. N. Lokken

246.   Lagana, Michael P.   THE POLITICAL CAREER OF DE WITT CLINTON: A NEED FOR REINTERPRETATION.   *Niagara Frontier 1974 21(3): 74-77.* Evaluates the influence which the political career of DeWitt Clinton had in the state of New York, 1800-22.

247. Lagana, Michael P. THE POLITICAL CAREER OF DE WITT CLINTON: A NEED FOR REINTERPRETATION. *Niagara Frontier 1975 22(4): 74-77.* Examines Jabez Hammond's *History of Political Parties in the State of New York* (1842) and its treatment of DeWitt Clinton, a politician and a political theorist; though Hammond's work is considered seminal and definitive, new interpretations of Clinton are necessary.

248. Lambert, Paul F. FROM FEDERALISM TO JEFFERSONIANISM, THE CONSISTENCY OF BENJAMIN RUSH. *New Scholar 1974 4(2): 191-203.* Rush's link to the Federalists was their mutual support of the federal Constitution. His personal and political differences with Alexander Hamilton and John Adams strengthened his ideal of a republican utopia with the exportability and perfectibility of American institutions, held since the early days of the Revolution.
D. K. Pickens

249. Latner, Richard B. A NEW LOOK AT JACKSONIAN POLITICS. *J. of Am. Hist. 1975 61(4): 943-969.* Reviews interpretations of the nature of Jacksonian era politics and emphasizes the strong influence of Kentuckians Amos Kendall and Francis Blair in the Jackson administrations. Kendall and Blair were particularly important in supporting Jackson's stands in the Bank War and on the nullification issue. Together they embodied the "western" orientation and Jeffersonian heritage in Jacksonian politics. Based on the Blair-Lee papers, the Blair family papers, the Van Buren papers, Jackson's published correspondence, the Washington *Globe*, and secondary works; 93 notes.
J. B. Street

250. Ledbetter, Billy. HOUSE REPUBLICAN OPPOSITION TO THE ADMISSION OF THE STATE OF OREGON. *Pacific Historian 1975 19(2): 150-164.* Offers a reinterpretation of Republican opposition in the House of Representatives to the 1859 Oregon enabling act. Oregon was admitted as a free state, but historians have been puzzled by Republican opposition. Explains the seeming inconsistency as a matter of principle and argues that Republicans demanded Oregon be admitted under the same provisions which caused Kansas' rejection, or not at all. Primary and secondary sources; 53 notes.
G. L. Olson

251. Leonard, Ira M. THE POLITICS OF CHARTER REVISION IN NEW YORK CITY, 1847-1849. *New-York Hist. Soc. Q. 1979 63(1): 6-23.* In 1846 a revision of the 1830 New York City charter, drawn up by the Democrats in power, was defeated. Subsequent reform attempts also failed, and the Whig Party captured the city government in the next year. Citing alleged Democratic corruption, the new administration under Mayor William V. Brady pushed through another charter revision, which was approved by the voters in 1849. However, changes were minimal and the municipal government was not modernized. The new document did not meet the needs of a growing metropolis. Primary sources; 3 illus., 47 notes.
C. L. Grant

252. Leonard, Ira M. THE POLITICS OF CHARTER REVISION IN NEW YORK CITY, 1845-1847. *New York Hist. Soc. Q. 1978 62(1): 43-70.* By the 1840's the new professional politicians in both parties had taken over control of New York City politics from the more established families. The city charter of 1830 needed modernization to accommodate a city growing at the rate of almost

five percent a year and rapidly becoming a cosmopolitan, industrial center. Thus, without firm direction from the charter, partisan city politics had produced a municipal government identified with political democracy yet characterized by corruption, patronage, and waste. During his first term as mayor, William Frederick Havemeyer, a Democrat and respectable sugar merchant, attempted to bring about reform without realizing how the city was changing. Soon it was obvious that neither the Whig Party nor the press was very interested in reform; thus, Havemeyer's party decided not to follow his lead. Nothing of significance was done. Primary sources; illus., 56 notes.   C. L. Grant

253.   Levin, Alexandra Lee.   HENRY BEDINGER OF VIRGINIA: FIRST UNITED STATES MINISTER TO DENMARK.   *Virginia Cavalcade 1980* *29(4): 184-191.* Biography of Henry Bedinger (1812-58), the first United States minister to Denmark, focusing on his American political career as a Democrat in the House of Representatives, his law career, and his appointment as minister to Denmark from 1854-58.

254.   Levine, Peter.   THE RISE OF MASS PARTIES AND THE PROBLEM OF ORGANIZATION: NEW JERSEY, 1829-1844.   *New Jersey Hist. 1973* *91(2): 91-107.* Patronage provided manpower for political parties. The party which won each statewide election ran the joint meeting of the legislature and thus had the power of appointment. Discusses the awarding of compensatory positions and statistically analyzes those appointments to show the strength of party control. Based on primary and secondary sources; 7 illus., table, 27 notes.
                                                          E. R. McKinstry

255.   Levine, Peter.   STATE LEGISLATIVE PARTIES IN THE JACKSONIAN ERA: NEW JERSEY 1829-1844.   *J. of Am. Hist. 1975 62(3): 591-* *608.* Quantitatively analyzes the relationship of legislative parties to party organization and state government operation in New Jersey 1829-44. Establishes an "index of likeness" to measure party cohesion in appointments to state and local office, judgeships, and enactment of legislation, and finds that party cohesion increased through time. Concludes that legislative party action aimed primarily at satisfying party organizational interests and "underlined the absence of ideological conflict and of an agenda that required responsible party action." Based on published proceedings of the New Jersey general assembly, the journal of the New Jersey legislative council, newspapers, and secondary works; 5 tables, chart, 37 notes.   J. B. Street

256.   Lieberman, Carl.   GEORGE WASHINGTON AND THE DEVELOPMENT OF AMERICAN FEDERALISM.   *Social Sci. 1976 51(1): 3-10.* The origins and development of American federalism can be explained by reference to such factors as the existence of a common culture, favorable geographical conditions, and the shared experience of a war for independence. However, the actions of national leaders, including the president of the United States, have also affected the development of the federal system. This article describes some of the ways in which George Washington influenced the federal order while serving as the country's first chief executive.   J

257. Lizanich, Christine M. "THE MARCH OF THIS GOVERNMENT": JOEL BARLOW'S UNWRITTEN HISTORY OF THE UNITED STATES. *William and Mary Q. 1976 33(2): 315-330.* At the suggestion of Thomas Jefferson, Joel Barlow began to write a history of the American Republic. Discusses Barlow's views on politics and government, and his efforts at the organization and writing of the project. Reprints four essays intended as part of the history. They cover 1) differences between Federalists and Republicans, 2) political science in America, 3) the novelty of the American system, and 4) faith in the American government. Barlow considered the work a successor to *The Federalist*. Based on primary sources. 27 notes.   H. M. Ward

258. Lowe, Richard G. THE REPUBLICAN PARTY IN ANTEBELLUM VIRGINIA, 1856-1860. *Virginia Mag. of Hist. and Biog. 1973 81(3): 259-279.* The Republican Party in Virginia in the late 1850's was far more important that its small size would suggest. Virginia Republicans drew their strength from the northwestern counties of the state where non-slaveholding small farmers had long resented domination by easterners. Despite great hostility, Virginia Republicans almost succeeded in bringing the 1860 national convention to Wheeling, and only the volatile reaction to John Brown's raid at Harpers Ferry convinced the party to go to Chicago. Virginia Republicans continued to influence national and state affairs, first in shifting the convention from Seward to Lincoln, and later in organizing the secession movement for West Virginia. Based on newspapers, secondary accounts, and documents at West Virginia University; 47 notes.
                                                          R. F. Oaks

259. Madison, James H. BUSINESS AND POLITICS IN INDIANAPOLIS: THE BRANCH BANK AND THE JUNTO, 1837-1846. *Indiana Mag. of Hist. 1975 71(1): 1-20.* The Second State Bank of Indiana was created in 1834 when Jacksonian attacks on the Bank of the United States threatened to deprive the state of vital banking services. As one of the State Bank's 10 branches, the Indianapolis Branch Bank was initially dominated by a group of wealthy Whig businessmen which exercised favoritism toward mercantile interests in the granting of loans. Against a background of economic depression and bolstered by electoral gains, state Democrats mounted a steady attack on the Branch Bank and the business junto which controlled it. Unlike the experience in other states, however, Whig businessmen, led by Calvin Fletcher (1798-1866), directed a reform movement which corrected loan abuses, equalized political representation on the bank board, and effectively silenced Democratic critics. Primary and secondary sources; 81 notes.   K. F. Svengalis

260. Mann, Ralph. NATIONAL PARTY FORTUNES AND LOCAL POLITICAL STRUCTURE: THE CASE OF TWO CALIFORNIA MINING TOWNS, 1850-1870. *Southern California Q. 1975 57(3): 271-297.* Examines political activity in two California gold camps, Grass Valley and Nevada City, 1850-70. Initially miners were a transient class, and political offices were held by local entrepreneurs. Successful miners later increased their participation, although businessmen and professionals continued to be overrepresented in political offices proportionate to their numbers. Foreign-born people held office less on their ethnicity than on their occupational success; Chinese were excluded from political participation. The Civil War was a factor in concentrating the Democratic Party in Grass Valley and the Republicans at Nevada City. Political offices

and allegiances tended to follow practices in the East rather than ad hoc miners' institutions. Where a city was dominated by one party, occupational democracy was found in the minority party which was trying to build a larger political base. Based on census data, contemporary and secondary published works, and local newspapers; 14 tables, 13 notes.   A. Hoffman

261. Marshall, Jonathan. EMPIRE OR LIBERTY: THE ANTIFEDERAL-ISTS AND FOREIGN POLICY, 1787-1788. *J. of Libertarian Studies 1980 4(3): 233-254.* Discusses the role which the Antifederalists had in early foreign policy debates and their impact on the ratification of the Constitution.

262. Marsis, James L. AGRARIAN POLITICS IN RHODE ISLAND, 1800-1860. *Rhode Island Hist. 1975 34(1): 13-22.* Politics in Rhode Island, 1800-60, directed by the agrarian sector of the population, began the century in strict support of Jeffersonian democracy; but with the influx of Irish laborers, politics became more conservative, law-and-order-oriented, and (as the Civil War drew nearer) abolitionist, so that by 1860, Rhode Island was overwhelmingly Republican.

263. Matthews, J. V. "WHIG HISTORY": THE NEW ENGLAND WHIGS AND A USABLE PAST. *New England Q. 1978 51(2): 193-208.* Whigs believed that custom, tradition, and authoritarian government were losing their power to maintain a stable society during the 1840's-50's. In place of these controls the Whigs hoped to use history to develop a sense of self-restraint by showing that the first American settlers came to escape an overt, established authority but that they voluntarily submitted to a sterner self-imposed discipline and that the Revolution did not create a new governmental system but instead more firmly entrenched an already established political system. Based on Whig speeches and essays; 21 notes.   J. C. Bradford

264. May, Robert E. A "SOUTHERN STRATEGY" FOR THE 1850'S: NORTHERN DEMOCRATS, THE TROPICS, AND EXPANSION OF THE NATIONAL DOMAIN. *Louisiana Studies 1975 14(4): 333-359.* After 1847 much of the history of the Democratic Party represented an effort by northern leaders to satisfy the southern need to expand while at the same time not to offend the essentially free soil attitudes of their own constituents. Many northern Democratic leaders searched for an alternative outlet for the slavery expansion as a means of diverting the southern consciousness from the western United States. As a result, northerners adopted a southern strategy; if the South could be persuaded to accept expansion into the tropics in exchange for free soil control of the West, the vexing territorial problems might be resolved and the party kept intact. Democratic leaders who supported this approach included Stephen A. Douglas, William Marcy, Franklin Pierce, and James Buchanan. For northern Democrats a southern strategy was not the only reason for supporting expansion southward, since an amalgam of attitudes pervaded the northern Democrats; but it was an important element. Yet southern strategy floundered, primarily because northerners did not wholeheartedly support tropical expansion. Based on primary and secondary sources; 57 notes.   B. A. Glasrud

265. Mayo, Edward L. REPUBLICANISM, ANTIPARTYISM, AND JACKSONIAN PARTY POLITICS: A VIEW FROM THE NATION'S CAPITAL. *Am. Q. 1979 31(1): 3-20.* Describes the antiparty campaigns of Joseph Gales, Jr., and William Winston Seaton during Andrew Jackson's presidency. These long-time editors of the Washington, D.C., *National Intelligencer* had been steeped in the republican antipartyism of the Virginia presidents. Therefore, their long, sharp editorial criticisms depicted Jacksonian partisan politics in terms of factions, as divisive, and pictured such extraconstitutional organizations as Jackson's Kitchen Cabinet in conspiratorial terms. Their viewpoint may be regarded as reflective of a large number of Americans at the time, given their long experience, even though their audience was primarily of the elite. Based on *National Intelligencer* backfiles; 57 notes. D. G. Nielson

266. McCardell, John. JOHN A. QUITMAN AND THE COMPROMISE OF 1850 IN MISSISSIPPI. *J. of Mississippi Hist. 1975 37(3): 239-266.* Describes the varied, confused, and changing reactions of Mississippians toward the Compromise of 1850. Democrat John A. Quitman, elected governor by a large margin in 1849, led the forces opposed to the compromise, forces defeated in 1851 elections by a new Union Party composed mostly of Whigs and led by Democrat Henry S. Foote, the shrewd and skillful US Senator. Primary and secondary sources; 77 notes, appendix. J. W. Hillje

267. McClaughry, John. THE RISE AND FALL OF THE LOCO-FOCOS. *Reason 1979 10(11): 32-34.* Strongly antimonopoly and favoring hard money and Jeffersonianism, the Loco-Focos dominated the national Democratic Party doctrine, 1837-44.

268. McCoy, Drew R. AMERICAN POLITICAL IDEOLOGY IN THE 1790S: TWO APPROACHES. *Rev. in Am. Hist. 1978 6(4): 496-502.* Review article prompted by Lance Banning's *The Jeffersonian Persuasion: Evolution of a Party Ideology* (Ithaca, N.Y.: Cornell U. Pr., 1978) and John Zvesper's *Political Philosophy and Rhetoric: A Study of the Origins of American Party Politics* (Cambridge, Eng.: Cambridge U. Pr., 1977) which discuss American political ideology in the 1790's.

269. McCoy, Drew R. REPUBLICANISM AND AMERICAN FOREIGN POLICY: JAMES MADISON AND THE POLITICAL ECONOMY OF COMMERCIAL DISCRIMINATION, 1789 TO 1794. *William and Mary Q. 1974 31(4): 633-646.* The development of American commercial policy was connected with the rise of political parties. Madison's views on manufactures and his reasons for discrimination, reflected his Republican ideology. Actually Madison wanted an unrestricted international order which would expand the human mind and humanity. American economic independence would not exclude Americans from foreign markets. Also describes Hamilton's conception of a sectionally interdependent economy as a means for the United States to contend for reciprocity, rather than Madison's coercive proposals. Based on primary and secondary sources; 42 notes. H. M. Ward

270. McCrary, Royce C. GEORGIA POLITICS AND THE MEXICAN WAR. *Georgia Hist. Q. 1976 60(3): 211-227.* The Mexican War was particularly divisive in American politics; the Georgia Whig and Democratic Parties

both experienced splits as a result of it. In the congressional election of 1846, the legislative, senatorial, and gubernatorial elections of 1847, and the 1848 presidential and congressional election, the war was an important issue. The Georgia Whigs did better than the Democrats in all but the gubernatorial election, but their organization suffered and never recovered. The Democratic Party has since controlled the state. Primary and secondary sources; 31 notes.

G. R. Schroeder

271. McCrary, Royce C.   JOHN MAC PHERSON BERRIEN AND THE KNOW-NOTHING MOVEMENT IN GEORGIA.   *Georgia Hist. Q. 1977 61(1): 35-42.* Traces the influence of retired politician John M. Berrien (1781-1856) on the Know-Nothings in Georgia. Beginning with his letter "To the People of Georgia" of 4 September 1855, he encouraged a party emphasis on preserving the Union rather than on anti-Catholicism and nativism. He died before his ideas could take root, and the party reverted to their former views. Primary and secondary sources; 28 notes.

G. R. Schroeder

272. McCrary, Royce, ed.   A FEDERALIST VIEW OF GEORGIA POLITICS IN 1808: A LETTER BY JOHN MACPHERSON BERRIEN.   *Georgia Hist. Q. 1974 58(4): 447-449.* The Federalists lost the election of 1796 and lost considerable strength in Georgia. Berrien suggested a strategy to use the Federalist members of the Georgia legislature to select Federalist electors and thus win the election in the Electoral College. The strategy was defeated primarily due to serious Federalist failures in northern states. Primary and secondary sources; 14 notes.

M. R. Gillam

273. McFaul, John M.   EXPEDIENCY VS. MORALITY: JACKSONIAN POLITICS AND SLAVERY.   *J. of Am. Hist. 1975 62(1): 24-39.* Reinterprets the attitudes of the political parties toward the slavery issue during the Jackson administrations. The majority of the Jacksonian Democrats believed that government neutrality, as embodied in the Pinckney resolutions, on the slavery issue was necessary to preserve the union. Only political outsiders and some Whigs raised the slavery issue on a moral basis. In this era national parties and slavery agitation were mutually exclusive. Based on newspapers and secondary works; 45 notes.

J. B. Street

274. McGregor, Robert C.   BETWEEN THE TWO WARS: ALABAMA IN THE HOUSE OF REPRESENTATIVES 1849-1861.   *Alabama Hist. Q. 1980 42(3-4): 167-200.* Of the 21 men from Alabama serving in the US House of Representatives during 1849-61, 12 were radical Southern rights men and nine were conservatives. Slavery was a crucial issue, and sectional unity was seen as beneficial for preserving this Southern practice. The radicals gained in popularity as tensions between North and South grew. Several situations occurred that made the radicals appear to be the defenders of Southern institutions. Primary sources; 59 notes.

A. Drysdale

275. McLaughlin, Tom L.   GRASS-ROOTS ATTITUDES TOWARD BLACK RIGHTS IN TWELVE NONSLAVEHOLDING STATES, 1846-1869.   *Mid-America 1974 56(2): 175-181.* One test of the common wisdom that the rights of free Negroes were eroding in the North during the age of the common man is an evaluation of the voting patterns in 22 popular referenda held

in 12 northern states. The evidence suggests that the Republican Party's ideological program was not far in advance of national opinion in stressing the basic humanity of Negroes and their need for protected civil rights. Based on primary sources; table, 9 notes.

T. D. Schoonover

276. McManus, Michael J. WISCONSIN REPUBLICANS AND NEGRO SUFFRAGE: ATTITUDES AND BEHAVIOR, 1857. *Civil War Hist 1979 25(1): 36-54.* The debated existence and extent of Republican Party involvement in Negro rights can be tested in Wisconsin. This young, heterogeneous state voted on the Negro franchise in 1857. Hard necessity forced a party dedicated philosophically to spell out the practical effects. The Democrats made sure of this. The Republican state convention exposed the split on principle. Later, party candidates avoided mentioning suffrage; party editors proclaimed it. Wisconsin blacks joined the fray. Negro suffrage was defeated, but not by Republicans, who either voted for suffrage, or simply abstained. A majority of all voters in some manner called racism into question. Based on state documents, published and unpublished, newspapers, and some secondary sources; 67 notes. R. E. Stack

277. Meerse, David E. BUCHANAN'S PATRONAGE POLICY: AN ATTEMPT TO ACHIEVE POLITICAL STRENGTH. *Pennsylvania Hist. 1973 40(1): 37-57.* President James Buchanan's (1791-1868) policy of selective rotation or the "rule of rotation" was partly a response to the fact that the previous national administration had also been Democratic. Rotation was not applied extensively in the South. In the North, selective rotation was applied to unify the party. The administration was even willing to subordinate past political friendship to demonstrated political strength. Provides case studies. Based on the Buchanan papers and other manuscript collections; illus., 33 notes.

D. C. Swift

278. Meerse, David E. THE NORTHERN DEMOCRATIC PARTY AND THE CONGRESSIONAL ELECTIONS OF 1858. *Civil War Hist. 1973 19(2): 119-137.* Statistical analysis of the congressional election of 1858 which tends to refute the common belief that it was a debacle for the Democrats. A number of factors suggest that "contemporaries saw neither the . . . elections . . . as a great struggle over Kansas nor the results as an epic defeat for a repudiated party." Based on primary and secondary sources; tables, notes. E. C. Murdock

279. Meyer, D. H. CONSERVATIVE FEDERALISTS AND THE LIBERAL ARTS: TWO OLD-TIME COLLEGE PRESIDENTS. *Hist. of Educ. Q. 1976 16(2): 229-234.* Review article prompted by Stephen E. Berk's *Calvinism versus Democracy: Timothy Dwight and the Origins of American Evangelical Orthodoxy* (Hamden, Connecticut: Archon Books, 1974) and Robert A. McCaughey's *Josiah Quincy, 1772-1864: The Last Federalist* (Cambridge, Massachusetts, Harvard U. Pr., 1974).

280. Meyer, Lysle E. PIONEER REPUBLICANS JOIN THE FRAY: ASPECTS OF THEIR FIRST PRESIDENTIAL NOMINATING CONVENTION OF 1856. *Lincoln Herald 1975 77(1): 15-26.* Amidst the social turmoil and the dissolution of the Whig Party in the early 1850's emerged the Republican Party. The party began at the local level in 1854, and by the fall of that year had organizations in the Mississippi Valley and some eastern states. A national con-

vention to nominate candidates for President and Vice-President was held in Philadelphia in 1856. The party nominated John C. Frémont for President and William L. Dayton for Vice-President. Based on primary and secondary sources; 7 illus., 68 notes.   B. J. LaBue

281. Miller, Richard G. THE TARIFF OF 1832: THE ISSUE THAT FAILED. *Filson Club Hist. Q. 1975 49(3): 221-230.* The tariff issue posed many dangers for the Democratic Party in the election of 1832, but adroit political action by Andrew Jackson eliminated the potential dangers. Jackson was under pressure from southern Democrats to reduce or end the tariff rates passed in 1828. Henry Clay championed manufacturing interests and Western farmers, claiming that the Democrats reflected only southern farmers. On the other side, John C. Calhoun threatened to lead a Southern nullification movement if the tax was not defeated. Jackson defused the issue by backing a moderate reduction of the tariff that proved to be so popular that Clay supported it and Calhoun was unable to rally the South to his position. Documentation comes from manuscripts at the Library of Congress including the Clay and Jackson Papers; 41 notes.
                                                                    G. B. McKinney

282. Morrison, Howard Alexander. GENTLEMEN OF PROPER UNDER-STANDING: A CLOSER LOOK AT UTICA'S ANTI-ABOLITIONIST MOB. *New York Hist. 1981 62(1): 61-82.* The antiabolitionist riot in Utica, New York on 21 October 1835 was politically motivated. Democratic politicians seeking reelection and other Democratic Party leaders led the riot in order to identify themselves and their party with the antiabolitionist majority. The Utica riot, moreover, was orchestrated by a Democratic political machine in order to strengthen the presidential candidacy of Martin Van Buren. Based on the Martin Van Buren Papers, James Watson Williams Papers, and contemporary newspapers and books; 6 illus., 52 notes.   R. N. Lokken

283. Moss, Richard J. JACKSONIAN DEMOCRACY: A NOTE ON THE ORIGINS AND GROWTH OF THE TERM. *Tennessee Hist. Q. 1975 34(2): 145-153.* The term "Jacksonian Democracy" was not used in the period of Jackson, and people who lived through the Jacksonian era would not have been able to define it, though they believed that Jackson represented a further democratization of America. Not until the 1890's, in the writing of historians such as Frederick Jackson Turner, did the term begin to take on the broad connotations it has today. Primary and secondary sources; 23 notes.   M. B. Lucas

284. Mulkern, John. WESTERN MASSACHUSETTS IN THE KNOW-NOTHING YEARS: AN ANALYSIS OF VOTING PATTERNS. *Hist. J. of Western Massachusetts 1980 8(1): 14-25.* Examines the factors behind the victory of the American or Know-Nothing Party in the statewide election of 1854 and the vote on the 1853 state constitution. These elections began the process of realignment that was completed by 1858 when the Republican Party won a majority in that statewide election. Newspapers, contemporary publications, and secondary sources; 3 tables, 21 notes.   W. H. Mulligan, Jr.

285. Neely, Mark E. RICHARD W. THOMPSON: THE PERSISTENT KNOW NOTHING. *Indiana Mag. of Hist. 1976 72(2): 95-122.* Discusses the anti-Catholic Know-Nothing Party, popular in the 1850's in American politics,

and gives an in-depth view of the Party's leader and major speaker, Richard W. Thompson.

286. Penney, Sherry. DISSENSION IN THE WHIG RANKS: DANIEL DEWEY BARNARD VERSUS THURLOW WEED. *New-York Hist. Soc. Q. 1975 59(1): 71-92.* Throughout the life of the Whig Party, Daniel Dewey Barnard was a leading New York member. Serving as state legislator, congressman, and foreign diplomat, he was always numbered among the conservative members of the party. A study of his career reveals that struggle within the party was for more than just leadership; there was always a difference of opinion over the nature of the party. Thus Barnard's differences with Thurlow Weed assume importance and point up the significance of the struggle. In the end, Barnard's pressure on Weed and the liberal wing undoubtedly aided in the breakup of the party after a short history of only two decades (1834-55). Based on contemporary newspapers and correspondence; 3 illus., 44 notes.　　　　　C. L. Grant

287. Perkal, M. Leon. AMERICAN ABOLITION SOCIETY: A VIABLE ALTERNATIVE TO THE REPUBLICAN PARTY? *J. of Negro Hist. 1980 65(1): 57-71.* The American Abolition Society molded radical abolitionism into an independent movement during 1855-58. Avoiding the disunionist sentiment of the Garrisonians, the Society exerted moral influence upon the new Republican Party. The American Abolition Society served as a link between idealism and practical politics. Based on primary materials; 57 notes.　　　N. G. Sapper

288. Phillips, Kim T. WILLIAM DUANE, PHILADELPHIA'S DEMO-CRATIC REPUBLICANS, AND THE ORIGINS OF MODERN POLITICS. *Pennsylvania Mag. of Hist. and Biog. 1977 101(3): 365-387.* In early 19th-century Pennsylvania, significant political conflict, not mere factionalism, occurred within political parties. In Philadelphia, the Republicans split between the socially disparate Quids and William Duane's Democrats. The Quids entertained older, elitist notions of consensus; the Democrats prefigured Jacksonian partisan politics. Primary and secondary sources; 68 notes.　　　T. H. Wendel

289. Pocock, J. G. A. CIVIL WARS, REVOLUTIONS, AND POLITICAL PARTIES. Bonomi, Patricia U., ed. *Party and Political Opposition in Revolutionary America* (Tarrytown, N.Y.: Sleepy Hollow Pr., 1980): 1-12. Compares the development of political parties as national organizations in Great Britain and the United States and reviews the historiography on party development during the 18th century. Parties in both countries connected the electorate to the government, but the English parliamentary democracy was an extension of the idea of community of the realm, while American republican democracy evolved from the idea of the balance of component parts. Secondary sources; 16 notes.　　S

290. Prince, Carl E. NEW JERSEY CUSTOMS: PARTIES AND PORTS IN THE ERA OF THE YOUNG REPUBLIC. *New Jersey Hist. 1980 98(1-2): 29-36.* Even though New York and Philadelphia handled most of the shipping in the Middle Atlantic region, New Jersey had six ports open to both foreign and domestic commerce. Infighting regarding the appointment of customs officials at each port reflected the political concerns of the United States as the two party system began to operate under John Adams and Thomas Jefferson. These six ports were symbolic battlegrounds whose significance extended beyond the con-

fines of the state. Based on the papers of customs officials, government records, and secondary sources; illus., map, 8 notes.   E. R. McKinstry

291.   Ratcliffe, Donald J.   POLITICS IN JACKSONIAN OHIO: REFLEC-TIONS ON THE ETHNOCULTURAL INTERPRETATION.   *Ohio Hist.* *1979 88(1): 5-36.* Sorts out and analyzes influences on voters which kept Ohio a strong Jacksonian Democrat state during the 1830's and '40's. Historians differ as to the strength of ethnoculture and socioeconomic factors in elections of the period. It is possible that party alignments formed during the presidential contest between Henry Clay, Andrew Jackson, and John Quincy Adams in the 1820's had a distinct bearing upon party loyalties in the '30's and '40's. However, during this latter period, great economic and social changes were taking place which make very difficult any clear-cut explanation involving ethnic, cultural, or economic factors exclusively. 2 maps, 2 tables, 87 notes.   H. F. Thomson

292.   Ratcliffe, Donald J.   THE ROLE OF VOTERS AND ISSUES IN PARTY FORMATION: OHIO 1824.   *J. of Am. Hist. 1973 59(4): 847-870.* The presidential election of 1824 in Ohio was a race among three candidates: Henry Clay, Andrew Jackson, and John Quincy Adams. Historians have traditionally viewed that election, narrowly won by Clay, as one in which ambitious politicians created catch-all party organizations designed to attract voters who were insensitive to political issues or ideology. In fact, issues were of predominant importance, and political organizations were built around constituency interests. Clay attracted votes from counties hoping to benefit from his "American system" of federally-supported internal improvements, Adams got support from New Englanders repelled by Clay's involvement in slavery, and Jackson gathered support from depression-ridden Cincinnati, Scotch-Irish and German voters, and a general antipolitical animus. These alignments continued into the Whig Democrat era. 4 tables, 69 notes.   K. B. West

293.   Reichard, Maximilian.   URBAN POLITICS IN JACKSONIAN ST. LOUIS: TRADITIONAL VALUES IN CHANGE AND CONFLICT. *Missouri Hist. Rev. 1976 70(3): 259-271.* A local political crisis in 1833 ended traditional politics in St. Louis. Dr. Samuel Merry was denied the office of mayor by the aldermen because he held a federal job. The controversy which followed involved the right of the council to challenge the executive, the right of the people to elect the mayor, and whether the mayor was an officer of the state or of his community. The controversy also pitted Whigs against Democrats and the northside against downtown St. Louis. By 1838 the Democrats were well on their way toward breaking traditional political patterns by securing legislation that extended the suffrage and made more city offices elective. Primary and secondary sources; illus., 29 notes.   W. F. Zornow

294.   Renner, Richard Wilson.   IN A PERFECT FERMENT: CHICAGO, THE KNOW-NOTHINGS, AND THE RIOT FOR LAGER BEER.   *Chicago Hist. 1976 5(3): 161-169.* Discusses Chicago's Know-Nothing government of 1855 which alienated German supporters with a temperance law that provoked a major riot.

295. Reynolds, John F.   PIETY AND POLITICS: EVANGELISM IN THE MICHIGAN LEGISLATURE, 1837-1861. *Michigan Hist. 1977 61(4): 322-351.* Statistical analysis of roll-call votes in the Michigan House of Representatives during 1837-60 confirms the complexity of political motive during the Jacksonian Era. Neither the class conflict theory nor the ethnocultural, or "evangelical," approach fully explains voting on such issues as slavery, temperance, adultery, and public prayer. Although non-Democrats supported evangelical legislation in greater number, the major political parties were generally similar in their stands regarding such measures. Bills and resolutions regarding slavery were the most divisive partisan issues. Although there was a degree of evangelical cleavage, neither the Democrats nor the Whigs capitalized on it. Primary sources; 30 notes, 8 illus., 2 photos, 4 tables.
                                                                            D. W. Johnson

296. Riccards, Michael P.   PHILIP MAZZEI: THE JEFFERSONIAN AS INTERNATIONALIST. *Italian Americana 1980 6(2): 210-221.* Biography of Italian-born Philip Mazzei, republican, supporter of the American Revolution, and close friend of Thomas Jefferson, focusing on his writings on politics and government.

297. Richards, Leonard L.   THE JACKSONIANS AND SLAVERY. Perry, Lewis and Fellman, Michael, ed. *Antislavery Reconsidered: New Perspectives on the Abolitionists* (Baton Rouge: Louisiana State U. Pr., 1979): 99-118. Examines the charge by John Quincy Adams that his defeat by Andrew Jackson in the presidential election of 1828 was a defeat rather than a victory for democracy and concludes that Adams's claim is not without merit. While northern and southern Democrats presented a generally solid front of anti-Negro and proslavery sentiment, northern Whigs were divided on these issues. Jackson's Indian policy and political maneuvers, even in engineering the election of the northerner Martin Van Buren as president, were consistently more advantageous to the South than to the North. 27 notes.
                                                                                        S

298. Ridgway, Whitman H.   COMMUNITY LEADERSHIP: BALTIMORE DURING THE FIRST AND SECOND PARTY SYSTEMS. *Maryland Hist. Mag. 1976 71(3): 334-348.* Borrowing concepts of strategic elites (positional and traditional) versus decisional elites from modern community power studies, focuses on the changing power structure of Baltimore from the conservative merchant oligarchy of the postrevolutionary era down to 1806, to the younger professional-skilled artisan polyarchy of the Jacksonian era, 1827-36. Studies the decisionmakers in the salient local concerns of internal improvements and the creation of a water company in the first era, and internal improvements and political reform in the second. "The most important difference . . . was the opportunity for men without ties to the old elite to rise to power during the second party period." While still landed, the new elite was younger, held fewer slaves, and was increasingly drawn from nonmerchant ranks. Primary and secondary works; 4 tables, 36 notes.
                                                                            G. J. Bobango

299. Ridgway, Whitman H.   MC CULLOCH VS. THE JACKSONIANS: PATRONAGE AND POLITICS IN MARYLAND. *Maryland Hist. Mag. 1975 70(4): 350-362.* Discusses political realignments produced by the elections of 1824 and 1828, with stress on the new "second party system" in Maryland led by second-generation Jacksonians such as William Frick, Philip Laurenson, and

John W. Wilmer. Earlier leaders such as Roger B. Taney and Virgil Maxcy had been "assimilated into the federal bureaucracy outside the state" by 1833-34, and the retirement of Gen. Samuel Smith from the Senate, who was "the key figure behind Maryland's patronage policy," brought basic alterations in the prevailing system. Benjamin Chew Howard took up Smith's role by the mid-1830's but was forced to compromise with the rank-and-file as Smith had not done. A major defection from the Jackson party brought about the short-lived Workingmen's Pary, adding to the clamor to actually initiate "rotation in office," which had not yet been the case in Maryland, long dominated by Smith's influence. Cohesion and purpose in the Maryland Jacksonian ranks came ironically only toward the close of Old Hickory's Presidency. Based on many contemporary letters, the Baltimore *Republican*, and secondary sources; 44 notes.   G. J. Bobango

300.   Risjord, Norman K. and DenBoer, Gordon.   THE EVOLUTION OF POLITICAL PARTIES IN VIRGINIA, 1782-1800.   *J. of Am. Hist. 1974 60(4): 961-984.* Analysis of roll call votes in the Virginia House of Delegates reveals that by the time of the Constitutional Convention a political group had emerged which could be designated "creditor/nationalist" in its orientation toward payment of prewar debts, a lenient attitude toward returned Loyalists, tax powers to the national government, and judicial reforms to assist debt collection. Another group oriented around Patrick Henry could be considered "debtor/antinationalists." The Henry faction tended to become Antifederalists in the debate over the constitution, while Madison and the "creditor/nationalist" faction became Federalists. In later debates over Hamilton's fiscal policies some Federalists became Republicans, but within the state a clearly large majority of 1788's Federalists remained Federalists by 1791. A similar continuity is to be noted when issues of neutrality and Jay's Treaty were raised. By 1800 more cohesive and disciplined political parties had emerged, making conscious appeals to the electorate. 9 tables, 76 notes.   K. B. West

301.   Rock, Howard B.   THE AMERICAN REVOLUTION AND THE MECHANICS OF NEW YORK CITY: ONE GENERATION LATER.   *New York Hist. 1976 57(3): 367-394.* Inspired by Revolutionary ideals, the mechanics of New York City a generation after Independence attacked the deferential system that excluded them from full political participation and equal status in American society. In their quest for recognition, the mechanics identified themselves with the Democratic-Republicans against the Federalists and sought to organize for protection against capitalist employers. Illus., 67 notes.
        R. N. Lokken

302.   Rosentreter, Roger L.   MICHIGAN AND THE COMPROMISE OF 1850.   *Old Northwest 1980 6(2): 153-173.* Anti-slavery sentiment was strong in Michigan in the 1830's and 1840's. By the late 1840's both Democrats and Whigs in Michigan were loosely allied in opposition to its extension. The Mexican War, which ended in 1848, intensified feelings over the question of whether land acquired by the war would be open to slavery. By 1850 the debate had come to a head, and when Congress enacted a compromise, the Compromise of 1850, many Michiganians realized that the best interests of the nation demanded acceptance, but not before they reaffirmed their opposition to the extension of slavery by electing "free soil" congressmen. Based on primary sources; 45 notes.
        J. Powell

303. Rozett, John M. RACISM AND REPUBLICAN EMERGENCE IN ILLINOIS, 1848-1860: A REEVALUATION OF REPUBLICAN NEGROPHOBIA. *Civil War Hist. 1976 22(2): 101-115.* Challenges the James Rawley-Eugene Berwanger thesis that Negrophobia was the predominant component in the Free Soil-Republican Party philosophy during 1848-60. While conceding that racism was a factor in the opposition to slavery extension and that the Rawley-Berwanger theory supplies an important corrective to the traditional view, the author argues that basically the antislavery parties were hostile to slavery on moral grounds and that this was not true of the Democrats. Abraham Lincoln is the best example of the free soil position although he did not believe in racial equality. Supports arguments with a quantitative analysis of Illinois elections in 1848 and 1860. E. C. Murdock

304. Scheina, Robert L. BENJAMIN STODDERT, POLITICS, AND THE NAVY. *Am. Neptune 1976 36(1): 54-68.* Stoddert was extremely partisan in his "high Federalist" politics, but when he served as Secretary of the Navy (1798-1801) he supported President John Adams rather than the Hamiltonian Federalists. Furthermore, "Stoddert was a Federalist second and Secretary of the Navy first. When the two conflicted, the Navy won out." Based on manuscript and published sources; 57 notes. G. H. Curtis

305. Schelin, Robert C. A WHIG'S FINAL QUEST: FILLMORE AND THE KNOW-NOTHINGS. *Niagara Frontier 1979 26(1): 1-11.* History of the American, or Know-Nothing, Party in the United States, which originated in European anti-Catholicism and American nativism, becoming a political force in the 1850's; focuses on the Party's nomination of ex-President Millard Fillmore as presidential candidate at the 1856 nominating convention, and his vain attempts, as a pro-Union candidate, to resurrect the Whig Party.

306. Scherr, Arthur. THE SIGNIFICANCE OF THOMAS PINCKNEY'S CANDIDACY IN THE ELECTION OF 1796. *South Carolina Hist. Mag. 1975 76(2): 51-59.* During the campaign of 1796 federalists and Republicans seriously considered Thomas Pinckney of South Carolina for president. His election might have enabled Jeffersonians and Hamiltonians to settle their differences rather than polarizing the nation into two political parties as did the election of John Adams. Primary sources; 38 notes. R. H. Tomlinson

307. Schneider, John C. RIOT AND REACTION IN ST. LOUIS, 1854-1856. *Missouri Hist. R. 1974 68(2): 171-185.* Discusses the buildup, culmination, and aftermath of local political tension in St. Louis in the 1850's. Central to the conflict was a growing nativism and the emergence of the Know-Nothing Party which caused alarm among the Democrats. This resulted in rioting on election day, 7 August 1854, with a counterattack led by members of the Irish community. As a result of the conflict, the regular police force was reorganized and professionalized, the state passed a stronger riot law effective only in St. Louis County, and election procedures were restructured. The elections of 1855 and 1856 were again emotional races between the Know-Nothing Party and the Democrats, but order was kept during both, although the above changes were actually partisan in nature. Based on contemporary newspaper reports, St. Louis city documents, primary and secondary sources; 7 illus., 22 notes. N. J. Street

308.   Schroeder, John H.   CONGRESS AND OPPOSITION TO THE MEXI-
CAN WAR.   *Capitol Studies 1975 3(1): 15-30.* Discusses congressional opposition to President James Polk and the Mexican War, 1846-48, emphasizing the
activities of Whigs and Democrats led by John C. Calhoun.

309.   Seavoy, Ronald E.   THE ORGANIZATION OF THE REPUBLICAN
PARTY IN MICHIGAN, 1846-1854.   *Old Northwest 1980-81 6(4): 343-376.*
Recounts the movement in Michigan between 1846 and 1854 to organize a new
political party to halt the expansion of slavery into the territories. The fusion
process that resulted in the formation of the Michigan Republican Party can be
attributed to professional politicians who focused public attention on the national
issue of slavery extension and away from divisive local issues. This strategy, which
was very successful in the Michigan elections of 1854, was later used by antislavery politicians to build the Republican Party in other Northern states. Based on
the Blair Papers in the Burton Historical Collection at the Detroit Public Library,
and other primary sources; 68 notes.   P. L. McLaughlin

310.   Senkewicz, Robert M.   RELIGION AND NON-PARTISAN POLI-
TICS IN GOLD RUSH SAN FRANCISCO.   *Southern California Q. 1979
61(4): 351-378.* Examines the makeup and strategies of the 1856 San Francisco
Vigilance Committee. The vigilante movement was the effort of importers and
merchants who had earlier made several nonpartisan campaigns in local elections.
Their effort lacked success until they linked their interests with the Know-
Nothing Party in 1854. There followed a series of issues which made religious
questions significant in local politics: public aid to Catholic schools, Catholic
influence in government operations such as the county hospital, and similar
charges. Use of the Catholic issue broadened the base of the merchants, made
local government nonpartisan, and through the mechanism of the Vigilance
Committee rid San Francisco not only of accused criminals but also of political
opponents, including Irish Catholics. The People's Party, as the merchants called
themselves, continued as an important political faction until they merged with the
Republicans in 1864. 83 notes.   A. Hoffman

311.   Shalhope, Robert E.   SOUTHERN FEDERALISTS AND THE FIRST
PARTY SYNDROME.   *Rev. in Am. Hist. 1980 8(1): 45-51.* Review essay of
James H. Broussard's *The Southern Federalists, 1800-1816* (Baton Rouge: Loui-
siana State U. Pr., 1978).

312.   Shelden, Aure.   HISTORY IN HIDING.   *New-England Galaxy 1975
17(2): 39-43.* Recounts a Whig political convention held during July 1840 on a
300-acre clearing west of Stratton, Vermont. More than 10,000 spectators heard
an address by Daniel Webster. Portrays the camping, eating, and recreational
activities of the crowd, the traffic jams on the roads leading to the site, and
reactions of the audience. Photo.   P. C. Marshall

313.   Shortridge, Ray M.   THE VOTER REALIGNMENT IN THE MID-
WEST DURING THE 1850'S.   *Am. Pol. Q. 1976 4(2): 193-222.* Focuses on the
shift of party loyalties in the 1850's which created the Republican party. The
Whigs, Free Soilers, and American party faded from the political scene by 1860
and were superseded by the Republicans. The vote-flow among the political
parties of the Midwest in the 1850's is examined. The realignment process varied

among the most populous midwestern states. The 1850's realignment involved the 1856 fusion of Free Soilers and Whigs into a core of Republican voters, and the movement of many 1856 nativist voters and some 1856 innovators into the Republican ranks in 1860.   P. Travis

314. Shortridge, Ray M.   VOTING FOR MINOR PARTIES IN THE AN-TEBELLUM MIDWEST.   *Indiana Mag. of Hist. 1978 74(2): 117-134.* Examines the midwestern electoral support for the three minor parties—the Liberty Party, Free Soil Party, and American Party—and the role they played in the antebellum electoral system, ca. 1840-60.

315. Smith, Harold T.   THE KNOW-NOTHINGS IN ARKANSAS. *Arkansas Hist. Q. 1975 34(4): 291-303.* The Arkansas Know-Nothing Party, organized in Little Rock by August 1855, was composed mainly of former Whigs with a sprinkling of Democrats opposed to the Kansas-Nebraska Act. Major ideological divisions in the campaign of 1856 were over Kansas-Nebraska and southern rights. After losing most elections within the state in 1856 the Know-Nothings made a poor showing in the national canvass and soon passed from existence. Based on primary and secondary sources; 28 notes.   T. L. Savitt

316. Stagg, J. C. A.   JAMES MADISON AND THE "MALCONTENTS": THE POLITICAL ORIGINS OF THE WAR OF 1812.   *William and Mary Q. 1976 33(4): 557-585.* Discounts previous interpretations of the causes of the War of 1812. Also considers the roles of Congress and the War Hawks as less decisive than other historians have believed. Granting the importance of the crisis in Anglo-American relations, Stagg emphasizes the disunity and dissension within the Republican Party against Madison and his foreign and domestic policies. Middle state politicians resented the domination of Virginians in national politics. The "malcontents" thought Madison soft on Great Britain. Out of expediency Madison moved to the position of his critics. The war helped to restore unity in the Republican Party. Based on personal correspondence, newspapers, and foreign affairs documents; 102 notes.   H. M. Ward

317. Stanley, Gerald.   RACISM AND THE EARLY REPUBLICAN PARTY: THE 1856 PRESIDENTIAL ELECTION IN CALIFORNIA. *Pacific Hist. R. 1974 43(2): 171-187.* Develops the thesis that California Republicans in the presidential election of 1856 were concerned over the geographical expansion of the black race rather than matters relating to freedom and racial equality. Republicans repeatedly declared that they opposed the extension of slavery because it would encroach upon the rights of the white race. "They never disapproved of slavery because of its injustice to the slave. . . . It was the geographical location, not the status of black Americans that vexed California's Republicans in 1856." 67 notes.   R. V. Ritter

318. Stanley, Gerald.   SLAVERY AND THE ORIGINS OF THE REPUBLICAN PARTY IN CALIFORNIA.   *Southern California Q. 1978 60(1): 1-16.* The slavery issue was a major factor in the formation of California's Republican Party in 1856. Not many members of the new party came from the defunct Whig Party. Statistical evidence, while imperfect, suggests that the Republicans found their strength in recruitment of Anti-Nebraska Democrats rather than in former Whigs or the American Party. Recent studies indicate that Republican emergence

in other states did not resemble the California experience, where the national slavery issue predominated over local concerns. Primary and secondary sources; table, 45 notes.   A. Hoffman

319. Stegemoeller, James E.   THAT CONTEMPTIBLE BAUBLE: THE BIRTH OF THE CINCINNATI WHIG PARTY, 1834-1836.   *Cincinnati Hist. Soc. Bull. 1981 39(3): 201-223.* Examines the turmoil as two factions of the Cincinnati, Ohio, Whig Party fought for control from 1834-36; a group of young businessmen fought and lost to an older, conservative group of ex-National Republicans.

320. Strum, Harvey.   NEW YORK FEDERALISTS AND OPPOSITION TO THE WAR OF 1812.   *World Affairs 1980 142(3): 169-187.* Discusses New York Federalists' reaction to the War of 1812, to better understand dissent during America's first declared war.

321. Stuart, Reginald C.   JAMES MADISON AND THE MILITANTS: RE-PUBLICAN DISUNITY AND REPLACING THE EMBARGO.   *Diplomatic Hist. 1982 6(2): 145-167.* The failure of the embargo against Great Britain caused a crisis within the divided Democratic Republican Party in 1809. James Madison, a passive leader, wanted Congress to formulate a more vigorous policy. The militant Madison supporters, joined by the "invisibles," urged limited reprisals. Federalists, Quids, and conservative Republicans prevented extreme measures. Voting patterns and the militants' diversity indicate that party affiliation was more significant than region. The majority wanted the embargo repealed and Republican unity maintained, but shrank from war and accepted the Non-Intercourse Act (US, 1809). The militants, by suggesting an active policy in 1809, took the first step toward establishing a consensus for war. Based on the papers of James Madison, *Annals of Congress,* and other primary sources; table, 43 notes.
                                                             T. J. Heston

322. Suppiger, Joseph E.   AMITY TO ENMITY: NINIAN EDWARDS AND JESSE B. THOMAS.   *J. of the Illinois State Hist. Soc. 1974 67(2): 200-211.* Two Illinois territorial and later Illinois state senators, Jesse B. Thomas and Ninian Edwards, rivaled each other for political appointments of supporters. Each advanced into state and national offices during Illinois' early statehood. Eventually both Thomas and Edwards lost prestige and backing, Edwards through ill-advised political attacking and Thomas (a Whig) through the rise of Jacksonian Democracy. Based on the Thomas Papers in the Illinois Historical Society Library and the published Edwards Papers; 45 notes.   A. C. Aimone

323. Sweeney, Kevin.   RUM, ROMANISM, REPRESENTATION, AND REFORM: COALITION POLITICS IN MASSACHUSETTS, 1847-1853.   *Civil War Hist. 1976 22(2): 116-137.* Examines the Democratic-Free Soil Party coalition which controlled Massachusetts during 1850-52, in the context of local and statewide issues. Too much stress has been placed on the coalition's success in terms of national politics. The Massachusetts Free Soilers and the Democrats cooperated on state issues such as constitutional reform and representation and minimized their respective national differences. Thus the Free Soilers avoided the fate of most "one-cause" third parties and paved the way for the rise of Republicanism in Massachusetts a few years later.   E. C. Murdock

324.   Taishoff, Sue.   NEW HAMPSHIRE STATE POLITICS AND THE
CONCEPT OF A PARTY SYSTEM, 1800-1840.   *Hist. New Hampshire 1976
31(1-2): 17-43.* Assesses the development of New Hampshire political parties,
1800-40, in light of the prevailing assumption that there was a "progression from
the anti-partyism of the 1790's to the new politics of the 1830's . . .," involving
a total transformation in political attitudes and practices. Concludes that "there
were striking affinities in political behaviour" throughout the period, but that
electoral patterns underwent "significant shifts and disruptions usually not noted
in the literature of early party development." Illus., 43 notes.   D. F. Chard

325.   Turner, John J., Jr.   THE TWELFTH AMENDMENT AND THE
FIRST AMERICAN PARTY SYSTEM.   *Historian 1973 35 (2): 221-237.* The
12th Amendment partly was intended to extend and strengthen the safeguards
against factionalism which were institutionalized in the Electoral College. In fact,
the amendment facilitated the emergence of the modern party system by legaliz-
ing party control of both officers in the executive branch. Shows the state of
opinion about political parties at this stage in American history. Based on records
of the Constitutional Convention, the Federalist papers, and secondary sources;
61 notes.   N. W. Moen

326.   Waldrep, Christopher R.   WHO WERE KENTUCKY'S WHIG VOT-
ERS? A NOTE ON VOTING IN EDDYVILLE PRECINCT IN AUGUST
1850.   *Register of the Kentucky Hist. Soc. 1981 79(4): 326-332.* Voters in
Eddyville precinct in Caldwell County, Kentucky were mostly farmers. The
Whigs were the minority party in the August 1850 election for state senator,
receiving only 26% of the vote. Most Whigs were farmers and perhaps a bit
younger than the Democrats. Only the precinct's craftsmen preferred the Whig
Party.   Primary sources including census and tax rolls; illus., 16 notes.
                                                                          J. F. Paul

327.   Wallace, Doris Davis.   THE POLITICAL CAMPAIGN OF 1860 IN
MISSOURI.   *Missouri Hist. Rev. 1976 70(2): 162-183.* The four national parties
in 1860 held township, county, district, and state conventions to elect delegates,
nominate candidates, ratify nominations and party action, and increase unity.
The audiences at these meetings and other impromptu gatherings gave the speakers a chance to clarify issues, state their positions, and tell why the party supported those positions. Voters believed they could evaluate candidates' character
and ability by their manner of speaking as well as by the content of the speeches.
After pointing out that the speakers tried to win support by logical, emotional
and ethical proof, the author examines in detail the campaign approach of each
party. He concludes that if campaign speakers had great influence in a conservative state like Missouri they may have had an even greater effect in states where
the voters held extreme views. Based on primary and secondary sources; illus.,
76 notes.   W. F. Zornow

328.   Walton, Brian G.   ARKANSAS POLITICS DURING THE COMPRO-
MISE CRISIS, 1848-1852.   *Arkansas Hist. Q. 1977 36(4): 307-337.* Dividing
Arkansas into three sections (black, white, and intermediate) depending on the
percentage of slaves in each county, discusses the activities of the Whig and
Democratic parties in elections during 1848-52. Despite Democratic Party divi-
sions, the Whigs were never able to establish a coalition resulting in victory.
Primary and secondary sources; 3 illus., map, table, 92 notes, appendix.
                                                                  G. R. Schroeder

329.   Walton, Brian G.   ELECTIONS TO THE UNITED STATES SENATE IN ALABAMA BEFORE THE CIVIL WAR. *Alabama R. 1974 27(1): 3-38.* Political factionalism in the decade 1819-30 yielded thereafter to stability and regularity under the aegis of the Jacksonian Democratic Party, which elected every United States senator between 1831 and 1861. Disruptions in 1847 and 1849 proved temporary and atypical compared to most other Southern states. The Whig opposition, although numerically viable, was inconsistent, divided, and passive. Alabama senators represented northern and southern sections within the state according to time-honored tradition. Radical sentiment gained ascendancy after 1844, when the moderate northern element of the predominant Democratic party began losing control of the legislature. Based on primary and secondary sources; 2 tables, 86 notes.   J.F. Vivian

330.   Walton, Brian G.   ELECTIONS TO THE UNITED STATES SENATE IN NORTH CAROLINA, 1835-1861. *North Carolina Hist. R. 1976 53(2): 168-192.* Close two-party rivalry, similar to that which existed on the national level, characterized North Carolina politics during 1835-61. Senatorial elections, which took place in the state legislature, typified the competition that existed between the Whig and Democratic parties. Pervading settlement of all Senate elections were questions of personal, regional, and ideological rivalries, both within and between parties. Usually the majority party caucus' candidate won the election, unlike the experience of other southern states. Based on manuscripts, family and public papers, newspaper articles, and secondary sources; 10 illus., 4 tables, 60 notes.   T. L. Savitt

331.   Warner, Lee H.   THE PERPETUAL CRISIS OF CONSERVATIVE WHIGS: NEW YORK'S SILVER GRAYS. *New York Hist. Soc. Q. 1973 57(3): 212-236.* The New York Whig Party was a "negative coalition." Most Whigs believed that government should assume a positive role in society through tariffs, a national bank, and internal improvements. Despite agreement on such matters, the party was continually hurt by internal disputes. By the 1840's two factions had emerged. Thurlow Weed and William Henry Seward led one, and Millard Fillmore and Francis Granger the other. The latter group, known as the "Silver Grays," maintained that the Union was the first consideration and bolted over the concessions to the South in the Compromise of 1850. The Kansas-Nebraska Act (1854) killed the faction, which disappeared by 1856. Based on primary and secondary sources; 9 illus., 45 notes.   C. L. Grant

332.   Whitmore, Allan R.   "A GUARD OF FAITHFUL SENTINELS": THE KNOW-NOTHING APPEAL IN MAINE, 1854-1855. *Maine Hist. Soc. Q. 1981 20(3): 151-197.* Traces the rise and fall of the Know-Nothing Party in Maine from the summer of 1854 through 1855. Support for the anti-Catholic nativism grew rapidly among the working class, a result of irrational fears, the appeal of a highly secretive organization, and its leaders' demagoguery. When Know-Nothing aid helped Anson P. Morrill win the gubernatorial election of September 1854, the party reached its pinnacle. Its decline began in early 1855. Morrill generally ignored its claims, the national party's apparent proslavery position alienated Mainers, the newly formed (February 1855) Maine Republican Party had a wider appeal, and the local party was tainted with corruption and its basic fanaticism recognized. Most defectors moved into the Republican Party. Illus., 131 notes.   C. A. Watson

333. Wilentz, Sean. WHIGS AND BANKERS. *Rev. in Am. Hist. 1980 8(3): 344-350.* Review essay of Daniel Walker Howe's *The Political Culture of the American Whigs* (Chicago: U. of Chicago Pr., 1979); 1840's-50's.

334. Willingham, William F. GRASS ROOTS POLITICS IN WINDHAM, CONNECTICUT DURING THE JEFFERSONIAN PERIOD. *J. of the Early Republic 1981 1(2): 127-148.* Local political struggles are the backbone of national party structures. In Windham, these struggles represented an ideological debate over state issues: the ability of the existing constitution to preserve republican values and government, and whether or not to separate church and state. The Old Whig standing order became the Federalist Party, and dominated the state and Windham until 1805. Both parties used the more open political tactics introduced by the Democratic-Republicans in 1800. Declining economic and social basis for Windham Federalists led to increasing politcial power of new commerical and professional interests represented by the Democratic-Republican Party. By 1818 this, and growth of dissenters and the Toleration Party, led to ratification of a new state constitution separating church and state. Based on town and state records and on contemporary newspaper accounts; 3 tables, 59 notes.   C. B. Schulz

335. Wire, Richard Arden. JOHN M. CLAYTON AND THE RISE OF THE ANTI-JACKSON PARTY IN DELAWARE, 1824-1828. *Delaware Hist. 1973 15(4): 256-268.* John M. Clayton (1796-1856) labored to establish a republic of order. Clayton immersed himself in local and state politics as a young man, finally achieving the office of Delaware secretary of state. In 1824 he garnered only one of Delaware's electoral votes for John Quincy Adams. Clayton consistently argued for limited constitutional change within Delaware and for the development of a strong Adams party. In Delaware, party formation in the fluid Adams years "was characterized more by a concern with state than with national affairs and more by a preoccupation with personalities than with issues." From his position as secretary of state Clayton wielded immense power. He adroitly used patronage, printing contracts, and speaking tours to advance his party and his friends. The Adams press portrayed the Louis McLane Democratic Jacksonians as bloated aristocrats who sought to perpetuate their dominance through placemen and corruption. Assiduously courting favors and votes and building on the Federalist foundations in lower Delaware, Clayton's Adams party became an effective counterweight to McLane's Democrats. Clayton delivered Delaware's three electoral votes to Adams in 1828, and in the state sweep was rewarded with a U.S. Senate seat. 25 notes.   R. M. Miller

336. Wire, Richard Arden. JOHN M. CLAYTON AND WHIG POLITICS DURING THE SECOND JACKSON ADMINISTRATION. *Delaware Hist. 1978 18(1): 1-16.* Describes the Senatorial career of John M. Clayton during the second administration of Andrew Jackson. Clayton was active in trying to unite the anti-Martin Van Buren forces in the Senate, in criticizing Jackson's foreign policy and policy toward the Indians, in passing resolutions censuring Jackson for removing government deposits from the Bank of the United States, and in promoting the economic policies of Henry Clay. Clayton took particular interest in defense and foreign policy questions, particularly the question of French debts to the United States. Clayton Papers, contemporary newspapers, and secondary accounts; 44 notes.   R. M. Miller

337. Woodman, Harold D. THE OLD SOUTH: GLOBAL AND LOCAL PERSPECTIVES ON POWER, POLITICS, AND IDEOLOGY. *Civil War Hist. 1979 25(4): 339-351.* Raimondo Luraghi's *The Rise and Fall of the Plantation South* traces southern ideology to a premodern "seigneurial" system flowing through Canada from the Italian Renaissance. From colonial beginnings, Puritan bourgeois northern ideology opposed it. Industrialism brought northern aggression, including ideological offensives, eventuating in war and a "sort of Southern state socialism," comparable to Russia's and China's. J. Miller Thornton III's *Politics and Power in a Slave Society: Alabama, 1800-1860* traces secession to small farmers' efforts to restore government to protect individual autonomy against Republicans and emerging Yankee-type planters. Planters promoted diversification, but never at their expense; costs ruined small farmers. Republican strength and border-state hesitancy frightened and disillusioned them. Secondary sources; 11 notes.   R. E. Stack

338. —. MENNONITES AND THE POLITICAL ELECTIONS OF 1856: JOHANNES RISSER ON POLITICS AND THE SLAVERY ISSUE. *Mennonite Hist. Bull. 1976 37(4): 1-3.* Reprints three letters from Johannes Risser to his sister and brother-in-law in 1857 discussing the slavery issue, the Democratic Party, and the general state of politics at the time.

339. —. [PARTY FORMATION]. *William and Mary Q. 1973 30(2): 307-324. Henderson, H. James.* QUANTITATIVE APPROACHES TO PARTY FORMATION IN THE UNITED STATES: A COMMENT, pp. 307-323. Mary P. Ryan's quantitative analysis of party formation in the U.S. Congress 1789-96, from *William and Mary Quarterly* 1971 28(4): 523-542 (see abstract 9:2821), distorted reality by stressing a conservative and radical alignment. After identifying factional groupings, Ryan ignored many issues that did not bring forth a dichotomous voting pattern. Ryan's essay is useful as a refinement in the analysis of roll-call votes. 2 tables, 28 notes. Ryan, Mary P. REPLY, pp. 323-324. "I still maintain that congressional voting parties were not mere 'groupings and fumbling inventions' [Chambers] or 'missteps and misunderstandings' [Hofstadter] along the path to the modern party system."
                                                        H. M. Ward and S

340. —. [POLITICAL FACTIONS, EXPANSION, AND REVOLUTION]. Bonomi, Patricia U., ed. *Party and Political Opposition in Revolutionary America* (Tarrytown, N.Y.: Sleepy Hollow Pr., 1980): 43-69.
Egnal, Marc. THE PATTERN OF FACTIONAL DEVELOPMENT IN PENNSYLVANIA, NEW YORK, AND MASSACHUSETTS, 1682-1776, *pp. 43-60.* The political parties that emerged by the 1740's continued until the 1770's and underlay the choice of loyalties during the American Revolution. Divisions over local issues were replaced after 1740 by disputes over territorial expansion and imperial regulation. The ideology of the revolutionaries was based on expansionism rather than on constitutional rights. 69 notes.
Olson, Alison Gilbert. EMPIRE AND FACTION: A COMMENT, *pp. 61-69.* Expansionism appears to have been effective in creating political divisions but other factors were involved, too, and their roles must be assessed before expansionism is called the most significant factor. 12 notes.
                                                                              S

341. —. [POLITICAL IDEAS AND CONSTITUTIONALISM IN PENN-SYLVANIA]. Bonomi, Patricia U., ed. *Party and Political Opposition in Revolutionary America* (Tarrytown, N.Y.: Sleepy Hollow Pr., 1980): 98-118.
Dargo, George. PARTIES AND THE TRANSFORMATION OF THE CONSTITUTIONAL IDEA IN REVOLUTIONARY PENNSYLVANIA, 98-118. Despite the growing tendency to tolerate political parties by the 1760's and the success of political parties in Pennsylvania during the American Revolution in legitimizing the new government, integrating the new elite into the power structure, and increasing political participation, opposition to them increased. Political theory had changed. Leaders believed that the principles of good government had been discovered and enshrined in the state constitutions. Freedom was secure and parties were no longer desirable. 63 notes.
Patterson, Stephen E. CONSTITUTIONAL FORMALISM OR THE POLITICS OF VIRTUE?: A COMMENT, *pp. 115-118.* Challenges the thesis that political parties led to consensus rather than to political conflict. 4 notes.
S

3

THE REPUBLICAN ASCENDANCY
(1860-1932)

342. Abrams, Douglas Carl. A PROGRESSIVE-CONSERVATIVE DUEL: THE 1920 DEMOCRATIC GUBERNATORIAL PRIMARIES IN NORTH CAROLINA. *North Carolina Hist. Rev. 1978 55(4): 421-443.* The 1920 North Carolina gubernatorial Democratic primary campaign illustrates well the conservative-progressive split which existed in that state's Democratic Party politics. Three issues, "machine" politics, women's suffrage, and state press coverage of the campaign, divided the three candidates, conservative Cameron Morrison, and progressives Robert Newton Page and O. Max Gardner. While Page ran a mundane but solid campaign on the issues, Morrison and Gardner threw mud and barbs at each other and sensationalized the issues. Page was eliminated in the first primary; Gardner lost the second. Newspaper accounts, published and unpublished family papers, and secondary sources; 11 illus., 2 maps, 35 notes.
T. L. Savitt

343. Adams, David Wallace. ILLINOIS SOLDIERS AND THE EMANCIPATION PROCLAMATION. *J. of the Illinois State His. Soc. 1974 67(4): 406-421.* Provides evidence that Illinois Volunteers supported the Republican Party and the Emancipation Proclamation. Their absence from the polls in 1862 was detrimental to the Republican Party's success. Based on contemporary newspaper reports, Illinois State documents, and primary and secondary sources; 2 illus., 9 photos, 51 notes.
N. J. Street

344. Agan, Thomas. THE NEW HAMPSHIRE PROGRESSIVES: WHO AND WHAT WERE THEY? *Hist. New Hampshire 1979 34(1): 32-53.* New Hampshire's progressives emerged in the state's Republican Party in the late 19th century as a reaction to the political power of the Boston and Maine Railroad. The movement became prominent in 1906 when novelist Winston Churchill unsuccessfully sought the gubernatorial nomination but managed to create progressivism's power base. In 1910 the progressive candidate, Robert P. Bass, became governor. In many ways the progressives were similar to regular Republicans, although they were interested in some civil rights questions. Based on the Churchill and Bass collections at Dartmouth College and on secondary sources. 2 illus., 43 notes.
D. F. Chard

345. Ahern, Wilbert H. LAISSEZ FAIRE VS. EQUAL RIGHTS: LIBERAL REPUBLICANS AND LIMITS TO RECONSTRUCTION. *Phylon 1979 40(1): 52-65.* Traces the development of the Liberal Republican movement of 1872 and the reasons for the Liberal departure from the main party line. Elaborates on the role of racism, which, in contrast to other scholarship, is determined not to be the cause of the split. 42 notes. G. R. Schroeder

346. Albright, Claude. DIXON, DOOLITTLE, AND NORTON: THE FORGOTTEN REPUBLICAN VOTES. *Wisconsin Mag. of Hist. 1975-76 59(2): 90-100.* Discusses US Senators James Dixon of Connecticut, James R. Doolittle of Wisconsin, and Daniel S. Norton of Minnesota, three Republicans who voted for the acquittal of President Andrew Johnson during his impeachment trial in 1868. Although most historians mention seven Republicans who abandoned their party to support acquittal along with a Democratic minority, the author argues that Dixon, Doolittle, and Norton should be added to the list. He believes that these moderate Republicans over the length of their careers represented their party more closely than their radical colleagues in Congress. 8 illus., 4 tables, 34 notes. N. C. Burckel

347. Allen, Howard W. and Clubb, Jerome. PROGRESSIVE REFORM AND THE POLITICAL SYSTEM. *Pacific Northwest Q. 1974 65(3): 130-145.* A study of Progressivism concerned with certain basic but unanswered questions: the relation between the several components of the reform movement and the isolation and identification of fundamental conflicts and differences, the sources and extent of popular support for progressive reform and the degree to which reform proposals were popularly perceived and supported, the degree to which progressive reforms were to bring about basic changes in American life, institutions, and the distribution of political and economic power within the nation. Statistical analysis of congressional response, reformer characteristics, and popular response suggest that the movement was largely one of the substantial middle class. 7 tables, 33 notes. R. V. Ritter

348. Allison, Hildreth M. HASSLE FOR THE TOP SPOT: THE REPUBLICAN GUBERNATORIAL CONVENTION OF 1906. *Hist. New Hampshire 1981 36(1): 73-84.* There were four main contenders for the Republican gubernatorial nomination in 1906. Of these, Winston Churchill of Cornish, an author who had represented his town in the legislature in 1903 and 1905, was a dark horse reform candidate. The party machine took his candidacy lightly at first. Charles M. Floyd eventually won the nomination, but Churchill's support had surpassed that of political stalwarts Rosecrans W. Pillsbury and Charles H. Greenleaf. In addition, the party platform embodied his ideas for the abolition of free railroad passes for legislators and repudiated corrupt lobbying. 4 illus., 19 notes. D. F. Chard

349. Alsobrook, David E. MOBILE'S FORGOTTEN PROGRESSIVE: A. N. JOHNSON, EDITOR AND ENTREPRENEUR. *Alabama Rev. 1979 32(3): 188-202.* Andrew N. Johnson (1865-1922) was a reform-minded black businessman, newspaper editor, and civic leader in Mobile (Alabama) and Nashville (Tennessee). An active Republican, he opposed Alabama's lily-white faction, unsuccessfully tried to persuade President Theodore Roosevelt to remove Jim Crow proponents from patronage positions, and supported the National Negro Business League. Primary and secondary sources; 51 notes. J. F. Vivian

350.   Anders, Evan.   BOSS RULE AND CONSTITUENT INTERESTS: SOUTH TEXAS POLITICS DURING THE PROGRESSIVE ERA.   *Southwestern Hist. Q. 1981 84(3): 269-292.* From 1882 through 1920, Democratic machine politics prevailed in Cameron County, Texas, under boss James B. Wells. The Wells political machine was astutely sensitive to constituents' needs, particularly those of ranchers, businessmen, and Mexican Americans. After 1905, however, railroad transportation and the development of irrigation lured large numbers of Anglo Americans into the county. These newcomers did not have ties to the political machine and this new majority resented boss-rule, political manipulation, and Mexican American participation in the governmental process. As a result, insurgent influence in local politics, together with Mexican border raids in 1915 and 1916 and growing racial hatred, caused the collapse of the Wells political machine in 1920. Based on the James B. Wells papers and newspapers; 12 illus., 28 notes.   R. D. Hurt

351.   Anders, Evan.   THE ORIGINS OF THE PARR MACHINE IN DUVAL COUNTY, TEXAS.   *Southwestern Hist. Q. 1981 85(2): 119-138.* At the turn of the 20th century, Democratic machine politics dominated the counties which form the southern tip of Texas; and, after 1907, Duval County came under the control of Archer "Archie" Parr. Although Parr was a typical machine politician, he was exceptionally ruthless and corrupt. Progressives believed he represented the worst features of machine politics. Parr's control, however, went virtually unchecked, and he was able to establish a political machine that dominated Duval County government for nearly 60 years. Based on records in the National Archives and in the University of Texas, newspapers, and state and federal publications; 35 notes.   R. D. Hurt

352.   Appleton, Thomas H., Jr.   PROHIBITION AND POLITICS IN KENTUCKY: THE GUBERNATORIAL CAMPAIGN AND ELECTION OF 1915.   *Register of the Kentucky Hist. Soc. 1977 75(1): 28-54.* Prohibition was the main issue in the 1915 Democratic gubernatorial primary in Kentucky. Augustus Owsley Stanley led those who opposed statewide prohibition. Henry V. McChesney led the drys. After a heated campaign, Stanley won. In the fall election, he narrowly defeated Republican Edwin P. Morrow, in a campaign not seriously affected by the prohibition issue. Yet, by 1918, Kentucky, along with the nation, was ready for prohibition. Even Governor Stanley urged speedy approval of a state constitutional amendment. Primary and secondary sources; 100 notes.   J. F. Paul

353.   Archdeacon, Thomas J.   THE ERIE CANAL RING, SAMUEL J. TILDEN, AND THE DEMOCRATIC PARTY.   *New York Hist. 1978 59(4): 409-429.* The economic decline of New York State's Erie and Oswego Canals culminated in post-Civil War allegations of corruption by contractors and politicians who had a common interest in profiting from canal repairs—the Erie Canal Ring. Samuel J. Tilden, elected governor in 1874, appointed an independent commission to investigate canal repairs since 1868 and the Ring's operations. Few convictions resulted from the commission's findings, but canal management was reformed. The Canal Ring investigation enchanced Tilden's popularity on the eve of the 1876 presidential race. Suggests that Tilden was a timid reformer motivated by political ambition. 6 illus., 35 notes.   R. N. Lokken

354. Arconti, Steven J. TO SECURE THE PARTY: HENRY L. DAWES AND THE POLITICS OF RECONSTRUCTION. *Hist. J. of Western Massachusetts 1977 5(2): 33-45.* Henry L. Dawes was a moderate Republican congressman, until 1875, when he was elected to the Senate. He initially supported President Andrew Johnson; but after the president's veto of the Civil Rights Act of 1866 he became convinced that Johnson had to be removed in order to save the Republican Party from factionalism, and the country from disunion. Illus., 56 notes. W. H. Mulligan, Jr.

355. Argersinger, Peter H. "A PLACE ON THE BALLOT": FUSION POLITICS AND ANTIFUSION LAWS. *Am. Hist. Rev. 1980 85(2): 287-306.* In the scholarly debate over the origins of the dramatic changes in American political behavior occurring around the turn of this century, scholars have neglected the political context of electoral legislation and accordingly have misunderstood its significance. This essay examines the interaction between politics and ballot reform in the 1890's by focusing on antifusion legislation and answering the questions of legislative intent: who urged the passage of these laws and why? Under the mild cover of a procedural reform prohibiting the listing of a candidate's name more than once on the ballot, antifusion legislation served the interests of the Republican Party by obstructing the fusion politics characteristic of the period, disrupting opposition parties, revising traditional campaign and voting practices, and weakening the 19th-century tradition of strong third parties. These effects were deliberately sought by the sponsors of such laws in the northern states and cannot be viewed as "unintended consequences" of reforms in the structural properties of the electoral system. Based on newspaper files, legislation, and personal letters; 61 notes. A

356. Avillo, Philip J., Jr. BALLOTS FOR THE FAITHFUL: THE OATH AND THE EMERGENCE OF SLAVE STATE REPUBLICAN CONGRESSMEN, 1861-1867. *Civil War Hist. 1976 22(2): 164-174.* Surveys loyalty oath legislation in the Border States. The disfranchising measures gave Republicans control of the legislatures of those states and enhanced Republican control of Congress. Concludes that without this added Republican Party strength in the national legislature, important legislation such as the 13th and 14th Amendments, Civil Rights Act, Freedmen's Bureau Act, and First Reconstruction Act, would not have been passed. E. C. Murdock

357. Avillo, Philip J., Jr. PHANTOM RADICALS: TEXAS REPUBLICANS IN CONGRESS, 1870-1873. *Southwestern Hist. Q. 1974 77(4): 431-444.* Texas elections in 1869 gave control to the Radical Republicans in the state and its congressional delegation. The 1871 elections sent a Democratic-dominated delegation to Congress. Examines the performance of these alleged radicals. In civil rights and amnesty matters, two measures of radicalism, their records do not support the label. 53 notes. D. L. Smith

358. Baggett, James A. BIRTH OF THE TEXAS REPUBLICAN PARTY. *Southwestern Hist. Q. 1974 78(1): 1-20.* Covers 1865-68.

359. Baggett, James Alex. ORIGINS OF EARLY TEXAS REPUBLICAN PARTY LEADERSHIP. *J. of Southern Hist. 1974 40(3): 441-454.* Texas' three Republican governors all served during the Reconstruction years and symbolized

the tie between prewar Unionism and the post-Civil War Republican party. Traces the changing allegiance of many Whigs in Texas from the Know-Nothing Party to Unionism and then to the Republican Party. The Texas Republican party had little carpetbag influence, and while the black membership was larger than the white, the blacks did not rise to leadership positions. The few carpetbaggers who rose in the party were usually Union Army officers stationed in Texas, while some ex-Rebel officers also joined the Republican leadership group. There is no evidence to show that the early Republican leaders were not sincere, aware, experienced men. Based on manuscripts and published primary and secondary sources; table, 48 notes.   T. D. Schoonover

360.   Bailey, John W., Jr.   THE PRESIDENTIAL ELECTION OF 1900 IN NEBRASKA: MC KINLEY OVER BRYAN.   *Nebraska Hist. 1973 54(4): 561-584.* Bryan won his home state over McKinley in 1896 by more than 13,000 votes, but lost it in 1900 by more than 7,000 votes. Prosperity, the decline of Populism, the intensive Republican campaign in the state, and Bryan's partial neglect of his home state all explain the results in 1900.   R. Lowitt

361.   Baker, Jean H.   A LOYAL OPPOSITION: NORTHERN DEMO-CRATS IN THE THIRTY-SEVENTH CONGRESS.   *Civil War Hist. 1979 25(2): 139-155.* Analyzes the 1,176 roll-call votes of the three sessions of the 37th Congress (summer 1861-spring 1863), to examine the operation and values of the minority Democratic Party's 12 senators and 57 representatives. Divides the roll-call voting issues into: procedural, partisan, military, trampled rights, black, economic, Confederate, and general. Far from being Copperheads, the Democrats supported war measures to save the Union even while they dissented from some Republican war goals, thus showing the working of the two-party system in which the parties agreed on the overall end but not on how to attain it. Only a few Democrats favored peace at any price or southern independence. The issues of black rights, federal interference with states, and administration usurpations of power and violations of civil rights did cause Democrats to dissent. They were motivated by their special relationship to the South, by their aim to return to power after the war, and by their conviction that the Republicans were violating the natural order of society by enforcing emancipation and harsh reconstruction. 2 tables, 49 notes.   S

362.   Baker, John D.   THE CHARACTER OF THE CONGRESSIONAL REVOLUTION OF 1910.   *J. of Am. Hist. 1973 60(3): 679-691.* The Insurgent Republican revolution against "Cannonism" in 1910, which limited the authority of Speaker Joseph G. Cannon, has often been characterized inaccurately as part of the Progressive movement for responsible government. Comparison of voting records, however, shows that relatively few of the Insurgents were Progressives. Many had supported the Payne-Aldrich tariff and therefore were in trouble with their constituents. "Cannonism" was unpopular, and a blow against him would help congressmen to escape abuse for their tariff stand and to attack a man who had denied committee chairmanships to some of them. The revolt merely stripped Cannon of his chairmanship of the Rules Committee and hardly remedied the worst evils of the system. 2 tables, 42 notes.   K. B. West

363. Barjenbruch, Judith. THE GREENBACK POLITICAL MOVE-MENT: AN ARKANSAS VIEW. *Arkansas Hist. Q. 1977 36(2): 107-122.* The Greenback movement in Arkansas was short-lived (1876-82) but significant in revealing the vicissitudes of post-Reconstruction state politics. The movement provided an alternative to the Republican and Democratic Parties. It often re-placed the Republican Party by briefly allying itself with the Democrats. Major issues included national "hard money" laws, state and local politics, and race relations. The Greenback Party's greatest appeal in Arkansas was to agrarian radicals. Among its leaders were Charles E. Tobey and Rufus King Garland. Based on two contemporary Democratic Little Rock newspapers, primary and secondary sources; illus., 42 notes.   T. L. Savitt

364. Bates, J. Leonard. POLITICS AND IDEOLOGY: THOMAS J. WALSH AND THE RISE OF POPULISM. *Pacific Northwest Q. 1974 65(2): 49-56.* Studies the ideology, apparent motivations, and methods of Thomas J. Walsh (1859-1933), and his move toward populism. An analysis of his early political speeches reveals a Jeffersonian Democrat of liberal ideology. Walsh often expressed populist ideas but did not join the movement, choosing rather to contribute to the liberalization of the Democratic Party while advancing his own career. 21 notes.   R. V. Ritter

365. Baulch, J. R. GARNER HELD THE COW WHILE JIM WELLS MILKED HER. *West Texas Hist. Assoc. Year Book 1980 56: 91-99.* Texas Democratic politician John Nance Garner (a congressman after 1902) was an instrument of Texas political boss Jim Wells, 1896-1923.

366. Baum, Dale. THE "IRISH VOTE" AND PARTY POLITICS IN MAS-SACHUSETTS, 1860-1876. *Civil War Hist. 1980 26(2): 117-141.* Discusses Irish voter participation in Massachusetts politics in various elections during 1860-76. Ecological regression techniques are used to analyze the effects of their votes, which were largely Democratic, although Republicans frequently at-tempted to win Irish loyalty and used the Fenian issue in the 1860's to some advantage. Based on census and voting records, other primary and secondary sources; 9 tables, 57 notes.   G. R. Schroeder

367. Baum, Dale. "NOISY BUT NOT NUMEROUS": THE REVOLT OF THE MASSACHUSETTS MUGWUMPS. *Historian 1979 41(2): 241-256.* In a pioneering electoral study, Lee Benson challenged the accepted notion that the Mugwumps influenced enough Republican votes toward Cleveland to defeat Blaine; instead he suggested that the decline of Republican votes in Massachusetts from 1880-84 was best explained by support for Benjamin F. Butler. Reexamines this hypothesis through a more detailed analysis of Massachusetts voting returns by ecological regression. Argues that Butler failed to attract Republican votes, and that apathy was more important in the decline of Republican fortunes. Exaggerated importance given to restore political factions plus unsophisticated procedures for estimating voting patterns from aggregate statistics have combined "to give the celebrated bolt of the Mugwumps an importance out of proportion to their raw numerical strength, not only in the 1880's but also later in accounts of the period by many historians." Primary and secondary sources; 9 tables, 29 notes.   R. S. Sliwoski

368.   Bayliss, Garland E.   THE ARKANSAS STATE PENITENTIARY UNDER DEMOCRATIC CONTROL, 1874-1896.   *Arkansas Hist. Q. 1975 34(3): 195-213.* Between 1874 and 1896 the state penitentiary in Little Rock was leased out to private individuals and nominally supervised by state government representatives. In effect, this system resulted in the use of prisoners, a majority of whom were black, for labor in private and public works. Initiated during the Reconstruction Republican government, convict-lease was continued by Democratic administrations throughout the rest of the century, despite well-publicized abuse of prisoners. Based on newspaper accounts, published documents, manuscript records, and secondary works; 2 illus., 32 notes.   T. L. Savitt

369.   Belz, Herman.   THE FREEDMEN'S BUREAU ACT OF 1865 AND THE PRINCIPLE OF NO DISCRIMINATION ACCORDING TO COLOR. *Civil War Hist. 1975 21(3): 197-217.* Traces the evolution of the Freedmen's Bureau Act (1865) in Congress. Had not a provision supporting assistance to white southern refugees, sponsored by conservative rather than radical Republicans, been incorporated in the bill, it would not have passed. The original legislation dealing only with the care of freed slaves would have had insufficient backing in Congress for passage. Broadening the scope of the bill to include white refugees, an effort led by the American Union Commission and Republican Congressman Robert C. Schenck of Ohio, insured the measure's success.
E. C. Murdock

370.   Belz, Herman.   PROTECTION OF PERSONAL LIBERTY IN REPUBLICAN EMANCIPATION LEGISLATION OF 1862.   *J. of Southern Hist. 1976 42(3): 385-400.* Most historiographical concern over the motivation behind the Emancipation Proclamation has focused on Lincoln's motivation. Still, understanding of this crucial event can be advanced by examination of the 1862 measures of the Republican Party. These legislative items reveal little concern about Negro liberty and much about securing military advantage to the Union through depriving the South of labor. Guided by expediency, Congress no less than Lincoln's administration ignored or slighted the problem of the freed slaves' personal liberty.   T. Schoonover

371.   Benedict, Michael Les.   EQUALITY AND EXPEDIENCY IN THE RECONSTRUCTION ERA: A REVIEW ESSAY.   *Civil War Hist. 1977 23(4): 322-335.* Essayists in James C. Mohr's *Radical Republicans in the North* touch most neglected Reconstruction areas through northern state politics. Local Republicans stressed unpopular national issues, particularly black equality. Herman Belz's *A New Birth of Freedom* chronicles the development of this Republican commitment. Although motivation for rights legislation was mixed, Republicans shared a humanitarian concern. Glenn M. Linden's *Politics or Principle* uses congressional voting statistics to confirm the same idea. These books show Republican 1850's antislavery agitation growing into postwar rights legislation, but do not explain the inconsistency of legislation mixed with continued intense northern racism. Secondary sources; 28 notes.   R. E. Stack

372.   Benedict, Michael Les.   SOUTHERN DEMOCRATS IN THE CRISIS OF 1876-1877: A RECONSIDERATION OF REUNION AND REACTION. *J. of Southern Hist. 1980 46(4): 489-524.* C. Vann Woodward's thesis that Reconstruction represented an effort by northern capitalists to secure their interests

against a revived agrarianism has remained strongly embedded in the textbooks and synthesis works despite general agreement that racial rather than economic issues determined the course of Reconstruction. An analysis of the House votes on the proposed filibuster of late February 1877 reveals that both northern and southern Democrats defected from the Democratic ranks. Thus, fear of violence rather than any economic bargaining played the major role in the events of 1877. Based on personal manuscripts of congressmen and newspapers; 2 tables, 93 notes, 2 appendixes.   T. D. Schoonover

373. Bernard, Kenneth H. LINCOLN AND THE CIVIL WAR AS VIEWED BY A DISSENTING YANKEE OF CONNECTICUT. *Lincoln Herald 1974 76(4): 208-214.* Expresses the dissenting opinion of Richard Harvey Phelps of Connecticut, an ardent member of the Democratic Party who opposed the Civil War and Abraham Lincoln's running of it on nearly all fronts.

374. Berwanger, Eugene H. ROSS AND THE IMPEACHMENT: A NEW LOOK AT A CRITICAL VOTE. *Kansas Hist. 1978 1(4): 235-242.* Edmund Ross (1826-1907) was one of seven Republicans who voted to acquit President Andrew Johnson (1808-75). His vote had less to do with idealism than it did with a belief that an attempt was being made to destroy his political career. He intimated that the trial had degenerated into a scheme by certain Republicans to retain control of the government through patronage. Letters to President Johnson reveal the degree to which Ross believed this to be true. A letter from Henry C. Whitney (1831-1905) to the editor of the Burlington *Kansas Patriot* on 13 June 1868 reveals the degree to which Ross feared Kansas Senator Samuel C. Pomeroy (1816-91) and Representative Sidney Clarke (1831-1909) were conspiring to turn out all of Ross's friends after the conviction of Johnson. Illus., 35 notes.
                                                                                        W. F. Zornow

375. Berwanger, Eugene. THREE AGAINST JOHNSON: COLORADO REPUBLICAN EDITORS REACT TO RECONSTRUCTION. *Social Sci. J. 1976 12(3): 149-158.* The three leading Republican newspapers of Colorado, finding President Andrew Johnson's Reconstruction overtures to Democrats political treason, attacked him as an odious character in 1865-67.

376. Bethauser, Margaret O'Connor. HENRY A. REEVES: THE CAREER OF A CONSERVATIVE DEMOCRATIC EDITOR, 1858-1916. *J. of Long Island Hist. 1973 9(2): 34-43.* Focuses on the consistency in Reeves' thought as owner and editor of the Democratic *Republican Watchman* of Greenport, Long Island. As "Peace Democrat" he aired conservative, eastern views favoring low tariff and hard money rather than those of the Democratic Party. In political and social philosophy he was essentially a Jeffersonian-Jacksonian proponent of local autonomy and responsibility. Photo.   C. A. Newton

377. Bicha, Karel D. THE CONSERVATIVE POPULISTS: A HYPOTHE-SIS. *Agric. Hist. 1973 47(1): 9-24.* Populists were neither liberals nor reactionaries, but rather conservatives dedicated to classical laissez-faire economics. Populism offered no positive solutions to the problems of depression, unemployment, natural disasters, or welfare, believing them to be beyond the legitimate scope of government. Based mainly on newspapers, federal and State records, and correspondence; 58 notes.   D. E. Brewster

378.   Bicha, Karel D.   PECULIAR POPULIST: AN ASSESSMENT OF JOHN R. ROGERS.   *Pacific Northwest Q. 1974 65(3): 110-117.* A study and evaluation of John R. Rogers, the Populist and Democratic governor of Washington from 1897-1901, including his significance as a publicist, ideologue, and advocate of reform. Rogers began his career as a monetary reformer and ended with a complete obsession with land use and land tenure reform. His intransigent agrarianism, as exemplified by his free homestead proposal, was socialistic in its implications, even though he was a champion of individualism. 36 notes.

R. V. Ritter

379.   Bicha, K. D.   WESTERN POPULISTS: MARGINAL REFORMERS OF THE 1890'S.   *Agricultural Hist. 1976 50(4): 626-635.* The People's Party of the 1890's showed little interest in reform in the legislatures of the plains and mountain states where it was strong. Except for railroad bills, Populists initiated and passed no more reform legislation than Republicans or Democrats. Populists may have encouraged other parties to sponsor reform measures but were not themselves reformers. Table, 16 notes.

D. E. Bowers

380.   Binning, F. Wayne.   THE TENNESSEE REPUBLICANS IN DECLINE, 1869-1876. PART I.   *Tennessee Hist. Q. 1980 39(4): 471-484.* Discusses political reconstruction in Tennessee, 1869-70. By controlling balloting, DeWitt Clinton Senter earned the support of those enfranchised by his maneuvers, and was elected governor. His extension of the franchise, however, opened the way for the return of the Democrats to power. When the Democratic legislature elected in 1869 met, it undid Radical legislation. The Republican tide of 1865-69 receded. In 1870 the Democrats further extended their power with the election of John Calvin Brown as governor. Democrats captured the legislature and Supreme Court and remodeled the state constitution to suit their needs. Primary sources; 32 notes.

J. Powell

381.   Binning, Wayne F.   CARPETBAGGERS' TRIUMPH: THE LOUISIANA STATE ELECTION OF 1868.   *Louisiana Hist. 1973 14(1): 21-39.* Carpetbaggers and blacks were the two principal factions of the Louisiana Republican Party after the Civil War. Their struggle culminated during the election of 1868 when the Radical Republicans refused to support the party nominee, Henry Clay Warmoth, and nominated James Govan Taliaferro as an opposition candidate. The more moderate Carpetbaggers were vindicated when Warmoth strongly defeated Taliaferro. Thereafter, the "free colored class" was "effectively excluded from politics," although they kept the civil rights issue alive. Based on published documents, newspapers, and the H. C. Warmoth Papers in the Southern Collection, University of North Carolina at Chapel Hill; 3 photos, 47 notes.

R. L. Woodward

382.   Blakey, George T.   CALLING A BOSS A BOSS: DID ROOSEVELT LIBEL BARNES IN 1915?   *New York Hist. 1979 60(2): 195-216.* Theodore Roosevelt, defendant in a $50,000 libel suit brought against him by William Barnes, Jr., used the courtroom as a forum for his attack on political bossism and corruption, defense of democratic principles against political machine rule, and an attempt to restore his political prestige. Barnes, long influential in New York Republican politics, sued Roosevelt for having publicly called him a corrupt political boss. The trial revealed the contrasting political styles and philosophies

of the principals. Based on the New York State Supreme Court trial records. 10 illus., 45 notes.

R. N. Lokken

383. Bland, Gaye K. POPULISM IN THE FIRST CONGRESSIONAL DISTRICT OF KENTUCKY. *Filson Club Hist. Q. 1977 51(1): 31-43.* The combination of a relatively small black population and an economically depressed farming population made the Populist party a major factor in Kentucky's First Congressional District. The financial difficulties were caused in part by the policies of the American Tobacco Company monopoly. Populist and Republican Fusion failed to materialize, and the Democrats retained the seat in 1892. Based on contemporary newspapers; 97 notes.

G. B. McKinney

384. Block, Robert Hoyt. SOUTHERN CONGRESSMEN AND WILSON'S CALL FOR REPEAL OF THE PANAMA CANAL TOLL EXEMPTION. *Southern Studies 1978 17(1): 91-100.* In 1913, President Woodrow Wilson (1856-1924) asked Congress to remove American exemption from tolls for use of the Panama Canal. Although the Hay-Pauncefote Treaty of 1901 had called for usage by all nations "on terms of entire equality," Congress established rates, in 1912, exempting American ships. The British protested, and Wilson decided to seek repeal. This was in opposition to the Democratic Party platform and Wilson's own views of a year earlier. To secure passage, Wilson enlisted the aid of southern congressmen and government officials, who supported him primarily out of party loyalty. In both houses, southern Democrats voted for repeal to a larger degree than northern Democrats. Primary and secondary sources; 46 notes.

J. Buschen

385. Bogue, Allan G. THE RADICAL VOTING DIMENSION IN THE U.S. SENATE DURING THE CIVIL WAR. *J. of Interdisciplinary Hist. 1973 3(3): 449-474.* A study of the quantitative approach to the definition of Radicals and non-Radicals in the Civil War Senate. Approaches used in the past have unexpected hazards, while scaling allows a more satisfactory analysis, particularly because it frees individual voting records from aggregate analysis. 3 tables, 6 figs., 23 notes, appendix.

R. Howell

386. Boles, David C. EFFECT OF THE KU KLUX KLAN ON THE OKLAHOMA GUBERNATORIAL ELECTION OF 1926. *Chronicles of Oklahoma 1977-78 55(4): 424-432.* Despite Republican attempts to closely link Democratic gubernatorial candidate Henry S. Johnston to the Ku Klux Klan, Johnston won the 1926 Oklahoma election with a greater margin than any predecessor. Though affiliated with the Klan earlier and carrying its backing in this election, Johnston did not seek its support nor make Klan activity a political issue. Newspaper accounts; 2 photos, 46 notes.

M. L. Tate

387. Bradford, Richard H. RELIGION AND POLITICS: ALFRED E. SMITH AND THE ELECTION OF 1928 IN WEST VIRGINIA. *West Virginia Hist. 1975 36(3) 213-221.* In the 1928 Democratic presidential primary, New York Governor Alfred E. Smith faced Missouri Senator James A. Reed in West Virginia. Although Smith never set foot in the state while Reed campaigned vigorously, and although Smith was a Catholic running in a 95% Protestant state, he won the primary, 82,000 to 76,000. In November, Hoover won; but West Virginia had been a Republican state for some time, and Smith did better than

previous Democratic candidates. Based on newspapers and secondary sources; 50 notes.
                                                                        J. H. Broussard.

388.   Bromberg, Alan B.   THE WORST MUDDLE EVER SEEN IN N.C. POLITICS: THE FARMERS' ALLIANCE, THE SUBTREASURY, AND ZEB VANCE.   *North Carolina Hist. Rev. 1979 56(1): 19-40.* Zebulon B. Vance's (1830-94) opposition to the Farmers' Alliance planned subtreasury in 1890 almost cost him his Senate seat and disrupted North Carolina Democratic Party politics. The Democrats were forced to discuss the substantive issue over which they were split: farmers favored the subtreasury plan, conservatives opposed it as government intervention. Before 1890 patronage and competition among state politicians had been issues dividing the party. To insure continued support and to save the party, Vance agreed to follow instructions from his legislature on the subtreasury matter, although he later broke this agreement. The Democratic Party was never the same. Journal and newspaper articles, personal letters, and secondary sources; 16 illus., 40 notes.
                                                                        T. L. Savitt

389.   Brown, Ira V.   WILLIAM D. KELLEY AND RADICAL RECONSTRUCTION.   *Pennsylvania Mag. of Hist. and Biog. 1961 85(3): 316-329.* Traces the life and accomplishments of William Darrah Kelley, a Philadelphian who served in Congress as a Republican from 1861 until his death in 1890, concentrating on his role as an exponent of Radical Reconstruction policies for the South, woman suffrage, and the civil rights of blacks.

390.   Brown, Kenny L.   WILLIAM C. GRIMES: ACTING GOVERNOR OF OKLAHOMA TERRITORY, 1901.   *Chronicles of Oklahoma 1975 53(1): 93-108.* William C. Grimes came to Oklahoma Territory from Nebraska and participated in the 1889 land rush into the Unassigned Lands. Active participation in Republican Party affairs secured for him an appointment as territorial marshal in August 1890 and the more lucrative post of territorial secretary 11 years later. He became closely identified with the Dennis Flynn wing of the Republican Party, wielded considerable power, and made some notable behind-the-scenes contributions to the territory. As secretary, Grimes became acting governor on 30 November 1901 when Governor William Jenkins was removed from office. But his term lasted only 10 days until a new governor was appointed. Continuing as secretary, he faced charges of corruption from various political circles and retired from politics upon reaching the expiration of his term in January 1906. Despite his short stint as territorial governor, Grimes considerably helped shape the history of Oklahoma Territory. Based on primary and secondary sources; 4 photos, 38 notes.
                                                                        M. L. Tate

391.   Brownlee, W. Elliot, Jr.   INCOME TAXATION AND THE POLITICAL ECONOMY OF WISCONSIN, 1890-1930.   *Wisconsin Mag. of Hist. 1976 59(4): 299-324.* The anticorporate bias of rural voters in the 1890's was an important ingredient in the progressivism of Republicans under Robert Marion La Follette. As a means of redistributing income and relieving the property taxes of farmers, progressives succeeded in 1911 in passing a state corporate income tax that fell most heavily on the manufacturing sector of the economy. Primarily this was because manufacturing interests were not strongly organized against the tax and did not represent a dominant position in the business community. An important result of this shift in taxation was the development of Wisconsin's

agricultural service-state which had its roots in the 1870's. The relative weakness of manufacturing interests accounts for the more radical character of Wisconsin's progressivism when compared with that of other industrial states. 11 illus., 78 notes.

N. C. Burckel

392. Buenker, John D. DYNAMICS OF CHICAGO ETHNIC POLITICS, 1900-1930. *J. of the Illinois State Hist. Soc. 1974 67(2): 175-199.* Reviews Chicago's Italian, Irish, Swedish, Bohemian, German, Polish, and black city wards and why they supported the more effective Democratic Party. Native-stock politicians were to lose out to ethnic-orienated politicians despite financial, educational, and social advantages. The Chicago Irish took particular advantage of their numbers and group cohesiveness, and were successful on such issues as the repeal of Prohibition. Based on political biographies and recent political studies; 37 notes.

A. C. Aimone

393. Buenker, John D. THE POLITICS OF RESISTANCE: THE RURAL-BASED YANKEE REPUBLICAN MACHINES OF CONNECTICUT AND RHODE ISLAND. *New England Q. 1974 47(2): 212-237.* The principle of representation by town rather than population allowed the political machines of J. Henry Roraback of Connecticut and Charles R. Brayton of Rhode Island to operate freely. For example, 12% of the population in Connecticut elected a majority of the senate in 1910. Malapportionment guaranteed the supremacy of the small town over the city, of Yankee Protestants over the more recent immigrants, and of the Republicans over the Democrats. 45 notes.

E. P. Stickney

394. Bullough, William A. HANNIBAL VERSUS THE BLIND BOSS: THE "JUNTA," CHRIS BUCKLEY, AND DEMOCRATIC REFORM POLITICS IN SAN FRANCISCO. *Pacific Hist. Rev. 1977 46(2): 181-206.* The clash in San Francisco municipal politics during the 1890's between Democratic Blind Boss Christopher A. Buckley (1845-1922) and the Junta, an elite reform coalition, sheds light on the historiographic controversy concerning progressive reformers. Changed conditions had eroded Buckley's personal power by the 1890's, but his continued presence challenged the business and professional men who were seeking to establish their own authority and at the same time provided them with a moral issue to justify their manipulations. In reality, the reformers supplanted the Blind Boss by using more sophisticated versions of his political tactics. Based on newspapers; 71 notes.

W. K. Hobson

395. Bullough, William A. THE STEAM BEER HANDICAP: CHRIS BUCKLEY AND THE SAN FRANCISCO MUNICIPAL ELECTION OF 1896. *California Hist. Q. 1975 54(3): 245-262.* Describes the comeback attempt by blind politician Christopher A. Buckley in San Francisco's 1896 municipal election. Denied representation by opponents controlling Democratic party machinery, Buckley created the Regular Democratic Party, transforming it into the Anti-Charter Democrats when the former party was refused a place on the ballot. He also infiltrated the Populist party and managed to place candidates of his choosing on its ticket. Suspicion of collusion between Buckley and John D. Spreckels came to light but ended when the sugar heir lost power in the Republican party. During the campaign Buckley was actively opposed by Democrats as well as a hostile press, and in the election his candidates were roundly defeated,

signaling the end of the political bossism that had dominated in the 1880's and marking the emergence of the professional man in politics, a product of changing urban conditions in cities across the country. Based on primary and secondary sources; 103 notes.   A. Hoffman

396.   Burbank, Garin.   THE POLITICAL AND SOCIAL ATTITUDES OF SOME EARLY OKLAHOMA DEMOCRATS.   *Chronicles of Oklahoma 1974/75 52(4): 439-455.* Discusses the status and actions of leading Oklahoma Democrats in the years following statehood. Uses Robert Lee Williams, chief justice of the state supreme court and later governor, as a typical representative of Oklahoma Democratic leaders. Most were privileged property owners and used their position to garner political power and distribute favors. This elite group was self-seeking and indifferent or hostile to land and financial reform unless it favored their interests. They encountered strong Socialist opposition and worked to discredit the Socialist party. Based on contemporary newspaper reports, primary and secondary sources; 4 photos, 58 notes.   N. J. Street

397.   Burckel, Nicholas C.   GOVERNOR ALBERT B. WHITE AND THE BEGINNING OF PROGRESSIVE REFORM 1901-05.   *West Virginia Hist. 1978 40(1): 1-12.* The leadership of West Virginia's Republican Party in the early 20th century was in the hands of young businessmen. Albert B. White, raised in the Midwest, moved to West Virginia in 1887 and became owner-editor of the Parkersburg *State Journal.* He was elected governor in 1900 on a platform of tax reform and constitutional revision, but Republican Senator Stephen B. Elkins opposed any taxation of business. White also pushed conservation, election reform, railroad regulation, and a food and drug act, but the reluctant legislature did little on any of his recommendations. Primary and secondary sources; 28 notes.   J. H. Broussard

398.   Burckel, Nicholas C.   WILLIAM GOEBEL AND THE CAMPAIGN FOR RAILROAD REGULATION IN KENTUCKY, 1888-1900.   *Filson Club Hist. Q. 1974 48(1): 43-60.* Uses the career of William Goebel to show that political ambition and reform ideas combined to form the basis of Progressivism. Goebel had built his career on a record of favoring state regulation of railroads and induced a state constitutional convention to include a railroad commission in the Kentucky constitution of 1891. In 1898, he supported a partisan election law which centralized election administration in the Democratically controlled state legislature. After Goebel received the 1899 Democratic gubernatorial nomination, the Republican candidate William S. Taylor stated that Goebel would use the election law to have himself counted into office, a charge that Goebel ignored. Taylor won the election by a small plurality, and Goebel was assassinated in the midst of his contest to overturn the results. Documentation from contemporary newspapers; 57 notes.   G. B. McKinney

399.   Campbell, Allen.   REPUBLICAN POLITICS IN DEMOCRATIC ARIZONA: TOM CAMPBELL'S CAREER.   *J. of Arizona Hist. 1981 22(2): 177-196.* The author's father, Tom Campbell, achieved prominence in Arizona and national political events despite being a Republican in a Democratic state. Besides being governor, Tom Campbell played a leading role in state labor laws, tax laws, US relations with Mexico, the Bureau of Reclamation, and the US Civil Service Commission from 1901-32. Based on unpublished memoirs and secondary sources; 2 photos, 39 notes.   G. O. Gagnon

400.   Chandler, Robert.   THE FAILURE OF REFORM: WHITE ATTI-
TUDES AND INDIAN RESPONSE IN CALIFORNIA DURING THE
CIVIL WAR ERA.   *Pacific Hist. 1980 24(3): 284-294.* Republicans came into
power in California in the 1860's and brought the belief of equality for all under
the law. Reformism and the Civil War modified white attitudes toward blacks and
Chinese but not Indians. Indians were thought to be both racially inferior and
culturally barbaric. The Indian population rapidly declined. It was about 310,000
in 1769; by 1845 it was 150,000; by 1850 it was 100,000; and by 1900 it was only
20,000. California Indians were called "Diggers" by the Americans. Attempts
were made to place some Indians on reservations. Other attempts were made to
kill them or to enslave them (through apprentice programs). The whites thought
that the Indians were dying out as a race and that killing them aided nature. The
reformers failed because the Indian was placed so low on the scale of humanity
he could not contribute to civilization and therefore did not try to. Based on local
newspapers, 1850 and 1860 California Statutes; 28 notes.   G. L. Lake

401.   Christensen, Lawrence O.   THE RACIAL VIEWS OF JOHN W.
WHEELER.   *Missouri Hist. R. 1973 67(4): 535-547.* Discusses the racial views
of John W. Wheeler, a Republican member of the St. Louis black community and
editor of the *St. Louis Palladium*. Holding a respected position within society,
Wheeler was able to persuade Negroes to join the Republican Party. Like Booker
T. Washington, he urged Negroes to take on the responsibility of improving
themselves, maintaining high moral standards, and supporting racial solidarity.
Wheeler defended blacks against racial attacks, fought segregation attempts, and
opposed black emigration to Africa in 1903. Based on contemporary newspaper
reports, US government documents, and secondary sources; 5 illus., photo, 54
notes.   N. J. Street

402.   Clark, J. Stanley.   CAREER OF JOHN R. THOMAS.   *Chronicles of
Oklahoma 1974 52(2): 152-179.* Gives a biographical account of John Robert
Thomas (1846-1914), Republican politician and lawyer. As a congressman from
Illinois he actively supported naval development. Later appointed a federal dis-
trict judge in Indian Territory, he moved to Muskogee; he also served on the first
Oklahoma Code Commission. While visiting McAlester, he was shot to death
during a prison outbreak. Illus., 4 photos.   N. J. Street

403.   Coben, Stanley.   A. MITCHELL PALMER AND THE REORGA-
NIZATION OF THE DEMOCRATIC PARTY IN PENNSYLVANIA, 1910-
1912.   *Pennsylvania Mag. of Hist. and Biog. 1960 84(2): 175-193.* Discusses
Congressman A. Mitchell Palmer's role in reforming the Democratic Party,
1910-12 in Republican-run Pennsylvania, focusing on his ability to bridge the gap
between the progressive faction of the party and the professional politicians who
preferred maintaining a safe, subservient position with respect to the ruling
Republican Party.

404.   Cochran, William C.   "DEAR MOTHER: ..." AN EYEWITNESS
REPORT ON THE REPUBLICAN NATIONAL CONVENTION OF 1876.
Hayes Hist. J. 1976 1(2): 88-97. Presents an eyewitness account of the Republican
Party Convention of 1876, in Cincinnati, and traces how James G. Blaine, initially
the most widely supported candidate, lost the nomination to Rutherford B. Hayes
of Ohio. The role of the press, rumors about the candidates, and the attempt of

Blaine supporters to force a vote for President and Vice-President, are highlighted
as deciding factors in the nomination of Hayes. Primary source; 4 illus.
                                                                    J. N. Friedel

405.   Coker, William L.   THE UNITED STATES SENATE INVESTIGA-
TION OF THE MISSISSIPPI ELECTION OF 1875.   *J. of Mississippi Hist.*
1975 37(2): 143-163. Describes the US Senate investigation of the Mississippi
election of 1875 in which, after "an intensive political campaign frequently accompanied by violence and intimidation," Democrats overthrew Radical Republican rule. Although concerned with human rights, the Republicans were
motivated chiefly by a desire to use testimony for political gain in the presidential
election of 1876. Primary sources; 55 notes.   J. W. Hillje

406.   Colbert, Thomas Burnell.   POLITICAL FUSION IN IOWA: THE
ELECTION OF JAMES B. WEAVER TO CONGRESS IN 1878.   *Arizona and*
the West 1978 20(1): 25-40. After two decades in the Republican Party, Civil War
General James B. Weaver was alienated by advocating prohibition and accepting
the tenets of greenbackism. By 1878 he was ready to bolt his party and to accept
the nomination of the Iowa Independent (Greenback) Party for a seat in Congress. Weaver succeeded w1th the support of local Democrats and he soon gained
national prominence as an agrarian leader. 3 illus., 37 notes.   D. L. Smith

407.   Coletta, Paolo.   BRYAN AT BALTIMORE, 1912: WILSON'S WAR-
WICK.   *Nebraska Hist. 1976 57(2): 200-225.* Detailed examination of William
Jennings Bryan's crucial role at the 1912 Democratic Party convention. As a
result of his stance in opposing any candidate who had the support of "the
financiers of Wall Street," Woodrow Wilson was able on the 46th ballot to secure
the nomination.   R. Lowitt

408.   Connor, William P.   RECONSTRUCTION REBELS: THE *NEW OR-*
LEANS TRIBUNE IN POST-WAR LOUISIANA.   *Louisiana Hist. 1980*
21(2): 159-181. Upon the demise in 1864 of *L'Union,* the French language
newspaper of the New Orleans gens de couleur, Dr. Louis Charles Roudanez
(1823-90), a well-educated free man of color, began publishing the bilingual *New*
Orleans Tribune. This paper briefly prospered with state and federal printing
contracts. Its most prominent editor, Jean-Charles Houzeau (1820-88), a Belgian
intellectual, advocated full social, economic, and political equality for all
Negroes. *Tribune* editorials also espoused cooperatives managed by labor and
supported Radical Republicanism. This black owned daily and its program both
failed in 1868 with the splintering of Louisiana's Republican Party. Based primarily on contemporary newspapers; 86 notes.   D. B. Touchstone

409.   Cox, LaWanda.   REVOLUTION IN THE BLACK MAN'S LEGAL
STATUS: PRODUCT OF WAR AND THE REPUBLICAN PARTY.
Rev. in Am. Hist. 1977 5(3): 348-353. Review article prompted by Herman Belz's
A New Birth of Freedom: The Republican Party and Freedmen's Rights, 1861
to 1866 (Westport, Conn.: Greenwood Pr., 1976).

410.   Crofts, Daniel W.   THE UNION PARTY OF 1861 AND THE SECES-
SION CRISIS.   *Perspectives in Am. Hist. 1977-78 11: 325-376.* The Union
Party, which took political shape in the upper South between Abraham Lincoln's
election and his decision to move on Fort Sumter, had political potential. Party

members did not want to secede, and most residents of the upper south shared their views. If Lincoln had not forced their hand by his decision on Sumter, the Civil War might have been averted.   W. A. Wiegand

411. Crosson, David. JAMES S. CLARKSON AND THEODORE ROOSEVELT, 1901-1904: A STUDY IN CONTRASTING POLITICAL TRADITIONS. *Ann. of Iowa 1974 42(5): 344-360.* Theodore Roosevelt's appointment of James S. Clarkson as surveyor of the Port of New York renewed Clarkson's political career. A Radical Republican, as opposed to the Progressivism of the President, Clarkson nevertheless used his post to gather information about New York City's business and financial elites and to organize labor and minority support for the President. Clarkson's success certainly contributed to Roosevelt's election in 1904.   C. W. Olson

412. Crow, Jeffrey J. "FUSION, CONFUSION, AND NEGROISM": SCHISMS AMONG NEGRO REPUBLICANS IN THE NORTH CAROLINA ELECTION OF 1896. *North Carolina Hist. Rev. 1976 53(4): 364-384.* Seeking the best political strategy for protecting their interests, black Republican voters were deeply divided over the gubernatorial candidacy of Daniel L. Russell (1845-1908) in 1896. Conservatives opposed Russell (an advocate of fusion with the Populist Party), fearing loss of status in the Republican Party and disliking his public racial insults. Fusionists favored Russell as a means of avoiding Democratic rule and their expected prejudice and violence. Democratic antiblack campaign rhetoric and good Republican organization brought a majority of blacks into the victorious Russell fold on election day. Based on collections of personal papers, local newspaper articles, and secondary sources; 11 illus., 63 notes.   T. L. Savitt

413. Current, Richard N. THE POLITICS OF RECONSTRUCTION IN WISCONSIN, 1865-1873. *Wisconsin Mag. of Hist. 1976-77 60(2): 82-108.* Traces the success of Wisconsin Republicans in dealing with the issues of racism, nativism, materialism, sectionalism, idealism, and antimonopolism which kept them in power during Reconstruction. The article is the concluding chapter in Current's published volume, *The History of Wisconsin, Volume II: The Civil War Era, 1848-1873.* 18 illus., 40 notes.   N. C. Burckel

414. Curry, Earl R. PENNSYLVANIA AND THE REPUBLICAN CONVENTION OF 1860: A CRITIQUE OF MC CLURE'S THESIS. *Pennsylvania Mag. of Hist. and Biog. 1973 97(2): 183-198.* In 1892 Whig politician and journalist Alexander K. McClure recorded that William H. Seward was prevented from securing the presidential nomination at the Republican National Convention of 1860 by the Pennsylvania delegation's refusal to support him. Pennsylvania was recognized, and rightly so, as the Keystone State—an essential state to carry in any national election. According to McClure, Pennsylvania's leaders realized that if Seward was nominated, strong opposition from Pennsylvania's Know-Nothings spelled ultimate defeat for the national ticket. Contrary to McClure's thesis, however, the Know-Nothings were so weak in Pennsylvania by 1860 that Republican leaders did not even feel it necessary to consider their views. Republican leaders did not support Seward because they feared that his outspoken attacks on slavery would become the chief focus of the campaign, thereby obscuring the tariff issue—which topic the Republican leaders wanted to make

the dominant campaign issue. Based on primary and secondary sources; 46 notes.
E. W. Carp

415.   Daly, James J.   WILLIAM JENNINGS BRYAN AND THE RED
RIVER VALLEY PRESS, 1890-1896.   *North Dakota Hist. 1975 42(1): 27-37.*
The Republican newspapers saw Bryan as an anti-Christ, a fool, a danger to
American freedoms, an anarchist, and a disloyal American. Before his nomination as Democratic Presidential candidate, Bryan was either ignored, treated
neutrally, or slightly disparaged in the Red River Valley press; yet following his
nomination, the free-wheeling and outspoken Republican editors vilified him.
The few Democratic newspapers came to his defense but they were a fairly
insignificant minority in a heavily Republican area. Based on primary newspaper
research and secondary sources.   N. Lederer

416.   Delatte, Carolyn E.   THE ST. LANDRY RIOT: A FORGOTTEN IN-
CIDENT OF RECONSTRUCTION VIOLENCE.   *Louisiana Hist. 1976 17(1):
41-49.* A riot of major proportions in St. Landry in 1868 resulted in weeks of
unprecedented brutality. A majority of voters rejected the Radical constitution
since the Republican Party had no roots in the parish. A small group of white
radicals in St. Landry provided effective leadership for the large Negro population. "The entire white population joined ranks to insure Negro subordination."
36 notes.   E. P. Stickney

417.   Di Nunzio, Mario R.   LYMAN TRUMBULL, THE STATES' RIGHTS
ISSUE, AND THE LIBERAL REPUBLICAN REVOLT.   *J. of the Illinois
State Hist. Soc. 1973 66(4): 364-375.* Senator Lyman Trumbull (1813-96) from
Illinois was one of those who left the Republican Party in the post-Civil War era
and rejoined the Democratic Party in 1872. The regulation of federal power and
its corruption were the major reasons for changing parties. Trumbull opposed the
abuse of constitutional government that prevailed in the Grant administration.
The Ku Klux Klan bill of 1871, which authorized suspension of habeas corpus
and other extraordinary measures in order to suppress the Klan, was opposed by
Trumbull as a dangerous trend toward centralization of federal power. Based on
the Trumbull Papers in the Illinois State Historical Library, and on Trumbull
publications and biographies; illus., 28 notes.   A. C. Aimone

418.   Dillard, Tom.   TO THE BACK OF THE ELEPHANT: RACIAL CON-
FLICT IN THE ARKANSAS REPUBLICAN PARTY.   *Arkansas Hist. Q.
1974 33(1): 3-15.* Chronicles the struggle of blacks for equal participation in the
state's Republican activities, 1867-1928.   S

419.   Dillard, Tom W.   FIGHTING THE LILY WHITES: RACIAL CON-
FRONTATION IN THE ARKANSAS REPUBLICAN PARTY, 1920-1924
DOCUMENTS.   *Red River Valley Hist. Rev. 1979 4(2): 63-71.* Traces efforts
by white Republicans to eliminate black participation in the party between the
1890's and 1920, and the resulting counteroffensive by blacks between 1920 and
1924, based on documents now in the Pratt C. Remmel Collection at the University of Arkansas Library Special Collections, which show how hard the blacks
fought.

420. Drago, Edmund L. THE BLACK PRESS AND POPULISM, 1890-1896. *San Jose Studies 1975 1(1): 97-103.* Black newspapers between 1890 and 1896 were almost unanimous in their support of the Republican Party and condemnation of populism. S

421. Drew, Donna. THE LOUISIANA ELECTION OF 1892 RE-EXAMINED. *Louisiana Studies 1976 15(2): 161-177.* The gubernatorial election of 1892 in Louisiana was characterized by fraud on the part of the two major candidates and also the governor of the state. Both major candidates were from factions within the Democratic Party. Murphy J. Foster (1849-1921) led the faction opposed to the rechartering of the Louisiana State Lottery Company while Samuel D. McEnery (1837-1910) headed the faction reputed to be in favor of the lottery. Although a decision of the US Supreme Court rendered the issue of the lottery nugatory, both factions practiced fraud in the primary, which Foster won. In the actual election, Governor Francis R. Nicholls (1834-1912) used his influence to manipulate vote counting, and Foster won by a large and fradulent majority. Based on New Orleans and Baton Rouge newspaper accounts, theses at Louisiana State U., and secondary sources; table, 62 notes. J. Buschen

422. Edwards, John Carver. HERBERT HOOVER'S PUBLIC LANDS POLICY: A STRUGGLE FOR CONTROL. *Pacific Historian 1976 20(1): 34-45.* During the 1920's, Republicans developed few positive programs for dealing with Western lands. Herbert C. Hoover's Secretary of Interior, Ray Lyman Wilbur, supported efforts to turn lands over to states for administration, as recommended by a special committee headed by James R. Garfield. Opponents, such as Gifford Pinchot, raised the specter of Teapot Dome, and the plan was defeated. Primary and secondary sources; 3 illus., 16 notes.
G. L. Olson

423. Eggert, Gerald G. "I HAVE TRIED SO HARD TO DO RIGHT." *Am. Hist. Illus. 1978 12(9): 10-23.* Stephen Grover Cleveland (1837-1908) of New York defeated Blaine for the Presidency in 1884. A Democratic reformer known for thoroughness and integrity, Cleveland used the veto "to do right." Vetoing pension bills cost him the support of the GAR and possibly the 1888 election, but he defeated Harrison in an 1892 rematch. The Panic of 1893, Coxey's Army's march, the Pullman Strike, and Hawaiian and Cuban expansion moves occupied his second term. Cleveland retired to "Oakview" in Princeton, New Jersey. His dying words furnished the title and theme of the article. Cleveland was philosophically conservative, politically lucky, and mentally unimaginative, but morally honest. Secondary sources; 14 illus. D. Dodd

424. Eisenberg, John M. A HOUSE DIVIDED: SILVER DEMOCRATS AND THEIR PARTY. *West Tennessee Hist. Soc. Papers 1975 29: 86-99.* A convention of silver Democrats in Memphis called for a bimetallic meeting in Memphis during June 1895 to counteract an earlier meeting of gold Democrats which had been held in Memphis in May. More than 2,000 delegates attended. While most were Democrats, Republicans were also present, and the convention's declarations were bipartisan. The importance of the convention was that it was the first non-Congressional meeting of silver Democrats which transcended state boundaries. It also proved to be a splendid opportunity to resolve the debate between those favoring a fight within the party over the silver issue and those who

wanted to leave the party. The latter group finally decided to remain in the party. The following year in Chicago William Jennings Bryan delivered his famous "Cross of Gold" speech and was subsequently nominated as the Democrats' standard-bearer, largely as the result of the Memphis convention. Based on secondary materials; 52 notes, 2 appendixes.   H. M. Parker, Jr.

425.   Elbert, E. Duane.   SOUTHERN INDIANA IN THE ELECTION OF 1860: THE LEADERSHIP AND THE ELECTORATE.   *Indiana Mag. of Hist. 1974 70(1): 1-23.* A statistical study of a cross-section of the electorate and party leaders in six select Indiana counties. Examines Republicans, Democrats, and Constitutional Unionists from the perspectives of place of birth, average age, occupation, and wealth. The existing correlations are evident. There was no positive correlation between foreign birth and political party; age was not a distinction among the parties; there were definite occupation correlations; and wealth was about the same with Democrats and Republicans, while Constitutional Unionists were on the whole better off than the leaders and members of the other two parties. Concludes that party leadership in all three parties in the six counties studied was strongly southern and midwestern in origin. Based on secondary sources; 12 tables, 23 notes.   N. E. Tutorow

426.   Ellis, William E.   PATRICK HENRY CALLAHAN: A KENTUCKY DEMOCRAT IN NATIONAL POLITICS.   *Filson Club Hist. Q. 1977 51(1): 17-30.* Patrick Henry Callahan of Louisville, Kentucky, was an innovative businessman and a major spokesman for Catholics in the national Democratic Party. Callahan achieved fame by introducing a highly successful profit sharing plan in his Louisville Varnish Company. His strong commitment to prohibition was strengthened by his friendship with William Jennings Bryan and led Callahan to oppose Al Smith's presidential nomination in 1928. Callahan was an early supporter of Franklin D. Roosevelt and the New Deal. He defended the Roosevelt administration against attacks on its Mexican policy and from the challenge of Father Charles Coughlin. Based on the Callahan Papers at Catholic University and the Roosevelt, Bryan, and Woodrow Wilson Papers; 50 notes.
                    G. B. McKinney

427.   Ellsworth, S. George.   SIMON BAMBERGER: GOVERNOR OF UTAH.   *Western States Jewish Hist. Q. 1973 5(4): 231-242.* Simon Bamberger, a German, Jewish immigrant active in railroads and charity work, was elected the first non-Mormon, Democratic governor of Utah in 1916.

428.   Falzone, Vincent J.   TERENCE V. POWDERLY: POLITICIAN AND PROGRESSIVE MAYOR OF SCRANTON, 1878-1884.   *Pennsylvania Hist. 1974 41(3): 289-309.* Terence V. Powderly served as mayor of Scranton during 1878-84. First elected as a Greenbacker, he found it necessary to run as a Democrat in 1882. Though an able mayor, he faced a variety of political problems, and in 1884 lost the fight for renomination to his long-time foe Frank A. Beamish. Powderly's political difficulties account in part for his belief that the Knights of Labor should avoid partisan political activity. Based on Powderly Papers, Scranton municipal records, and newspapers; illus., 78 notes.   D. C. Swift

429. Faries, Clyde J. CARMACK VERSUS PATTERSON: THE GENESIS OF A POLITICAL FEUD. *Tennessee Hist. Q. 1979 38(3): 332-347.* Traces the fierce 1896 battle for Tennessee's 10th Congressional District to its tragic end. Incumbent Democrat Josiah Patterson's (1837-1904) support for the Gold Standard led to his defeat by Edward Ward Carmack, who was supported by "Private" John Mills Allen (1846-1917), the congressman from Tupelo, Mississippi. The result was contested, exacerbating the feud, which continued until 1908 when Carmack was shot to death in a gunfight with Duncan and Robin Cooper, supporters of Patterson's son Malcolm (1861-1935), then Governor of Tennessee. Primary sources; 59 notes.
W. D. Piersen

430. Faulkner, Ronnie W. NORTH CAROLINA DEMOCRATS AND SILVER FUSION POLITICS, 1892-1896. *North Carolina Hist. Rev. 1982 59(3): 230-251.* During 1892-96 the issue of free silver coinage greatly affected North Carolina politics. State Democrats opposed 1892 presidential nominee Grover Cleveland's "gold bug" stand. Cleveland was elected and then blamed for the panic of 1893 and other fiscal problems. Therefore, North Carolina Populists swung support to Republicans in 1894 causing Democratic defeats in many races. State Democrats and Populists supported William Jennings Bryan's bid for president, but ran separate gubernatorial candidates, giving the Republicans a victory. But Populists quickly dissolved ties with Republicans as the Democratic free silver movement won reformists' support. Based on papers of numerous North Carolina political figures and local newspapers; 16 photos, 62 notes.
T. L. Savitt

431. Feinman, Ronald L. THE PROGRESSIVE REPUBLICAN SENATE BLOC AND THE PRESIDENTIAL ELECTION OF 1932. *Mid-America 1977 59(2): 73-91.* During the early 1930's the progressive Republican bloc consisted of 12 senators from Midwestern and Western states. Most of them opposed Herbert Hoover's policies and sought options which would further progressivism. A third party alternative was rejected. Several considered opposing Hoover in the 1932 primaries, but this failed to materialize. Only two of the 12, Charles McNary of Oregon and Arthur Capper of Kansas, actively supported Hoover during the Presidential campaign. The others remained neutral or supported Roosevelt as the most progressive candidate. Based on archival material; 43 notes.
J. M. Lee

432. Feinstein, Estelle F. TOWARD A MEANING FOR MUGWUMPERY. *R. in Am. Hist. 1975 3(4): 467-471.* Gerald W. McFarland's *Mugwumps, Morals & Politics, 1884-1920* (Amherst: U. of Massachusetts Pr., 1975) outlines the profile, values, and subsequent political history of 420 Mugwumps in New York City who left the Republican Party in 1884 over a matter of principle.

433. Fink, Leon. "IRRESPECTIVE OF PARTY, COLOR OR SOCIAL STANDING": THE KNIGHTS OF LABOR AND OPPOSITION POLITICS IN RICHMOND, VIRGINIA. *Labor Hist. 1978 19(3): 325-349.* The Knights of Labor in Richmond turned to political action in 1886 by supporting a reform slate in municipal elections. A coalition with Negro Republicans threatened existing Democratic control, but racial divisions generated by the meeting of the 10th General Assembly of the Knights helped divide the coalition and ensured

defeat. By 1888 the reform movement vanished, and Negroes steadily lost political influence. Based on newspapers; 50 notes.   L. L. Athey

434. Fink, Leon. POLITICS AS SOCIAL HISTORY: A CASE STUDY OF CLASS CONFLICT AND POLITICAL DEVELOPMENT IN NINE-TEENTH-CENTURY NEW ENGLAND. *Social Hist. [Great Britain] 1982 7(1): 43-58.* The political and institutional transformation of the marble-quarrying town of Rutland, Vermont, 1880-95, shows the inadequacy of accepted views of urban political development in the United States, and the intimate connections between politics and social history. The key to change was the organized working-class challenge to the elite in the 1880's, involving Knights of Labor and United Labor election slates. This led to the division of Rutland into three: the company town of Proctor run through paternalistic consensus; a democratic consensus in West Rutland where the Democrats gained the support of ethnic working-class voters; and the rest of Rutland where a dominant Republican machine was challenged by a Democrat minority with labour support. Thus class conflict broke the political edifice and forced its reconstruction in new forms. Based on documents in the Proctor Free Library and Vermont State Library, newspapers, and other printed sources; 28 notes.   D. J. Nicholls

435. Fischer, Le Roy H. OKLAHOMA TERRITORY, 1890-1907. *Chronicles of Oklahoma 1975 53(1): 3-8.* Following the 1889 land rush into the Unassigned Lands, Congress created Oklahoma Territory on 2 May 1890. George W. Steele was appointed the first territorial governor, and by August a general election was held for positions in the territorial legislature. A bitter contest erupted between several towns seeking the capital, and it was not settled until 1910 when Oklahoma City received that prize. Meanwhile, Stillwater secured the Agricultural and Mechanical College, Norman acquired the University, and Edmond accepted the Normal School. By 1895 additional lands taken from Indian reservations were opened to homesteaders, and in the following year Greer County was added. Throughout the territorial period from 1890 to 1907, the Republican Party dominated political office because many settlers were Union Army veterans who profited from the Republican Homestead Act of 1862. Map.
                                    M. L. Tate

436. Folmar, J. Kent. REACTION TO RECONSTRUCTION: PENNSYL-VANIA REPUBLICANS IN THE FORTY-SECOND CONGRESS, 1871-1873. *Western Pennsylvania Hist. Mag. 1978 61(3): 203-222.* Discusses the declining importance of the Southern Question with northern Republicans in the 42d Congress, emphasizing the 13-member Pennsylvania delegation.

437. Folsom, Burton W. TINKERERS, TIPPLERS, AND TRAITORS: ETHNICITY AND DEMOCRATIC REFORM IN NEBRASKA DURING THE PROGRESSIVE ERA. *Pacific Hist. Rev. 1981 50(1): 53-75.* In Nebraska prohibition was of central importance in progressive politics before World War I. Many British-stock Protestants advocated prohibition as a solution to social problems, while German and other ethnic Lutherans and Catholics attacked prohibition as a menace to their social customs and personal liberty. Prohibitionists supported direct democracy to enable voters to bypass the state legislature in lawmaking. The Republican Party championed the interests of the prohibitionists, while the Democratic Party represented ethnic group interests. After 1914

the issue shifted to the Germans' opposition to Woodrow Wilson's foreign policy. Then both Republicans and Democrats joined in reducing direct democracy in order to reduce German influence in state politics. Based on contemporary newspapers, legislative journals, and other primary sources; 36 notes.

R. N. Lokken

438. Fry, Joseph A. and Tarter, Brent. THE REDEMPTION OF THE NINTH: THE 1922 CONGRESSIONAL ELECTION IN THE NINTH DISTRICT OF VIRGINIA AND THE ORIGINS OF THE BYRD ORGANIZATION. *South Atlantic Q. 1978 77(3): 352-370.* The Virginia Ninth District is located in the southwest corner of the state, comprising 13 mountainous counties and the city of Bristol. From 1902 it had been represented by the Republican C. Bascom Slemp. Details the successful efforts of the Democrats to win the 1922 election, thus wiping out the last Republican bastion in the state. A major contributor to the victory was Harry F. Byrd, apple-grower, editor, and state Democratic Party chairman. Because of his endeavors whereby the Democratic candidate, George Peery, was elected, this campaign was the beginning of "Byrdocracy" which dominated Virginia's political scene for several decades. Based on the Byrd Papers, MSS Departments, Alderman Library, University of Virginia, other collections and newspapers; 40 notes.

H. M. Parker, Jr.

439. Fry, Joseph A. SENIOR ADVISER TO THE DEMOCRATIC "ORGANIZATION": WILLIAM THOMAS REED AND VIRGINIA POLITICS, 1925-1935. *Virginia Mag. of Hist. and Biog. 1977 85(4): 445-469.* Historians studying the career of Harry F. Byrd, Sr. have not given enough attention to the role of his closest friend and adviser, William Thomas Reed. During and after Byrd's governorship, Reed's behind-the-scenes activity made him one of the most influential men in Virginia. Based on the Byrd Papers, U. of Virginia, and the Reed Family Papers, Virginia Hist. Soc.; photo, 95 notes.

R. F. Oaks

440. Fuke, Richard Paul. HUGH LENNOX BOND AND RADICAL REPUBLICAN IDEOLOGY. *J. of Southern Hist. 1979 45(4): 569-586.* The "new orthodoxy" of Radical historiography asserts that Radical ideology was conservative and unwilling to challenge northern racism. This view has slighted the progressive and genuine reform elements of Radical Republicanism. In Maryland, Hugh Lennox Bond proposed adjusting the general attitude of Marylanders to permit changes allowing "equal access to law, education and economic opportunity by both white and black citizens." While failing in the immediate post-Civil War years, Bond and others believed that progress on the race question could have induced economic progress into Maryland. Covers ca. 1861-68. Based on manuscript and printed primary and secondary sources; 97 notes.

T. D. Schoonover

441. Funchion, Michael F. IRISH NATIONALISTS AND CHICAGO POLITICS IN THE 1880'S. *Éire-Ireland 1975 10(2): 3-18.* The Chicago branch of the Clan na Gael, an American Irish nationalist organization, was "a highly effective local political machine." Those Clan members who were mavericks or Republican Party members, however, could not sway Irish Americans from voting Democratic, especially in presidential elections. Mentions Alexander Sullivan's pragmatic leadership of the Clan, a split in the Clan by followers of New York-based John Devoy in 1885, John Finerty's congressional campaigns in 1882

and 1884, and the presidential elections of 1884 and 1888. Based on newspapers, secondary sources, and the Devoy Papers in the National Library of Ireland; 39 notes.   D. J. Engler

442. Gabel, Jack.   BROOKLYN'S LAST MAYORALTY CAMPAIGN: EDWARD MORSE SHEPARD AND THE IRONY OF REFORM POLITICS. *J. of Long Island Hist. 1979 15(2): 23-40.* Brooklyn's reformers began their campaign against the Democratic Party machine in 1880 under the leadership of Edward Morse Shepard. Shepard organized the Brooklyn Civil Service Reform Association, the Young Men's Democratic Club, and the Brooklyn Democratic Club. These reform organizations were able to defeat the party machine led by Hugh McLaughlin and control Brooklyn's mayoralty elections from 1882 to 1894. In the process, they destroyed Brooklyn's Democratic Party so that when Brooklyn became a borough of New York City in 1898 the city's Tammany machine filled the political vacuum. Based on newspapers; 4 illus., 43 notes.   J. K. Ehrlich

443. Gaboury, William J.   GEORGE WASHINGTON MURRAY AND THE FIGHT FOR POLITICAL DEMOCRACY IN SOUTH CAROLINA. *J. of Negro Hist. 1977 62(3): 258-269.* George Washington Murray, a former slave, represented the Seventh District of South Carolina as a Republican congressman during 1893-97. Contrary to most accounts, his major political contribution was a determined struggle against the white Democrats bent upon the destruction of Negro suffrage in South Carolina. One of the first victims of the resurgent white Democrats was Congressman Murray. Primary and secondary sources; 64 notes.   N. G. Sapper

444. Garcia, George F.   BLACK DISAFFECTION FROM THE REPUBLICAN PARTY DURING THE PRESIDENCY OF HERBERT HOOVER, 1928-1932. *Ann. of Iowa 1980 45(6): 462-497.* During the presidency of Herbert Hoover, several factors contributed to growing black defections from the ranks of the Republican Party: Hoover's efforts to strengthen the southern wing of his party by purging black Republicans from leadership positions; his nomination of John J. Parker, a North Carolina judge with a racist past, to the Supreme Court; the president's failure to condemn the segregation of Gold Star mothers during a War Department sponsored trip to American cemeteries in France; and the reduction of black military units. By 1932 much of the black press was portraying Hoover as a racist and a shift of black allegiance from the Republicans to the Democrats was underway even before Franklin D. Roosevelt took office. Based on the Colored Question file, Presidential Papers, Herbert Hoover Presidential Library, West Branch, Iowa, and other primary sources; 40 notes.
                                                                       P. L. Petersen

445. Garson, Robert A.   POLITICAL FUNDAMENTALISM AND POPULAR DEMOCRACY IN THE 1920'S. *South Atlantic Q. 1977 76(2): 219-233.* The 1920's fundamentalist backlash against cosmopolitan modernity was an expression of popular democracy in the Jacksonian tradition. Alienated and frustrated by the crumbling of Victorian mores, the fundamentalists, including pietistic Christian evangelists and the Ku Klux Klan, attempted to preserve traditional ways at the local level. Their vigilantism was intended to keep unpopular new ideas out of local communities and to silence any local adherents. Not

sophisticated enough to focus their attack on the mass media, they spent most of their efforts in minimizing the effects of the professional elites in public education on local youth and in carrying punishment to the moral lawbreakers left untouched by civil authorities. In this the fundamentalists evoked the issue of accountability in local education and politics. 24 notes.   W. L. Olbrich

446.   Gatewood, Willard B., Jr.   A BLACK EDITOR ON AMERICAN IM-PERIALISM: EDWARD E. COOPER OF *THE COLORED AMERICAN, 1898-1901*. *Mid-America 1975 57(1): 3-19.* Faltering only at the mustering out of blacks following the Spanish-American War, Edward E. Cooper, editor of *The Colored American*, never deviated from support of the Republican Party and the McKinley administration. Cooper hoped that imperialism would strengthen the federal government at the expense of segregationist state governments. Democrats, he believed, were anti-imperial for the same reasons that they were anti-black, while Negroes would receive a rich harvest from the policy of expansion. Based on *The Colored American*, and other secondary sources; 47 notes.
T. H. Wendel

447.   Geary, James W.   CLEMENT L. VALLANDIGHAM VIEWS THE CHARLESTON CONVENTION.   *Ohio Hist. 1977 86(2): 127-134.* Reproduces a previously unpublished letter from Clement L. Vallandigham to Alexander H. Stephens discussing the Democratic National Convention of April 1860. Held in Charleston, South Carolina, this convention was organized to select a Presidential candidate and platform. However, the delegates were hopelessly split over the choice of Stephen A. Douglas and his popular sovereignty program throughout the convention, and many delegates, both northern and southern, left before the convention formally adjourned ten days after it began. Vallandigham, secretary to the Charleston Convention, wrote this letter after the convention had ended and it reveals an eye-witness view of the occasion. The letter is housed at Emory University. 2 illus., 25 notes.   J

448.   Gelston, Arthur Lewis.   RADICAL VERSUS STRAIGHT-OUT IN POST-RECONSTRUCTION BEAUFORT COUNTY.   *South Carolina Hist. Mag. 1974 75(4): 225-237.* During Reconstruction in Beaufort County, South Carolina, the radical wing of the Republican Party dominated politics with Negro and white Republicans electing congressmen and local officials. But during the 1880's, when the National Republicans adopted Reconciliation (attempting to attract conservative white southerners by dropping the Negro cause), Beaufort County Republicans divided, radicals versus reconciliationists, giving Democrats control of the county and ending Negro political power in Beaufort. Primary and secondary sources; 58 notes.   R. H. Tomlinson

449.   Gerber, Richard Allan.   THE LIBERAL REPUBLICANS OF 1872 IN HISTORIOGRAPHICAL PERSPECTIVE.   *J. of Am. Hist. 1975 62(1): 40-73.* Reviews major trends in the historiography on the Liberal Republicans of 1872 over the past 100 years. Earlier schools of history described the Liberal Republicans from a "Reunionist" viewpoint (James Ford Rhodes, William A. Dunning, Claude G. Bowers, Paul Buck) or from a "Reformist" viewpoint (Earl D. Ross, Matthew Josephson, Eric F. Goldman). More recent interpretations of Liberal Republicanism center around Revisionist attacks on the "Reunionists" (Robert F. Durden, James M. McPherson) and on the "Reformists" (Ari A. Hoogen-

boom, Matthew Downey, John G. Sproat). The recent work of Patrick Rid-
dleberger and Michael Les Benedict shows the continued research needed to
illuminate the relationship between Liberal and Radical Republicanism. Based on
secondary works; 72 notes.   J. B. Street

450.   Gergel, Richard M.   WADE HAMPTON AND THE RISE OF ONE
PARTY RACIAL ORTHODOXY IN SOUTH CAROLINA.   *Pro. of the
South Carolina Hist. Assoc. 1977: 5-16.* Analyzes state politics in South Carolina
and the development of one-party racial orthodoxy under the leadership of Wade
Hampton during 1876-78. By making the Democratic Party all-white, Hampton
destroyed the Republican Party and influenced South Carolina's political development for 90 years. Based on manuscript sources; 24 notes.
                                                         J. W. Thacker, Jr.

451.   Gerteis, Louis S.   SALMON P. CHASE, RADICALISM AND THE
POLITICS OF EMANCIPATION, 1861-1864.   *J. of Am. Hist. 1973 60(1):
42-62.* Radical Republicans may have been sincere in their desire to help southern
blacks to full and meaningful freedom, but a study of the efforts of Salmon
Portland Chase (1808-73) indicates that they were not successful. Chase pressed
Lincoln at every turn to bring about emancipation but was content to stress
military expediency as the rationale. He urged early enlistment of blacks in the
Union Army, but was critical of the work of Lorenzo Thomas in utilizing landless
blacks as labor in the Mississippi Valley. Chase urged the leasing of lands to
blacks and supported the preemption of land by freedmen in the Sea Islands of
South Carolina. He pressed the land issue in his 1864 election plans, but when
his chances evaporated the land reform failed too, reflecting the weaknesses of
the Radicals. The promise of the Freedmen's Bureau bill was meaningless because
no land was available to implement it. 61 notes.   K. B. West

452.   Gerz, Richard J., Jr.   URBAN REFORM AND THE MUSSER COA-
LITION IN THE CITY OF LANCASTER, 1921-1930.   *J. of the Lancaster
County Hist. Soc. 1974 78(2): 49-110.* Analyzes the nature of the urban reform
movement in Lancaster, Pennsylvania, 1921-30, drawing parallels to the national
movement, 1900-16; chronicles and compares the concurrent Coalition Movement in which members of the Republican Party grew dissatisfied with the party
machine and switched to the Democratic Party, forming a Coalition Party in
order to bring about modernization and progressivism to Lancaster. 4 photos, 274
notes, 10 appendixes, biblio.   G. A. Hewlett

453.   Giffin, William.   BLACK INSURGENCY IN THE REPUBLICAN
PARTY OF OHIO, 1920-1932.   *Ohio Hist. 1973 82(1/2): 25-45.* Complaints of
lack of patronage and the dissociation of white Republicans from black candidates led to fission in the Republican Party of Ohio. In Cincinnati, Columbus,
and Cleveland (where black efforts were most successful) blacks ran for city
council as independents, having failed to win Republican primary elections. The
lack of an anti-KKK stand by the Republicans in the presidential election of 1924
led to some disenchantment with the party of Lincoln. The net results of blacks'
frustrations with the Republican Party during the 1920's was alienation that
prepared the way for the mass desertion of blacks to the Democratic Party in the
1930's. Based particularly on newspapers; 2 illus., 73 notes.   S. S. Sprague

454. Gill, Jerry L. THOMPSON BENTON FERGUSON: GOVERNOR OF OKLAHOMA TERRITORY, 1901-1906. *Chronicles of Oklahoma 1975 53(1): 109-127.* Arriving in Oklahoma Territory in 1889, Thompson Benton Ferguson gradually gained influence in the Dennis Flynn wing of the Republican Party, and somewhat reluctantly accepted the territorial governorship in 1901. Ferguson's honesty and nonpartisanship helped temporarily restore a degree of Republican unity and produced important party victories at the polls. He also provided guidance for new legislation involving education, aid to farmers and cattlemen, and a balanced budget. Though statehood was not achieved during Ferguson's tenure, he played a major role in ultimately bringing it about. By 1905 the Republican followers of Bird McGuire began an all-out assault on Ferguson's administration and convinced President Theodore Roosevelt to replace him with someone more agreeable to their faction. After serving the longest continuous term of any of Oklahoma's territorial governors—four years and six weeks— Ferguson stepped down on 13 January 1906. Based on primary and secondary sources; 4 photos, 55 notes. M. L. Tate

455. Ginzl, David J. PATRONAGE, RACE AND POLITICS: GEORGIA REPUBLICANS DURING THE HOOVER ADMINISTRATION. *Georgia Hist. Q. 1980 64(3): 280-293.* Accusations of irregularities in the dispensing of Republican Party patronage and the collection of "contributions" in Georgia resulted in the rise of political factions that struggled for control of the state party throughout Hoover's presidency. Factions were also based on race. Based on correspondence, newspapers and secondary sources; 30 notes.

G. R. Schroeder

456. Ginzl, David J. THE POLITICS OF PATRONAGE: FLORIDA RE- PUBLICANS DURING THE HOOVER ADMINISTRATION. *Florida Hist. Q. 1982 61(1): 1-19.* Herbert Hoover's presidential sweep in 1928 raised hopes of returning Republicans to state offices. The Depression retarded reorga- nization efforts. The Hoover administration failed to heal rifts within the state and demonstrated political ineptness in dispensing patronage. Florida state Re- publican leaders resented outside interference. The result was confusion and division with the loss of all hope for reestablishing the party within the state. Based on the Hoover Presidential Papers (Hoover Presidential Library, West Branch, Iowa), state newspapers, and other sources; 4 fig., 45 notes.

N. A. Kuntz

457. Giroux, Vincent A., Jr. THE RISE OF THEODORE G. BILBO (1908- 1932). *J. of Mississippi Hist. 1981 43(3): 180-209.* Traces the political awaken- ing of the poorer whites of Mississippi and Bilbo's rise to power in state politics with their support. The author describes the state's four distinct topographical regions—the Delta, the prairie region, the Gulf coast, and the hill country—and discusses the political and racial attitudes, factional splits in the state democratic party, and economic aspirations in each region. Political reforms, like the open primary law passed in 1903, allowed Bilbo, a hill country spokesman from the piney woods section, to obtain political support from most rural whites in all sections. Bilbo's colorful and checkered machinations in the state's public offices are sketched. Bilbo became Mississippi's most loved and at the same time most hated leader in the early 20th century. M. S. Legan

458.   Goldberg, Joyce S.   PATRICK EGAN: IRISH-AMERICAN MINIS-
TER TO CHILE.   *Éire-Ireland 1979 14(3): 83-95.* Discusses the political and
diplomatic careers of Patrick Egan (1841-1919). Egan, a successful entrepreneur
and an active Irish nationalist from at least 1860, left Ireland in the early 1880's
to avoid imprisonment by the British. In Nebraska he rebuilt his finances. He
became prominent in the national Republican Party and a good friend of James
G. Blaine, who in 1889 arranged for Egan's appointment as US minister to Chile,
possibly to oppose Great Britain's great commercial influence there. In Chile in
1891, Egan through his reports to Washington seemed to favor the elected president, José Manuel Balmaceda, against a revolution of the congress and the navy
(with which Great Britain sympathized). After the revolution succeeded in August, anti-American sentiment was high. Eventually the Chileans tolerated Egan,
who had defended US interests and growing hemispheric responsibility. Secondary sources and Egan correspondence; 33 notes.   D. J. Engler

459.   Gould, Lewis L.   THEODORE ROOSEVELT, WILLIAM HOWARD
TAFT, AND THE DISPUTED DELEGATES IN 1912: TEXAS AS A TEST
CASE.   *Southwestern Hist. Q. 1976 80(1): 33-56.* Reexamines Texas' 40 disputed delegates to the 1912 Republican national convention. Texas party leaders
split between President William Howard Taft and ex-President Theodore Roosevelt, but the Taft group claimed nearly all the delegates. The Republican national
convention rejected a Roosevelt challenge and gave Taft 31 of the 40 votes.
Impartial analysis of each district indicates that a fair division would have been
21 for Roosevelt, 19 for Taft, but both factions were interested in political
advantage rather than fairness. Based on primary sources; table, 49 notes.
                                                                  J. H. Broussard

460.   Grant, Philip A., Jr.   CONGRESSIONAL LEADERS FROM THE
GREAT PLAINS 1921-1932.   *North Dakota Hist. 1979 46(1): 19-23.* During
the 1920's and early 1930's congressmen and senators from the Great Plains states
of North and South Dakota were important figures in Congress owing to the
Republican Party domination of the federal legislature and to their longevity in
office. Representative James A. Sinclair was important in Mississippi and Missouri River flood relief legislation and Thomas Hall, like Sinclair from North
Dakota, was deeply involved in farm relief bills. William Williamson of South
Dakota emphasized work in government efficiency and cost effectiveness. Congressman Charles A. Christopherson of South Dakota concerned himself in part
with prohibition and federal bankruptcy legislation, while Senator Gerald P. Nye
of North Dakota dealt with federal election expenditure abuse regulation. Lynn
J. Frazier of North Dakota concerned himself with bettering the farmer's lot
through Congressional action. Senator Porter J. McCumber of North Dakota
dealt with the tariff while Peter Norbeck of South Dakota dealt with the plight
of the farmer in the Depression.   N. Lederer

461.   Grassman, Curtis E.   PROLOGUE TO CALIFORNIA REFORM:
THE DEMOCRATIC IMPULSE, 1886-1898.   *Pacific Hist. R. 1973 42(4):
518-536.* Traces the growth of the spirit of reform in the Democratic Party from
the era of dominance by the corrupt San Francisco boss, Christopher Buckley,
to the establishment and success of state Senator Stephen White's progressive
coalition. Significant reforms emerged as a result of the coalition's efforts, the
Buckley machine was discredited, and the lessons learned in the 1890's were later
effectively used by a reform group within the Republican Party. 45 notes.

C. W. Olsen

462. Green, James. POPULISM, SOCIALISM AND THE PROMISE OF DEMOCRACY. *Radical Hist. Rev. 1980 (24): 7-40.* Traces the histories of Populism and socialism in the United States since the 1890's in light of the recently growing appeal of Populism "among many socialists as the U.S. left seems more fragmented and isolated," and addresses Lawrence Goodwyn's *Democratic Promise: The Populist Movement in America* (1976) and the author's own *Grass-Roots Socialism: Radical Movements in the Southwest, 1895-1943* (1978).

463. Greenberg, Irwin F. PINCHOT, PROHIBITION AND PUBLIC UTILITIES: THE PENNSYLVANIA ELECTION OF 1930. *Pennsylvania Hist. 1973 40(1): 21-36.* The election of 1930 in Pennsylvania was complicated by the wet-dry issue, Republican factionalism, and the Depression. Former Governor Gifford Pinchot (1865-1946) won the Republican nomination for governor and had the strong backing of the Grundy faction of the G.O.P. John Hemphill, the Democratic nominee, received considerable assistance from the Vare faction of the G.O.P. which opposed Pinchot's plans for regulating the utilities. As nominee of the Liberal Party, Hemphill was also in a position to attract wet Republican votes. Despite these factors, Pinchot won by only 58,000 votes. The election was won in Pittsburgh where Pinchot retained the support of wet Republicans through patronage promises. Based on Raskob papers, Pinchot papers, and newspapers; illus., 43 notes. D. C. Swift

464. Greene, Suzanne Ellery. BLACK REPUBLICANS ON THE BALTIMORE CITY COUNCIL, 1890-1931. *Maryland Hist. Mag. 1979 74(3): 203-222.* Failure in Maryland of post-Reconstruction moves to disenfranchise blacks insured continued presence of at least one black Republican member on Baltimore's city council through 1931. Harry Sythe Cummings, John Marcus Cargill, and Hiram Watty before World War I, and William L. Fitzgerald, Warner T. McGuinn, and Walter S. Emerson afterward were regularly reelected from predominantly black wards. All fought for improved status, facilities, and faculty of segregated schools for Negroes, an improved share of patronage jobs for blacks, and against white Democratic attempts to disenfranchise blacks and institute legal residential segregation. Based on Baltimore *City Council Journals,* newspaper accounts, papers of the six councilmen, and interviews with their descendants; chart with 18 notes, 85 notes. C. B. Schulz

465. Grinde, Gerald S. THE EMERGENCE OF THE "GENTLE PARTISAN": ALBEN W. BARKLEY AND KENTUCKY POLITICS, 1919. *Register of the Kentucky Hist. Soc. 1980 78(3): 243-258.* Alben W. Barkley's address to the Kentucky state Democratic convention in 1919 demonstrated his rhetorical style and his ability to placate diverse interests within his party. He further demonstrated these qualities and his total partisanship in his later years. Primary sources, including the Barkley papers at the University of Kentucky Library; 2 illus., 21 notes. J. F. Paul

466. Grinde, Gerald S. POLITICS AND SCANDAL IN THE PROGRESSIVE ERA: ALBEN W. BARKLEY AND THE MC CRACKEN COUNTY CAMPAIGN OF 1909. *Filson Club Hist. Q. 1976 50(2): 36-51.* Deals with an

incident in the early political career of Alben W. Barkley. Barkley, later a Congressman, Senator, and Vice President, was the Democratic candidate for judge in McCracken County, Kentucky. He was forced to defend his personal record in the light of political corruption committed by other Democratic county officials. Despite some Republican gains in the normally Democratic county, Barkley was reelected. Based on local newspapers, 45 notes.   G. B. McKinney

467. Haas, Edward F.   JOHN FITZPATRICK AND POLITICAL CONTINUITY IN NEW ORLEANS, 1896-1899. *Louisiana Hist. 1981 22(1): 7-29.* In the spring of 1896 Mayor John Fitzpatrick of New Orleans, leader of the city's Bourbon Democratic organization, left office after a scandal-ridden administration, his chosen successor badly defeated by reform candidate Walter C. Flower. But Fitzpatrick and his associates quickly regrouped, organizing themselves on 29 December into the Choctaw Club, which soon received considerable patronage from Louisiana governor and Fitzpatrick ally Murphy Foster. Fitzpatrick, a power at the 1898 Louisiana Constitutional Convention, was instrumental in exempting immigrants from the new educational and property requirements designed to disenfranchise blacks. In 1899 he managed the successful mayoral campaign of Bourbon candidate Paul Capdevielle. Based on contemporary reports and editorials in the Louisiana press; 84 notes, table.   L. Van Wyk

468. Hall, Charles.   ASA S. MERCER AND "THE BANDITTI OF THE PLAINS": A REAPPRAISAL. *Ann. of Wyoming 1977 49(1): 53-64.* Reinterprets Asa Mercer's *The Banditti of the Plains.* Contrary to legend, Mercer encountered no suppression of the book by cattlemen involved in the Johnson County War. Mercer wrote the book to discredit the cattle barons and to win favor from Wyoming Democrats in the state. He sought this political patronage hoping to save his failing newspaper, but miscalculated. Covers the 1890's. Primary sources; 22 notes.   M. L. Tate

469. Hall, Kermit L.   THE CIVIL WAR ERA AS A CRUCIBLE FOR NATIONALIZING THE LOWER FEDERAL COURTS. *Prologue 1975 7(3): 177-186.* At least in their institutional structure, the federal courts proved resistant to the impact of the Civil War and the early years of Reconstruction. "The changes made in 1862 and 1869, and those proposed in 1866, were more cosmetic than substantial." Republicans burdened the federal courts with new jurisdictional obligations, but proved "surprisingly tradition-minded," unwilling to break from their notions of parsimonious government and judicial representation that emphasized regional diversity over central authority. They clung to local judicial representation and circuit riding even when confronted by overcrowded dockets and southern resistance to Reconstruction. Primary and secondary sources; 59 notes.   W. R. Hively

470. Hammarberg, Melvyn.   INDIANA FARMERS AND THE GROUP BASIS OF THE LATE NINETEENTH-CENTURY POLITICAL PARTIES. *J. of Am. Hist. 1974 61(1): 91-115.* Statistical analysis of the political and religious affiliations of a group of Indiana farmers in 1870 as contrasted to townspeople reveals that among both groups there was a tendency for those giving census evidence of generalized Protestant or specific denominational ties to stipulate a more Republican party allegiance than those giving "No Religious Affiliation." At the same time on a scaled continuum running from Republican through

Independent to Democratic, and involving all religious groups, there was for both propertied and nonpropertied farmers a normless party identification with Independents holding a balance. This suggests a fluid lack of institutional linkage among farmers that might in time of economic depression lead to directionality toward one or another major party or a third party. 9 tables, 6 figs., 32 notes.

K. B. West

471.   Haney, James E.   BLACKS AND THE REPUBLICAN NOMINATION OF 1908.   *Ohio Hist. 1975 84(4): 207-221.* Joseph B. Foraker was a strong candidate for the Republican presidential nomination in 1908 among blacks, who regarded him as their agent in repudiating the dishonorable discharge of 167 black soldiers for alleged involvement in a disturbance at Brownsville, Texas in 1906. When Taft was nominated, many blacks in the North opposed him because of his views on Negro suffrage, the reduction of Southern representation in the House, and the Brownsville Affair; but a campaign of black journalists on behalf of Taft was highly successful. With the race arrayed in his favor, blacks could expect political rewards. Illus., 56 notes.   E. P. Stickney

472.   Hanna, William F., III.   ABRAHAM LINCOLN'S 1860 VISIT TO RHODE ISLAND.   *Lincoln Herald 1979 81(3): 197-201.* Describes Abraham Lincoln's two visits to Rhode Island in 1860 in the months before the 1860 presidential election, and discusses the political climate in Rhode Island during 1860 when the state's Republicans were split between the conservatives and the moderates.

473.   Hardaway, Roger D.   JEANNETTE RANKIN: THE EARLY YEARS.   *North Dakota Q. 1980 48(1): 62-68.* Discusses Jeannette Rankin (1880-1973), the first woman in the House of Representatives, and focuses on her fight for woman suffrage and campaign strategy on the Republican Party ticket in Montana in 1916.

474.   Harmond, Richard.   TROUBLES OF MASSACHUSETTS REPUBLICANS DURING THE 1880'S.   *Mid-America 1974 56(2): 85-99.* The historians Carl Degler and H. Wayne Morgan argue that the Republican Party's appeal to urban dwellers made it better able to deal with new urban and industrial problems than the Democratic Party. Other historians, like Paul Kleppner and Richard Jensen, discern no trend toward urban power in the Republican Party, and suggest that local, ethnic-cultural commitments are a better gauge of party success or failure than national political ideology. A case study of Massachusetts Republicans' mismanagement of local liquor and school issues suggests support for the Kleppner-Jensen hypothesis. Based on primary and secondary sources; 42 notes.   T. D. Schoonover

475.   Harris, Carl V.   RIGHT OR LEFT FORK? THE SECTION-PARTY ALIGNMENT OF SOUTHERN DEMOCRATS IN CONGRESS, 1873-1897. *J. of Southern Hist. 1976 42(4): 471-506.* The restored southern Democratic faction soon became one of the largest party-sectional blocs in Congress. It has usually been ascribed the role proposed by Professor C. Vann Woodward, namely, that the southern Democrats confronted a forked road in the 1870's. The right fork led to the economically conservative eastern faction of the Democratic party, and the left fork to the radical agrarian western faction. Choosing the right

fork, the southern Democrats became a bulwark of, instead of a menace to, the new order. Using quantitative tests to measure cohesion within blocs and to test likeness between blocs, reveals that, in general as well as on specific issues, the southern Democrats shifted their ties to other factions depending upon the issue being tested. On the crucial economic issues, focal to Woodward's thesis, the southern Democrats maintained a consistent left-fork alliance with the western left fork rather than the eastern right fork.   T. Schoonover

476.   Harris, D. Alan.   CAMPAIGNING IN THE BLOODY SEVENTH: THE ELECTION OF 1894 IN THE SEVENTH CONGRESSIONAL DISTRICT.   *Alabama R. 1974 27(2): 127-138.* Scurrility and violence attended the 1894 congressional campaign in the Seventh District. Populist victor Milford W. Howard beat Democrat William H. Denson, who failed to win major Populist support despite his strong agrarian leanings. Denson's tactics and charges enhanced Howard's image and popularity. Ballot stuffing and electoral fraud failed to blunt the Populist tide. The district's "bloody" reputation survived beyond the turn of the century. Based on primary and secondary sources, including the Howard family papers; 37 notes.   J. F. Vivian

477.   Harris, William C.   MISSISSIPPI: REPUBLICAN FACTIONALISM AND MISMANAGEMENT.   Olsen, Otto H., ed. *Reconstruction and Redemption in the South* (Baton Rouge: Louisiana State U. Pr., 1980): 78-108. Mismanagement, ineptitude in office, and rampant factionalism in the Republican Party ruined Reconstruction efforts in Mississippi. The lack of experience in politics, the lack of favorable attitudes to Negroes, and the war between conservatives and radicals within the party provided the wedges that the Democratic Party used to regain power. The effort was completed with a variety of techniques to drive remaining Republicans from office and pretty much return to the status quo antebellum. 60 notes.   V. L. Human

478.   Hauser, Robert E.   "THE GEORGIA EXPERIMENT": PRESIDENT WARREN G. HARDING'S ATTEMPT TO REORGANIZE THE REPUBLICAN PARTY IN GEORGIA.   *Georgia Hist. Q. 1978 62(4): 288-303.* When Warren G. Harding won the presidential election of 1920, he began planning to extend the Republican Party in the South, beginning in Georgia. Many members of the two factions in the existing Georgia party refused to unite behind John Louis Philips, Harding's man. This opposition, plus scandal, led to Republican defeat in the congressional election of 1922. Eventually the experiment failed and the old leadership, particularly Henry Lincoln Johnson, returned to power. Primary sources; 56 notes.   G. R. Schroeder

479.   Hawkes, Robert T., Jr.   THE EMERGENCE OF A LEADER: HARRY FLOOD BYRD, GOVERNOR OF VIRGINIA, 1926-1930.   *Virginia Mag. of Hist. and Biog. 1974 82(3): 259-281.* During his term as Governor of Virginia, Harry Flood Byrd achieved many reforms in state government which previous governors had attempted in vain. While achieving national recognition for the state, Byrd established control over the state Democratic Party, and though ineligible for re-election, chose his successor and assured himself of a future in politics. Based on primary and secondary sources; 2 cartoons, 69 notes.   R. F. Oaks

480. Hays, Brooks. A POLITICAL FANTASY. *Arkansas Hist. Q. 1975 34(3): 268-274.* Personal reminiscence of the 1908 Pope County Democratic Convention. Rather than holding himself strictly to facts, the author conveys the flavor of this kind of political gathering by presenting the types of delegates and their actions. T. L. Savitt

481. Heinemann, Ronald L. "HARRY BYRD FOR PRESIDENT": THE 1932 CAMPAIGN. *Virginia Cavalcade 1975 25(1): 28-37.* Discusses the political campaign of Virginia governor Harry Flood Byrd for the presidential nomination of the Democratic Party convention in Chicago in 1932, emphasizing his competition with Franklin D. Roosevelt.

482. Hennesey, Melinda Meek. RACE AND VIOLENCE IN RECONSTRUCTION NEW ORLEANS: THE 1868 RIOT. *Louisiana Hist. 1979 20(1): 77-92.* The New Orleans race riot, September-October 1868, grew out of efforts by white Democrats to reduce the Republican vote in New Orleans in the upcoming presidential election and to emasculate the recently created Metropolitan Police Force, one-third of whom were black. The worst phase of the violence began on the evening of 24 October 1868 in a clash between white Democratic and black Republican marching clubs, during their processions on Canal Street. During the next few nights Negroes indiscriminately attacked whites on the streets, and whites retaliated by ransacking the homes and businesses of black political leaders and relieving black citizens of their registration certificates. The crisis was defused when General Jame Steedman agreed to assume command of the Metropolitan Police Force. The result was 6-7 white deaths, at least 13 black deaths, and an overwhelming Democratic majority in the November election. Primary and secondary sources; 43 notes. L. N. Powell

483. Hennessey, Melinda M. RECONSTRUCTION POLITICS AND THE MILITARY: THE EUFAULA RIOT OF 1874. *Alabama Hist. Q. 1976 38(2): 112-125.* During the election of 1874, Democrats caused riots all over Alabama to defeat the Republican Party. The military refused to aid in protecting the rights of the people compounding the violence. This study discusses the situation in Eufaula County as a model of what was happening all over the state. 41 notes. E. E. Eminhizer

484. Himelhoch, Myra. ST. LOUIS OPPOSITION TO DAVID R. FRANCIS IN THE GUBERNATORIAL ELECTION OF 1888. *Missouri Hist. R. 1974 68(3): 327-343.* Discusses the public opposition in St. Louis to its mayor and Democratic candidate, David R. Francis, during the gubernatorial election in 1888. The Republican victory in St. Louis was due in part to anti-Cleveland sentiment and possible election irregularities involving blacks and foreigners. Francis, however, had difficulties with the labor vote, losing to the Union Labor or Republican tickets. Anti-Prohibitionists were also suspected of voting against him, and the mayor was additionally hurt by the reform-Democrat campaign led by the St. Louis *Post-Dispatch*. Francis was elected governor but was soundly defeated in St. Louis, which had later repercussions on his political career. Based on contemporary newspaper reports, US census reports, and secondary sources; table, 4 illus., 4 photos, 34 notes. N. J. Street

485.   Hinckley, Ted C.   THE POLITICS OF SINOPHOBIA: GARFIELD, THE MOREY LETTER, AND THE PRESIDENTIAL ELECTION OF 1880. *Ohio Hist. 1980 89(4): 381-399.* Presidential elections of the late 19th century often provided a necessary outlet to public tensions and articulated public issues that would influence subsequent legislation; the presidential struggle of 1880 provides an example that magnified Americans' anti-Chinese labor feelings with the controversy over the "Morey Letter." James A. Garfield's purported letter to H. L. Morey, first published in New York City's *Truth* and endorsed as genuine by Democratic leaders Abram S. Hewitt and William H. Barnum, threatened to anathematize the Republican candidate to western voters already panicked by the negotiation of the Burlingame Treaty, increased Chinese immigration, and the 1870's business depression. Although proven to be a forgery, the letter revealed the Chinese labor question to be a volatile issue in the voters' minds and accelerated the passage of the 1882 Chinese Exclusion Act. Based on the papers of James A. Garfield, Ohio Historical Society Archives, the collections of the Rutherford B. Hayes Memorial Library, and other primary sources. 2 illus., 50 notes.   L. A. Russell

486.   Hoffecker, Carol E.   THE POLITICS OF EXCLUSION: BLACKS IN LATE NINETEENTH-CENTURY WILMINGTON, DELAWARE. *Delaware Hist. 1974 16(1): 60-72.* "Wilmington seemed to offer several major prerequisites for the success of blacks in the political system. Not only was there a large black community but Republicans and Democrats fought a see-saw battle for control of city elections throughout the late nineteenth century. Politicians were forced to seek out every potential vote. The Republicans in particular recognized their dependence upon the support of black voters." Blacks, however, were ill-served in their loyalty to the GOP. Black voters sided with but received few benefits from Republicans, who remained "complacent about their relations with blacks and were unable to accommodate black men into the framework of economic issues that dominated late nineteenth-century politics." Based largely on newspaper sources; 46 notes.   R. M. Miller

487.   Holli, Melvin G.   MAYOR PINGREE CAMPAIGNS FOR THE GOVERNORSHIP. *Michigan Hist. 1973 57(2): 151-173.* Hazen S. Pingree, wealthy shoe manufacturer, won four successive Detroit mayoralty elections. His administrations (1889-97) brought him national acclaim as the leading social-reform mayor in the country. He built a political machine, purged his opponents, and transformed Detroit from a Democratic into a Republican city. After the Republican-dominated state legislature voided reforms for which he was responsible, Pingree challenged the state political apparatus, won the gubernatorial nomination in 1896, and won the election, far outdistancing the GOP presidential candidate. 7 illus., 37 notes.   D. L. Smith

488.   Holt, Wythe W.   THE SENATOR FROM VIRGINIA AND THE DEMOCRATIC FLOOR LEADERSHIP: THOMAS S. MARTIN AND CONSERVATISM IN THE PROGRESSIVE ERA. *Virginia Mag. of Hist. and Biog. 1975 83(1): 3-21.* In spite of the idealistic goals of many progressives to reform the government, the realities of politics enabled conservative Democrats to prevent many changes while Woodrow Wilson was President. A firm supporter of Wilson, conservative Senator Thomas S. Martin of Virginia helped save the seniority system by resigning his position as Democratic floor leader in 1913. The

need for party unity enabled conservatives to retain the seniority system and to re-elect Martin as Senate floor leader in 1917 with the tacit approval of Wilson. Based on the Wilson Papers in the Library of Congress, collections at the University of Virginia, College of William and Mary, and Duke University, newspapers, and secondary sources; 75 notes. R. F. Oaks

489. Holzer, Harold. AN ALL-PURPOSE CAMPAIGN POSTER. *Lincoln Herald 1982 84(1): 42-45.* Discusses the three political posters rendered by the lithography firm of H. H. Lloyd & Company of lower Manhattan, New York City, for the 1860 campaign: the pro-Lincoln "National Republican Chart," the "Political Chart" that portrayed a number of political candidates of different political persuasions, and the "National Political Chart" issued after Lincoln's victory.

490. Hood, James Larry. FOR THE UNION: KENTUCKY'S UNCONDITIONAL UNIONIST CONGRESSMEN AND THE DEVELOPMENT OF THE REPUBLICAN PARTY IN KENTUCKY, 1863-1865. *Register of the Kentucky Hist. Soc. 1978 76(3): 197-215.* Kentucky politics underwent a severe transformation during the Civil War. Three dissident Union Democrats, Lucien Anderson, Green Clay Smith, and William Harrison Randall, supported the national administration and helped form the basis for a permanent Republican Party in the state. These three, elected to Congress in 1863 as Union Democrats, shocked Kentuckians by voting with the Republicans to organize the Congress. The attitude of northern Republicans toward the South ruined the efforts of Anderson, Smith, and Randall to overcome Kentuckians' strong southern loyalties. Although these three and their followers laid the groundwork for a Republican resurgence, it would be many years before the minority Republicans would make their presence felt. Primary and secondary sources; illus., 58 notes. J. F. Paul

491. Hopper, Stanley D. FRAGMENTATION OF THE CALIFORNIA REPUBLICAN PARTY IN THE ONE-PARTY ERA, 1893-1932. *Western Pol. Q. 1975 28(2): 372-386.* This article applies V. O. Key's theories of American state politics to California's one-party era. Employing simple statistical techniques made familiar by Key's work, the analysis shows that the Republican party, overwhelmingly dominant in the 1920s, became highly factionalized. The analysis shows that there was not an organized party-like bifactional politics pitting "progressives" against "conservatives" in the Republican primaries of the 1920s. Instead, the Republican party is shown to have degenerated as a political party nominating structure. The analysis, consequently, helps to account for the weaknesses of the Republican party during and after the realignment of the California electorate in the 1930s. J

492. Horowitz, Murray M. BEN BUTLER AND THE NEGRO: "MIRACLES ARE OCCURRING." *Louisiana Hist. 1976 17(2): 159-186.* Details the career of Democratic General Benjamin F. Butler 1861-64 and analyzes his complete reversal of positions in such a brief time. The former "pro-slavery Democrat of the worst school" had become the darling of the Radicals. The actual experiences of war in the deep South, especially his contact with Negroes, caused the reversal. Illus., 43 notes. E. P. Stickney

493.   Howard, Victor B.   THE KENTUCKY PRESS AND THE NEGRO TESTIMONY CONTROVERSY, 1866-1872.   *Register of the Kentucky Hist. Soc. 1973 71(1): 29-50.* The press played a substantial role in Kentucky, after the Civil War, on deciding the right of blacks to testify in court. Despite the 13th Amendment, slave codes remained on the books in many states. The Freedmen's Bureau exerted pressure for repeal of Kentucky's slave codes and was bitterly denounced by the Democratic press. Early in 1866, all legal restrictions were removed except the provision prohibiting black testimony against whites. In April 1866, the Civil Rights Bill reversed this, but attacks from the press continued and in 1867 the Kentucky Court of Appeals declared the bill inoperative. Generally, the rural press attacked black testimony while the Louisville *Courier-Journal* was the strongest voice for it. In 1871, the issue was central to state elections, and the election of a Democratic governor led to adoption of a new law of evidence in 1872. Based on newspapers and primary sources; 91 notes.   J. F. Paul

494.   Huch, Ronald K.   "TYPHOID" TRUELSEN, WATER AND POLITICS IN DULUTH, 1896-1900.   *Minnesota Hist. 1981 47(5): 189-199.* Duluth fearfully endured typhoid fever and needed clean water in the 1890's. The private water utility would not incur the expense of the necessary changes and would only sell to the city at an inflated price. Caspar Henry Truelson rose in Democratic and Populist politics from his Danish-German immigrant background to become a two-term mayor on the popular support of his stand against a sudden purchase. Once in office he bought the utility at his price and, during the second term, revised the city charter to give it a stronger hand in any future utility purchase battles. He nearly won reelection in 1900 and was defeated for election in 1902, but he remained a local hero until his death. Based on a variety of local documents, manuscripts, and newspapers; 12 illus., 35 notes.   C. M. Hough

495.   Hume, Richard L.   THE ARKANSAS CONSTITUTIONAL CONVENTION OF 1868: A CASE STUDY IN THE POLITICS OF RECONSTRUCTION.   *J. of Southern Hist. 1973 39(2): 183-206.* Historians generally agree that southern constitutional conventions, necessitated by the abolition of slavery, were dominated by Negroes and outside whites. A close study of the Arkansas convention reveals that this was not the case in Arkansas. Southern whites outnumbered the other two groups combined, and therefore controlled the convention. Blacks and outside whites consistently supported Republican objectives; the majority southern whites were more independent. Thus Arkansas reconstruction policies on the state level were primarily a product of southern whites. Table, 75 notes, appendix.   V. L. Human

496.   Hume, Richard L.   THE MEMBERSHIP OF THE VIRGINIA CONSTITUTIONAL CONVENTION OF 1867-1868: A STUDY OF THE BEGINNINGS OF CONGRESSIONAL RECONSTRUCTION IN THE UPPER SOUTH.   *Virginia Mag. of Hist. and Biography 1978 86(4): 461-484.* Studies the 1867 Reconstruction Act-induced Convention's membership and activities. Classifies delegates as "Radicals," those voting to aid blacks, restrict ex-Confederates, or help the Republican Party; "Conservatives," those opposing such; and nonaligned; and by hereditary class: "Outside White," "Southern White," and Negro. Concludes that Outside Whites, some Southern Whites, and Negroes made an effective coalition to pass a Radical document, notably failing only in requiring racial integration in public schools. Includes revisionist findings about delegates' education, income, and constituencies. 2 charts, 54 notes.   P. J. Woehrmann

497. James, Edward T. BEN BUTLER RUNS FOR PRESIDENT: LABOR, GREENBACKERS, AND ANTI-MONOPOLISTS IN THE ELECTION OF 1884. *Essex Inst. Hist. Collections 1977 113(2): 65-88.* Before the 1954 accession by the Library of Congress of Benjamin F. Butler's (1818-1893) papers, scholars inadequately understood his campaign as a third-party presidential candidate in 1884. Even with support from the Anti-Monopoly Convention, Greenbackers, and labor, Butler's People's Party failed to stop Grover Cleveland's nomination at the Democratic convention and subsequent election. Discusses causes for failure, chiefly the Republican subsidy. Based on the Butler Papers, primary and secondary sources; 3 illus., photo, 78 notes.   R. S. Sliwoski

498. James, Felix. THE CIVIC AND POLITICAL ACTIVITIES OF GEORGE A. MYERS. *J. of Negro Hist. 1973 58(2): 166-178.* George A. Myers, a black barber from Cleveland, was a power broker for the black constituency of William McKinley. Myers, the most important black leader within the organization forged by Marcus A. Hanna, displaced such black Republican leaders as Norris Wright Cuney, Perry Carson, Blanche K. Bruce, John R. Lynch, and William A. Pledger. Based on primary sources in the collections of the Ohio Historical Society and on secondary sources; 45 notes.   N. G. Sapper

499. Jarrell, Ann Margaret. DID AN ORATORICAL SPARK IGNITE THE KENTUCKY EXPLOSION? *Register of the Kentucky Hist. Soc. 1976 74(1): 40-50.* Attempts to ascertain the role of William Goebel in Kentucky politics during the late 1890's. An anti-corporation lawyer and state legislator, Goebel attempted to assume control of the state's Democratic Party in 1897. Ex-governor John Y. Brown and the L and N Railroad were his greatest obstacles. In 1899 Goebel ran for governor in an election so heated and disputed that he was shot on 31 January 1900, while still contesting the outcome. Sworn in as governor on 3 February Goebel died the next day. Concludes that the link between Goebel and the "Kentucky Explosion" of the 1890's remains unclear. Based on secondary sources; 36 notes.   J. F. Paul

500. Jones, Allen W. POLITICAL REFORM AND PARTY FACTIONALISM IN THE DEEP SOUTH: ALABAMA'S "DEAD SHOES" SENATORIAL PRIMARY OF 1906. *Alabama R. 1973 26(1): 3-32.* Reform agitation for the direct primary system in Alabama was strong by 1905. Conservative forces, including Governor William Dorsey Jelks, Senator Edmund Winston Pettus, and Congressman John Hollis Bankhead, hoped to retain control under an "ingenious" arrangement that provided, in part, for the election of "alternate senators" should the two aging incumbents, Senators Pettus and John Tyler Morgan, die in office. The ensuing "dead shoes" primary of 1906 pitted seven prominent aspirants. Bankhead and ex-Governor Joseph Forney Johnston were the surprise victors. Governor Braxton Bragg Comer, reform forces leader, reluctantly appointed both men to Morgan's and Pettus' unexpired terms in 1907. The 1906 elections, "the most significant political contest in the state since Reconstruction," placed Alabama in step with the movement toward popular election of senators, witnessed the demise of the Black Belt in state affairs, and showed that honest elections could prevail with the black vote neutralized. Based on state archival sources, newspapers, theses, and secondary sources; 98 notes.   J. F. Vivian

501.   Jones, James P.   RADICAL REINFORCEMENT: JOHN A. LOGAN RETURNS TO CONGRESS.   *J. of the Illinois State Hist. Soc. 1975 68(4): 324-336.* John A. Logan, a Democratic Congressman before the Civil War, was reelected as a Radical Republican from Illinois in 1866. Allied with the anti-Johnson forces in the House, he pursued a strong line toward the former Confederate states. He was considered as a possible contender for the governorship of Illinois or even the Republican nomination for the Presidency in 1868 by some observers. Appointed as one of the managers for the House of Representatives in the impeachment of Andrew Johnson, Logan played a minor role in the deliberations. Based on primary sources.   N. Lederer

502.   Kaplan, Michael.   THE JOKER IN THE REPUBLICAN DECK: THE POLITICAL CAREER OF OTTO MEARS 1881-1889.   *Western States Jewish Hist. Q. 1975 7(4): 287-302.* Otto Mears was very influential in Colorado politics in the late 19th century. By 1876 he was an important Republican Party boss. He was elected to the state legislature in 1882 and served for one term. While a legislator he discovered that lobbyists held the real power to get laws passed. He began to lobby for laws that were favorable to his railroad business. In 1884 and 1886, he backed German-born William Meyer for governor. In 1889, Governor Job Cooper appointed Mears to the committee to build a state capitol building. 2 photos, 54 notes.   R. A. Garfinkle

503.   Kelemen, Thomas A.   A HISTORY OF LYNCH, KENTUCKY, 1917-1930.   *Filson Club Hist. Q. 1974 48(2): 156-176.* The coal town of Lynch, Harlan County, Kentucky, was created in 1917 by the US Coal and Coke Company. The company, a subsidiary of US Steel, exploited the rich coal reserves in Harlan County to meet the fuel crisis caused by World War I. Management attempted to build an ideal company town, with well constructed houses, attractive churches, and a sewer and water system. Still, it was a company town where housing was only for workers, the company store dominated the local economy, and the workers were strongly encouraged to vote Republican. Documentation by contemporary newspapers; 93 notes.   G. B. McKinney

504.   Kertman, G. L.   BOR'BA V RESPUBLIKANSKOI PARTII SSHA PO VOPROSAM NALOGOVOI POLITIKI (1925-1928)   [The struggle in the US Republican Party on tax policy (1925-28)]. *Vestnik Moskovskogo U., Seriia 8: Istoriia [USSR] 1980 (5): 42-55.* Among the Republicans there was a division on the income tax system. Andrew W. Mellon, the Secretary of the Treasury under Calvin Coolidge, wanted to lower taxes to encourage production. The issue of the inheritance tax also became important but a compromise, which retained it, was passed in 1926. By 1927, the growth in the size of the government and governmental expenses, as well as the proposal of agrarian Republicans to establish an agricultural stabilization fund, forced the "Old Guard" and Coolidge to keep the inheritance tax. 76 notes.   D. Balmuth

505.   Kilar, Jeremy W.   ANDREW JOHNSON "SWINGS" THROUGH MICHIGAN: COMMUNITY RESPONSE TO A PRESIDENTIAL CRU-SADE.   *Old Northwest 1977 3(3): 251-273.* President Andrew Johnson (1808-1875) included southern Michigan in his "swing around the circle" of 1866 attempting to advance his moderate reconstruction policy. Speaking in Detroit and eight other towns he was defended by the Democratic press, attacked by the

Republican. His press relations were bad, and he was upstaged by the military heroes who accompanied him. In spite of this Johnson won some favorable results in areas visited. The Democrats carried Wayne County (Detroit) and barely lost other counties along Johnson's route. Based on newspaper reports and secondary works; map, 67 notes.   J

506. King, Willard L. LINCOLN AND THE ILLINOIS COPPERHEADS. *Lincoln Herald 1978 80(3): 132-137.* Early in the Civil War, Illinois was the most ardent prowar Union state. Even local Democrats, to avoid disloyalty, refused to campaign against Abraham Lincoln in 1862. After Lincoln's Emancipation Proclamation in 1863, Illinois Democrats began to repudiate and condemn him. A majority of them became Copperheads and caused considerable trouble south of Springfield. Because Lincoln hated slavery, he refused to abandon his policy, even though friends told him it would cost him reelection in 1864. After the war a few Illinois Democrats were still considered Copperheads, a word implying disloyalty. 2 photos.   T. P. Linkfield

507. Klingman, Peter D. INSIDE THE RING: BISBEE-LEE CORRESPONDENCE, FEBRUARY-APRIL 1880. *Florida Hist. Q. 1978 57(2): 187-204.* Reprints 12 letters between Congressman Horatio Bisbee, Jr. (1839-1916) and Joseph E. Lee (d. 1920), an influential black Republican of Jacksonville. The correspondence reveals intraparty feuding and Republican thinking in post-Reconstruction Florida. The letters are in the Joseph E. Lee Memorial Library, Jacksonville. 27 notes.   P. A. Beaber

508. Klingman, Peter D. JOSIAH T. WALLS AND BLACK TACTICS OF RACE IN POST CIVIL WAR FLORIDA. *Negro Hist. Bull. 1974 37(3): 242-246.* Examines the political attitudes of the Republican Party and Josiah T. Walls, a black Florida member of the House of Representatives, during and after Reconstruction, 1867-85.

509. Klingman, Peter D. and Geithman, David T. NEGRO DISSIDENCE AND THE REPUBLICAN PARTY, 1864-1872. *Phylon 1979 40(2): 172-182.* Negro leaders tried to work in a moderate way in and with the Republican Party during 1864-72, to make as many gains for their race as possible. Describes the Southern States Convention in Columbia, South Carolina, October 1871. 41 notes.   G. R. Schroeder

510. Kolchin, Peter. SCALAWAGS, CARPETBAGGERS, AND RECONSTRUCTION: A QUANTITATIVE LOOK AT SOUTHERN CONGRESSIONAL POLITICS, 1868-1872. *J. of Southern Hist. 1979 45(1): 63-76.* Increased historical attention to Reconstruction politics has refined our image of the identity, ideology, and political behavior of the southern Republican parties without determining who—blacks, carpetbaggers, or scalawags—dominated them. Examination of the members of the U.S. House of Representatives from the 11 ex-Confederate states reveals that healthy southern Republican parties were controlled by blacks and carpetbaggers. The rise in scalawag leadership indicated an increasingly strong Democratic competition and suggested the decline of the Republican Party. Primary and secondary materials; 6 tables, 28 notes.   T. D. Schoonover

511. Kramer, Rita. "WELL, WHAT ARE YOU GOING TO DO ABOUT IT?" *Am. Heritage 1973 24(2): 17-21, 94-97.* Richard Croker (1843?-1922), better known as "Boss Croker," became the leader of Tammany Hall and usually dominated politics in New York City 1886-1901. He seemed immune to bitter satirical attacks against the graft and corruption of his reign, and his typical response to muckrakers' detailed charges of police corruption was, "Well, what are you going to do about it?" He lost bids to get control of the state and national Democratic Party mechanisms, and he retired to the splendor of his English, Irish, and Florida estates. 7 illus.   D. L. Smith

512. Kremer, Gary R. BACKGROUND TO APOSTASY: JAMES MILTON TURNER AND THE REPUBLICAN PARTY. *Missouri Hist. Rev. 1976 71(1): 59-75.* James Milton Turner, who served as minister to Liberia for seven years, looked to the Radical Republicans for financial and political support of black education and suffrage. He did not identify with those who regarded blacks as oppressed; rather, he believed that the Republicans would soon rectify whatever injustices existed. After returning from Liberia in 1877, Turner found his bid for election to the House of Representatives in 1878 blocked on racial grounds. The disillusioned Turner concluded that the party of General Grant was insincere in its dealings with blacks. Based on primary and secondary sources; illus., 34 notes.   W. F. Zornow

513. Kremm, Thomas W. CLEVELAND AND THE FIRST LINCOLN ELECTION: THE ETHNIC RESPONSE TO NATIVISM. *J. of Interdisciplinary Hist. 1977 8(1): 69-86.* Politics in Cleveland, Ohio, on the eve of the Civil War did not revolve exclusively around the question of slavery extension. Accepted theories on the election do not adequately explain ethnic voting patterns in the city. The major division within the electorate was one of Catholics versus non-Catholics. The Republican Party was as much an anti-Catholic coalition as it was an anti-slavery extension organization and non-Catholic voters, ethnic and native-American, voted accordingly. Newspapers and printed sources; 8 tables, 19 notes.   R. Howell

514. Krenkel, John H. THE DISPUTED ARIZONA GUBERNATORIAL ELECTION OF 1916. *J. of the West 1974 13(4): 59-68.* Examines the 1916 Arizona gubernatorial election dispute. A question of accurate counting was raised when Republican Thomas E. Campbell defeated incumbent Democrat George W. P. Hunt by 30 votes. Briefly relates the differing backgrounds and campaigns of the two candidates. Hunt filed a charge of fraud with the Superior Court and demanded a recount. The court decided in Campbell's favor. Hunt then appealed to the State Supreme Court which decided in his favor. Hunt became governor again in 1917. Based on contemporary journal reports, the *George W. P. Hunt Diary*, and secondary sources; 35 notes.   N. J. Street

515. Krug, Mark M. LINCOLN, THE REPUBLICAN PARTY AND THE EMANCIPATION PROCLAMATION. *Hist. Teacher 1973 7(1): 48-61.* The Emancipation Proclamation was a turning point in the Civil War because it made slavery a central issue. Lincoln had a long record of criticizing slavery, and he wished to see it abolished. He was not forced to issue the proclamation by the Radicals; rather, he issued it to help the military situation and to right a moral wrong. The proclamation was endorsed by all factions of the Republican Party. Based on primary and secondary sources; 49 notes.   P. W. Kennedy

516. Kuepper, Stephen L. BOMBS, BULLETS AND BALLOTS: CHICAGO'S 'PINEAPPLE PRIMARY' OF 1928. *Mankind 1976 5(9): 12-16, 46-47.* The Republican city primary of 1928 in Chicago pitted the faction of Charles S. Deneen against the machine of William Hale Thompson. The primary electoral campaign was fraught with violence, murder, and irregularities; each faction relied considerably on gangster support. The Thompson faction upheld its own in the election for city ward committee positions but lost significant city-wide and state primary contests. Legal proceedings against persons for criminal actions during the campaign resulted in acquittals or lenient sentences. N. Lederer

517. Lambert, Franklin T. FREE SILVER AND THE KENTUCKY DEMOCRACY, 1891-1895. *Filson Club Hist. Q. 1979 53(2): 145-177.* Investigates the role of the controversy over monetary policy in splitting the Kentucky Democratic Party of the 1890's. Conservative Democrats such as Henry Watterson and Secretary of the Treasury Carlisle battled free silver advocates Senator J. C. S. Blackburn and 1895 gubernatorial candidate P. W. Hardin for control of the party. The split became so bad that both free silver and conservative voters deserted the party in 1895; that allowed the election of the first Republican governor in Kentucky's history. Based on the *Louisville Courier-Journal* and other newspapers; map, 6 tables, 62 notes. G. B. McKinney

518. Larson, Bruce L. SWEDISH AMERICANS AND FARMER-LABOR POLITICS IN MINNESOTA. Hasselmo, Nils, ed. *Perspectives on Swedish Immigration* (Chicago: Swedish Pioneer Hist. Soc. and Duluth: U. of Minnesota, 1978): 206-224. Politicians of Swedish and other Scandinavian origins were important in the history of Minnesota state politics in general and of the Farmer-Labor Party in particular. Swedish Americans Charles A. Lindbergh, Sr., Magnus Johnson, Ernest Lundeen, Elmer Benson, and Floyd Olson were key figures in the party. Swedes in Minnesota gave slightly stronger support than most other Minnesotans to the Farmer-Labor Party, especially in the peak periods of the early 1920's and the mid-1930's. The Farmer-Labor Party merged with the Democratic Party in 1944. Illus., table, fig., 37 notes, appendix. S

519. Ledbetter, Billy D. THE ELECTION OF LOUIS T. WIGFALL TO THE UNITED STATES SENATE, 1859: A REEVALUATION. *Southwestern Hist. Q. 1973 77(2): 241-254.* Unionist Democrats swept the state and congressional elections in Texas in August 1859. In December the state legislature elected Louis T. Wigfall, the most radical states' righter in Texas, to the U.S. Senate. Discounts the conventional explanation that the turnabout was a repercussion from John Brown's mid-October raid at Harpers Ferry. It was due to a regrouping of the ultra-states'-righters who had controlled the party and dominated state politics during the 1850's and to the careful preparation of the Wigfall supporters for his campaign. 3 tables, 31 notes. D. L. Smith

520. Lee, David D. RURAL DEMOCRATS, EASTERN REPUBLICANS, AND TRADE-OFFS IN TENNESSEE, 1922-1932. *East Tennessee Hist. Soc. Publ. 1976 48: 104-115.* In 1922 Governor Austin Peay and his close advisor Luke Lea divided the Democratic Party in Tennessee into urban and rural factions. Peay took an interest in Eastern Tennessee and his rural faction of the Democratic Party often was supported by eastern Tennessee Republicans. 22 notes. D. A. Yanchisin

521.   Lee, David D.   THE TRIUMPH OF BOSS CRUMP: THE TENNES-
SEE GUBERNATORIAL ELECTION OF 1932.   *Tennessee Hist. Q. 1976*
35(4): 393-413. After the death of Austin Peay in 1927 Edward Crump led an
urban assault on Peay's successors who ran Tennessee politics until 1932. In a
three-way primary campaign, Crump supported State Treasurer Hill McAlister
in a campaign which witnessed rampant fraud and appeals to racism. McAlister
won a narrow victory over Lewis Pope, the independent candidate who protested
fraud, bolted the Democratic Party, and ran in the general election. Once again
in a three-cornered campaign, Crump's candidate won. This began the 16-year
domination of Tennessee politics by the Shelby County boss. Primary and secondary sources; 7 tables, 77 notes.   M. B. Lucas

522.   Lee, David L.   THE ATTEMPT TO IMPEACH GOVERNOR HOR-
TON.   *Tennessee Hist. Q. 1975 34(2): 188-201.* The close relationship between
Governor Henry Horton and Rogers Caldwell led to an investigation of Caldwell's financial activities involving state funds upon the collapse of his empire in
1930. An investigation led by Horton's political opponent, E. H. Crump, soon
implicated the Tennessee governor in negligent, if not fraudulent, handling of
state money. In 1931, to avoid impeachment, Horton and his allies began making
blatant political deals with Democrats and Republicans, a controversial policy
which proved successful in the end. 37 notes.   M. B. Lucas

523.   Leff, Michael C. and Mohrmann, G. P.   LINCOLN AT COOPER
UNION: A RHETORICAL ANALYSIS OF THE TEXT.   *Q. J. of Speech 1974*
60(3): 346-358. "Seeking the presidential nomination, Lincoln attempts to in-
gratiate himself with a Republican audience, and after an extensive attack upon
Douglas, he creates a mock debate with the South and appeals for Republican
unity. Each section features controlled argument, builds in intensity, and rests
upon an association between Republicans and the founding fathers, Lincoln using
arrangement, argument, and style to associate self and party with the fathers and
to dissociate self and party from his chief rivals."   J

524.   Leitman, Spencer L.   THE REVIVAL OF AN IMAGE: GRANT AND
THE 1880 REPUBLICAN NOMINATING CAMPAIGN.   *Missouri Hist.*
Soc. Bull. 1974 30(3): 196-204. Analyzes maneuvers by admirers and Stalwart
factionalists to obtain the Republican Party's presidential nomination in 1880 for
Ulysses S. Grant (1822-85). The boom for Grant foundered on the shoals of
intraparty factionalism and widespread antipathy toward a third presidential
term for Grant. Based on newspapers and secondary sources; 41 notes.
                                                                    H. T. Lovin

525.   Levi, Steven C.   THE MOST EXPENSIVE MEAL IN AMERICAN
HISTORY.   *J. of the West 1979 18(2): 62-73.* In the summer of 1916 Charles
Evans Hughes, Republican candidate for president, attempted to bring disaffected Progressives back into the Republican Party. His campaign in California
coincided with a period of labor unrest in San Francisco. Hughes unwisely
followed the advice of conservative Republicans and attended a banquet in an
antiunion restaurant on 19 August 1916. This act marked Hughes as an enemy
of labor and was a major cause of his failure to carry California in the presidential
election. Based on newspapers and other published sources; 4 photos, 59 notes.
                                                                    B. S. Porter

526. Lindstrom, Andrew F. LAWRENCE STRINGER: A WILSON DEMOCRAT. *J. of the Illinois Hist. Soc. 1973 66(1): 20-40.* Lawrence Beaumont Stringer of Lincoln, Illinois, was a leading state Democrat from 1891 to 1915. An early backer of Woodrow Wilson, reformer Stringer was an effective spokesman for downstate progressives. Irving Shuman and William F. McCombs, Wilson's volunteer campaign manager, joined Stringer in opposing machine politics. They were opposed by U.S. House Speaker Champ Clark (also a recognized Progressive), who overwhelmingly won the 1912 Illinois Democratic primary. The Illinois Democratic Party split three ways between Chicago precinct committeeman Roger Sullivan, anti-Wilson Chicago mayor Carter Harrison, and Stringer's downstate faction, finally compromised when Sullivan sided with Stringer. As Logan County Judge, Stringer campaigned for fellow Democrats until his death in 1942. Based on Stringer papers and on newspapers; 5 illus., 60 notes.
A. C. Aimone

527. Lonsdale, David L. CHICANERY IN COLORADO. *Red River Valley Hist. Rev. 1979 4(3): 33-43.* Political infighting between Republicans and Democrats for hegemony in the state legislature during 1902-04 scuttled attempts to have an eight-hour work day written into the state constitution, and instead limited determination of work days to a fairly ineffectual statute passed in 1905.

528. Loveland, Anne C. THE "SOUTHERN WORK" OF THE REVEREND JOSEPH C. HARTZELL, PASTOR OF AMES CHURCH IN NEW ORLEANS, 1870-1873. *Louisiana Hist. 1975 16(4): 391-407.* "Like most other Northern Methodist missionaries to the South, Hartzell saw no conflict in linking religious endeavors and Republican politics." Hartzell supervised three Methodist institutions for Negroes: Union Normal School, Thomson Institute, and the Freedmen's Orphan Home which combined educational and missionary efforts. The response of Southern Whites to the educational and missionary work of the Northern Methodists among the freedmen was generally unsympathetic. Another reason for the loss of support was the Republicans ultimately abandoned the social and political goals of Reconstruction. Based largely on correspondence from the Hartzell and Baldwin Papers. Illus., 42 notes.
E. P. Stickney

529. Lovett, Bobby L. MEMPHIS RIOTS: WHITE REACTION TO BLACKS IN MEMPHIS, MAY 1865-JULY 1866. *Tennessee Hist. Q. 1979 38(1): 9-33.* The bloody racial riots in Memphis, Tennessee, on 1-2 May 1866, were the result of demographic changes caused by the influx of large numbers of black refugees, thus creating an urban black community and new race relationships. The claim that the presence of black troops caused the riots is a myth. The results of the riot were the opposite of what the white instigators desired since the riot helped convince national and state Republicans to pass protective civil rights legislation for blacks. Primary and secondary sources; 2 illus., 49 notes.
M. B. Lucas

530. Lowden, Lucy. NEW HAMPSHIRE AT CHICAGO—1860: "THE ONLY FIT AND PROPER NOMINATION . . . ." *Hist. New Hampshire 1974 29(1): 20-41.* Examines the New Hampshire delegation's decision at the Republican National Convention to vote for the presidential nomination of Abraham Lincoln instead of William H. Seward.
S

531.   Lunde, Erik S.   THE AMBIGUITY OF THE NATIONAL IDEA: THE
PRESIDENTIAL CAMPAIGN OF 1872.   *Can. Rev. of Studies in Nationalism
[Canada] 1978 5(1): 1-23.* The 1872 presidential campaign in the United States,
pitting the incumbent Ulysses S. Grant against newspaper editor Horace Greeley,
also represented a clash between two views of the American nation and of
nationalism. The Republicans supporting Grant saw the Civil War as a great
triumph which had bound the United States into a united nation, linked not only
by sentiment but by rapidly increasing stretches of roads, railways, telegraph
lines, and other modes of communication. The Democrats, among whom were
many former Confederates, and their Liberal Republican allies, among whom
were Carl Schurz and Greeley himself, looked upon the war as a tragedy and upon
Republican centralism with distaste. America needed to recapture the unity and
the purity of prewar days through reconciliation and respect for the autonomy
of the states. The elections of 1872 saw Greeley's benevolent image of nationalism
defeated by the centralizing, "blood and iron" concept of Grant and his Republicans, but the latter's triumph would be short-lived; the Liberal vision would win
in the end. 46 notes.   J. C. Billigmeier

532.   Lunde, Erik S.   THE CONTINUED SEARCH FOR NATIONAL
UNITY: THE UNITED STATES PRESIDENTIAL CAMPAIGN OF 1876.
Can. Rev. of Studies in Nationalism [Canada] 1981 8(1): 131-149. The contest
between Samuel J. Tilden and Rutherford B. Hayes in the year of the American
centennial was the occasion for a renewed surge of nationalist spirit. Still suffering
from the legacy of the Civil War, the political parties disagreed on the exact
nature of nationalism, the role of government, and regionalism; only increased
disunity resulted from the polemics. 43 notes.   R. Aldrich

533.   Lyman, E. Leo.   A MORMON TRANSITION IN IDAHO POLITICS.
Idaho Yesterdays 1977 20(4): 2-11, 24-29. Mormons in Idaho generally voted
Democratic in the years preceding statehood. However, the conflicts over polyg-
amy and political domination by church leaders led to support of Republicans,
because the church received more sympathetic treatment from them. When the
immediate issues were resolved, Mormons divided their votes equally between the
two parties. Covers the 1880's. Primary and secondary sources; 7 illus., 61 notes.
                                                              B. J. Paul

534.   Mackle, Elliott.   CYRUS TEED AND THE LEE COUNTY ELEC-
TIONS OF 1906.   *Florida Hist. Q. 1978 57(1): 1-18.* Cyrus R. Teed (d. 1908)
was founder and leader of the Koreshan Unity, a celibate religious community
of socialists, numbering about 200. In 1894 he established a settlement at Estero
near Fort Myers in Lee County. By 1904 Teed desired control of county politics
as a part of his plan to unite the whole society under his leadership. Opportunity
arose in 1906 when he opposed disfranchisement aimed at blacks and Koreshans
in county elections by forming the Progressive Liberty Party (PLP). This consisted of Koreshans, socialists, Republicans, and dissatisfied Democrats who
voiced political sentiment through their newly formed newspaper, the *American
Eagle.* Although defeated politically, Teed still retained followers after the election and was seen as a prophet upon his death in 1908. Based mainly on newspaper sources; illus., 48 notes.   P. A. Beaber/G. Fox

535. Maddex, John P., Jr. VIRGINIA: THE PERSISTENCE OF CEN-
TRIST HEGEMONY. Olsen, Otto H., ed. *Reconstruction and Redemption in
the South* (Baton Rouge: Louisiana State U. Pr., 1980): 113-155. Unlike the
situation in most other southern states, Virginia succeeded in holding the carpetbaggers and scalawags at bay. Both Conservatives and Republicans tended to
moderation. Insofar as the Negro was concerned, the results were the same, but
much unnecessary ratifying and repealing was avoided. Curiously, the Republican Party could not elect a governor during Reconstruction, but succeeded in
doing so afterward as a consequence of a tax revolt, which temporarily united
Negroes and the whites of the mountains. 44 notes.   V. L. Human

536. Malone, Dumas and Hochman, Steven H.   A NOTE ON EVIDENCE:
THE PERSONAL HISTORY OF MADISON HEMINGS.   *J. of Southern
Hist. 1975 41(4): 523-528.* A review of the controversy surrounding Madison
Hemings, supposedly the son of President Thomas Jefferson by a Negro slave.
The first account of Hemings appeared in 1873 in a Republican newspaper in
Democrat-dominated Waverly, Ohio. A review of the circumstances surrounding
publication suggests that it was done for the sake of political gain. The editor's
introduction to the article is included, along with a rebuttal by a rival Democratic
paper. 10 notes.   V. L. Human

537. Margulies, Herbert F.   LA FOLLETTE, ROOSEVELT AND THE RE-
PUBLICAN PRESIDENTIAL NOMINATION OF 1912.   *Mid-Am. 1976
58(1): 54-76.* Despite Robert Marion La Follette's claims to the contrary, it was
he and not Theodore Roosevelt who played a double game during the nomination
campaign. Following the successful 1910 fall elections, La Follette created the
National Progressive Republican League to work toward replacement of Taft. La
Follette's strategy of a united front against Taft collapsed as Roosevelt's candidacy slowly emerged. The ill La Follette, advised by his wife, accused the Roosev-
eltians of treachery and continued the race. Ultimately, La Follette preferred
Wilson's victory to that of his rivals; he was again the leading progressive Republican. Based on the La Follette Family Collection, Library of Congress and other
MS. sources, and on published sources and secondary works; 78 notes.
                                                                    T. H. Wendel

538. Matthews, John M.   NEGRO REPUBLICANS IN THE RECON-
STRUCTION OF GEORGIA.   *Georgia Hist. Q. 1976 60(2): 145-164.* The
Georgia Equal Rights Association and the Union League were forerunners of the
Republican Party in Georgia. Among the Republican's problems were the split
between the radical and the moderate factions and the disastrous governorship
of Rufus B. Bullock during 1868-71. The Party's inability to hold the allegiance
of its black supporters was a significant factor in its defeat in the 1870's. The
blacks were rarely rewarded with leadership or offices by the Republicans. Many
blacks ended up being manipulated by the Democrats. Primary and secondary
sources; 44 notes.   G. R. Schroeder

539. Mattson, Robert Lee.   POLITICS IS UP! GRIGSBY'S COWBOYS
AND ROOSEVELT'S ROUGH RIDERS, 1898.   *South Dakota Hist. 1979
9(4): 303-315.* Political influence played a vital role in the organization, recruiting, equipping, and internal promotions of the three cowboy regiments authorized
by Congress during the Spanish-American War in 1898. While Melvin Grigsby,

Jay L. Torrey, and Leonard Wood (1860-1927) were authorized to recruit and command regiments, the effects of political pressure caused the Rough Riders regiment led by Wood and Theodore Roosevelt (1858-1919) to gain immortality while the others became lost in obscurity. Although Theodore Roosevelt's courage and ability cannot be denied, his political influence may have been more important in his becoming a war hero than any of his other qualities. Based on the Grigsby Papers at the Center for Western Studies, Augustana College, Sioux Falls, South Dakota, and other primary sources; 4 photos, 44 notes.

P. L. McLaughlin

540.   Mauer, John Walker, ed.   WILLIAM ALEXANDER'S POLITICAL TRICK: THE "SECRET CIRCULAR" OF 1875.   *Southwestern Hist. Q. 1978 81(3): 283-298.* Presents a bogus letter supposedly from the Texas Democratic central committee to local Democrats concerning the election of delegates to the Texas Constitutional Convention of 1875. Actually written by William Alexander, a leading Texas Republican, it satirized the Democratic Party's leadership troubles with young office-seekers, Grangers, and the press. Primary and secondary sources; illus., 22 notes.

J. H. Broussard

541.   McCarthy, G. Michael.   THE BROWN DERBY CAMPAIGN IN WEST TENNESSEE: SMITH, HOOVER, AND THE POLITICS OF RACE. *West Tennessee Hist. Soc. Papers 1973 (27): 81-98.* The hard-fought political campaign between Alfred E. Smith and Herbert C. Hoover in Tennessee dredged up racial, religious, ethical, and political mud and ultimately resulted in Hoover's breaking the solid South for the first time since Reconstruction.

542.   McCarthy, G. Michael.   COLORADO'S POPULIST PARTY AND THE PROGRESSIVE MOVEMENT.   *J. of the West 1976 15(1): 54-75.* Using Richard Hofstadter's hypotheses describing populism, the author examines populism in Colorado and finds some similarities and some differences. Agreeing with Hofstadter's thesis, it was found that the leaders of the Colorado populists were, by and large, professional men and professional reformers. Contrary to the thesis, few of the Colorado populists made the transition to progressivism. The stumbling block appears to have been that the doctrine of natural resource conservation ran counter to Colorado beliefs.

R. Alvis

543.   McCarthy, G. Michael.   SMITH VS. HOOVER: THE POLITICS OF RACE IN WEST TENNESSEE.   *Phylon 1978 39(2): 154-168.* When the Democrats in 1928 nominated for President of the United States Al Smith of New York, a big-city, Catholic, anti-prohibition, pro-immigration, professional politician, there were wide defections in parts of the South, which was overwhelmingly rural and small-town, Protestant, prohibitionist, and anti-immigration. Herbert Hoover won over many southern Democrats because he was from a rural background, was a Protestant, a prohibitionist, and an old stock American. West Tennessee resisted this anti-Smith trend for racial reasons. Blacks were one-third the population in West Tennessee, and the whites feared that they might become politically powerful. The Republican Party had always been the party of the blacks, and in 1928 it reinforced this image by including in its platform a strong anti-lynching plank. The result was white, Democratic solidarity behind Al Smith. Of the 19 counties west of the Tennessee River, only 4 went for Hoover. 71 notes.

J. C. Billigmeier

544. McCarthy, Michael P.   PRELUDE TO ARMAGEDDON: CHARLES E. MERRIAM AND THE CHICAGO MAYORAL ELECTION OF 1911. *J. of the Illinois State Hist. Soc. 1974 67(5): 505-518.* Charles E. Merriam, a progressive, intellectual professor, easily won the Republican mayoral nomination when the incumbent Fred A. Busse declined to seek reelection. Taking advantage of the new direct primary, the progressives broke the hold of downtown Republican bosses. But the Progressives could not stay in power without a victory on election day. This they failed to deliver. Merriam's overzealous campaign was wrecked by Democrat Carter Harrison II, who won the blue-collar vote, and by the opposition from regular Republicans on his own ticket. After Harrison became mayor, the machine politicians regained control of the battered Republican organization. Primary and secondary sources; 9 illus., 27 notes.
W. R. Hively

545. McCarthy, Michael P.   THE SHORT, UNHAPPY LIFE OF THE ILLINOIS PROGRESSIVE PARTY. *Chicago Hist. 1977 6(1): 2-11.* As an offshoot of the Republican Party, the Illinois Progressive Party was born during the state nominating convention, 1912, but died in 1916 when the 1912 candidate, Theodore Roosevelt, declined to run for office again.

546. McCormick, Richard L.   PRELUDE TO PROGRESSIVISM: THE TRANSFORMATION OF NEW YORK STATE POLITICS, 1890-1910. *New York Hist. 1978 59(3): 253-276.* Studies the transformation from 19th-century patterns of political partisanship and public policymaking, exemplified by the political strategy of New York State Republican Party boss Thomas C. Platt, to the reforms of the progressive era. Weakening of party discipline and demands for divisive economic policies reshaped traditional New York politics. Republican Party leaders in New York State kept their party in power by compromising with the demands of independent reformers. Suggests that the progressive movement generally should be studied as the interaction between politicians in power and people who had grievances against the existing political system. 7 illus., 32 notes.
R. N. Lokken

547. McCormick, Richard L.   THE THOMAS COLLIER PLATT PAPERS. *Yale U. Lib. Gazette 1975 50(1): 46-58.* Reviews the career of Thomas Collier Platt, three-term US Senator and long-time leader of the New York State Republican Party from the late 1880's until his death in 1910. "While primary sources abound on New York State politics in Platt's era, relatively few of his own manuscript materials have been available to scholars." The recent gift by his grandson to Yale University of letters and newspaper clippings dating from 1896 to 1902 when Platt's power was at its height is a substantial contribution to the political history of the state and the nation—"these papers shed fascinating light on the inner workings of the political system of New York State in a seminal period of political change." 7 notes.
D. A. Yanchisin

548. McDaniel, George W.   PROHIBITION DEBATE IN WASHINGTON COUNTY, 1890-1894: SMITH WILDMAN BROOKHART'S INTRODUCTION TO POLITICS. *Ann. of Iowa 1981 45(7): 519-536.* Contrary to widely held historical opinion, Smith Wildman Brookhart did not begin his political career as an antirailroad politician. Rather his introduction to politics came in 1894 when the dry faction of the Washington County, Iowa, Republican Party

succeeded in gaining Brookhart's nomination for the office of county attorney. Brookhart easily won the office and thus began a career in politics that would eventually lead to the US Senate. Based on local newspapers; 3 photos, 38 notes.
P. L. Petersen

549. McDaniel, Ruth Currie. BLACK POWER IN GEORGIA: WILLIAM A. PLEDGER AND THE TAKEOVER OF THE REPUBLICAN PARTY. *Georgia Hist. Q. 1978 62(3): 225-239.* William A. Pledger (b. 1852) felt that black Republicans in Georgia were not receiving their share of the patronage. Campaigning at party conventions and through his newspaper, the Athens *Blade,* he helped John Emory Bryant (a sympathetic white) be elected to the state Republican Party chairmanship in 1876 and achieved that position himself in 1880. However, the party was still weak and lost at the polls, and party divisions kept the blacks from making any real progress despite their temporary power. Based on newspaper and other primary sources; 35 notes.   G. R. Schroeder

550. McFeely, William S. THE JACKSONIAN NAVAL PERSON IN LINCOLN'S CABINET. *R. in Am. Hist. 1974 2(3): 394-401.* The influence of Jacksonian Democrats in the political history of the 1820's-1870's is illustrated in John Niven's biography of Gideon Welles, Secretary of the Navy during the Civil War, *Gideon Welles: Lincoln's Secretary of the Navy* (New York: Oxford U. Pr., 1973).

551. McHugh, Christine. MIDWESTERN POPULIST LEADERSHIP AND EDWARD BELLAMY: "LOOKING BACKWARD" INTO THE FUTURE. *Am. Studies 1978 19(2): 57-74.* Analyzes the thrust and impact of the 1888 *Looking Backward 2000-1887,* as well as Bellamy's impact on his contemporaries. His ideas "permeated the midwestern Populist heartland." Populist editors urged readers to become familiar with Bellamy's ideas about producerism, and reprinted his articles widely. They focused on work as a divine blessing, economic grievances, and the devaluation of labor by nonproductive market forces. Primary and secondary sources; 62 notes.   J. A. Andrew

552. McKinney, Gordon B., ed. THE KLAN IN THE SOUTHERN MOUNTAINS: THE LUSK-SHOTWELL CONTROVERSY. *Appalachian J. 1981 8(2): 89-104.* Reproduces the account provided in 1923 by Virgil Lusk of his violent encounter in 1869 with Randolph Shotwell in Asheville, North Carolina, which grew out of these men's political and personal differences over Republican Party policies during Reconstruction and out of Lusk's opposition to and Shotwell's support of Ku Klux Klan terrorism.

553. McKinney, Gordon B. THE POLITICAL USES OF APPALACHIAN IDENTITY AFTER THE CIVIL WAR. *Appalachian J. 1980 7(3): 200-209.* Discusses how regional identity associated with the mountain people of Appalachia was exploited by politicians, particularly Republicans, during 1860-99, citing the 1860-61 secession crisis and the Civil War as cases in point.

554. McKinney, Gordon B. THE POLITICS OF PROTEST: THE LABOR REFORM AND GREENBACK PARTIES IN NEW HAMPSHIRE. *Hist. New Hampshire 1981 36(2-3): 149-170.* In 1870, rapid industrialization and rural population decline led to the formation of the Labor Reform Party of New Hampshire, which received 10.6% of the popular vote in the 1870 state elections,

making it the most successful third party in New Hampshire between 1856 and 1912. But it failed to achieve any of its objectives, as its support came from disaffected Democrats, allowing Republicans to sweep into power. In the late 1870's the Greenback Party began organizing in New Hampshire, and workers alienated by the two major parties turned to it with great interest. It also failed to provide an effective vehicle for reform and amounted only to a protest party. 57 notes.

D. F. Chard

555. McKinney, Gordon B.   SOUTHERN MOUNTAIN REPUBLICANS AND THE NEGRO, 1865-1900.   *J. of Southern Hist. 1975 41(4): 493-516.* The end of the Civil War witnessed Republican efforts to build a political base in the South. Reconstruction policies strengthened the Democrats everywhere but in the mountains. Republicans sought the black vote because they needed all the votes they could get. Strengthening of anti-Negro statutes forced the Republicans to disguise their position, and gradually to forsake it. There were few Negroes in the mountains; race was not an issue. Blacks were eventually excluded from all party positions, either directly or indirectly. 3 tables, 115 notes.   V. L. Human

556.   McKnight, Gerald D.   THE PERILS OF REFORM POLITICS: THE ABORTIVE NEW YORK STATE CONSTITUTIONAL REFORM MOVE-MENT OF 1915.   *New-York Hist. Soc. Q. 1979 63(3): 202-227.* Following the Republican defeat in 1912, reform-minded young party members in New York state attempted to introduce changes to the constitution to increase centralization in the state government. Led by such young Republicans as Henry L. Stimson and Ogden Mills, a constitutional convention was held, such innovations as a short ballot and the executive budget were included in a new constitution, and the document was presented to the voters in 1915. It went down to a resounding defeat. Primarily responsible was the opposition of staunch Progressives and old-line Republicans. Many of the changes would be brought about during the next decade but, for the moment, it was obvious that the Republican Party badly needed some remodeling to have much chance of winning the presidency in 1916. Primary sources; 4 illus., 65 notes.

C. L. Grant

557.   McKnight, Gerald D.   REPUBLICAN LEADERSHIP AND THE MEXICAN QUESTION, 1913-1916: A FAILED BID FOR PARTY RESUR-GENCE.   *Mid-America 1980 62(2): 105-122.* During Woodrow Wilson's first term, conservative Republican leaders looked to foreign policy to convince the electorate that the Republican Party was the party of constructive leadership. The Mexican Revolution seemed to be a tailor-made foreign policy issue. The major reason for the lack of consistent criticism on the Mexican question was the interjection of the Panama Canal tolls controversy into national politics. This showed that the Republicans were too divided to capitalize on the situation in Mexico. 8 notes.

M. J. Wentworth

558.   Melcher, Daniel P.   THE CHALLENGE TO NORMALCY: THE 1924 ELECTION IN CALIFORNIA.   *Southern California Q. 1978 60(2): 155-182.* Analyzes the influence of the La Follette Progressive Party ticket on California in the 1924 presidential election. The third party movement was supported by Republicans who failed to share in Coolidge prosperity, including workers in the depressed gold, timber, and agricultural industries, plus urban working class voters. Their vote was a protext against the upper and middle class orientation

of the Republican party; disaffected Democrats also turned to the Progressives in the belief that the Democratic party failed to represent their needs. The La Follette ticket provided the means for a major realignment in the electorate as Republicans went through the Progressive Party in 1924 and into the Democratic party in 1928. "More than any other factor, the election of 1924 turned on the economic well-being of the electorate." Thus the Progressives were not a reminder of prewar reform as much as the beginnings of what by 1932 became a Democratic coalition. Census and voting records, contemporary and secondary published works; 6 tables, 59 notes.   A. Hoffman

559.   Mering, John V.   THE CONSTITUTIONAL UNION CAMPAIGN OF 1860; AN EXAMPLE OF THE PARANOID STYLE.   *Mid-America 1978 60(2): 95-106.* Studies the Constitutional Union Party campaign in 1860, using as a basis the "paranoid" style of politics as articulated by the late Richard Hofstadter. The Constitutional Unionists were paranoid in that they did not see much difference between the Republicans and the abolitionists. Although they opposed secession, they saw the Republicans as an organized conspiracy to abolish slavery and acted accordingly during the campaign. Based on campaign speeches and diaries; 45 notes.   J. M. Lee

560.   Mering, John V.   THE SLAVE-STATE CONSTITUTIONAL UNIONISTS AND THE POLITICS OF CONSENSUS.   *J. of Southern Hist. 1977 43(3): 395-410.* The traditional view of the Constitutional Union party of 1860 as revealing the ambivalent nature of southern opinion in the crisis of the mid-19th century is incorrect. A close study of the rise of the opposition Democratic faction in the South in the state and local campaigns of 1859 and 1860, as well as in the national ones, reveals the deeply held consensus between the southern Democrats and the Constitutional Union parties within the framework of party competition. Both parties roundly condemned black republicans and took similar ambivalent stands on secession. They proclaimed their love of union yet denied they were submitting to Republican rule. The Constitutional Union party did not exist during the contests over secession in 1860-61 because it did not contest that policy. Based on manuscripts, printed primary and secondary sources; 50 notes.
                                                        T. D. Schoonover

561.   Miglian, Robert Murken.   CALIFORNIA'S REACTION TO THE DISPUTED PRESIDENTIAL ELECTION OF 1876.   *J. of the West 1976 15(1): 9-28.* Unlike in the East, in California there was little reaction to the Hayes-Tilden election. Provides résumés of the party platforms for 1876, and the election returns.   R. Alvis

562.   Mikkelsen, D. Craig.   THE POLITICS OF B. H. ROBERTS.   *Dialogue 1974 9(2): 25-43.* Roberts, a turn-of-the-century Utah Democrat, supported the Mormon Church but opposed the church leaders' (particularly President Joseph F. Smith's) use of their religious authority to promote the Republican Party. On the other hand, Roberts used his own position as a church official to promote the League of Nations. Other political issues discussed are women suffrage, prohibition, and the Mormon Church's "Political Manifesto" of 1896. Primary sources; 78 notes.   D. L. Rowe

563. Miller, Grace L. THE ORIGINS OF THE SAN DIEGO LINCOLN-ROOSEVELT LEAGUE, 1905-1909. *Southern California Q. 1978 60(4): 421-443.* Traces the development of the progressive political reform movement in San Diego, California. Progressive Republicans opposed the control of their city by the Southern Pacific and by "Boss" Charles Hardy. Beginning with the 1905 municipal election, reformers sought an end to machine politics and boss rule. On 24 May 1906, the Roosevelt Republican Club was organized to support progressivism within the Republican Party framework. In 1907 progressive Republicans backed a Nonpartisan League, and under the leadership of Edgar Luce, George Marston, Ed Fletcher, and other reformers, the Roosevelt Republican Club was revitalized as the Lincoln-Roosevelt Republican League. A major test came in the mayoralty election of 1909; it marked a complete victory for the league. Whem Hiram Johnson opened his campaign for governor in March 1910, his first speech was in San Diego, a city that had been won over to the support of progressive goals. Primary and secondary sources; 73 notes.   A. Hoffman

564. Mills, Todd. PENCIL PUSHERS AND INK SLINGERS: THE GLOBE NEWSPAPER WAR OF 1911. *J. of Arizona Hist. 1980 21(2): 147-170.* Describes the convoluted efforts of the national Republican Party to discredit Democratic gubernatorial candidate George Hunt on the eve of Arizona's admission to the union. The primary means chosen was to acquire the Democratic newspapers in Globe as a vehicle of apparent independent criticism of the Democrats and their candidate. The means were gained but the effort failed. 11 photos, 51 notes.   G. O. Gagnon

565. Montgomery, David. RADICAL REPUBLICANISM IN PENNSYLVANIA, 1866-1873. *Pennsylvania Mag. of Hist. and Biog. 1961 85(4): 439-457.* The conventional view of Radical Republicanism sees it as a platform for advancing northern economic interests and advocating social reform in the South. Pennsylvania Radical Republicans, however, reflected social changes such as industrialization and urbanization, which were unrelated to regional disputes or the aftermath of the Civil War.

566. Moore, James Tice. REDEEMERS RECONSIDERED: CHANGE AND CONTINUITY IN THE DEMOCRATIC SOUTH, 1870-1900. *J. of Southern Hist. 1978 44(3): 357-378.* Originally enjoying a reputation as saviors of the South from carpetbag rule, during the 1920's-50's, the redeemers were critically reinterpreted to become the builders of the New South with urban, industrial, and whiggish qualities. However, the revisionist image of the redeemers greatly overemphasizes the break with traditional values which took place in the 1870's and 1880's. The persistent, traditionalist South continued to align with the agricultural West after redemption. Secondary materials; 58 notes.
T. D. Schoonover

567. Morgan, James F. WILLIAM CARY RENFROW: GOVERNOR OF OKLAHOMA TERRITORY, 1893-1897. *Chronicles of Oklahoma 1975 53(1): 46-65.* A businessman and civic figure from Norman, William Cary Renfrow was elevated to the territorial governorship by President Grover Cleveland. He thus became the first Democratic governor of Oklahoma Territory and the first former Confederate soldier to hold the office. His first year was a stormy one as he received criticism from the *Daily Oklahoma State Capital*, a leading Republican

newspaper in Guthrie, and from Republican office holders whom he purged. Renfrow successfully pressured for more Indian land to be opened to white settlement and tried unsuccessfully to merge Indian Territory with Oklahoma Territory. Though primarily a conservative Democrat, he promoted some Populist causes and garnered Populist support by 1896. Renfrow's efforts toward creation of Langston University won support from some blacks, but his veto of a poorly written civil rights bill undercut much of that support. Based on primary and secondary sources; 7 photos, 43 notes.   M. L. Tate

568. Mugleston, William F.   THE 1912 PROGRESSIVE CAMPAIGN IN GEORGIA. *Georgia Hist. Q. 1977 61(3): 233-245.* The situation of the Progressive Party in Georgia was representative of the problems Theodore Roosevelt had throughout the South during the campaign of 1912. White southerners were particularly suspicious of Progressive attitudes toward Negroes, which caused party splits in Georgia and three other states. This third party and its supporters were very weak in campaign ability and received little support in the South. Their position was even more difficult since they were opposing Woodrow Wilson who was a southern Democrat. Primary and secondary sources; 27 notes.
                                                                 G. R. Schroeder

569. Murray, Lawrence L.   BUREAUCRACY AND BI-PARTISANSHIP IN TAXATION: THE MELLON PLAN REVISITED. *Business Hist. Rev. 1978 52(2): 200-225.* Disagrees with the traditional portrait of Andrew W. Mellon as an archconservative Secretary of the Treasury who successfully advocated a tax reduction program that primarily benefited his own higher income constituency. The Mellon tax approach would have been the basis of Treasury Department policy even if the Democrats had won the 1920 election, because it was the product of earlier departmental bureaucratic planning and not Mellon's own initiative. Based principally on government documents and private papers; 98 notes.   C. J. Pusateri

570. Murray, Lawrence L.   THE MELLONS, THEIR MONEY, AND THE MYTHICAL MACHINE: ORGANIZATIONAL POLITICS IN THE REPUBLICAN TWENTIES. *Pennsylvania Hist. 1975 42(3): 221-241.* Though the Mellon family possessed considerable political influence in Pittsburgh and Pennsylvania in the 1920's, it did not command an organization or machine. As Secretary of the Treasury, Andrew W. Mellon became deeply involved in Pennsylvania Republican affairs as a means of obtaining support for his programs. His nephew, William Larimer Mellon, president of Gulf Oil Corporation, functioned as his political alter ego. Though the Mellons had some initial successes in Pennsylvania intraparty affairs, their money and national political influence were not matched by an ability to deliver votes, particularly in the primaries. The defeat of Senator George Wharton Pepper by William Vare in the 1926 primary demonstrated the weakness of the Mellons. The sound defeat of Mellon-backed candidates in the 1930 primary again demonstrated that the family did not control a political organization. Illus., 45 notes.   D. C. Swift

571. Murray, Robert K.   THE DEMOCRATS VS. FRUSTRATION CITY: IT WAS NO MIX. *Smithsonian 1976 7(1): 48-55.* Reviews a chapter in Robert K. Murray's *The 103rd Ballot: The Democrats and the Disaster in Madison Square Garden* (Harper-Row, 1976), concerning the Democratic convention in

New York City in 1924, a convention which reflected American social cleavage, e.g. urban vs. agricultural, wet vs. dry, and featured the candidacy of William Gibbs McAdoo (1863-1941) and Alfred E. Smith (1873-1944). Many favorite sons were antagonistic about the convention location, and this, plus misunderstanding, influenced the candidates and the convention results. By 10 July (the convention began 24 June) the delegates, after voting for 59 different persons on 103 Presidential ballots (both records), reached a compromise. 6 illus., 20 photos.

K. A. Harvey

572. Mushkat, Jerome. BEN WOOD'S 'FORT LAFAYETTE': A SOURCE FOR STUDYING THE PEACE DEMOCRATS. *Civil War Hist. 1975 21(2): 160-171.* Analyzes the anti-Civil War novel *Fort Lafayette*, written in 1862 by Ben Wood, New York Peace Democrat journalist brother of Fernando Wood, New York Peace Democrat politician. Unsuccessful in making his arguments heard through the press, Wood resorted to fiction to detail his opposition to war and emancipation, and his belief that the war was destroying civil liberties. Though ignored by students of Civil War fiction because of its archaic style, blatant racism, and Wood's own politics, *Fort Lafayette* should be recognized as an important primary source for the study of the Peace Democrats.

E. C. Murdock

573. Neely, Mark E., Jr. LINCOLN AND THE MEXICAN WAR: AN ARGUMENT BY ANALOGY. *Civil War Hist. 1978 24(1): 5-24.* Gives an historiographical analysis of Abraham Lincoln's opposition to the Mexican War. Compares Albert Beveridge's ideas in *Abraham Lincoln, 1809-1858* (1928): that Lincoln, an inexperienced politician, was overwhelmed by experienced eastern Whigs, forgot the expansionist sentiments of his Illinois constituents, and opposed the war, with G. S. Boritt's contention that Lincoln's antiwar sentiments stemmed from moral grounds, and were not disputed by his constituents. Analyzes the inconsistencies in the records of Lincoln's stand on the war, and concludes that Lincoln's position on the war reflected that of the Whig Party, and "he picked his way through the political solutions to the Mexican War with a politician's care." S

574. Nelsen, Clair E. HERBERT HOOVER, REPUBLICAN. *Centennial R. 1973 17(1): 41-63.* Herbert Clark Hoover's political collapse was due largely to his relationship with the Republican party. His failure to affiliate with the Republicans until 1920 and his liberal and internationalist stance affronted the "Old Guard," who opposed his selection as secretary of commerce in 1921. Although Hoover was head of the Republican party after winning the 1928 presidential nomination, he did not become part of it. As president, he often diverged from Republican policy and lost congressional support. Hoover's efforts at governmental intervention during the Depression made him a "transitional figure in American politics between the old and the new ideas of government." He had been elected to maintain the status quo and his failure was "the party's excuse for repudiating him in 1932." 40 notes. A. R. Stoesen

575. Nelson, Larry E. BLACK LEADERS AND THE PRESIDENTIAL ELECTION OF 1864. *J. of Negro Hist. 1978 63(1): 42-58.* The presidential campaign and election of 1864 was marked by political campaigning by Afro-American leaders. Although generally denied the vote, they spoke publicly to the

central issue of the campaign: the fate of black people after the Civil War. Although the Republican Party received support as the lesser of two racist evils, the political culture of Afro-Americans had its beginnings in the election of 1864. Based on periodical literature of 1864 and secondary material; 88 notes.

N. G. Sapper

576. Niswonger, Richard L.   ARKANSAS AND THE ELECTION OF 1896. *Arkansas Hist. Q. 1975 34(1): 41-78.* Arkansas Democratic Party politics during 1893-96 reflected changes in the national party. Arkansans joined other Southern and Western states against President Cleveland and for free silver. Silverite Daniel Jones gained the party's gubernatorial nomination in 1896, and conservative bimetallite Senator James K. Jones won re-election. Senator Jones, prominent in national party politics, played significant roles at the Populist fusion convention at the 1896 Chicago convention which nominated William Jennings Bryan. Based on private papers, newspapers, published documents, and secondary works; 2 illus., 91 notes.

T. L. Savitt

577. Noah, Elmer, II.   POLITICS AND RECONSTRUCTION IN MORE-HOUSE PARISH, 1872-1877.   *North Louisiana Hist. Assoc. J. 1975 7(1): 12-19.* In the 1870's, most of the political conflicts in Morehouse Parish occurred between "factions of the resurgent Democratic Party and the declining Republican Party." During the political campaigns of 1874, for example, several teachers were forced to leave the parish. Then, during the hotly contested election of 1876, assaults were "committed by Democrats on Republicans . . . by Republicans on Democrats, Republicans on Republicans, and by parish officials on freedmen." Although most of the people of the parish felt that the voting in November was peaceful and constituted a valid election, most of the votes, which were for Samuel Tilden, were rejected by the State Returning Board "on the grounds of intimidation of voters." A later investigation by a House Committee concluded the returns had been rejected because of "a predetermined plan" and that there had been little intimidation of voters. "But it would be many years before the region would recover" from the effects of "the black period of Reconstruction." Photo, 36 notes.

A. N. Garland

578. O'Brien, Patrick G.   SENATOR JOHN J. BLAINE: AN INDEPENDENT PROGRESSIVE DURING "NORMALCY."   *Wisconsin Mag. of Hist. 1976 60(1): 25-41.* Analyzes John J. Blaine's record as Senator 1927-33 and concludes that he was an insurgent Republican whose progressivism, as reflected in key Congressional votes, was exceeded only by a few Republicans during his single term in office. Some of the major issues which reflected Blaine's stand included his repudiation of Hoover for President, his opposition to the Republican party's choice for president pro tempore of the Senate and for committee assignments, his defense of civil liberties and opposition to the Ku Klux Klan, his support for an excess-profits tax to end privilege and redistribute income, and his opposition to "dollar diplomacy" which he saw as the policy of imperialism and colonialism. 10 illus., 78 notes.

N. C. Burckel

579. Oder, Broeck N.   ANDREW JOHNSON AND THE 1866 ILLINOIS ELECTION.   *J. of the Illinois State Hist. Soc. 1980 73(3): 189-200.* President Andrew Johnson and the 36th Congress disagreed over Reconstruction. Johnson supported rapid readmission of the ex-Confederate states. The Republican Con-

gress favored a more gradual policy. With the congressional elections of 1866 only a few months away, Johnson made a speaking tour of the United States in order to create a Democratic Congress that would favor his policy. This article discusses his tour of Illinois and the probable effects of his tour in voting in that state. Though he may have inspired increased voting by his tour, he did not influence the voter's minds as he had hoped. Based on archival material and other primary sources; 3 tables, 27 notes. J. Powell

580. Olsen, Otto H. NORTH CAROLINA: AN INCONGRUOUS PRESENCE. Olsen, Otto H., ed. *Reconstruction and Redemption in the South* (Baton Rouge: Louisiana State U. Pr., 1980): 156-197. Reviews Reconstruction in North Carolina. That the state had experienced complicated politics and division of mood before the war would color the postwar period. The Republican Party experienced some initial success, but was rent with the ineptness and factionalism which weakened it in other states. The Conservatives were clever, exploiting opportunities as they arose without contesting the basic Republican Reconstruction objectives. Behind the state's many faces was strong unity on issues central to Reconstruction; without the use of federal military power the unregenerate southerner was destined to prevail. Reconstruction policy had no force behind it and no support within the state. 46 notes. V. L. Human

581. Palermo, Patrick F. THE MIDWESTERN REPUBLICAN TRADITION: FROM PARTY TO INSURGENCY. *Capitol Studies 1977 5(1): 43-56.* Midwestern Progressivism, 1900-12, in the Republican Party (led primarily by Albert Beveridge, William Borah, Victor Murdock, George Norris, and Robert LaFollette) was a movement toward preservation of political order threatened by growing urban-industrialism.

582. Palmer, Bruce. AMERICAN HISTORY'S HARDY PERENNIAL: POPULISM FROM THE 1970S. *Am. Q. 1978 30(4): 557-566.* Review article prompted by Stanley Parson's *The Populist Context: Rural Versus Urban Power on a Great Plains Frontier* (Westport, Conn.: Greenwood Pr., 1973), Peter H. Argersinger's *Populism and Politics: William Alfred Peffer and the People's Party* (Lexington: U. Pr. of Kentucky, 1974), James M. Youngdale's *Populism: A Psychohistorical Perspective* (Port Washington, N.Y.: Kennikat Pr., 1975), and Lawrence Goodwyn's *Democratic Promise: The Populist Moment in America* (New York: Oxford U. Pr., 1976). These works attempt to provide an understanding of the Populist idea which gave rise to the short-lived party during the 1890's, but whose concepts still continue. The Populists were unwilling to exchange democratic beliefs for prosperity, but one must also closely examine the society to which they were responding. R. V. Ritter

583. Palmer, Bruce. THE ROOTS OF REFORM: SOUTHERN POPULISTS AND THEIR SOUTHERN HISTORY. *Red River Valley Hist. Rev. 1979 4(2): 33-62.* Traces Populism in the American South between the 1850's and the 1890's, and discusses the southern Populists' view of the history of the South.

584. Palmer, Bruce. SOUTHERN POPULISTS REMEMBER: THE REFORM ALTERNATIVE TO SOUTHERN SECTIONALISM. *Southern Studies 1978 17(2): 131-149.* Southern Populists of the late 19th century looked upon the antebellum South with neither nostalgia for the Old South nor admira-

tion for the industrialization of the New South. They were hostile to any form of aristocracy, opposed sectionalism, were ant1monopoly and pro-Greenback, and were concerned with the effects of black slavery on white labor. They viewed the Civil War as necessary to destroy slavery and criticized their own period of the 1890's for enslaving blacks and whites in the new industrialization. The Civil War was an unfortunate tragedy best forgotten, not glorified. The disappearance of the Populist Party after 1896 removed the last viable political opposition to the Democratic solid South. Based on Southern newspapers and secondary sources; 72 notes.   J. Buschen

585.   Palsson, Mary Dale.   THE ARIZONA CONSTITUTIONAL CON-VENTION OF 1910: THE ELECTION OF DELEGATES IN PIMA COUNTY.   *Arizona and the West 1974 16(2): 111-124.* Heated debates over progressive issues attended the county election campaigns to choose delegates to a constitutional convention for the new state of Arizona. In Pima County, how-ever, these issues remained in the background. Political debate, as reported in the newspapers, was concerned with Republican bossism, corporation control, and the Enabling Act. The county elected Republican delegates, five of the 11 from the entire territory. Reform as an issue throughout the territory on the eve of statehood needs reexamination. 4 illus., 28 notes.   D. L. Smith

586.   Parker, James R.   PATERNALISM AND RACISM: SENATOR JOHN C. SPOONER AND AMERICAN MINORITIES, 1897-1907.   *Wisconsin Mag. of Hist. 1974 57(3): 195-200.* Although conservative Republican Senator John Coit Spooner of Wisconsin posed as a champion of civil rights, and his biographer has characterized him as such, the author draws a different conclu-sion. Spooner was first a Republican politician and then a defender of civil liberties, as his defense of President Theodore Roosevelt's action in the Browns-ville incident illustrated. His attitude toward Indians and Mexican Americans was even less enlightened than toward blacks. On the issue of minority rights Spooner often had the power to affect policy, but he seldom moved beyond rhetoric to positive action. 2 illus., 40 notes.   N. C. Burckel

587.   Petersen, Peter L.   STOPPING AL SMITH: THE 1928 DEMOCRATIC PRIMARY IN SOUTH DAKOTA.   *South Dakota Hist. 1974 4(4): 439-454.* Rural "dry" Democrats failed to defeat Al Smith's nomination in 1928 in the first primary of the year. Although Smith won by less than 2,000 votes, opposition among Democrats nationwide melted away after the attempt in South Dakota. The attempt failed owing to the well-established Smith campaign, the reluctance of Thomas Walsh of Montana to announce his candidacy, and the ascendency of the urban East. Internally, South Dakota Democrats patched up differences to reelect the state's first Democratic governor. 3 photos.   A. J. Larson

588.   Pickens, Donald K.   THE HISTORICAL IMAGES IN REPUBLICAN CAMPAIGN SONGS, 1860-1900.   *J. of Popular Culture 1981 15(3): 165-174.* Seen by politicians as encouraging voting participation, Republican campaign songs were basically shaped by the Civil War. Although growing urbanization would alter their content, they continued to maintain and sustain the perspectives of localism, limited government, and racism. Based on songbooks in the Music Collection, Library of Congress; 64 notes.   D. G. Nielson

589.   Pleasants, Julian M.   "BUNCOMBE BOB" AND RED RUSSIAN FISH EGGS: THE SENATORIAL ELECTION OF 1932 IN NORTH CAROLINA. *Appalachian J. 1976 4(1): 51-62.* Discusses the political campaigns of Robert R. Reynolds, Cameron Morrison, Franklin D. Grist, and Thomas C. Bowie in the Democratic Party primaries for the 1932 senatorial election in North Carolina.

590.   Polakoff, Keith Ian.   DEMOCRATIC FACTIONALISM IN CALIFORNIA AND TEXAS, 1880-1920. *Rev. in Am. Hist. 1974 2(4): 535-540.* Review essay which describes the contents and major conclusions of R. Hal Williams' *The Democratic Party and California Politics, 1880-1896* (Stanford, Calif.: Stanford U. Pr., 1973) and Lewis L. Gould's *Progressives and Prohibitionists: Texas Democrats in the Wilson Era* (Austin: U. of Texas Pr., 1973), and assesses the books' contributions to understanding some of the political and ethnocultural issues during 1880-1919.

591.   Porter, David L.   ATTITUDES OF THE GEORGIA PRESS IN THE PRESIDENTIAL ELECTION OF 1860. *Georgia Hist. Q. 1975 59(Supplement): 127-133.* Discusses the divided loyalties of 17 Georgia newspapers in the 1860 presidential election, emphasizing support of Kentucky Democrat John Breckinridge.

592.   Powell, Lawrence N.   REJECTED REPUBLICAN INCUMBENTS IN THE 1866 CONGRESSIONAL NOMINATING CONVENTIONS: A STUDY IN RECONSTRUCTION POLITICS. *Civil War Hist. 1973 19(3): 218-237.* Analyzes the failure to renominate Republican congressional incumbents in 1866. Tests the validity of the theory that Republican congressmen who backed President Andrew Johnson in his fight with Congress were retired by their own party as punishment. Concludes that Reconstruction politics played a minor role in all but one instance. Local issues, party jealousies, and rotating rules better explain the fate of the defeated. E. C. Murdock

593.   Powers, Joseph P.   "YOURS VERY TRULY, THOS. T. CRITTENDEN": A MISSOURI DEMOCRAT'S OBSERVATIONS OF THE ELECTIONS OF 1896. *Missouri Hist. R. 1974 68(2): 186-203.* Presents the views of Thomas T. Crittenden, Democratic congressman, governor of Missouri, and diplomat, during the "free silver" election in 1896. Crittenden, a supporter of free silver until he observed the weakness of Mexico's silver-based economy, expressed concern when the Democratic Party divided on the issue and urged moderation in order to face the strong Republican force. When the party selected William Jennings Bryan as presidential candidate on a pro-silver platform, Crittenden was torn between his monetary views and party loyalty, but chose to support his party. His published report on Mexico's economic affairs was censored by the US government, and Crittenden became an unwilling martyr of the free silver cause. Based on contemporary newspaper reports, Missouri and US government documents, primary and secondary sources; 9 illus., 46 notes. N. J. Street

594.   Poyo, Gerald E.   CUBAN REVOLUTIONARIES AND MONROE COUNTY RECONSTRUCTION POLITICS, 1868-1876. *Florida Hist. Q. 1977 55(4): 407-422.* Cubans exerted considerable influence in the politics and economy of Monroe County from 1868, when they began immigrating to Florida. Initially Cubans voted Republican in hopes of aiding the independence cause in

Cuba. When the United States showed no interest in becoming involved in the insurrection, Cubans turned to more direct radical involvement in Cuban politics. Cubans continued to influence Monroe County politics after 1876. 7 illus., 42 notes.   P. A. Beaber

595.   Press, Donald E.   KANSAS CONFLICT: POPULIST VERSUS RAIL-ROADER IN THE 1890'S.   *Kansas Hist. Q. 1977 43(3): 319-333.* In the 1890's, Kansas Populists alarmed railroaders by calling for maximum freight rates and state ownership of the railroads. In 1896 they won control of the governorship and both houses of the legislature, but were able to agree on railroad legislation only at a last-minute session after their defeat in 1898. At this time they created the Court of Visitation, with broad regulatory powers, which was declared unconstitutional two years later by the Republican-controlled state supreme court. Many of the measures that the Populists advocated but failed to implement in the 1890's, including a maximum freight rate, became law under the Republicans in the succeeding decade. Based on proceedings of the Kansas legislature, contemporary publications (especially *Railway Age),* and secondary sources; 2 illus., 3 tables, 42 notes.   L. W. Van Wyk

596.   Pruitt, Paul, Jr.   A CHANGING OF THE GUARD: JOSEPH C. MANNING AND POPULIST STRATEGY IN THE FALL OF 1894.   *Alabama Hist. Q. 1978 40(1-2): 20-36.* Details the attempt of Joseph C. Manning, 1892-96, to unite Populists against the Jeffersonian Democratic machine in Alabama. 80 notes.   E. E. Eminhizer

597.   Pusateri, C. Joseph.   RURAL-URBAN TENSIONS AND THE BOURBON DEMOCRAT: THE MISSOURI CASE.   *Missouri Hist. R. 1975 69(3): 282-298.* Republican victories in 1894 have been attributed to the depression of 1893, the inept response to it by Grover Cleveland, and the conservative (Bourbon) wing of the Democratic Party. The Bourbons have been regarded as businessmen, conservative in outlook, dedicated to laissez faire, and at odds with the rural wing of their party. This study of Governor David R. Francis and the Missouri Bourbons shows that they were consistently moderate and conciliatory toward the rural wing. However, they found it impossible to maintain the rural-urban alliance in the face of the farmers' desire to push the silver issue. Based on primary and secondary sources; illus., 44 notes.   W. F. Zornow

598.   Rabinowitz, Howard N.   FROM RECONSTRUCTION TO REDEMPTION ON THE URBAN SOUTH.   *J. of Urban Hist. 1976 2(2): 169-194.* Discusses the rise, operation, and fall of Republican Party government in Southern cities during 1865-75. Primary and secondary sources; 80 notes.
                                                                                    T. W. Smith

599.   Rable, George C.   SOUTHERN INTERESTS AND THE ELECTION OF 1876: A REAPPRAISAL.   *Civil War Hist. 1980 26(4): 347-361.* Southerners, especially in Louisiana and South Carolina, were far more interested in the election of Democratic governors in 1876 (Francis J. Nicholls and Wade Hampton respectively) than in who became president. They saw Samuel J. Tilden as a weak character and refused to fight to have him elected. They were willing to accept Rutherford B. Hayes as president, if they could oust the Republican governors from their states. Based on correspondence and other sources; 31 notes.
                                                                                    G. R. Schroeder

600. Rhodes, Benjamin D. HERBERT HOOVER AND THE WAR DEBTS, 1919-33. *Prologue 1974 6(2): 130-144.* Settlement of World War I war debts devolved early about the person of Herbert Hoover who originally favored a conciliatory approach, but was forced by political considerations to reverse his course. Election to the presidency and the coming of the Great Depression again caused Hoover's reversion to the soft-line position, with opposition in Congress remaining adamant. Hoover further failed to win over president-elect Roosevelt to his viewpoint, which represented the end of the line for his program. 46 notes.
V. L. Human

601. Roberts, George C. WOODROW WILSON, JOHN W. KERN AND THE 1916 INDIANA ELECTION: DEFEAT OF A SENATE MAJORITY LEADER. *Presidential Studies Q. 1980 10(1): 63-73.* Overall Democratic Party relations between Woodrow Wilson and his first Senate leader warrant more extensive examination; John W. Kern, the personification of social justice, backed up Wilson's legislative program. The 1916 Indiana election, with Wilson and Kern electoral partners, clearly illuminates their relationship. It also indicates why Kern lost his bid for reelection. 77 notes.
G. E. Pergl

602. Roberts, Susan Ann. THE POLITICAL TRIALS OF CARL C. MAGEE. *New Mexico Hist. R. 1975 50(4): 291-311.* Carl C. Magee was an Albuquerque newspaper editor who was a defendant in one of the most unusual political trials in New Mexico history. This trial occurred during June 1923-July 1924. The trial of Magee revealed the willingness of some Republican leaders to use the courts as political weapons. The judge sentenced Magee to 360 days in jail and fined him and the Magee Publishing Company $4,050. Almost immediately Governor James F. Hinkle gave Magee a full pardon. The Magee trial revealed the bitterness of New Mexico politics. Based primarily on newspaper articles.
J. H. Krenkel

603. Robinson, Armstead L. EXPLAINING THE FAILURE OF DEMO-CRATIC REFORM IN RECONSTRUCTION SOUTH CAROLINA. *Rev. in Am. Hist. 1980 8(4): 521-530.* Review essay of Thomas Holt's *Black Over White: Negro Political Leadership in South Carolina during Reconstruction* (Urbana: U. of Illinois Pr., 1977); 1865-77.

604. Robinson, John W. COLONEL EDWARD J. C. KEWEN: LOS AN-GELES' FIRE-EATING ORATOR OF THE CIVIL WAR ERA. *Southern California Q. 1979 61(2): 159-181.* Edward J. C. Kewen (1825-1879), was a prominent southern California attorney noted for his oratory and support of the Democratic Party in the Civil War era. Born in Mississippi, Kewen came to California in 1849. During the 1850's he participated in William Walker's filibustering adventures in Nicaragua. Initially a Whig, Kewen became an active Democrat when he returned to California and took up residence in the Los Angeles area, buying for his home a mill now well known as El Molino Viejo. A defender of southern rights, Kewen was an outspoken supporter of the Democratic party and a strong critic of the Lincoln Administration. During the Civil War he held several political posts, including state assemblyman, but he was also briefly detained on charges of treasonable activity. Hot-tempered in personality, he fought several gun duels. His last effort at politics was for Congress in 1872, but by then fiery oratory was out of style, and he lost the election. His funeral in 1879

was attended by many prominent Los Angeles citizens. Primary and secondary sources; photos, 76 notes.

A. Hoffman

605. Rodabaugh, Karl. CONGRESSMAN HENRY D. CLAYTON, PATRIARCH IN POLITICS: A SOUTHERN CONGRESSMAN DURING THE PROGRESSIVE ERA. *Alabama Rev. 1978 31(2): 110-120.* As Democratic Congressman from Alabama during 1897-1914, Henry D. Clayton managed to retain his posture as "Patriarch of his people, not the Tribune of his constituents." His inherited sense of family leadership and noblesse oblige, his careful dispensation of patronage, and his selected culling of federal largesse successfully offset the extension of civil service regulations, broadening of the franchise, and heightened local competition. Primary and secondary sources; 14 notes.

J. F. Vivian

606. Rodabaugh, Karl. CONGRESSMAN HENRY D. CLAYTON AND THE DOTHAN POST OFFICE FIGHT: PATRONAGE AND POLITICS IN THE PROGRESSIVE ERA. *Alabama Rev. 1980 33(2): 125-149.* Examines the spoils system at the local political level through the reform of civil service, and the administrations of William Howard Taft and Woodrow Wilson in order to shed light on the removal of Byron Trammell Dothan, Alabama's postmaster. Trammell had supported Theodore Roosevelt at the 1912 Republican National Convention. Despite the influence of Alabama Congressman Henry D. Clayton, Taft removed Trammell from office, and the spoils systems claimed another victim. Primary sources; 41 notes.

J. Powell

607. Rodabaugh, Karl. THE DOTHAN POST OFFICE FIGHT: A CASE STUDY OF THE CONFLICT OF LOCAL AND TRANSLOCAL FORCES DURING THE PROGRESSIVE ERA. *Southern Studies 1980 19(1): 65-80.* Conflicts between local interests and the centralized, bureaucratized national government have always existed in American politics. The struggle over the appointment of a new postmaster for Dothan, Alabama in 1912, affords one example. Two local Democratic factions attempted to impose candidates. The conflict between local and translocal forces largely determined members' group allegiances in state and national politics. Based on Judy Henry DeLamar Clayton Papers in the University of Alabama Library and newspaper accounts; 35 notes.

J. J. Buschen

608. Rodabaugh, Karl. "KOLBITES" VERSUS BOURBONS: THE ALABAMA GUBERNATORIAL ELECTION OF 1892. *Alabama Hist. Q. 1975 37(4): 275-321.* The election of 1892 saw Democrat Thomas Goode Jones defeating Reuben F. Kolb. The campaign saw agriculture opposing industry. The election also indicated something of the Farmers' Alliance involvement in politics. 102 notes.

E. E. Eminhizer

609. Rodabaugh, Karl. THE ALLIANCE IN POLITICS: THE ALABAMA GUBERNATORIAL ELECTION OF 1891. *Alabama Hist. Q. 1974 36(1): 54-80.* The Farmers' Alliance in Alabama had by 1889 become convinced that the Democratic Party was going to do nothing to promote their ends. At their convention in 1889 Commissioner of Agriculture Reuben F. Kolb, their choice for Democratic nominee as governor, suggested that a list of grievances of farmers be adopted. Those in control of the Democratic Party attempted to bring the race

question into the debate to weaken Kolb's support, and tension over racial issues and declining farm prices grew. Although Kolb was the only announced candidate, opposition to him was strong, and the settlement of contested delegates at the Democratic convention went to Thomas G. Jones, who was nominated. The hope of the Alliance went down with the nomination of Jones, who won the election.   E. E. Eminhizer

610. Rogers, William Warren. THE BOYD INCIDENT: BLACK BELT VIOLENCE DURING RECONSTRUCTION. *Civil War Hist. 1975 21(4): 309-329.* Discusses the murder, in rural Alabama, of Republican county prosecutor Alexander Boyd during March 1870, by 30 members of the Ku Klux Klan and examines the political ramifications of the killing. Along with other acts of violence, murder, and intimidation, this event helped the Democrats regain political control of several Black Belt Alabama counties in the fall elections of 1870.
                                                                                                    E. C. Murdock

611. Rogers, William Warren. POLITICS AS ART: "THE CONQUERED ROOSTER." *Alabama Hist. Q. 1978 40(3-4): 169-172.* Reprints, from the Republican newspaper the *Alabama State Journal,* 11 November 1868, the anonymous satirical poem, "The Conquered Rooster," modeled on Father Abram Joseph Ryan's pro-Confederate lament of 1865, "The Conquered Banner." The 1868 satire exulted over the Democrats' defeat in the recent presidential election, lampooned Montgomery Democratic editor Joseph Hodgson, and taunted southern romanticism.   S

612. Russell, Marvin F. THE RISE OF A REPUBLICAN LEADER: HARMON L. REMMEL. *Arkansas Hist. Q. 1977 36(3): 234-257.* Harmon L. Remmel (1852-1927) was a follower of Arkansas Republican Powell Clayton and eventually succeeded him to the state party leadership in 1913. During his rise to power, Remmel ran for governor three times (1894, 1896, and 1900, all unsuccessfully), served in many party offices and appointive state positions, was involved with patronage, and dealt with state party factions and the Republican Party's relationship with Theodore Roosevelt. Primary and secondary sources; illus., 127 notes.   G. R. Schroeder

613. Salisbury, Robert H. and MacKuen, Michael. ON THE STUDY OF PARTY REALIGNMENT. *J. of Pol. 1981 43(2): 523-530.* Party realignment has traditionally been interpreted as the conversion of voters from one party to another, ignoring the increase in the voting population. From 1860 to 1900, the adult, white, male population increased from seven to 20 million, with an average increase of one million voters in each presidential election. In the election of 1896, Republican efforts to suppress nativism enabled the party to attract British, Scandinavian, and some German immigrants. After 1890, immigration from these regions decreased while immigration from southern and eastern Europe increased. Some of the decline in voting after 1896 may be explained by the disinterest of professional, urban party organizations in mobilizing these new immigrant groups. 16 notes.   A. W. Novitsky

614. Sarasohn, David. THE ELECTION OF 1916: REALIGNING THE ROCKIES. *Western Hist. Q. 1980 11(3): 285-305.* Woodrow Wilson's electoral victory in the election of 1916 is traditionally explained as a consequence of the

split in the Republican Party and of the unique wartime circumstances. Outside the Old South, Wilson and the Democratic Party gained their most sweeping victories in the eight Rocky Mountain states. The conventional explanations are not satisfactory for the mountain states. Here the voters saw fundamental long-range issues at stake and responded emphatically; they remained in the Democratic ranks throughout the 1920's. 6 tables, 34 notes.   D. L. Smith

615.   Sarasohn, David.   THE INSURGENT REPUBLICANS: INSURGENT IMAGE AND REPUBLICAN REALITY.   *Social Sci. Hist. 1979 3(3-4): 245-261.* Insurgent Republicans of the Taft era have a generally good image among historians. Democrats of the same period do not. Finds little difference in their actual positions. Democrats consistently supported progressive-insurgent causes. Contemporary image-makers, however, misled later historians by making sharp distinctions between the positions and effectiveness of insurgents and Democrats. Based on primary sources in the Library of Congress; 3 notes.
                                                                L. K. Blaser

616.   Schewel, Michael J.   LOCAL POLITICS IN LYNCHBURG, VIRGINIA, IN THE 1880'S.   *Virginia Mag. of Hist. and Biog. 1981 89(2): 170-180.* Narrates attempt of populist groups to gain control of local government and use it for purposes more egalitarian than practiced by dominant conservative Democrats. Using the names Regulators, Coalitionists, and Republicans, biracial working-class voters achieved a narrow success in the mid-1880's in controlling the city council by subsuming themselves within the Knights of Labor. Their biggest success was building a public school for black children. City expenses overall increased only marginally while the coalition was in power. After the national failure of the Knights, racial animosity split the ranks and the Democrats returned to power. The principle cause of division was competition for jobs in the local tobacco industry, which in prosperity had brought liberally inclined voters to Lynchburg, but was now in decline. Based primarily on local newspapers of the period and secondary sources; 32 notes.   P. J. Woehrmann

617.   Schlup, Leonard.   ADLAI E. STEVENSON AND THE SOUTHERN CAMPAIGN OF 1892.   *Q. Rev. of Hist. Studies [India] 1977-78 17(1): 7-14.* Reviews vice-presidential candidate Adlai E. Stevenson's efforts to hold the solid south for the Democratic Party during the presidential election of 1892. Farm economics were unfavorable; southern states threatened to go for the Populist candidate. Stevenson campaigned in North Carolina and Virginia, and when he was finished, victory was assured. He was successful because: 1) his family was from the south, 2) Republicans and Populists refused to merge, 3) the Populists nominated a northerner repugnant to the south, and 4) he played heavily on the racial issue to overcome economic fears. Ref.   V. L. Human

618.   Schlup, Leonard.   ADLAI E. STEVENSON AND THE 1900 CAMPAIGN IN DELAWARE.   *Delaware Hist. 1977 17(3): 191-198.* As the vice-presidential candidate on the William Jennings Bryan ticket in 1900, Adlai Stevenson of Illinois played the role of party accommodator, trying to win over conservative Democrats to Bryan. In mid-October, 1900, he made several significant speeches in Delaware, focusing on foreign policy, and ignoring local issues such as the John Addicks controversy in Delaware. Argues that Stevenson was anti-expansionist and, in many ways, backward in his conception of American

foreign policy. Although his speeches were well attended, the Democrats did not carry the state. 17 notes.

R. M. Miller

619. Schlup, Leonard. ADLAI E. STEVENSON AND THE 1892 CAMPAIGN IN VIRGINIA. *Virginia Mag. of Hist. and Biog. 1978 86(3): 345-354.* Democratic Vice-Presidential nominee Adlai E. Stevenson campaigned vigorously in Virginia during the 1892 campaign. His efforts headed off a serious threat by the Populist Party and helped carry the state for the Democratic Party. Based on manuscript material, newspapers, and secondary accounts; 26 notes.

R. F. Oaks

620. Schlup, Leonard. ADLAI E. STEVENSON AND THE PRESIDENTIAL ELECTION OF 1896. *Social Sci. J. 1977 14(2): 117-128.* Examines the unifying role which Adlai E. Stevenson had on the Democratic Party in the presidential election of 1896, including the stand which he took on the otherwise confusing currency issue.

621. Schlup, Leonard. ADLAI E. STEVENSON AND THE 1892 CAMPAIGN IN ALABAMA. *Alabama R. 1976 29(1): 3-15.* Vice-presidential nominee Adlai E. Stevenson was instrumental in preserving the Democratic majority in the South in 1892. He spent two months campaigning in five southern states, including Alabama. His speeches consistently portrayed the Federal Elections Bill (1890), although twice defeated, as indicative of the direct threat that awaited regional interests should the Republicans recapture the White House. Stevenson's efforts successfully neutralized the Populist challenge. Primary and secondary sources; 22 notes.

J. F. Vivian

622. Schlup, Leonard. ADLAI E. STEVENSON AND THE PRESIDENTIAL CAMPAIGN OF 1900. *Filson Club Hist. Q. 1979 53(2): 196-208.* Adlai E. Stevenson won the Democratic vice-presidential nomination in 1900 despite little organized efforts on his behalf. As Grover Cleveland's Vice-President from 1893 to 1897, Stevenson had become identified with the conservative wing of the party. At the same time, he was a moderate supporter of increased silver money. Thus, he was acceptable to the reform Democrats and presidential candidate William Jennings Bryan. Based on the Stevenson, Bryan, and Carter Harrison Papers; 34 notes.

G. B. McKinney

623. Schlup, Leonard. ALTON B. PARKER AND THE PRESIDENTIAL CAMPAIGN OF 1904. *North Dakota Q. 1981 49(1): 48-60.* Brief biography of Democratic Party presidential nominee in 1904, Alton Brooks Parker (1852-1926), focusing on his political career, particularly the circumstances surrounding his defeat by Teddy Roosevelt.

624. Schlup, Leonard. BRYAN'S PARTNER: ARTHUR SEWALL AND THE CAMPAIGN OF 1896. *Maine Hist. Soc. Q. 1977 16(4): 189-211.* Describes the role played by Arthur Sewall, wealthy ship-builder from Bath, Maine, as the vice-presidential nominee on the Democratic ticket in 1896. Sewall's selection by the Democratic Party was doubly unwise since Sewall was unknown nationally, and Maine, with few electors, constituted no power base. 60 notes.

P. C. Marshall

625. Schlup, Leonard.   CHARLES A. TOWNE AND THE VICE-PRESI-
DENTIAL QUESTION OF 1900.   *North Dakota Hist. 1977 44(1): 14-20.*
Charles A. Towne of Minnesota was an ardent silverite and William Jennings
Bryan's own choice for running mate on the Democratic ticket in 1900. Following
the Populists' nomination of Bryan for President and Towne for Vice President,
the Democrats were pressured by their Free Silver wing to adopt the same ticket.
Counterpressures from the Eastern wing of the Party and more conservative
factions prevailed. Towne's supporters lost to those of Adlai E. Stevenson at the
Democratic National Convention. Towne nevertheless campaigned hard for the
ticket and probably would have been offered a cabinet position had Bryan won
the election.   N. Lederer

626. Schlup, Leonard.   COE I. CRAWFORD AND THE PROGRESSIVE
CAMPAIGN OF 1912.   *South Dakota Hist. 1979 9(2): 116-130.* Coe Isaac
Crawford (1858-1944), elected successively as a Republican Governor and Sena-
tor between 1907 and 1915, was the founder of the progressive movement in
South Dakota. During the Republican Party split in 1912 Crawford supported
Theodore Roosevelt while officially remaining within the Republican Party and
used his influence to aid the cause of reform. When Roosevelt carried South
Dakota by 10,000 votes, Crawford saw the results as a progressive victory.
Although defeated by the Republican stalwarts in the 1914 senatorial primary,
Crawford left behind a legacy of progressive reform in South Dakota. Primary
sources; 3 illus., 5 photos, 29 notes.   P. L. McLaughlin

627. Schlup, Leonard.   DEMOCRATIC TALLEYRAND: ADLAI STE-
VENSON AND POLITICS IN THE GILDED AGE AND PROGRESSIVE
ERA.   *South Atlantic Q. 1979 78(3): 182-194.* Adlai Stevenson (1835-1914), 23d
Vice President, has been largely neglected by historians; yet in his day he was
considered a very shrewd politician. He has remained an enigma largely because
his political letters have not been found. Cites 16 of his letters, which bring to
light certain of his characteristics. They were written during 1876-1908 and
disclose his reactions to various events, the support he sought or gave, his concern
over political developments, and his determination to serve the Democratic Party.
A faithful party member, he was no maverick. He served as a transitional figure
between the conservative tradition of Democracy under Cleveland to the progressive brand under Bryan and Wilson. But his most lasting contribution was the
founding of an American political dynasty. Based on Stevenson's correspondence
located in scattered collections; 30 notes.   H. M. Parker, Jr.

628. Schlup, Leonard.   GROVER CLEVELAND AND HIS 1892 RUN-
NING MATE.   *Studies in Hist. and Society 1977 2(1-2): 60-74.* Discusses the
political activity of Adlai Ewing Stevenson during 1888-92, particularly his role
in Grover Cleveland's 1892 presidential campaign. Stevenson was selected as
Cleveland's running mate, and was a moderate force who represented Democratic
Party liberals. Coming from Illinois, Stevenson attracted votes from the Midwest;
Cleveland was from the East. Stevenson was on very cordial terms with Cleveland, who had nominated him for a judgeship in 1889 before leaving office during
his first presidential term. Stevenson's campaigning in the South was extremely
important in 1892 because Populist forces were eroding the strength of the
Democrats. Discusses antecedents of the Democratic Convention, where Stevenson played an important role in nominating Cleveland, and his activity leading

up top the victory of their ticket. Stevenson's earlier support of a "soft" money policy was his only vulnerable position; he publicly modified his views to conform with the Party platform. 59 notes.

629. Schlup, Leonard. PHILOSOPHICAL CONSERVATIVE: PORTER JAMES MC CUMBER AND POLITICAL REFORM. *North Dakota Hist. 1978 45(3): 16-21.* A conservative Republican senator from North Dakota, Porter James McCumber was the product of the political machine of Alexander John McKenzie. Serving in the US Senate during 1898-1922, McCumber, despite his conservative beliefs and those of his Party, voted for such reforms as women's suffrage and the direct election of senators. He deeply believed in voting according to the desires of his constituents even if taking their position violated his own convictions. McCumber was a loyal party stalwart, supporting the "Old Guard" of the GOP during the factional battles with Theodore Roosevelt and the "Bull Moosers." He bitterly attacked Roosevelt for the latter's defection from Republican Party ranks. In his political philosophy McCumber favored gradual change in accordance with the Constitution.   N. Lederer

630. Schlup, Leonard. POLITICAL MAVERICK: SENATOR HANSBROUGH AND REPUBLICAN PARTY POLITICS, 1907-1912. *North Dakota Hist. 1978 45(4): 32-39.* During his last senatorial term, Henry Clay Hansbrough (1848-1933) broke off his previously close political relationship with Theodore Roosevelt. Believing that Roosevelt, a friend of George Perkins, was in league with the International Harvester Trust, Hansbrough turned initially toward supporting William Howard Taft and, eventually, the Democrat Woodrow Wilson. As he became more oriented toward Progressive political views, Hansbrough broke sharply with the stalwart Republican Party machine in North Dakota headed by Alexander John McKenzie. Based mainly on primary sources.   N. Lederer

631. Schlup, Leonard. RELUCTANT EXPANSIONIST: ADLAI E. STEVENSON AND THE CAMPAIGN AGAINST IMPERIALISM IN 1900. *Indiana Social Studies Q. 1976 29(1): 32-42.* Discusses foreign policy attitudes of Democratic Party Presidential and Vice-Presidential candidates William Jennings Bryan and Adlai E. Stevenson in the 1900 election, emphasizing the Philippines.

632. Schlup, Leonard. VICE-PRESIDENT STEVENSON AND THE POLITICS OF ACCOMMODATION. *J. of Pol. Sci. 1979 7(1): 30-39.* Adlai Ewing Stevenson (1835-1914), Vice-President of the United States from 1893 to 1897, based his political philosophy upon accommodation; as reformer and conformer he conciliated differences within the Democratic Party. Stevenson's most lasting contribution to American politics was in founding a political dynasty; he thrust his family onto the political stage and developed a tradition of service to the nation that has continued to the present. Based on published sources and interviews; 31 notes.   T. P. Richardson

633. Schlup, Leonard. WILLIAM LINDSAY AND THE 1896 PARTY CRISIS. *Register of the Kentucky Hist. Soc. 1978 76(1): 22-33.* William Lindsay (1835-1909), who held many political offices in Kentucky, refused to support the Democratic Party ticket headed by William Jennings Bryan in 1896 because

of the free silver issue. Instead, Senator Lindsay gave his support to the fledgling National Democratic Party (Gold Democrats) which nominated two native Kentuckians, Senator John M. Palmer and Lieutenant General Simon B. Buckner. McKinley carried Kentucky, but narrowly enough to suggest that the Gold Democrats had held the balance of power. Lindsay appeared satisfied with the results in Kentucky and the nation. Primary and secondary sources; 39 notes.
J. F. Paul

634.   Schmelzer, Janet.   THOMAS M. CAMPBELL: PROGRESSIVE GOVERNOR OF TEXAS. *Red River Valley Hist. Rev. 1978 3(4): 52-63.* Discusses reasons for the rise of Progressivism and describes the efforts of the Democratic governor of Texas (1907-11), Thomas M. Campbell, to regulate big business.

635.   Schott, Matthew J.   PROGRESSIVES AGAINST DEMOCRACY: ELECTORAL REFORM IN LOUISIANA, 1894-1921. *Louisiana Hist. 1979 20(3): 247-260.* By advocating such electoral reforms as the secret ballot, stiff requirements for voter registration, and the omission of party labels and symbols, Louisiana Progressives hoped to restrict and discourage lower-class voting. These elitist, moralistic reformers did eventually elect their leader, John M. Parker (1863-1939) to the governorship. However, in the long run they failed either to achieve their brand of electoral reform or to destroy the corrupt Regular Democrats, much of whose strength came from the New Orleans Machine and its poor, illiterate, immigrant supporters. Based on the John M. Parker Papers, Southwestern Archives, University of Southwestern Louisiana, Lafayette, and contemporary New Orleans newspapers, 28 notes.   D. B. Touchstone

636.   Schulp, Leonard S.   VILAS, STEVENSON AND DEMOCRATIC POLITICS 1884-1892. *North Dakota Q. 1976 44(1): 44-52.* The closely connected political careers of two midwestern Democrats—William Freeman Vilas of Wisconsin (1840-1908) and Adlai E. Stevenson of Illinois (1835-1914)—revolved around the political campaigns (1884 and 1892) and administrations of President Grover Cleveland.

637.   Schweninger, Loren.   ALABAMA BLACKS AND THE CONGRESSIONAL RECONSTRUCTION ACTS OF 1867. *Alabama Rev. 1978 31(3): 182-198.* The Reconstruction Acts prompted Alabama blacks to organize during March-October 1867 under able, moderate leadership, most of it former slaves. There was no call for retribution against whites or for forced redistribution of white lands. Republicans and Democrats alike failed to reciprocate; both parties declined to assimilate the black cause. Primary and secondary sources; 51 notes.
J. F. Vivian

638.   Schweninger, Loren.   BLACK CITIZENSHIP AND THE REPUBLICAN PARTY IN RECONSTRUCTION ALABAMA. *Alabama R. 1976 29(2): 83-103.* Throughout the Reconsturction era the Republican Party in Alabama was badly divided on the question of enfranchising the freedmen. A moderate wing defended the federal government and the 14th and 15th Amendments, while a conservative wing, led in part by Judge J. Haralson, an ex-slave, opposed the Constitution, the Grant Administration, and several federal patronage appointees. Tension and conflict plagued the party, and "doomed Alabama Reconstruction to failure from the outset." Based on primary and secondary sources; 88 notes.   J. F. Vivian

639. Shade, William G.; Hopper, Stanley D.; Jacobson, David; and Moiles, Stephen E. PARTISANSHIP IN THE UNITED STATES SENATE: 1869-1901. *J. of Interdisciplinary Hist. 1973 4(2): 185-205.* Senate partisanship in the 1890's did not differ from Senate partisanship in the earlier post-Reconstruction years. V. O. Key's theories of party cohesiveness and Angus Campbell's theory of the impact of "occasional cataclysmic events" on party groups are of more use in discussing the evolution of partisanship in the Senate from 1869-1901 than is the more generalized "organizational revolution" theory of David Rothman. 6 figs., 20 notes, appendix.

R. Howell

640. Shankman, Arnold. SOLDIER VOTES AND CLEMENT L. VAL-LANDIGHAM IN THE 1863 OHIO GUBERNATORIAL ELECTION. *Ohio Hist. 1973 82(1/2): 88-104.* Ohio's best known peace Democrat ran for governor in 1863. Until mid-September it appeared that the soldier ballots would be decisive. Using letters from troops in the field, the author illustrates the harsh feelings towards Vallandigham. The soldier vote went approximately 18-to-1 against Vallandigham. Based on primary sources; 2 illus., table, 46 notes.

S. S. Sprague

641. Shipps, Jan. THE PUBLIC IMAGE OF SEN. REED SMOOT, 1902-32. *Utah Hist. Q. 1977 45(4): 380-400.* Reed Smoot (1862-1941), Utah senator during 1903-33, was a Mormon, senator, businessman, family man, Republican, and conservative. His public image altered significantly during his three decades in the Senate. Uses the contemporary periodical press as a reasonably accurate picture of Reed Smoot's public image. The original conception of lawbreaker and libertine was displaced by the picture of a virtuous, patriotic public servant of vast influence and power. Primary and secondary sources; 6 illus., 36 notes.

J. L. Hazelton

642. Shoemaker, Raymond L. HENRY LANE WILSON AND REPUBLI-CAN POLICY TOWARD MEXICO, 1913-1920. *Indiana Mag. of Hist. 1980 76(2): 103-122.* After President Woodrow Wilson demanded his resignation as ambassador to Mexico, Henry Lane Wilson pressed for defeat of the government's foreign policy. He helped formulate the Republican Party's platform, proposing recognition of Mexico, irrespective of General Huerta's coup, in the interest of American capital and investment in Mexico. Indianan Wilson achieved this through wide correspondence with Republican leaders and a public speaking campaign during the elections of 1916 and 1920. Based on US Senate documents, newspapers, and secondary sources; photo, 68 notes. A. Erlebacher

643. Shofner, Jerrell H. ANDREW JOHNSON AND THE FERNANDINA UNIONISTS. *Prologue 1978 10(4): 211-223.* The Civil War measure levying taxes on real property in Confederate areas taken over by Union forces resulted in large-scale forced sales of land in the Fernandina area, on Amelia island, in northeastern Florida. Many freedmen and southern Unionists gained property at the expense of absentee landowners and the Florida Railroad Company. The resultant political and legal controversy over these land sales and efforts of former landowners to regain their property retarded economic growth in the area until the 1890's. The pro-Conservative Democrat actions of President Andrew Johnson affected southern Unionists who subsequently returned to the political camp of their erstwhile enemies who had supported secession. Based mainly on primary sources in the National Archives.

N. Lederer

644.   Shofner, Jerrell H.   FLORIDA: A FAILURE OF MODERATE RE-PUBLICANISM.   Olsen, Otto H., ed. *Reconstruction and Redemption in the South* (Baton Rouge: Louisiana State U. Pr., 1980): 13-46. Florida was thinly populated, had played no great role in the war, and increasingly became a haven for frontier-hunting Northerners. Covers the establishment of the moderate Reconstruction regime, the complicated political maneuvering and political infighting, the draft of a conservative constitution, the fight between liberals and radicals in the Republican Party, which finally alienated so many voters that a Democratic administration was brought to power. The new administration acted quickly to rig elections, disfranchise Negro voters, and make the state a reliable component of the solid South. 50 notes.   V. L. Human

645.   Shofner, Jerrell H.   A NEW JERSEY CARPETBAGGER IN RECONSTRUCTION FLORIDA.   *Florida Hist. Q. 1974 52(3): 286-293.* Captain George B. Carse of New Jersey became a Freedmen's Bureau agent in Leon County after the Civil War. He was involved in Republican politics after his appointment as adjutant general in 1868, siding with Governor Harrison Reed in his political conflict with Thomas W. Osborn, leader of a competing faction of Republicans. After bribery charges were laid against him in 1870, Carse resigned, returned to New Jersey, and served three terms in that state's legislature. Manuscript, newspaper and secondary sources; 20 notes.
                                                                J. E. Findling

646.   Shofner, Jerrell H.   THE WHITE SPRINGS POST OFFICE CAPER.   *Florida Hist. Q. 1978 56(3): 339-347.* The election of a Republican president in 1888 precipitated two bizarre events by a group of angry white Democrats in Hamilton County. The first was the shooting of Republican C. L. Morrison, who was to be appointed postmaster of White Springs. The assailant was Fred P. Cone, later governor of Florida (1937-41). The second incident was a post office robbery and general harassment of Morrison until most federal offices once again were assumed by Democrats after the 1892 election. Primary and newspaper sources; 15 notes.   P. A. Beaber

647.   Shook, Cynthia.   RICHARD PARKS BLAND: ALMOST A CANDIDATE.   *Missouri Hist. R. 1974 68(4): 417-436.* Discusses the involvement of Missouri congressman Richard Parks Bland (1835-99) in the Free Silver movement and the Democratic nomination in 1896. Bland led the silverites in Congress for 20 years, and all his major efforts were for this cause, including the Bland-Allison Act (1878) and opposition to the Sherman Silver Purchase Act (1890). In 1895 the silverites actively sought control of the Democratic Party and many pro-silver men endorsed Bland as their presidential candidate. A seating and platform battle between gold and silver Democrats took place at the national convention, but the silver men took control. Bland was nominated, but eventually defeated by William Jennings Bryan for numerous reasons, particularly because he did not actively take part in the campaign in his behalf. Based on contemporary newspaper reports, documents of the Democratic Party, primary and secondary sources; 5 illus., 5 photos, 42 notes.   N. J. Street

648.   Shook, Robert.   TOWARD A LIST OF RECONSTRUCTION LOYALISTS.   *Southwestern Hist. Q. 1973 76(3): 315-320.* Various surveys were made to determine qualified Unionists to fill numerous local and state offices in

post-Civil War Reconstruction in Texas. By checking these against removal and appointment orders it is possible to determine the loyalists involved in Reconstruction. A preliminary list, by counties, is given herein. A demographic analysis of such persons would shed considerable light on Republican govern.nent in Texas in 1867-69. 7 notes.   D. L. Smith

649. Shover, John L.   THE EMERGENCE OF A TWO-PARTY SYSTEM IN REPUBLICAN PHILADELPHIA, 1924-1936.   *J. of Am. Hist. 1974 60(4): 985-1002.* Samuel Lubell has popularized the thesis that Al Smith's ethnic appeal in the 1928 election foreshadowed the urban, ethnic, "New Deal coalition" that Franklin D. Roosevelt put together so effectively after 1932. The evidence for Philadelphia voting patterns demonstrates that 1928 was *not* a critical election. Some major ethnic groups did vote Democratic in that year, but Jews, blacks, and Germans were not a part of the coalition till much later, and the Irish and Italian vote, heavily Democratic for Smith in 1928, did not persist in 1930 or even 1932. Furthermore, there was no great surge of voter protest against the Depression in 1932. Casts doubt upon the concept of a "critical election," emphasizing rather the importance of a critical, fluctuating period when new voter patterns start to crystallize. 4 tables, 43 notes.   K. B. West

650. Silverman, Robert A.   NATHAN MATTHEWS: POLITICS OF REFORM IN BOSTON, 1890-1910.   *New England Q. 1977 50(4): 626-643.* Traces Nathan Matthews's (1853-1927) role in forming the Yankee-Irish alliance in the Democratic Party and his chairmanship of the Boston Finance Commission during 1907-09. Focuses on his four terms as the reform mayor of Boston during 1891-95 when he achieved his main goal of cutting expenditures through better management and established the Board of Survey which provided Boston with its first coordinated planning. Based on Matthews' correspondence and secondary sources; 42 notes.   J. C. Bradford

651. Smith, Brian Lee.   THEODORE ROOSEVELT VISITS OKLAHOMA. *Chronicles of Oklahoma 1973 51(3): 263-279.* Recounts Theodore Roosevelt's visits to Oklahoma during 1900-12, describing his relationship to the issue of Oklahoma statehood and the local Progressive Party.   S

652. Smith, Duane A.   COLORADO: BIRTH OF THE CENTENNIAL STATE.   *J. of the West 1976 15(1): 29-53.*
PART I: COLORADO'S STRUGGLE FOR STATEHOOD,   *pp. 29-38.*
    Traces the creation of Colorado Territory in 1861 and the 15-year struggle toward statehood. Premature and divisive efforts in the 1860's were followed by efforts caught between Radical Republicans and President Johnson. Finally on 3 March 1875 Congress passed enabling legislation. On 1 July 1876 the voters voted three to one for statehood.
PART II: COLORADO MINING IN 1876,   *pp. 38-53.* Surveys silver, gold, and coal mining. Covers mine safety, smelting, and taxation of mine output.
                                                                       R. Alvis

653. Smith, Gary N.   ST. LOUIS HOSTS THE POLITICAL CONVENTIONS.   *Gateway Heritage 1981 1(4): 10-17.* St. Louis hosted Democratic national nominating conventions in 1876, 1888, 1904, and 1916, as well as the national Republican convention of 1896 and a national Populist convention in the

same year. Because of easy railroad access to St. Louis, the city's elegant hotels and expansive meeting facilities, and Democratic political sensitivity to the "Solid South," the Democratic Party frequently selected St. Louis for its conclaves. 13 photos.   H. T. Lovin

654.   Snapp, Meredith A.   DEFEAT THE DEMOCRATS: THE CONGRESSIONAL UNION FOR WOMAN SUFFRAGE IN ARIZONA, 1914 AND 1916.   *J. of the West 1975 14(4): 131-139.* Discusses an attempt in 1914 and 1916 by the Congressional Union for Woman Suffrage organizers to convince women voters in Arizona (one of nine states which enfranchised women) to vote against Democratic Party candidates—the party they held responsible for inaction on the woman suffrage question. 34 notes.

655.   Sorensen, Scott and LeDoux, John.   MANUSCRIPT COLLECTIONS: THE WILLIAM LLOYD HARDING PAPERS IN THE SIOUX CITY PUBLIC MUSEUM.   *Ann. of Iowa 1981 45(7): 568-573.* Describes the William Lloyd Harding Papers. One of the most controversial figures in Iowa politics, Harding served two terms as lieutenant governor (1913-17) and two terms as governor (1917-21). His position on issues such as prohibition, "good roads," and the banning of all foreign languages during World War I often put him at odds with his fellow Republicans. The Harding Papers will be of value to students of early 20th-century Iowa political history. 2 photos.   P. L. Petersen

656.   Spence, Clark C.   THE GOVERNOR HUNTS ANOTHER JUDGE: BENJAMIN POTTS AND THE OUSTER OF JOHN MURPHY.   *Montana 1979 29(3): 41-49.* Benjamin Franklin Potts, Republican Governor of Montana Territory, sought to remove Republican Judge John L. Murphy from the territorial bench and replace him with a man who was more competent and who would strengthen the party's position in the region. Potts succeeded in 1872, but in the process split the Republican Party further, paved the way for the election of Democrat Martin Maginnis as Delegate to Congress, and revealed Potts's own powerful political connections in Washington, D.C. Murphy had replaced Judge George G. Symes, whom Potts also had pressured into leaving the Montana bench. Potts's friend Francis Servis replaced Murphy. Based on Rutherford B. Hayes and James A. Garfield presidential papers, Montana territorial papers, materials in the Montana Historical Society archives, and contemporary newspapers; 8 illus., 42 notes.   R. C. Myers

657.   Spencer, Thomas T.   THE ROOSEVELT ALL-PARTY AGRICULTURAL COMMITTEE AND THE 1936 ELECTION.   *Ann. of Iowa 1979 45(1): 44-57.* Strategists for the Democratic Party in 1936 believed that the midwestern farm belt was crucial to Franklin D. Roosevelt's reelection bid. In August 1936, the Franklin D. Roosevelt All-Party Agricultural Committee was formed. William Settle of Indiana was chairman. Other important members included Representative Marvin Jones of Texas, William Bradley of Iowa, and Paul Porter, chief of the Agricultural Adjustment Administration's press section. A study of the All-Party Agricultural Committee's activities in 1936 justifies several conclusions. First, Democratic leaders saw the farm vote as important and sought to bring farmers into the Roosevelt coalition. Second, the Committee was able to counter criticisms of New Deal agricultural policy. Finally, farmers were politically active in 1936 and many saw Roosevelt as their best hope for the future. 28 notes.   P. L. Petersen

658. Stanley, Gerald. CIVIL WAR POLITICS IN CALIFORNIA. *Southern Calif. Q. 1982 64(2): 115-132.* The Republican Party in California changed its stance from opposition to abolition before the Civil War to endorsement of the Emancipation Proclamation and condemnation of slavery by the war's end. In 1860 little difference existed between Republicans and Democrats on race and slavery issues; Republicans argued that the central issue of the Civil War was to preserve the Union. Once the war began, however, Republicans found it politically expedient to justify emancipation as a military measure, and to condemn slavery on moral grounds and to insist that slavery must be ended to win the war. By 1864 Republicans and Democrats were sharply divided on the race issue. The Republican transformation thus mirrored Republican politics on the national scene, a change deserving more attention from California historians. 57 notes.
A. Hoffman

659. Stanley, Gerald. THE SLAVERY ISSUE AND ELECTION IN CALIFORNIA, 1860. *Mid-America 1980 62(1): 35-45.* In the 1860 four-party presidential election, Republicans won 32% of the total vote. The Republican Party campaigned against the extension of slavery because it encroached upon the rights of nonslave-owning whites in the West. Furthermore, they linked slavery and race to other issues such as homesteads, railroads, and daily overland mail in a deliberate appeal to race prejudice. The Democratic Party was divided, but exploitation of the slavery and race issues was the decisive factor in the Republican victory. Notes.
M. J. Wentworth

660. Stanley, Gerald. THE WHIM AND CAPRICE OF A MAJORITY IN A PETTY STATE: THE 1867 ELECTION IN CALIFORNIA. *Pacific Hist. 1980 24(4): 443-455.* In 1867 California voted Democratic in a white backlash to congressional Reconstruction. Republican candidates and the national party had worked for full Negro suffrage. California Democrats faced the issue of the Chinese in their state, pointing out that the logical end of Republican Radicalism for them was Chinese suffrage. Thus the force of the white majority silenced those who had advocated a change in the racial status quo, and the election was carried largely by Democrats. The Republicans' ideals, however sincere and worthwhile, proved fragile when pitted against "the whim and caprice of a majority in a petty state." Based on the Haight Papers and Miscellaneous Letters, Huntington Library, San Marino; Cole Papers, UCLA; Andrew Johnson Papers, Library of Congress; *Congressional Globe,* and California newspapers of the period; 5 pictures, 34 notes.
H. M. Parker, Jr.

661. Stern, Norton B. LOS ANGELES JEWISH VOTERS DURING GRANT'S FIRST PRESIDENTIAL RACE. *Western States Jewish Hist. Q. 1981 13(2): 179-185.* During the 1868 presidential race between Republican Ulysses S. Grant and Democrat Horatio Seymour, both sides in Los Angeles tried to attract Jewish voters. Democrats reminded Jews of Grant's infamous General Order No. 11, expelling Jews, as a class, from the Department of Tennessee in 1862—supposedly for illegal cotton speculation. Republicans charged the County Board of Supervisors, mostly Democrats, of assigning higher tax assessment to the property of Jews. The election verified the Democratic affiliation of Los Angeles' Jews, who voted overwhelmingly for Seymour. Based on newspaper accounts; 34 notes.
B. S. Porter

662.   Sternsher, Bernard.   THE EMERGENCE OF THE NEW DEAL PARTY SYSTEM: A PROBLEM IN HISTORICAL ANALYSIS OF VOTER BEHAVIOR.   *J. of Interdisciplinary Hist. 1975 6(1): 127-150.* Studies recent literature dealing with the transition from the "industrialized" political system of 1894-1932 to the "New Deal" political system from 1932 on. The concept of the 1928 election as a "critical" election is criticized both as a concept and with respect to the arguments used to support the concept. The "party-systems analytical framework" is open to several reservations. 4 graphs, 62 notes.

R. Howell

663.   Stevens, Susan.   THE CONGRESSIONAL ELECTIONS OF 1930: POLITICS OF AVOIDANCE.   Plesur, Milton, ed. *An American Historian: Essays to Honor Selig Adler* (Buffalo: State U. of N.Y., 1980): 149-158. Confusion over whether the Democrats or the Republicans would constitute the majority in the House of Representatives after the election of 1930 was compounded by a Republican insurgent faction, the prohibition problem, President Herbert C. Hoover, and the country's economic state, until 1931, when Democrat John Nance Garner was elected Speaker of the House.

664.   Stratton, David H.   TWO WESTERN SENATORS AND TEAPOT DOME: THOMAS J. WALSH AND ALBERT B. FALL.   *Pacific Northwest Q. 1974 65(2): 57-65.* Both Albert B. Fall, an intensely partisan Republican, and Thomas J. Walsh, an equally partisan Democrat, were molded and shaped in frontier environments, with western ideas about conservation and public lands. However, Fall "always remained an unredeemed 19th-century exploiter," but "Walsh was a man who combined party loyalty with a strict personal morality." Moreover, Fall "viewed government as a sort of concurrent majority of special interests with himself as their minister plenipotentiary." Walsh, as chairman of the senatorial committee investigating Teapot Dome oil leases, thoroughly and relentlessly followed every shred of evidence "which finally opened up the case revealing Edward L. Doheny and Harry F. Sinclair as the source of Fall's new-found affluence." Fall became the first US cabinet member to close his career in prison, while Walsh became nationally famous. 40 notes.   R. V. Ritter

665.   Swanson, Jeffrey L.   THAT SMOKE-FILLED ROOM: A UTAHN'S ROLE IN THE 1920 GOP CONVENTION.   *Utah Hist. Q. 1977 45(4): 369-379.* Reed Smoot, (1862-1941), Utah senator during 1903-33, played a pivotal role in writing the platform and in the presidential nomination at the 1920 Republican Party Convention. As a member of the platform subcommittee, he submitted Elihu Root's compromise plank which avoided a direct stand on the League of Nations, thus averting a party split. He pushed the nomination of Harding at the meeting of seven senators in George Harvey's smoke-filled hotel room. He placated other candidates to keep party unity. Primary and secondary sources; 2 illus., 40 notes.   J. L. Hazelton

666.   Theisen, Lee Scott.   A "FAIR COUNT" IN FLORIDA: GENERAL LEW WALLACE AND THE CONTESTED PRESIDENTIAL ELECTION OF 1876.   *Hayes Hist. J. 1978 2(1): 20-30.* General Lew Wallace, author of *Ben Hur,* and a member of the Republican committee to recount the Florida votes in the 1876 presidential election, played a significant role in the electoral outcome of this state, and in the victory of Rutherford B. Hayes. In exchange for his

efforts, Wallace's appointment as governor of the New Mexico Territory took almost two years; in the meantime, he became embroiled in Indiana state politics. Offers insight into the contested 1876 presidential election, state politics of the era, and the complicated late 19th-century spoils system. Primary sources; 7 illus., 31 notes. J. N. Friedel

667. Tingley, Ralph R. THE CROWDED FIELD: EIGHT MEN FOR THE SENATE. *South Dakota Hist. 1979 9(4): 316-336.* The campaign for the United States Senate in 1923-24 was a long and unique one in South Dakota politics. The Richards Primary Law of 1918 forced the election process to begin in November of 1923. Because of party factionalism and personal rivalries there were eight candidates competing for the Senate seat. The real contest, however, was between the official Republican and Democratic candidates, William Henry McMaster (1877-1962) and U. S. G. Cherry. The election ended in November, 1924 with a decisive victory by McMaster. Based on newspapers and other primary sources; 6 illus., 9 photos, 47 notes. P. L. McLaughlin

668. Tingley, Ralph R. PODIUM POLITICS IN SIOUX FALLS, 1924: DAWES VERSUS LAFOLLETTE. *South Dakota Hist. 1980 10(2): 119-132.* Recounts the presidential campaign of 1924 and its impact on South Dakota as seen from Sioux Falls. Charles Gates Dawes (1865-1951), the Republican Vice Presidential candidate, and Wisconsin Senator Robert Marion LaFollette (1855-1925), running as an independent presidential candidate, staged rallies in Sioux Falls within a few weeks of each other. Since South Dakota was considered LaFollette territory, Dawes attemped to paint LaFollette as a radical while praising South Dakota. In the final analysis, even though the LaFollette rally was more enthusiastic and better attended, Republican organization outweighed the emotion of the LaFollette forces and the Republican Party carried South Dakota. Based on newspapers and other primary sources; 2 illus., 3 photos, 24 notes. P. L. McLaughlin

669. Tobin, Eugene M. THE PROGRESSIVE AS POLITICIAN: JERSEY CITY, 1896-1907. *New Jersey Hist. 1973 91(1): 5-23.* In tracing the career of Mark Fagan, mayor of Jersey City, the author relates the failure of Progressivism in one American city. Discusses Fagan's Republican Party affiliation, his program of equal taxation, his fight with the railroads and utilities, and his demise as a leader due to a lack of patience with the customary workings of party machinery. Based on primary and secondary sources; 7 illus., 39 notes. E. R. McKinstry

670. Trask, David Stephens. A NATURAL PARTNERSHIP: NEBRASKA'S POPULISTS AND DEMOCRATS AND THE DEVELOPMENT OF FUSION. *Nebraska Hist. 1975 56(3): 419-438.* Discusses the movement for fusion between Nebraska Democrats and Populists, consummated successfully in 1894. The party situation in the 1890's explains how the Populists in Nebraska accepted fusion with the Democrats behind Bryan before free silver became the dominant issue. R. Lowitt

671. Travis, Anthony R. MAYOR GEORGE ELLIS: GRAND RAPIDS POLITICAL BOSS AND PROGRESSIVE REFORMER. *Michigan Hist. 1974 58(2): 101-130.* George E. Ellis, mayor of Grand Rapids during 1906-16,

was the most dynamic, innovative, and powerful chief executive in the city's history. Forging a coalition of ethnic working class and middle class voters, Ellis strove successfully to widen the spectrum of citizen participation in politics. Ellis' career as a left-wing progressive who was both machine politician and social reformer demonstrates that the "boss" versus "reformer" typology, advanced by Samuel P. Hays, James Weinstein, and others, inadequately describes the complexity of urban politics in the progressive period. Primary and secondary sources; illus., 7 photos, map, 2 tables, 45 notes.   D. W. Johnson

672.   Treadway, Sandra Gioia.   SARAH LEE FAIN: NORFOLK'S FIRST WOMAN LEGISLATOR.   *Virginia Cavalcade 1980 30(3): 124-133.* Brief biography of Sarah Lee Fain (1888-1962), focusing on her interest in the Democratic Party, and her election to the House of Delegates in 1923, when she and Democrat Helen T. Henderson became the first women elected in Virginia; she served three terms, later worked for the federal government under Franklin D. Roosevelt, and remained active in politics until her death.

673.   Trelease, Allen W.   THE FUSION LEGISLATURES OF 1895 AND 1897: A ROLL-CALL ANALYSIS OF THE NORTH CAROLINA HOUSE OF REPRESENTATIVES.   *North Carolina Hist. Rev. 1980 57(3): 280-309.* Despite the joining of the Republican Party and the Populist Party in the 1894 and 1896 elections to gain control of the North Carolina legislature from the Democrats, the fusion was not a tight one. The coalition failed and ultimately disintegrated over such large issues as business regulation, the gold standard, and race relations as well as over specific state issues, including local government, patronage, education, taxes, lynching, and railroads. Roll-call voting analysis reveals, for instance, consistent Republican support for blacks and for election and government reform, and consistent Populist support of public education, business regulation, and liquor and cigarette control. Based on newspaper and published legislature journals; 10 illus., table, 114 notes.   T. L. Savitt

674.   Trelease, Allen W.   REPUBLICAN RECONSTRUCTION IN NORTH CAROLINA: A ROLL-CALL ANALYSIS OF THE STATE HOUSE OF REPRESENTATIVES, 1868-1870.   *J. of Southern Hist. 1976 42(3): 319-344.* The federal legislature during the Civil War and Reconstruction era has been subjected to considerable statistical analysis, but state legislatures have been neglected. Using roll-call analysis, Rice internal cohesion, and Guttman scaling to evaluate party, the author identifies factional and sectional influences upon the North Carolina House of Representatives. Scalawags are key to understanding the extent of the Republican Party's success in North Carolina. North Carolina Republicans moved further and faster toward emulating and catching up with the northern states than economic conditions and public opinion would permit. Hence, the Democratic program of 1868-70 foretold a course which would lead Democrats to power in 1870.   T. Schoonover

675.   Tucker, Gary J.   WILLIAM E. GLASSCOCK AND THE WEST VIRGINIA ELECTION OF 1910.   *West Virginia Hist. 1979 40(3): 254-267.* William E. Glasscock, Republican governor of West Virginia, 1909-1913, tried to soothe party factionalism that he feared would cause a Republican defeat in the 1910 elections. A challenge to incumbent Senator Nathan B. Scott, contests for many legislative seats, and quarrels over patronage left bitter divisions, especially

over the prohibition issue. Democrats swept the fall legislative and congressional elections. Based on the Blasscock papers and other primary sources; 63 notes.

J. H. Broussard

676. Tyson, Carl N. "I'M OFF TO COOLIDGE'S FOLLIES": WILL ROGERS AND THE PRESIDENTIAL NOMINATIONS, 1924-1932. *Chronicles of Oklahoma 1976 54(2): 192-198.* Discusses press coverage and political commentary by Will Rogers about the national political conventions of 1924, 1928, and 1932.

677. Waksmundski, John. GOVERNOR MC KINLEY AND THE WORKING MAN. *Historian 1976 38(4): 629-647.* Unlike earlier Republican Party leaders, Ohio governor William McKinley (1843-1901) sought to align himself and his party with the working class. Elected in 1891, McKinley asked the legislature to enact laws on railroad worker safety, right of employees to join labor organizations, and arbitration. McKinley was reelected in 1893 with improved Republican vote totals in counties with a substantial worker voting bloc. McKinley's careful actions dealing with striking coal miners during the 1893 depression enabled him to keep labor support. Notes.

M. J. Wentworth

678. Webb, Ross A. THE BRISTOW PRESIDENTIAL BOOM OF 1876. *Hayes Hist. J. 1976 1(2): 78-87.* Traces the unsuccessful efforts of Benjamin Helm Bristow, an ardent reformer from Kentucky and Secretary of the Treasury during the Grant administration, to gain the Republican Party's presidential nomination in June 1876. Bristow continued to support his party by campaigning extensively for the election of Rutherford B. Hayes. Gives insight into the political maneuvering and compromises between the Democrats and Republicans, and within the Electoral Commission, in selecting Hayes as President. Primary sources; 6 illus., 38 notes.

J. N. Friedel

679. Westwood, Howard C. THE FEDERALS' COLD SHOULDER TO ARKANSAS' POWELL CLAYTON. *Civil War Hist. 1980 26(3): 240-255.* Ku Klux Klan violence in Arkansas in 1868 resulted in panic and disruption of normal law enforcement processes. Republican Governor Powell Clayton (1833-1914) corresponded with Secretary of War John M. Schofield and General C. H. Smith, commander of the federal troops in Arkansas, but no federal help came. Clayton organized his own militia and declared martial law in the affected areas. Klanism was wiped out, but so was support for Clayton and the Republican Party. Based on military reports and other sources; 53 notes.

G. R. Schroeder

680. Wetta, Frank J. "BULLDOZING THE SCALAWAGS": SOME EXAMPLES OF THE PERSECUTION OF SOUTHERN WHITE REPUBLICANS IN LOUISIANA DURING RECONSTRUCTION. *Louisiana Hist. 1980 21(1): 43-58.* Terrorism and ostracism were as important as racism in keeping Louisiana whites from Unionist or Republican sympathies during 1866-78. Coercion by groups such as the Ku Klux Klan, the Seymour Knights, and the White League drove 38 prominent southern white Republicans from public and party offices after 1868 and silenced most of their supporters. These violent tactics of "bulldozing" dealt a fatal blow (literally, in some cases) to Louisiana Republicans in the era of Reconstruction. Based on extensive archival research,

census returns, contemporary newspapers, and congressional reports; 43 notes.

D. B. Touchstone

681. Widener, Ralph W., Jr. CHARLES HILLMAN BROUGH. *Arkansas Hist. Q. 1975 34(2): 99-121.* Charles Hillman Brough, governor of Arkansas 1917-21, was native of Mississippi and former resident of Utah. He adopted Arkansas as his home when he began teaching at the state university in 1903. Brough was a staunch Democrat and a former student and personal friend of Woodrow Wilson. Based on primary and secondary sources; illus., 115 notes.

T. L. Savitt

682. Wiggins, Sarah Woolfolk. ALABAMA: DEMOCRATIC BULLDOZ-ING AND REPUBLICAN FOLLY. Olsen, Otto H., ed. *Reconstruction and Redemption in the South* (Baton Rouge: Louisiana State U. Pr., 1980): 47-77. Covers Republican efforts during Reconstruction to assume control of the state and Democratic efforts to prevent it. Every sort of trick was employed by both sides, but the Democratic Party always had the white voters on their side and eventually won. The Republican Party was rent by the usual factionalism, and by the fact that Republicans were essentially products of their age: they were more closely allied with the views of Democratic whites than Republican Negroes. Ineptitude in office contributed to their downfall. 64 notes.

V. L. Human

683. Wiggins, Sarah Woolfolk. OSTRACISM OF WHITE REPUBLICANS IN ALABAMA DURING RECONSTRUCTION. *Alabama R. 1974 27(1): 52-64.* Ostracism of white Republicans was mild, perhaps nonexistent until June 1867, when the Alabama Republican Party was formed. Abuse, intimidation, and slander intensified rapidly in 1868 and remained strong throughout Reconstruction regardless of Republican political fortunes. Ostracism was not indiscriminately applied, however. It was reserved for those Northern newcomers who were politically active, as opposed to those who invested in Alabama but shunned politics; and for scalawags more than carpetbaggers. Contemporary exaggeration notwithstanding, "ostracism was all too real for most Republicans." Based on private letters, government documents, and secondary sources; 53 notes.

J. F. Vivian

684. Williams, David A. CALIFORNIA DEMOCRATS OF 1860: DIVISION, DISRUPTION, DEFEAT. *Southern California Q. 1973 55(3): 239-252.* Recounts California's participation in the 1860 Democratic National Convention. Heavily pro-slavery and anti-Stephen A. Douglas, California and Oregon supported the Southern states at the Charleston meeting. Although Douglas supporters were in the majority at the convention, they lacked the two-thirds vote necessary to put their candidate and platform across. On a number of key issues California voted on the side of the South, and after 57 ballots the deadlocked convention adjourned. When it met again in Baltimore 45 days later, California and the southern states walked out. The Baltimore convention went on to nominate Douglas, while California and the southern states nominated John C. Breckinridge at a rump convention in Richmond. In November California narrowly went for Lincoln and the Republicans. Primary and secondary sources; 40 notes.

A. Hoffman

685. Williams, Nudie E. CASSIUS MC DONALD BARNES: GOVERNOR OF OKLAHOMA TERRITORY, 1897-1901. *Chronicles of Oklahoma 1975 53(1): 66-82.* Though awarded Oklahoma Territory's governorship for loyalty to the Republican Party and especially to President William McKinley, Cassius McDonald Barnes presided over a divided party and a politically volatile population. Despite attempts to reunify the two Republican factions in the territory, he alienated the group led by Dennis Flynn while at the same time he faced charges of political corruption from leading Democrats. The animosity arose from patronage problems and from Barnes' public welfare efforts in behalf of education, the aged, the disabled, and the insane. Few people objected to the efforts, but towns competed for the resulting institutions and when Barnes selected a site, he alienated the others. Though personally honest and deeply committed to improvements in Oklahoma, he had created too much controversy to be reappointed. Based on primary and secondary sources; 5 photos, 23 notes.

M. L. Tate

687. Wingo, Barbara C. THE 1928 PRESIDENTIAL ELECTION IN LOUISIANA. *Louisiana Hist. 1977 18(4): 405-415.* Although Alfred E. Smith's majority in Louisiana in 1928 (76.3%) was very similar to Democratic majorities in that state in the 1920 and 1924 elections, the composition of his support was markedly different. Reviews and analyzes the election, showing that his strength was in the "wet," Catholic, southern part of the state rather than in the "dry," Protestant north. Black participation remained a factor in the state's Republican Party. Notes some similarities in the support for Smith and Huey P. Long. Primary sources; 3 tables, 66 notes.

R. L. Woodward, Jr.

688. Wister, Owen. THE SECOND MISSOURI COMPROMISE. *Idaho Yesterdays 1976 20(1): 2-17.* After the Civil War, Democratic territorial legislators from Missouri fought with Idaho's territorial governor who was a Radical Republican. The governor forced the legislators to sign an oath of allegiance to the United States before receiving their pay. First published in *Harpers Monthly*, March, 1895. 8 illus., 22 notes.

B. J. Paul

689. Wolff, Gerald W. THE OHIO FARMER-LABOR VOTE IN THE ELECTION OF 1896: A CASE STUDY. *Northwest Ohio Q. 1975 47(3): 100-119.* Republicans and Democrats wooed farmers and labor for the presidential election of 1896.

690. Wood, Barry R. 'HOLY JOE' FOLK'S LAST CRUSADE: THE 1918 ELECTION IN MISSOURI. *Missouri Hist. Rev. 1977 71(3): 284-314.* In 1918 little-known Republican Selden Spencer defeated former governor Joseph W. Folk in the Missouri senatorial election. Writers have credited Spencer's victory to his appeal to sectionalism, a low Democratic turnout, wheat growers' dissatisfaction with Wilson's farm policies, and a desire to punish Wilson for getting into World War I. The Democrats' defeat is more closely related to factionalism centering around a long-standing distrust of Folk, the prohibition issue, and the party's rural bias at a time when Missouri was becoming urbanized. Illus., 60 notes.

W. F. Zornow

691. Zanjani, Sally Springmeyer.   LOSING BATTLES: THE REVOLT OF THE NEVADA PROGRESSIVES, 1910-1914.   *Nevada Hist. Soc. Q. 1981 24(1): 17-38.*   Unlike turn-of-the-century Progressivism in many areas, the Nevada movement was rooted almost exclusively in revolt against state Republican Party leaders deemed too subservient to the Southern Pacific Railroad. Nevada Progressives, moreover, cooperated with Theodore Roosevelt's national insurgency. Poorly financed and negligent about performing essential political organizational work, Nevada Progressives proved no match for enemies who commanded efficient political machines. In the end, these Progressives could only force Nevada Republican stalwarts to support reform. Based on newspaper and secondary sources; photo, table, 46 notes.   H. T. Lovin

692. Zieger, Robert H.   THE CAREER OF JAMES J. DAVIS.   *Pennsylvania Mag. of Hist. and Biog. 1974 98(1): 67-89.*   James John Davis' (1873-1947) career as US Secretary of Labor and senator from Pennsylvania (1930-45) has been largely neglected by historians. As Secretary of Labor under Presidents Harding, Coolidge, and Hoover, Davis earned a reputation for moderation, although he was rarely consulted as an advisor and thus had little impact on economic policy. As a moderately liberal Republican Senator for 15 years, Davis was noted by his colleagues for "his uncanny ability to maintain himself in public office rather than for intellectual distinction, legislative prowess, or political courage." Based on primary and secondary sources; 42 notes.   E. W. Carp

693. —.   [THE COMPROMISE OF 1877].   *J. of Am. Hist. 1973 60(1).*
Peskin, Allan.   WAS THERE A COMPROMISE OF 1877?, pp. 63-75. C. Vann Woodward's *Reunion and Reaction: The Compromise of 1877 and the End of Reconstruction* (Boston: Little, Brown & Co., 1951), contains the classic and almost universally accepted interpretation of the far-reaching compromise wherein southern Democrats accepted Hayes as president in return for withdrawal of federal troops, support for internal improvements in the South, assurance of federal subsidies, appointment of a southerner as postmaster general, and the admission that the South alone could resolve its racial problems. Argues that these terms of the "compromise" were not complied with, that no compromise in fact existed, and that the southern Democrats were outwitted by Republicans.
Woodward, C. Vann.   YES, THERE WAS A COMPROMISE OF 1877, pp. 215-223.   The Compromise of 1877 was as real as that of 1850, the major terms were complied with, particularly home rule for the South, and if anyone was outwitted it was the Republicans. 49 notes.   K. B. West

694. —.   PRAISE FOR THE "MOST AVAILABLE CANDIDATE." *J. of the Illinois State Hist. Soc. 1978 71(1): 71-72.* A letter from Scott County Chairman Nathan Knapp to Illinois Secretary of State Ozias M. Hatch praises Abraham Lincoln as "the biggest man in the lot" of Republicans in 1859. Illus., 7 notes.   J

695. —.   [TENNESSEE GUBERNATORIAL ELECTIONS].   *Tennessee Hist. R. 1974 33(1): 34-61.*
Parker, James C.   TENNESSEE GUBERNATORIAL ELECTIONS, I. 1869 —THE VICTORY OF THE CONSERVATIVES, *pp. 34-48.* Conservative interest in Tennessee elections was dampened by the restrictions on

ex-Confederates under Radical Republican Governor W. G. "Parson" Brownlow after his election in 1865. When the boundlessness of Brownlow's ambition became apparent by 1869, the Conservatives re-entered politics in an effort to stop Brownlow. The election of 1869 ended Radical rule. 66 notes.

Jones, Robert B.   TENNESSEE GUBERNATORIAL ELECTIONS, II. 1880 —THE COLLAPSE OF THE DEMOCRATIC PARTY,   *pp. 49-61.* Part II. In 1880 the Republican Party regained the governorship of Tennessee for the first time since Reconstruction. The reason for their return to power was a bitter split within the majority Democratic Party over the state debt. 31 notes.   M. B. Lucas

4

THE DEMOCRATIC RESURGENCE
(1932-1960)

696. Adams, J. W.   GOVERNOR GORDON BROWNING, CAM-
PAIGNER EXTRAORDINARY—THE 1936 ELECTION FOR GOVER-
NOR.   *West Tennessee Hist. Soc. Papers 1976 (30): 5-23.* Depicts the 1936
gubernatorial primary campaign of Gordon Browning in Tennessee. Portrays
Browning's method of hard-hitting stumping, the 1936 campaign being a classic
of this type of campaign strategy. He won the Democratic primary by a two to
one margin over his opponent and was swept into office in the general election
which followed. While Boss Crump of Memphis supported him in the campaign,
he and Browning split over appointments after the latter assumed office. In 1938
the loss of Crump's support cost Browning his reelection, even though he had
given Tennessee a splendid reform administration. Browning was later reelected
Governor in 1949 and 1951. Based largely on files of Nashville newspapers in the
Gordon Browning Memorial Library, McKenzie, Tennessee; illus., 39 notes.
H. M. Parker, Jr.

697. Annunziata, Frank.   THE PROGRESSIVE AS CONSERVATIVE:
GEORGE CREEL'S QUARREL WITH NEW DEAL LIBERALISM.
Wisconsin Mag. of Hist. 1974 57(3): 220-233. George Creel (1876-1953) was a
progressive Democrat long before his appointment as chairman of the Committee
on Public Information during World War I, and he remained an important
progressive well into the New Deal. Although an early advocate of Roosevelt and
the New Deal, (in his post as chairman of the National Advisory Board, Works
Progress Administration), Creel turned passionately against both during the war
years 1940-45. The causes of that change in attitude included his resentment of
certain advisors close to Roosevelt, his failure to win an important administrative
post during the war, and the death of his first wife. Ideologically, he felt that the
New Deal, by moving to create a welfare state that accommodated demands of
organized interest groups, had abandoned the major tenets "of the neutral regulatory progressive state." He then called unsuccessfully for a conservative coalition
of southern Democrats and Republicans to reverse the trend, and he was disappointed with the policies of both Presidents Truman and Eisenhower. 3 photos,
61 notes.
N. C. Burckel

698.   Antognini, Richard.   THE ROLE OF A. P. GIANNINI IN THE 1934 CALIFORNIA GUBERNATORIAL ELECTION.   *Southern California Q. 1975 57(1): 53-86.* Analyzes how A. P. Giannini, founder and head of the Bank of America, switched from traditional support of the Republican Party to endorsement of the Roosevelt candidacy in 1932, and eventual backing of the Republican gubernatorial candidate in 1934. Giannini came into conflict with the Federal Reserve Board, the head of San Francisco's Federal Reserve Bank, and the Reconstruction Finance Corporation. Unhappy with the Hoover Administration, Giannini endorsed Franklin D. Roosevelt in 1932; and in return Roosevelt promised to support policies friendly to Giannini's needs. After Upton Sinclair captured the 1934 Democratic gubernatorial nomination, the Giannini forces and Republican candidate Frank Merriam reached an agreement which permitted support of Merriam without damaging relations with the Roosevelt Administration. Primary and secondary sources, including the Bank of America Archives; 86 notes.   A. Hoffman

699.   Arnold, Joseph L.   THE LAST OF THE GOOD OLD DAYS: POLITICS IN BALTIMORE, 1920-1950.   *Maryland Hist. Mag. 1976 71(3): 443-448.* While Progressive-era reforms in Maryland did end classic-style bossism as embodied in the famous Rasin-Gorman machine, still the heirs of this machine continued to monopolize Baltimore city and county politics for 35 years, since "individual leaders and their relationships, not the total organizational structure, determine the continuing strength of machine control." Democrats successfully identified the Republicans with the voters' fear of black control during the 1920's, and both European and rural white immigrants registered heavily Democratic. Personal conflicts between Democratic bosses John J. (Sonny) Mahon and Frank Kelly, heirs of the two major machine factions, weakened their party's control at the center, and 15 years of battling between the forces led by William Curran and perennial mayor Howard Jackson splintered the party further. Local ward bosses were thus able to develop independent neighborhood machines, and control of city council and the mayoralty depended on shifting and temporary alliances of such local groups. Republicans, however, were never able to take advantage of such Democratic in-fighting. Primary and secondary sources; 13 notes.   G. J. Bobango

700.   Arthur, Thomas H.   AN ACTOR IN POLITICS: MELVYN DOUGLAS AND THE NEW DEAL.   *J. of Popular Culture 1980 14(2): 196-211.* Chronicle of the political activities of actor Melvyn Douglas during the Roosevelt New Deal era. Essentially apolitical before joining the Hollywood Anti-Nazi League in 1936, Douglas went on to become a liberal Democratic political activist, and gained substantial recognition at both the state and national levels prior to US entry into World War II. Subsequent to his service in the army during the war, however, Douglas did not play as active a role in politics, and in fact disagreed with many postwar Democratic Party policies. Based on interviews and Douglas's papers; 88 notes.   D. G. Nielson

701.   Barnard, William D.   THE OLD ORDER CHANGES: GRAVES, SPARKS, FOLSOM, AND THE GUBERNATORIAL ELECTION OF 1942. *Alabama R. 1975 28(3): 165-184.* Conservative Democrat Chauncey Sparks won the 1942 gubernatorial election by default upon the death of liberal Democratic candidate Bibb Graves, assuring the continuance of probusiness and antilabor

leadership since 1938. However, the runner-up was first-time candidate James E. Folsom who inherited major blocs of the Graves organization and whose sectional success in northern Alabama foreshadowed the emergence of a new liberal force that would dominate the state after 1946. Primary and secondary sources, including a private interview with Folsom; 56 notes.   J. F. Vivian

702.   Bernstein, Barton J.   TRUMAN, THE EIGHTIETH CONGRESS, AND THE TRANSFORMATION OF POLITICAL CULTURE.   *Capitol Studies 1973 2(1): 65-75.*

703.   Best, Gary Dean.   AN EVANGELIST AMONG SKEPTICS: HOOVER'S BID FOR THE LEADERSHIP OF THE GOP, 1937-1938.   *Pro. of the Am. Phil. Soc. 1979 123(1): 1-14.* Immediately after the smashing defeat which the Republican Party suffered in 1936, Herbert C. Hoover laid plans for a conference of Republican leaders for early 1938 to revitalize the party and to establish a basic philosophy true to the party's historical position which would be an affirmative alternate to the coercion of the New Deal. Alfred M. Landon opposed this effort, viewing it as a ploy of Hoover to gain the nomination in 1940. Delineates the moves and countermoves of these two party leaders. Ultimately Hoover was forced to compromise, both from the timing of the conference as well as in establishing a basic Republican philosophy. The Republicans were highly successful in the 1938 elections, and both men took the credit. Based on the correspondence found in the Hoover Papers (Hoover Presidential Library) and the Landon Papers (Kansas State Historical Society) and contemporary newspaper accounts; 112 notes.   H. M. Parker, Jr.

704.   Best, Gary Dean.   HERBERT HOOVER AS TITULAR LEADER OF THE GOP, 1933-35.   *Mid-America 1979 61(2): 81-97.* After the 1932 election Herbert C. Hoover was the discredited leader of the Republican Party. Between March 1933 and March 1935 he kept a self-imposed public silence on political affairs. In March 1935 he issued an off-the-cuff statement to a Tucson newspaper on the Roosevelt administration's abandonment of the gold standard. Later the same month he issued a letter to the California Republican Assembly attacking the New Deal. This ended his two-year silence, yet Hoover remained discredited. 86 notes.   J. M. Lee

705.   Biles, Roger.   "BIG RED IN BRONZEVILLE": MAYOR ED KELLY REELS IN THE BLACK VOTE.   *Chicago Hist. 1981 10(2): 99-111.* Discusses the tenure of Chicago mayor Edward J. Kelly, a big city boss who ran Chicago's Democratic machine, focusing on black support for Kelly, traditionally given to the Republicans, and how Kelly cornered and controlled the black vote; 1933-50.

706.   Biles, Roger.   JACOB M. ARVEY, KINGMAKER: THE NOMINATION OF ADLAI E. STEVENSON IN 1952.   *Chicago Hist. 1979 8(3): 130-143.* Democratic National Committeeman and Chicago politico Colonel Jacob M. Arvey, got the Democratic presidential nomination for Illinois Governor Adlai E. Stevenson, in 1952; briefly traces Arvey's political career from 1932.

707.   Boxerman, Burton Alan.   ADOLPH JOACHIM SABATH IN CONGRESS: THE ROOSEVELT AND TRUMAN YEARS.   *J. of the Illinois State Hist. Soc. 1973 66(4): 428-443.* Continued from a previous article (see abstract 11A:791). Congressman Sabath of Illinois became increasingly critical of Presi-

dent Herbert Hoover's Republican Party policies between 1930 and 1931. As a liberal who championed the cause of immigrants he was also a key defender of the rights of labor. As an unfailing supporter of Presidents Franklin D. Roosevelt and Harry S. Truman, Sabath particularly backed legislation to improve health, housing, and welfare. He had a limited knowledge of parliamentary procedure despite his seniority and chairmanship of the Rules Committee. However, Sabath helped guide significant legislation of the New Deal and Fair Deal through the Rules Committee. Based on the *Congressional Record,* interviews, and contemporary newspapers; 2 photos, 56 notes.

A. C. Aimone

708. Braeman, John. THE MAKING OF THE ROOSEVELT COALITION: SOME RECONSIDERATIONS. *Can. Rev. of Am. Studies [Canada] 1980 11(2): 233-253.* Six recent publications attempt anew to assess Franklin D. Roosevelt's New Deal of the 1930's: Kristi Andersen's *The Creation of a Democratic Majority, 1928-1936* (Chicago, 1979), Barbara Blumberg's *The New Deal and the Unemployed: The View from New York City* (Lewisburg, Pa., 1979), Sidney Fine's *Frank Murphy: The Detroit Years* (Ann Arbor, 1975) and *Frank Murphy: The New Deal Years* (Chicago, 1979), John W. Jeffries's *Testing the Roosevelt Coalition: Connecticut Society and Politics in the Era of World War II* (Knoxville, Tenn., 1979), and Martha H. Swain's *Pat Harrison: The New Deal Years* (Jackson, Miss., 1978). 37 notes.

H. T. Lovin

709. Bullock, Charles S., III. COMMITTEE TRANSFERS IN THE UNITED STATES HOUSE OF REPRESENTATIVES. *J. of Pol. 1973 35(1): 85-120.* Examines congressional committee transfers 1949-69 for northern Democrats, southern Democrats, and Republicans. Analyzes, for each group, the relationships between committee and chamber seniority, security before the electorate, and committee prestige. Raises basic questions and implications about the manner in which committee policymaking procedures are affected by imbalances of members from a particular section of the nation. 9 tables, 68 notes.

A. R. Stoesen

710. Bullock, Paul. *"RABBITS AND RADICALS"*: RICHARD NIXON'S 1946 CAMPAIGN AGAINST JERRY VOORHIS. *Southern California Q. 1973 55(3): 319-359.* An account of the 1946 Congressional campaign between Richard M. Nixon and Congressman Jerry Voorhis, describing the issues and events which contributed to Voorhis' defeat. Nixon campaigned over legitimate issues such as price controls, housing, and labor-management relations, but gained his greatest publicity from a simplistic presentation of artificial issues such as the Political Action Committee endorsement, Voorhis' legislative record, and the telephone smear. Nixon misrepresented the nature of an endorsement from the Political Action Committee and gave out misleading statistics on Voorhis' votes in Congress. A third issue was the controversial smear campaign over the telephone just before election day in which callers alleged Voorhis was a Communist. Nixon might have won on the issues alone, but Republicans had coveted the district for 10 years and made sure of their victory through use of controversial tactics. Based on the author's campaign recollections as a Voorhis supporter, newspapers, personal interviews, and published studies; 40 notes, 4 appendices.

A. Hoffman

711.   Canon, Bradley C.   FACTIONALISM IN THE SOUTH: A TEST OF THEORY AND A REVISITATION OF V. O. KEY.   *Am. J. of Pol. Sci. 1978 22(4): 833-848.* The nature of electoral divisiveness is often explained by one of two competing theories: Riker's size principle or as a function of election rules. . . . This paper tests these theories in the context of Democratic Party factionalism in the South . . . data from 1932-77 indicates that with only minor exceptions multifactionalism occurs in double primary states and bifactionalism in single primary states. . . .
J

712.   Cobb, James C.   THE BIG BOY HAS SCARED THE LARD OUT OF THEM.   *Res. Studies 1975 43(2): 123-125.* Examines Franklin D. Roosevelt's unsuccessful attempt in 1938 to purge the Democratic Party of conservative congressmen, particularly Walter F. George of Georgia.
S

713.   Cobb, James C.   NOT GONE, BUT FORGOTTEN: EUGENE TAL-MADGE AND THE 1938 PURGE CAMPAIGN.   *Georgia Hist. Q. 1975 59(2): 197-209.* Discusses the political career of Georgia Democratic governor Eugene Talmadge, 1926-38, emphasizing President Franklin D. Roosevelt's 1938 intervention to remove him from power due to attacks on the New Deal.

714.   Corlew, Robert E., III.   FRANK GOAD CLEMENT AND THE KEY-NOTE ADDRESS OF 1956.   *Tennessee Hist. Q. 1977 36(1): 95-107.* The rapid rise of Frank Goad Clement in Tennessee politics and his choice as keynote speaker for the 1956 Democratic Party convention indicated that his success would continue at the national level. After a fiery speech that received much praise, however, Clement was bitterly disappointed that he received scant consideration for national office. Primary and secondary sources; 26 notes.
M. B. Lucas

715.   Davis, Polly Ann.   ALBEN W. BARKLEY'S PUBLIC CAREER IN 1944.   *Filson Club Hist. Q. 1977 51(2): 143-157.* Examines the conflict between President Franklin D. Roosevelt and Senate Democratic Majority Leader Alben W. Barkley over a tax bill in February 1944. Roosevelt vetoed H.R. 3687 on 21 February because it did not raise enough revenue. Barkley, who regarded the bill as the best measure obtainable, made a major Senate speech on 23 February, called on Congress to override the veto, and then resigned as Majority Leader. The immediate result was the overwhelming passage of the legislation and the unanimous reelection of Barkley as Majority Leader. The speech helped Barkley to be reelected to the Senate in 1944, but it prevented him from receiving the Vice Presidential nomination that same year. Based on newspapers and the Barkley papers; 66 notes.
G. B. McKinney

716.   Davis, William L.   FRANK CLEMENT: THE FIRST CAMPAIGN.   *Tennessee Hist. Q. 1976 35(1): 83-91.* In the 1952 Democratic primary, Frank Goad Clement (1920-69) upset incumbent Tennessee Governor Gordon Weaver Browning on his way to becoming the nation's youngest governor. Governor Browning, whose campaign theme was "anti-bossism," appeared as an old-fashioned stump speaker. His actions at the Democratic National Convention, and the "Memorial Hotel deal," augmented this unfavorable image. Clement believed that God had called him to govern. His captivating religious oratorical style catered to the religious fervor of the 1950's, and complemented his youthfulness,

his unblemished past, and his well-organized campaign. Based on primary and secondary sources; 36 notes.

W. R. Hively

717. Dorsett, Lyle W. FRANK HAGUE, FRANKLIN ROOSEVELT AND THE POLITICS OF THE NEW DEAL. *New Jersey Hist. 1976 94(1): 23-35.* Frank Hague was not pro-Roosevelt at the 1932 convention, but he enthusiastically supported him in the general election and helped deliver New Jersey's electoral votes to the Democratic ticket. Hague's political power was again demonstrated in his control of the New Deal's WPA and FERA programs in New Jersey. Abuses of the programs soon became common and the President's personal distaste for the Jersey City mayor grew. Roosevelt supported Charles Edison for governor in 1940, hoping to circumvent Hague with a friend in Trenton. As time passed it became evident that Hague could be embarrassed but not destroyed. Based on primary and secondary sources; 4 illus., 27 notes.

E. R. McKinstry

718. Duram, James C. CONSTITUTIONAL CONSERVATISM: THE KANSAS PRESS AND THE NEW DEAL ERA AS A CASE STUDY. *Kansas Hist. Q. 1977 43(4): 432-447.* Analyzes the editorial treatment of constitutional law issues of the New Deal in 46 Kansas newspapers in 1934-35. The editorial response of the Kansas press to the New Deal was the product of the Republican backgrounds and probusiness attitudes of the editors. Many editorials excoriated the New Deal for excessive regulation of business, wild spending, socialistic concepts, dangerous experimentation, and hastily drawn legislation. Most of the Kansas papers welcomed the Supreme Court's decisions on legislation, and criticized some decisions for not being more conservative than they were. Primary sources; 2 tables, 46 notes.

A. W. Howell

719. Errico, Charles J. THE NEW DEAL, INTERNATIONALISM AND THE NEW AMERICAN CONSENSUS, 1938-1940. *Maryland Hist. 1978 9(1): 17-31.* Contrasts Republican victories in the 1938 elections with the Democratic victories of 1940. Franklin D. Roosevelt, prompted by James Farley and Henry Wallace, emphasized the need for national unity in a time of international crisis even while continuing the unpopular domestic policies which had caused defeat in 1938. Based on correspondence and secondary sources; illus., 43 notes.

G. O. Gagnon

720. Ficken, Robert E. POLITICAL LEADERSHIP IN WARTIME: FRANKLIN D. ROOSEVELT AND THE ELECTIONS OF 1942. *Mid-America 1975 57(1): 20-37.* Franklin D. Roosevelt mainly remained aloof during the 1942 campaign, fearing to alienate the Kelly machine in the Illinois race and staying clear of Democratic Party disputes in Texas and Pennsylvania. The Democratic setback in 1942 showed how decayed the party was becoming. Primary and secondary sources; 85 notes.

T. H. Wendel

721. Grant, Philip A. THE PRESIDENTIAL ELECTION OF 1932 IN IOWA. *Ann. of Iowa 1979 44(7): 541-550.* Franklin D. Roosevelt's resounding defeat of Herbert C. Hoover in the 1932 presidential election in traditionally Republican Iowa was the result of profound discontent over the precarious state of Iowa's economy. Roosevelt's victory was extremely helpful to many Democratic Party candidates for state, congressional, and legislative offices. The presi-

dential election of 1932 marks the beginning of a genuine two-party system in Iowa. Primary and secondary sources; photo, 39 notes.   P. L. Petersen

722. Grant, Philip A. THE 1952 REPUBLICAN PRESIDENTIAL PRI-MARY. *South Dakota Hist. 1977 8(1): 46-58.* The last Republican Party primary before the national convention was held in South Dakota. The state was generally expected to favor Senator Robert A. Taft, the more conservative and isolationistic candidate. Dwight Eisenhower was still in Europe and had not yet openly campaigned. The results gave Taft 50.3% of the votes, barely a slim margin of victory. Assesses the meaning of the vote, based on a wide range of national newspapers, a majority of which felt that Taft's prospects had been somewhat diminished. A minority of them felt neither candidate had benefited. In any case, no major newspaper predicted a winner for the Republican presidential primary. Based on secondary sources; 5 photos, 35 notes.   A. J. Larson

723. Grant, Philip A., Jr. EDITORIAL REACTION TO THE 1952 PRESI-DENTIAL CANDIDACY OF RICHARD B. RUSSELL. *Georgia Hist. Q. 1973 57(2): 167-178.* Senator Richard B. Russell (d. 1971) announced his candidacy for the Democratic presidential nomination on 28 February 1952. Although President Harry S. Truman had not indicated whether he would seek reelection, Russell's move was a southern conservative protest to many of the president's key domestic legislative proposals. Russell was overwhelmingly praised by the press but virtually none predicted success for him. 58 notes.   D. L. Smith

724. Grant, Philip A., Jr. THE ELECTION OF HARRY S TRUMAN TO THE UNITED STATES SENATE. *Missouri Hist. Soc. Bull. 1980 36(2, pt. 1): 103-109.* Of the three Missouri Democrats seeking their party's US senatorial nomination in 1934, only Harry S. Truman (1884-1972) had no prior congressional service, but all were liberals sympathetic to Franklin D. Roosevelt's New Deal. After prevailing in the primary election, Truman ignored opposition attacks on his ties with the Pendergast political machine, reasserted his fealty to the New Deal, and thundered against the rich whose interests Republicans assertedly served. Truman captured 59.9% of the votes in the general elections. Based on government documents and newspaper sources; 35 notes.   H. T. Lovin

725. Grant, Philip A., Jr. THE PRESIDENTIAL ELECTION OF 1932 IN MISSOURI. *Missouri Hist. Soc. Bull. 1979 35(3): 164-170.* During 1918-30, the Missouri electorate consistently chose Republican candidates for most national and state offices. But, in the 1932 elections, Democratic nominees prevailed because Missouri voters were angry with the Herbert C. Hoover administration failures to cope with the Great Depression. Showing their displeasure, electors voted more against Hoover than for Franklin D. Roosevelt. Based on governmental publications and newspaper sources; table, 43 notes.   H. T. Lovin

726. Grant, Philip A., Jr. THE PRESIDENTIAL ELECTION OF 1932 IN WESTERN MASSACHUSETTS. *Hist. J. of Western Massachusetts 1980 8(1): 3-13.* Franklin D. Roosevelt's success in western Massachusetts in the 1932 presidential election was related to widespread discontent with the regional economy, gains by the Democratic Party in the 1928 Al Smith campaign, and the unity and strength of that party in the region. Based on newspapers, convention proceedings, and secondary sources; 37 notes.   W. H. Mulligan, Jr.

727. Grant, Philip A., Jr. THE 1948 PRESIDENTIAL ELECTION IN VIR-GINIA: AUGURY OF THE TREND TOWARDS REPUBLICANISM. *Presidential Studies Q. 1978 8(3): 319-328.* In 1948, the Democrats in Virginia were divided over the presidential nomination of Harry S. Truman whose un-popular civil rights platform prompted the formation of the States Rights Demo-crats supporting South Carolina Governor J. Strom Thurmond for President. With the split in the Democratic Party, Republican candidate Thomas E. Dewey threatened to carry Virginia. Provides a county-by-county analysis of the vote and attributes Truman's 28,716 plurality to Thurman's weak 10.4% showing and Dewey's failure to campaign in the state. Truman's unimpressive victory is seen as a precursor of future Republican presidential wins in Virginia. Table, 47 notes.

S. C. Strom

728. Grant, Philip A., Jr. THE 1952 MINNESOTA REPUBLICAN PRI-MARY AND THE EISENHOWER CANDIDACY. *Presidential Studies Q. 1979 9(3): 311-315.* In a "political miracle," Dwight D. Eisenhower, a write-in candidate, received enough votes to place second behind Harold E. Stassen.

729. Grayson, A. G. NORTH CAROLINA AND HARRY TRUMAN, 1944-1948. *J. of Am. Studies [Great Britain] 1975 9(3): 283-300.* Analyzes responses in North Carolina to domestic policies of Harry S. Truman, particu-larly his positions on civil rights, labor, and other controversial issues. The North Carolina electorate at first supported Truman, but he lost support increasingly and was vigorously criticized by some North Carolina Democratic factions. However, he continued to enjoy more support in North Carolina than his contem-poraries believed. Based on manuscripts, newspapers, and secondary sources; 76 notes.

H. T. Lovin

730. Green, George N. MC CARTHYISM IN TEXAS: THE 1954 CAM-PAIGN. *Southern Q. 1978 16(3): 255-276.* Reviews the Texas gubernatorial race of 1954. Governor Allan Shivers, who had defected to the Republican Party, was running for a third term against Ralph Yarborough, who mounted a strong campaign appealing to liberals, workers, and public-spirited men. Shivers raised the spectre of Communism, which was much in vogue at the time, although Texas was notoriously poor soil for that ideology. Racism also was used; the Supreme Court decision of that year which mandated school integration aroused Shivers' wrath. Yarborough took a more moderate position, which weakened him. Shivers won the election primarily because Yarborough's legions failed to vote in suffi-cient number. McCarthyism, dead or dying elsewhere, was shown to be still very much alive in Texas. 34 notes.

V. L. Human

731. Greenberg, Irwin F. PHILADELPHIA DEMOCRATS GET A NEW DEAL: THE ELECTION OF 1933. *Pennsylvania Mag. of Hist. and Biog. 1973 97(2): 210-232.* In the 1920's Philadelphia "boss" William S. Vare, the local Republican leader, controlled the city's political affairs by dispensing patronage favors to his friend John O'Donnell, leader of Philadelphia's Democrats. In return O'Donnell did nothing to offend his GOP patrons. Reform-minded Demo-crats revolted against O'Donnell's leadership. Fielding its own candidates, the Independent Democratic Campaign Committee easily defeated O'Donnell's slate in the 1932 primary election. In the 1933 election the IDCC rode on the coattails of Franklin D. Roosevelt and the New Deal and defeated Vare and the Republi-

cans. The election of 1933 signified the return of two-party politics to Philadelphia. Based on primary and secondary sources; 69 notes.   E. W. Carp

732.   Greer, Edward.   SHOULD THE LEFT TRY TO "CAPTURE" THE
DEMOCRATIC PARTY?   *Monthly Rev. 1980 31(10): 58-62.* Review essay on
Kristi Andersen's *The Creation of a Democratic Majority, 1928-1936* (Chicago:
U. of Chicago Pr., 1979).

733.   Grody, Harvey P.   FROM NORTH TO SOUTH: THE FEATHER
RIVER PROJECT AND OTHER LEGISLATIVE WATER STRUGGLES IN
THE 1950'S.   *Southern California Q. 1978 60(3): 287-326.* Traces the course of
administrative efforts behind the passage of key water resource development
legislation in the 1950's, focusing on the legislative campaign of 1959. Governor
Edmund G. (Pat) Brown, in contrast to his predecessor Goodwin J. Knight who
had only moderate success in water policy legislation, brought a popular mandate
and aggressive leadership into the campaign to pass the Feather River Project and
other important programs. Brown's influence overcame such obstacles as reluctant northern Democrats, a north-south split, and many amendments to the bills
he supported. The time was also right as the electorate approved major commitments to the expansion of water resource programs in the state, voting $1.75
billion in bonds. Primary and secondary sources; 140 notes.   A. Hoffman

734.   Hall, Alvin L.   POLITICS AND PATRONAGE: VIRGINIA'S SENA-
TORS AND THE ROOSEVELT PURGES OF 1938.   *Virginia Mag. of Hist.
and Biog. 1974 82(3): 331-350.* Examines President Franklin D. Roosevelt's
attempt in 1938 to strip Virginia Senators Harry F. Byrd and Carter Glass of
federal patronage and give it to anti-Byrd Democrats in Virginia. Byrd and Flood
countered with the issue of "Senatorial Courtesy," and the overwhelming support
they received in the senate dealt a serious blow to the already diminished prestige
of the president. Based on primary and secondary sources; cartoon, 71 notes.
                                                                  R. F. Oaks

735.   Hammersmith, Jack L.   FRANKLIN ROOSEVELT, THE POLISH
QUESTION, AND THE ELECTION OF 1944.   *Mid-Am. 1977 59(1): 5-17.*
Examines Democratic Party strategies to retain Polish American voters in 1944.
The Republicans made major gains in the 1942 congressional elections and con-
centrated on winning ethnic minorities, especially Polish Americans, in 1944.
Roosevelt and the Democrats took special care to retain and woo the Polish
Americans by keeping the Polish-Russian question at arm's length and appealing
to the special interests of Poles. Although Roosevelt won by the narrowest margin
ever, it was perhaps the Polish-American vote which contributed the most to his
victory. Primary and secondary sources; 66 notes.   J. M. Lee

736.   Haney, Richard C.   THE RISE OF WISCONSIN'S NEW DEMO-
CRATS: A POLITICAL REALIGNMENT IN THE MID-TWENTIETH
CENTURY.   *Wisconsin Mag. of Hist. 1974/75 58(2): 90-106.* The rise of the
Democratic Party in Wisconsin after World War II can be attributed to several
factors: former Socialist mayor of Milwaukee Daniel Hoan's decision to run for
governor on the Democratic ticket in 1944 and 1946; Senator Robert La Follette,
Jr.'s decision to return to the Republican fold after leading the independent
Progressive Party; his subsequent defeat by Joseph McCarthy which forced many

liberals out of the party, and the later formation of the Democratic Organizing Committee (DOC). The DOC gained control of the Democratic Party, aligned itself with the Americans for Democratic Action (ADA) and ran issue-oriented campaigns to win labor, urban, liberal, and anti-McCarthy votes. Prominent in these efforts were Patrick Lucey, James Doyle, William Proxmire, Gaylord Nelson, and Horace Wilkie. 14 illus., 36 notes. N. C. Burckel

737. Harper, Alan D. DEMOCRATIC DOMINOES. *Rev. in Am. Hist.* *1976 4(2): 284-290.* Review article prompted by Robert A. Garson's *The Democratic Party and the Politics of Sectionalism, 1941-1948* (Baton Rouge: Louisiana State U., 1974); discusses the separation of the South from the mainstream of Democratic Party politics and the Dixiecrat revolt, 1941-48.

738. Henriques, Peter R. THE BYRD ORGANIZATION CRUSHES A LIBERAL CHALLENGE, 1950-1953. *Virginia Mag. of Hist. and Biog. 1979 87(1): 3-29.* Analyzes the several failures of Virginia liberals to defeat the "Organization" of Harry F. Byrd, Sr. Despite differences with the national democratic administration, and despite internal rivalries, Byrd and his allies decisively beat back challenges on a state budget, a governorship, a Federal Trade Commission appointment, and Byrd's Senate seat. Lacking patronage, the liberals were without grass roots support. Also, most Virginia voters preferred Byrd as their champion of states' rights, limited government, and conservatism in general. After this period, some liberal positions received greater popular favor. 3 illus., 3 tables, 104 notes. P. J. Woehrmann

739. Henriques, Peter R. THE ORGANIZATION CHALLENGED: JOHN S. BATTLE, FRANCIS P. MILLER, AND HORACE EDWARDS RUN FOR GOVERNOR IN 1949. *Virginia Mag. of Hist. and Biog. 1974 82(3): 372-406.* One of the few serious challenges to the political supremacy of Senator Harry F. Byrd's organization, which dominated Virginia politics for 40 years, occurred in the gubernatorial campaign of 1949. John Stewart Battle, Byrd's choice for the office, was challenged by Horace Edwards, a conservative who drew from the same constituency. Virginia liberals, encouraged by this split, nominated Francis P. Miller, who led in the early campaigning. Battle and the Byrd organization ultimately won, but only with the help of Republicans and the political skill of Byrd himself. Based on primary and secondary sources; 2 cartoons, 144 notes. R. F. Oaks

740. Hine, Darlene Clark. BLACKS AND THE DESTRUCTION OF THE DEMOCRATIC WHITE PRIMARY, 1935-1944. *J. of Negro Hist. 1977 62(1): 43-59.* The adoption of the white primary by southern states in the 1890's became the most effective subterfuge to disenfranchise blacks. A 25-year legal struggle by the National Association for the Advancement of Colored People (NAACP) resulted in the victory of the Supreme Court decision in the case of *Smith* v. *Allwright* (US, 1944). 72 notes. P. J. Taylorson

741. Hine, Darlene Clark. THE ELUSIVE BALLOT: THE BLACK STRUGGLE AGAINST THE TEXAS DEMOCRATIC WHITE PRIMARY, 1932-1945. *Southwestern Hist. Q. 1978 81(4): 371-392.* After the Texas white primary law was ruled unconstitutional in *Nixon* v. *Herndon* (1927), the Texas Democratic Party tried every conceivable way of avoiding black voting in primar-

ies. The state NAACP fought a losing battle against exclusion, as the Supreme Court allowed the party, but not the state, to impose a white primary: *Grovey* v. *Townshend* (1935). Nine years later the Court finally did outlaw a white primary under any pretext, in *Smith* v. *Allwright* (1944). Through this entire controversy, the state and national NAACP had led the campaign for black participation in Democratic politics. Primary and secondary sources; 49 notes.
J. H. Broussard

742. Jones, Gene Delon. THE ORIGIN OF THE ALLIANCE BETWEEN THE NEW DEAL AND THE CHICAGO MACHINE. *J. of the Illinois State Hist. Soc. 1974 67(3): 253-274.* In 1932, the Chicago political machine had tried to shout down Franklin D. Roosevelt's nomination, but by 1940, Mayor Edward J. Kelly could refer to him as "our beloved President." The "politics of relief" had allied Roosevelt with the bosses, to the dismay of reformers. Kelly's overwhelming mayoral victory in 1935 put him in excellent position to demand a large share of New Deal relief funds for Chicago. It also convinced Roosevelt that machine support was necessary to carry Illinois in 1936. Primary and secondary sources; 2 illus., 3 photos, 76 notes.
L. Woolfe

743. Kenneally, James. PRELUDE TO THE LAST HURRAH: THE MASSACHUSETTS SENATORIAL ELECTION OF 1936. *Mid-America 1980 62(1): 3-20.* Massachusetts Democratic Governor James Michael Curley (1874-1958) tied his 1936 senatorial campaign to President Franklin D. Roosevelt's reelection race. Roosevelt ignored Curley. Curley's opponent, ex-Democrat Thomas O'Brien, was endorsed by Fr. Charles Coughlin and ran as the candidate of the National Union for Social Justice. O'Brien's action threatened to weaken traditional Democratic support and enable Republican candidate Henry Cabot Lodge, Jr., (b. 1902) to win, but Curley actually lost the election (to Lodge) because his flamboyant and abrasive political style as governor and campaigner had alienated Boston's Irish Catholic voters. Because Curley had built his political base on championship of the Irish voters, their defection marked the beginning of his last hurrah. Notes.
M. J. Wentworth

744. Kiewiet, D. Roderick. POLICY-ORIENTED VOTING IN RESPONSE TO ECONOMIC ISSUES. *Am. Pol. Sci. Rev. 1981 75(2): 448-459.* Explores the hypothesis that voting in response to economic problems is policy-oriented: voters concerned about unemployment give greater support to Democratic candidates, while those concerned about inflation vote more Republican. Support is strongest for the unemployment side of the hypothesis. Voters personally affected by unemployment gave a modest boost to Democratic candidates in virtually every election. And in years of high unemployment the large percentage of voters who felt it was a serious national problem voted heavily Democratic as well. Covers 1956-78.
J/S

745. Koeniger, A. Cash. THE NEW DEAL AND THE STATES: ROOSEVELT VERSUS THE BYRD ORGANIZATION IN VIRGINIA. *J. of Am. Hist. 1982 68(4): 876-896.* Modifies two interpretations of President Roosevelt's patronage feud with the Byrd machine in Virginia during the middle and late 1930's: James T. Patterson's *The New Deal and the States: Federalism in Transition* (1969) and James MacGregor Burns's *Roosevelt: The Lion and the Fox* (1956). Senator Byrd's "organizaton" was even less secure than Patterson claimed

it was, but the US Senate viewed Roosevelt's attempt to undermine Byrd's supremacy in Virginia's Democratic Party as an attack on its procedures. Had Roosevelt pressed his attack, as Burns claimed he should have, he might have damaged seriously his leadership ability in Congress. Based on the Harry F. Byrd Papers, the Carter Glass Papers, and the Franklin D. Roosevelt Papers; 74 notes.

T. P. Linkfield

746. Koeniger, A. Cash. THE POLITICS OF INDEPENDENCE: CARTER GLASS AND THE ELECTION OF 1936. *South Atlantic Q. 1981 80(1): 95-106.* In the 1936 presidential election, Carter Glass of Virginia ran considerably behind Franklin D. Roosevelt in vote-gathering. He essentially sat out the campaign because he could not support the New Deal. His role in the election marked the beginning of a hallmark in Virginia politics for the next three decades. Unable to reconcile his conservative convictions with the presidential candidate and national platform of his party, yet wedded to Democratic traditions, Glass took the only course that would enable him to maintain his integrity and remain a Democrat. His conduct met the approval of the Virginia electorate. It would be emulated and refined in the famed "golden silence" of Harry F. Byrd. Based on the Carter Glass Papers and the Harry F. Byrd Papers (both in the University of Virginia), the R. Walton Moore Papers (Franklin D. Roosevelt Library), and contemporary newspaper accounts; 27 notes.   H. M. Parker, Jr.

747. Kyvig, David E. RASKOB, ROOSEVELT, AND REPEAL. *Historian 1975 37(3): 469-487.* A prohibition repeal advocate, John J. Raskob exploited his chairmanship (1928-32) of the Democratic National Committee to secure repeal of the 18th Amendment. In so doing he collided with the presidential course of Franklin D. Roosevelt who mistakenly questioned the political wisdom of making any party commitment to repeal. However, Raskob was successful, first at the Democratic National Convention of 1932 with passage of a strong anti-prohibition plank to which Roosevelt gave opportunistic endorsement, and finally with the actual repeal on 5 December 1933. 83 notes.

748. Lader, Lawrence. THE WALLACE CAMPAIGN OF 1948. *Am. Heritage 1976 28(1): 42-51.* Summarizes factors leading to the unsuccessful presidential bid by Henry A. Wallace in 1948 and analyzes the campaign. Wallace's split with President Truman became clear in 1946 when he urged the President to take a softer line toward the Soviet Union. His ouster as Secretary of Commerce and the ever-hardening Truman Cold War posture led Wallace to make his bid for the presidency on the Progressive Party ticket. His ties with Communist supporters, his soft line in time of a Cold War, and the President's urging of Democrats not to "waste" their votes, all hurt his chances. 7 illus.   J. F. Paul

749. Leader, Leonard. UPTON SINCLAIR'S EPIC SWITCH: A DILEMMA FOR AMERICAN SOCIALISTS. *Southern California Q. 1980 62(4): 361-385.* Traces Socialist Party reaction to Upton Sinclair's switch from the Socialist Party to the Democratic Party in order to run for the Democratic gubernatorial nomination in California in 1934. Sinclair believed that the power base of the Socialist Party had shrunk to insignificance and that he stood a good chance for election if he changed his party affiliation. The Socialist Party leadership rejected him, but most rank and file party members approved the move as a politically realistic one. Sinclair surprised state party leadership by his over-

whelming victory in the Democratic primary in August 1934. Sinclair lost the general election, but he compiled more than 800,000 votes to less than 3,000 for the Socialist candidate. Sinclair saw his campaign as a movement to educate the masses, and in this context he was far more successful than the Socialist Party's doctrinaire leaders. 61 notes.   A. Hoffman

750. Lear, Linda J. REMNANT WITHOUT A CAUSE. *Rev. in Am. Hist. 1981 9(4): 510-515.* Reviews Ronald L. Feinman's *Twilight of Progressivism: The Western Republican Senators and the New Deal* (1981), a study of the political activities and significance of twelve Republican senators from the West from the beginning of the Depression until 1941.

751. Leupold, Robert J. THE KENTUCKY WPA: RELIEF AND POLI-TICS, MAY-NOVEMBER, 1935. *Filson Club Hist. Q. 1975 49(2): 152-168.* Destroys the myth that the Democrats purchased votes with Works Progress Administration funds during the 1935 Kentucky gubernatorial campaign. States that the rapid increase of personnel hired in the two weeks before election day was caused by administrative difficulties created by the demise of the Federal Emergency Relief Administration and the transfer of its functions to the WPA. Notes that less than half of those in the FERA work program in the spring of 1935 were receiving aid in November. Attributes the Democratic victory to the depression and the personality of Democratic candidate A. B. "Happy" Chandler. Based on newspapers; 100 notes.   G. B. McKinney

752. Lewis, Mort R. LINCOLN, STEVENSON AND YOURS TRULY. *Manuscripts 1975 27(4): 280-284.* Reminisces about correspondence with Adlai E. Stevenson, II, and includes the copy of a letter suggesting that Stevenson, the Lincoln admirer, engage Dwight D. Eisenhower in a series of debates over national issues in the 1952 presidential election.   D. A. Yanchisin

753. Lovin, Hugh T. TOWARD A FARMER-LABOR PARTY IN ORE-GON, 1933-38. *Oregon Hist. Q. 1975 76(2): 135-151.* Analyzes the failure of attempts to establish a branch of the Farmer-Labor Party in Oregon. This party was composed of agrarians and labor unionists discontented with the New Deal's failure to combat the depression. It proposed as a cure an "economy of abundance" achieved by government encouragement of cooperatives and legislation ensuring the production of goods 'for use" rather than "for profit." In 1937 opponents of the New Deal formed the Oregon Commonwealth Federation but the new party failed because of its radical reputation, weak backing from agrarians and the American Federation of Labor, and a disinclination toward third parties. Many of the reform-oriented goals were ultimately achieved through political activities within the Oregon Democratic Party. Based on manuscript collections, newspapers, unpublished theses, and secondary sources; 57 notes.
                                                                        J. D. Smith

754. Lutz, Paul F. THE 1952 WEST VIRGINIA GUBERNATORIAL ELECTION. *West Virginia Hist. 1978 39(2-3): 210-235.* In 1952 Democrat William C. Marland was elected governor of West Virginia over Republican Rush D. Holt by only 27,000 votes. Marland, the state's attorney general and candidate of the "statehouse machine," defeated labor-backed E. E. Hedrick in a hard-fought primary. In the bitter general election campaign Holt ran as an anticorrup-

tion candidate but Marland won with a last-minute media attack on Holt's character, family, and political record. Primary sources; 88 notes.

J. H. Broussard

755. Maddox, Robert Franklin. THE MARTIN-ROSIER AFFAIR. *Capitol Studies 1977 5(1): 57-70.* Examines factionalism in West Virginia's Democratic Party when Harley M. Kilgore, Joseph Rosier, and Clarence E. Martin all claimed to be Senators in 1941.

756. Malone, Michael P. MONTANA POLITICS AT THE CROSSROADS, 1932-1933. *Pacific Northwest Q. 1978 69(1): 20-29.* Montana's 1932 election witnessed a landslide victory for Democratic candidates riding the coattails of Franklin D. Roosevelt. Never before and never again would one party so completely dominate the state and guarantee Montana a powerful position within national politics. The death of Senator Thomas J. Walsh in March 1933 created new tensions when Democratic Governor John E. Erickson maneuvered himself into the vacant Senate position, but efforts to unseat him were unsuccessful. Since then Montana Democrats have maintained their loyalty to Roosevelt's moderate liberalism. Primary and secondary sources; 2 illus., 41 notes. M. L. Tate

757. Manykin, A. S. RESPUBLIKANSKAIA PARTIIA S.SH.A. V POIS-KAKH AL'TERNATIVY "NOVOMU KURSU" [The Republican Party of the U.S.A. and the search for an alternative to the "New Deal"]. *Vestnik Moskovskogo U., Seriia 8: Istoriia [USSR] 1978 (5): 44-59.* The Republicans developed a neoconservative view to oppose the New Deal. Hoover represented the faction opposing the New Deal while A. Landon opposed monopolies and accepted the principle of state regulation. After the 1936 election, J. Hamilton became head of the National Committee and fought to have Hoover end his active role. As a coalition of conservative Democrats and Republicans formed on the Supreme Court issue, the Republicans ended their policy of pure negation. They accepted some limited government regulation. The new conservative philosophy was expressed in a work of a commission which preceded the Republican convention of 1940. The new philosophy accepted social security under state authority and limited government regulation. The Republican Party was strengthened and the functioning of the two party system restored. (See also abstract 929). 66 notes.

D. Balmuth

758. McGuire, Jack B. ANDREW HIGGINS PLAYS PRESIDENTIAL POLITICS. *Louisiana Hist. 1974 15(3): 273-284.* Discusses the political work of Andrew J. Higgins, a Louisiana-born campaign worker for the Democratic Party, and his work in helping to elect Franklin D. Roosevelt and Harry S. Truman, 1944.

759. Mead, Howard N. RUSSELL VS. TALMADGE: SOUTHERN POLITICS AND THE NEW DEAL. *Georgia Hist. Q. 1981 65(1): 28-45.* The 1936 Georgia senatorial Democratic primary was a bitter race between incumbent Senator Richard B. Russell and Governor Eugene Talmadge. Russell, with his "patrician" view strongly supported Franklin D. Roosevelt and the then popular and successful New Deal programs and was elected, while Talmadge with his "nigger-baiting," demagogic, anti-New Deal views was defeated. Based on newspaper and secondary sources; 47 notes. G. R. Schroeder

760. Melosi, Martin V.   POLITICAL TREMORS FROM A MILITARY DISASTER: 'PEARL HARBOR' AND THE ELECTION OF 1944. *Diplomatic Hist. 1977 1(1): 79-95.* Discusses the debate between Republicans and the Roosevelt administration over personal responsibility for the Pearl Harbor disaster. Republicans failed, however, to make this a vital issue in the 1944 presidential campaign. Criticism of Franklin D. Roosevelt's policies was difficult to achieve while the nation was still at war. Republican presidential nominee Thomas E. Dewey was "reluctant to make a stand on an issue that smacked of disloyalty," and he could not "exploit one spectacular issue—the breaking of the Japanese code—which might give the Republican criticisms legitimacy." Furthermore, the Roosevelt administration effectively denied the release of information which might aid the Republicans. Primary and secondary sources; 49 notes.

G. H. Curtis

761. Meltz, David B.   LEGISLATIVE PARTY COHESION: A MODEL OF THE BARGAINING PROCESS IN STATE LEGISLATURES.   *J. of Pol. 1973 35(3): 647-681.* Develops a majority party bargaining model for state legislatures. "The assumptions of this theory of party cohesion establish an isomorphism with one type of N-person, zero-sum game and involve two theorems. The theorems state that intraparty cohesion is an increasing function of both short- and long-term interparty competition. The two competition variables together explain 68 percent of the intersession variation in Republican majority party cohesion on party opposition roll calls from the Indiana House, 1931-62. Relaxing some assumptions yields an adequate explanation of democratic party activity within the framework of the model." 5 tables, 24 notes, appendix.

A. R. Stoesen

762. Morgan, Alfred L.   THE SIGNIFICANCE OF PENNSYLVANIA'S 1938 GUBERNATORIAL ELECTION.   *Pennsylvania Mag. of Hist. and Biog. 1978 102(2): 184-211.* The relatively noncontentious Republican primary explains the victory of their candidate, Arthur H. James. Internal dissension and charges of corruption disrupted the Democrats, who also bucked an anti-New Deal tide. The election reversed the trend of Democratic resurgence. Based on newspapers, officials records, and secondary works; 82 notes.   T. H. Wendel

763. Partin, John W.   ROOSEVELT, BYRNES, AND THE 1944 VICE-PRESIDENTIAL NOMINATION.   *Historian 1979 42(1): 85-100.* Reviews the internecine strife that enveloped the 1944 vice-presidential nomination between James F. Byrnes and Henry A. Wallace. Franklin D. Roosevelt very consciously played them off against each other so that Harry S. Truman could be nominated. Roosevelt was able to enter the campaign with the support of his entire party, but he had done nothing to repair the schisms in the Democratic Party that would remain to plague his successors. Primary sources; 34 notes.   R. S. Sliwoski

764. Patenaude, Lionel V.   THE GARNER VOTE SWITCH TO ROOSEVELT: 1932 DEMOCRATIC CONVENTION.   *Southwestern Hist. Q. 1975 79(2): 189-204.* Describes the complex political negotiations which led to the release of the delegates pledged to John Nance Garner and the nomination of Franklin D. Roosevelt on the fourth ballot at the Democratic Convention in Chicago, 1 July 1932. Sam Rayburn was the key man, aided by William Gibbs McAdoo head of the California delegation, and James A. Farley, Roosevelt's

campaign manager. It was Roosevelt who made the decision to run with Garner; Garner accepted the vice-presidency "reluctantly and only as a party-saving gesture." 10 illus., 22 notes.   C. W. Olson

765. Paul, Justus F.   BUTLER, GRISWOLD, WHERRY: THE STRUG-GLE FOR DOMINANCE OF NEBRASKA REPUBLICANISM, 1941-1946. *North Dakota Q. 1975 43(4): 51-61.* Describes the hegemony of the Republican Party in Nebraska through the personalities and struggle for dominance of Re-publican leaders Hugh Butler, Dwight Griswold, and Kenneth Wherry.

766. Paul, Justus F.   ISOLATIONISM VERSUS INTERNATIONALISM? THE REPUBLICAN SENATORIAL PRIMARY IN NEBRASKA, 1946. *Nebraska Hist. 1975 56(1): 145-156.* Though the press and other observers con-sidered the 1946 Republican primary in Nebraska between Dwight Griswold, three-time governor and an internationalist, and Hugh Butler, the incumbent and an "unredeemed" pre-war isolationist, as an indication of Midwestern public opinion concerning American foreign policy, Butler won handily because of his effective political organization.   R. Lowitt

767. Phillips, Waite and Trafzer, Clifford E.   VIEWS FROM THE RED RIVER VALLEY: A "LIBERAL" REPUBLICAN'S PHILOSOPHY.   *Red River Valley Hist. R. 1974 1(1): 70-77.* In two letters, Republican politician Waite Phillips expressed his political philosophy, his criticisms of the New Deal, and his assessment of the latter's impact on rugged individualism.   S

768. Plesur, Milton.   THE REPUBLICAN CONGRESSIONAL COME-BACK OF 1938.   Plesur, Milton, ed. *An American Historian: Essays to Honor Selig Adler* (Buffalo: State U. of New York, 1980): 167-182. Causes of the Republican Party's comeback in the congressional elections of 1938 included that party's attempts to unify itself and to shed its reactionary image, dangerous setbacks to the economy starting in 1937, a purge in the Democratic Party, President Franklin D. Roosevelt's ill-fated attempt to remodel the Supreme Court, labor unrest, popular dissatisfaction with contradictions and complexities in the New Deal, and Roosevelt's foundering anti-isolationist foreign policy. The election of 1938 represented not a rejection of the New Deal, however, but a call to moderation in which the Democrats and Roosevelt suffered reverses even as the Republicans began to join them in a trend toward progressivism that would see the election of a Republican president 14 years later. 49 notes. Abridged from *Review of Politics* 1962 24(3): 525-562.   S

769. Reeves, William D.   PWA AND COMPETITIVE ADMINISTRA-TION IN THE NEW DEAL.   *J. of Am. Hist. 1973 60(2): 357-372.* The compet-itive theory of administration developed by Franklin Delano Roosevelt has often been admired as producing efficiency. In the case of the Public Works Adminis-tration (PWA), however, the competition over the size of expenditure, the selec-tion of the administrator, and the appointment of staff at the state level, led to delays and to the ultimate failure of PWA as a recovery instrument. As director of the budget, Lewis Douglas overrode the views of leading senators in reducing appropriations to $3,500,000,000 and in transferring much of that money to other agencies in lieu of their own specific appropriations. The cautious and penurious Harold Ickes won out over the more imaginative Hugh S. Johnson as chief of

public works administration. Political competition between rival Democratic state organizations and between Democrats and Progressive Republicans led to delays in implementing PWA efforts on the local level. 60 notes.

K. B. West

770. Reichard, Gary W. DIVISIONS AND DISSENT: DEMOCRATS AND FOREIGN POLICY, 1952-1956. *Pol. Sci. Q. 1978 93(1): 51-72.* Traces the evolution of Democratic party thought and action on significant foreign policy issues during the first Eisenhower administration. Refuting the idea that bipartisanship prevailed in foreign policy during the 1950's, describes how Democratic leaders differed with Eisenhower's policies from 1952 to 1956 and why they developed a coherent alternative policy of their own after 1956.   J

771. Reiter, Howard L. THE PERILS OF PARTISAN RECALL. *Public Opinion Q. 1980 44(3): 385-388.* Questions the methodology in Kristi Andersen's "Generation, Partisan Shift, and Realignment: A Glance Back to the New Deal" in Norman H. Nie et al., *The Changing American Voter* (1976). Andersen's conclusion that there was no significant shift from Republican to Democratic affiliation in 1932 ignores the possibility that those whose affiliation changed may simply have forgotten that they were Republicans in the '20's. Illustrates this tendency using data—from Andersen's own source—on black and Jewish voters. Based on the University of Michigan's Survey Research Center surveys, 1952-72; 3 tables, note, 2 ref.   L. Van Wyk

772. Rosenof, Theodore. THE POLITICAL EDUCATION OF AN AMERICAN RADICAL: THOMAS R. AMLIE IN THE 1930'S. *Wisconsin Mag. of Hist. 1974 58(1): 19-30.* Wisconsin congressman Thomas R. Amlie served in the House of Representatives first as a La Follette Republican from 1931 to 1933 and then as a Progressive from 1935 to 1939. The author traces the intellectual evolution of Amlie's radicalism as he responded to the depression and the political philosophy of the New Deal. At first Amlie sought to alter society through the formation of a third party. He gradually abandoned that idea in hopes of transforming Franklin D. Roosevelt and the New Deal into a new radical force, but ended the decade disillusioned by 'the New Dealers' dogmatically limited solution." 5 illus., 36 notes.   N. C. Burckel

773. Ryan, Thomas G. THE EARLY YEARS OF THE IOWA DEMO-CRATIC REVIVAL, 1950-1956. *Ann. of Iowa 1981 46(1): 43-63.* Attributes revival of Democratic Party in Iowa in years 1950-56 to gubernatorial factionalism within the state's Republican Party. Based on election returns in the *Iowa Official Register* and other primary sources; 3 tables, 2 photos, 24 notes.

P. L. Petersen

774. Sanford, Dudley Gregory. YOU CAN'T GET THERE FROM HERE: THE PRESIDENTIAL BOOMLET FOR GOVERNOR GEORGE D. AIKEN, 1937-1939. *Vermont Hist. 1981 49(4): 197-208.* Six years after the Putney nurseryman entered politics, Aiken won national attention as a Republican who could be elected governor in the 1936 Democratic landslide. Aiken's "new Republicanism," formulated in *Speaking from Vermont* (1939), sought to win the votes of youth, labor, and small business by accepting more federal welfare without deficit spending and by fostering local "cooperation." The 1936

New England flood dramatized the need for regional flood control, and Aiken became the New England spokesman for one-purpose dams, leaving power and other rights to the states and private business. He campaigned outside Vermont, with the aid of Leo Casey, retiring publicity director of the Republican National Committee, less to win the 1940 presidential nomination than to rejuvenate the Republican Party as a bulwark against the New Deal flood control program. Based mainly on the Aiken Papers, University of Vermont; 30 notes.

T. D. S. Bassett

775. Sayles, Stephen. CLAIR ENGLE AND HIS POLITICAL DEVELOP- MENT IN TEHAMA COUNTY, 1911-1944. *California Hist. Q. 1975 54(4): 293-314.* A biographical study of Clair Engle (1911-64), a congressman and senator from California, focusing on his formative years. Engle's early involve- ment in politics began when he was twice elected high school student body president. Having passed the bar at age 22, Engle began his public career in 1934 by winning election as Tehama County's district attorney in an aggressive cam- paign. He became a Democrat in 1936 and in 1942 was elected to the state Senate. In a special election the following year he defeated a divided Republican opposi- tion to become congressman from the Second District. In 1944, at age 33, Engle won reelection to the House, establishing a firm political base in northern Califor- nia and launching an influential career in state and national politics. At times opportunistic and narrowminded, he also demonstrated a capacity for growth and flexibility as he advanced his political career. Based on personal interviews, correspondence and documents, and contemporary and secondary sources; photos, 93 notes. A. Hoffman

776. Schapsmeier, Edward L. and Schapsmeier, Frederick H. FARM POL- ICY FROM FDR TO EISENHOWER: SOUTHERN DEMOCRATS AND THE POLITICS OF AGRICULTURE. *Agric. Hist. 1979 53(1): 352-371.* Analyzes political alignments and policies in the South since the New Deal. Regardless of historic Jeffersonian principles, Southern agriculture pragmatically supported federal intervention, and resisted major reform of the post-New Deal parity-price-support acreage allotment system, thereby giving tacit approval for enlarging other aspects of the welfare state. They also were able to defy Presidents Roosevelt, Truman, and Eisenhower on the substance of farm programs. Added to this, southern power in Congress was evidenced in the use of seniority, parlia- mentary skill, and adroitness at forming voting coalitions. By such means they played a vital role in the formulation of major farm programs of the period. 71 notes. Comment by John E. Lee, Jr., pp. 372-376. R. V. Ritter

777. Schapsmeier, Edward L. and Schapsmeier, Frederick H. SCOTT W. LUCAS OF HAVANA: HIS RISE AND FALL AS MAJORITY LEADER IN THE UNITED STATES SENATE. *J. of the Illinois State Hist. Soc. 1977 70(4): 302-320.* Democrat Scott W. Lucas (1892-1968) used a homey style of politicking to win his first House seat in 1934 and Senate seat in 1938. His poor health and strong support of Truman's foreign policy made possible his defeat in 1950 by Everett M. Dirksen. Based on Lucas Papers; 18 illus., 67 notes. J

778. Schnell, J. Christopher. MISSOURI PROGRESSIVES AND THE NOMINATION OF F.D.R. *Missouri Hist. R. 1974 68(3): 269-279.* Reexam- ines the basis of support by Missouri Democratic delegates of Franklin D. Roose-

velt for the presidential nomination in 1932. Many historians claim that the influence of Kansas City boss Thomas J. Pendergast swung Missouri support to Roosevelt. The support, however, was the result of efforts by a group of Wilsonian progressives, including many anti-Pendergast forces, led by Ewing Y. Mitchell, William Hirth, Judge Eldridge Dearing, and Louis Gualdoni. Pendergast had publicly supported the favorite son candidate, James A. Reed. The pro-Roosevelt group was well organized and had strong rural and "outstate" support. At the national convention the Missouri delegation increased its support of Roosevelt with each ballot, and all of the initial Missouri support came from these non-Pendergast forces. Based on contemporary newspaper reports, primary and secondary sources; 5 photos, 28 notes.   N. J. Street

779.   Schonberger, Howard B.   THE GENERAL AND THE PRESIDENCY: DOUGLAS MAC ARTHUR AND THE ELECTION OF 1948.   *Wisconsin Mag. of Hist. 1974 57(3): 201-219.* Relies on recently opened archival sources to argue that General Douglas MacArthur wanted the Republican presidential nomination in 1948, encouraged friends and participated in important strategy decisions concerning that abortive campaign. His chief supporters agreed that for MacArthur to have a chance of being chosen the compromise candidate at a convention deadlocked over Thomas E. Dewey and Robert A. Taft, he would first have to win the primary contest in Wisconsin. In that campaign his fortunes rested with Philip F. La Follette, former three-term governor and colonel on MacArthur's staff during World War II. Twice elected governor on the Progressive ticket, La Follette had alienated many regular Republicans who did not appreciate his belated return to the Republican party a decade later. MacArthur ran second in a three-man race, behind Harold Stassen. From that point on, his chances for the nomination were negligible, although he continued to believe he could win at the national convention. 11 illus., 75 notes.   N. C. Burckel

780.   Scobie, Ingrid Winther.   HELEN GAHAGAN DOUGLAS AND HER 1950 SENATE RACE WITH RICHARD M. NIXON.   *Southern California Q. 1976 58(1): 113-126.* Democratic incumbent Sheridan Downey bowed out of the primary race because of ill health; newspaper publisher Manchester Boddy, with support from Downey, unsuccessfully contested Helen Gahagan Douglas for the Democratic nomination. The hotly contested primary race provided Richard M. Nixon with additional political ammunition for the general election. Badly divided, the Democrats ran a poor contest against the Republicans. Nixon, managed by Murray Chotiner, ran an aggressive campaign which included use of smear tactics. These included linking Douglas' voting record with radical Congressman Vito Marcantonio's, accusing her of being soft on Communism, and misrepresenting her political views and associations. By contrast, Douglas' approach was idealistic and defensive. Douglas lost by a 3-2 margin. Nixon might have won on the issues alone, given the disorganization of the Democrats, but that ambitious congressman took no chances. Based on primary and secondary sources; 40 notes.   A. Hoffman

781.   Sears, James M.   BLACK AMERICANS AND THE NEW DEAL. *Hist. Teacher 1976 10(1): 89-105.* A discussion of black support for Franklin D. Roosevelt and the New Deal. Blacks, disenchanted with the Hoover administration, anticipated inclusion in New Deal efforts to create jobs for the unemployed. Blacks benefitted from the New Deal in perhaps greater measure than they had

anticipated. Without specifically committing himself, Roosevelt gave black Americans a stake in the governmental process. Black political and religious leaders, the black press and organizations, and Roosevelt's charisma helped place Negroes firmly in the Democratic party. Based on primary and secondary sources; 63 notes, biblio.

P. W. Kennedy

782. Simmons, Jerold. DAWSON COUNTY RESPONDS TO THE NEW DEAL, 1933-1940. *Nebraska Hist. 1981 62(1): 47-72.* Reviews the response of central Nebraskans in Dawson County to the array of programs, agencies and measures comprising the New Deal. Initially, the New Deal won widespread approval and attracted voters to the Democratic Party. But these voters refused to commit themselves permanently. By 1940 they had overwhelmingly returned to their traditionally Republican voting habits. Ethnic, economic and social reasons could explain the county's political response during the 1930's.

R. Lowitt

783. Sinclair, Barbara. FROM PARTY VOTING TO REGIONAL FRAGMENTATION: THE HOUSE OF REPRESENTATIVES, 1933-1956. *Am. Pol. Q. 1978 6(2): 125-146.* Examination of the House of Representatives' roll-call voting during 1933-56 shows that heavily partisan voting during the 1930's gave way by the early 1950's to voting strongly influenced by region. The regional fragmentation was, in part, due to the development of new, party-splitting issues. The blurring of party lines occurred during political normality. Party realignments, however, were characterized by highly partisan voting alignments in the congress. Later, centrifugal constituency-related forces again predominated and the sharp differences between the parties became blurred. 6 tables, 3 notes, ref.

R. V. Ritter

784. Sinclair, Barbara. THE POLICY CONSEQUENCES OF PARTY REALIGNMENT: SOCIAL WELFARE LEGISLATION IN THE HOUSE OF REPRESENTATIVES, 1933-1954. *Am. J. of Pol. Sci. 1978 22(1): 83-105.* Burnham's theory of the policy consequences of realignments is applied to social welfare legislation during the New Deal realignment and its aftermath. As predicted, social welfare legislation does emerge as a direct response to the depression. The most clearly nonincremental programs were passed during the height of the realigning era (1935-38) and little nonincremental legislation passed during the remaining years under study. Throughout the 1930s, the increased issue distance between the parties was reflected in highly partisan voting alignments on non-labor social welfare legislation. During the 1940s, centrifugal constituency related forces reasserted themselves. By the 80th Congress, a single dominant and highly stable social welfare dimension had developed. Southern Democrats, who had been highly supportive of social welfare legislation during the 1930s, were now the least supportive regional grouping within the Democratic party. Northeastern Republicans, once the most conservative segment of the Republican party, became the most supportive while west north central Republicans followed the opposite path.

J

785. Singer, Donald L. UPTON SINCLAIR AND THE CALIFORNIA GUBERNATORIAL CAMPAIGN OF 1934. *Southern California Q. 1974 56(4): 375-406.* An account of the 1934 California gubernatorial campaign. Persuaded to change his affiliation from Socialist to Democrat, Upton Sinclair

captured the party's nomination in a major primary victory. His End Poverty In California (EPIC) program, however, alarmed conservatives, although the Democrats modified and compromised it. Sinclair was smeared viciously; his only editorial support came from his own *EPIC News*, and almost all the state's newspapers denied him coverage. Not only Republicans but Communists feared his candidacy. He failed to receive endorsement from President Franklin Roosevelt, and his opponent, Governor Frank Merriam, let underlings carry on smear tactics. Having lost by some 250,000 votes, Sinclair attributed his defeat to defections by prominent Democrats, the smear campaign, and lack of newspaper coverage. Despite its defeat, the EPIC campaign indirectly helped turn the New Deal towards social welfare legislation, increased California's registration of Democrats, and gave budding Democratic leaders a boost in politics. Based on primary and secondary sources; 155 notes.   A. Hoffman

786. Smith, Harold T. PITTMAN, CREEL, AND NEW DEAL POLITICS. *Nevada Hist. Soc. Q. 1979 22(4): 254-270.* Cecil Creel, a leading Nevada agricultural scientist, directed New Deal relief programs in Nevada until Frank Upman, Jr., replaced him in 1934. Although he was a competent administrator, Creel was ousted in response to demands of Nevada Senator Key Pittman (1872-1940). Pittman persuaded President Franklin Roosevelt and Harry Hopkins that Pittman's faction of Nevada Democrats should control New Deal relief work in the state. Based on primary materials in the National Archives and Franklin D. Roosevelt Library and newspaper sources; 50 notes.   H. T. Lovin

787. Snyder, Robert E. HUEY LONG AND THE PRESIDENTIAL ELECTION OF 1936. *Louisiana Hist. 1975 16(2): 117-143.* The rise in popularity of Huey Long's Share Our Wealth movement caused Franklin D. Roosevelt and his supporters well-founded concern as the election of 1936 approached, not because Long (1893-1935) had any chance of winning the presidency, but because his candidacy could have given a strong Republican a better chance. Moreover, Long's movement would have kept other pro-Roosevelt politicians from winning office. Based on primary and secondary sources; 73 notes.   R. L. Woodward

788. Soapes, Thomas F. THE FRAGILITY OF THE ROOSEVELT COALITION: THE CASE OF MISSOURI. *Missouri Hist. Rev. 1977 72(1): 38-58.* Franklin D. Roosevelt's impressive electoral mandate in 1936 did not achieve immediate permanence. In Missouri the Negroes, farmers, and workers were weak links in the new Democratic alignment, as the Republican Party began to revive during the 1940's. It was not until 1952 that the Democratic Party regained most of the offices they lost in the 1940's. Republican leaders were only interested in maintaining their power in the party, the party did not have a record to compete with the Democrats, and the Republican areas of the state lost population. Roosevelt's fragile coalition had become a well-organized force by 1952. Primary and secondary sources; illus., 45 notes.   W. F. Zornow

789. Soapes, Thomas F. THE GOVERNORSHIP "STEAL" AND THE REPUBLICAN REVIVAL. *Missouri Hist. Soc. Bull. 1976 32(3): 158-172.* Analyzes the 1940 gubernatorial election in Missouri between Forrest C. Donnell (b. 1885) and Lawrence McDaniel. Donnell, the Republican nominee, won the election despite Democratic victories for congressional and most state legislative offices. Donnell's victory in 1940 signaled increasing success for the Republican

Party in Missouri politics during the 1940's, partly because Donnell effectively exposed corruption by the Democratic machine of Thomas Pendergast (1873-1945). Based on manuscript and newspaper sources; 8 photos, 33 notes.

H. T. Lovin

790. Spackman, S. G. F. ROOSEVELT. *Hist. Today [Great Britain] 1980 30 (June): 38-43.* Analyzes Franklin D. Roosevelt's policies from the 1920's to his death in 1945 and concludes that he did much to create the modern presidency and to make the diplomatic transition from the balance of power system to that of the superpowers.

791. Spencer, Thomas T. "AS GOES MAINE, SO GOES VERMONT": THE 1936 DEMOCRATIC CAMPAIGN IN VERMONT. *Vermont Hist. 1978 46(4): 234-243.* Republican control of Vermont relief programs, low Democratic Party campaign expenditures with little emphasis on FDR, a Republican press, George D. Aiken's candidacy for governor, and a lively Republican campaign all resulted in a 19,000 plurality for Landon, compared to 23,000 for Hoover in 1932. Based on Democratic National Committee correspondence and on secondary sources; 35 notes.

T. D. S. Bassett

792. Spencer, Thomas T. AUXILIARY AND NON-PARTY POLITICS: THE 1936 DEMOCRATIC PRESIDENTIAL CAMPAIGN IN OHIO. *Ohio Hist. 1981 90(2): 114-128.* Discusses the 1936 presidential campaign in Ohio, and the successful Democratic Party strategy of going outside the party to attract voters by organizing auxiliary and nonparty committees. Especially important in appealing to labor, blacks, farmers, and women, Democratic auxiliary committees such as the Non-Partisan Labor League, the Good Neighbor League, and Roosevelt's All-Party Agricultural Committee helped to counter criticism of the New Deal by attracting those voters with a vital stake in its success. Although Democratic fears of losing the Midwestern states were exaggerated, the campaign appeal of such organizations led to their becoming a "vital part of the Democratic coalition in future elections." Based on the collections of the Franklin D. Roosevelt Library, Hyde Park, New York, the National Archives and Records Service, the University of Iowa, and other primary sources; illus., 42 notes.

L. A. Russell

793. Spencer, Thomas T. BENNETT CHAMP CLARK AND THE 1936 PRESIDENTIAL CAMPAIGN. *Missouri Hist. Rev. 1981 75(2): 197-213.* Clark won the Missouri senatorial election in 1932 without any help from the Democratic machine in Kansas City. His votes against New Deal bills often made him a thorn in President Franklin D. Roosevelt's side, but the president and party leaders recognized his ability and selected him for an important role in 1936. As chairman of the rules committee for the Democratic National Convention, Clark found his assignment to lead the fight against the two-thirds rule an easy one, since no strong support for the rule developed. His most challenging assignments were to deliver campaign speeches and to chair the Committee of One, an auxiliary organized to solicit support from individuals outside the regular party structure. Based on secondary sources, newspapers, James A. Farley Papers, Library of Congress, Frank Walker Papers, University of Notre Dame, Emil Hurja Papers and the Democratic National Committee Records, Franklin D. Roosevelt Library; illus., 37 notes.

W. F. Zornow

794. Spencer, Thomas T. THE GOOD NEIGHBOR LEAGUE COLORED COMMITTEE AND THE 1936 DEMOCRATIC PRESIDENTIAL CAMPAIGN. *J. of Negro Hist. 1978 63(4): 307-316.* The Good Neighbor League Colored Committee, along with the Colored Voters Division of the Democratic Party, was a vital force in making Afro-Americans part of the Franklin D. Roosevelt coalition in 1936. Since 1936, blacks have continued to play an important part in Democratic campaigns. Based upon records in the Franklin D. Roosevelt Presidential Library; 32 notes.   N. G. Sapper

795. Spencer, Thomas T. THE NEW DEAL COMES TO THE "GRANITE STATE": THE 1936 DEMOCRATIC PRESIDENTIAL CAMPAIGN IN NEW HAMPSHIRE. *Hist. New Hampshire 1980 35(2): 186-201.* Franklin D. Roosevelt surprised many political observers in defeating Alfred Landon in the 1936 presidential election in New Hampshire. Roosevelt's personal popularity and the success of New Deal relief and recovery programs probably account for the victory. The president carried only three of New Hampshire's 10 counties, but he carried populous Hillsborough County by more than 11,000 votes. Relief and recovery programs employed more than 9,000 workers in New Hampshire in the fall of 1936, mainly in urban areas. 34 notes.   D. F. Chard

796. Stickle, Warren E. EDISON, "HAGUEISM," AND THE SPLIT TICKET IN 1940. *New Jersey Hist. 1979 97(2): 69-86.* In the 1940 New Jersey gubernatorial election the Republican Party, its candidate Robert Hendrickson, and the Republican-controlled state legislature made Frank Hague and "Hagueism" the theme of the campaign. Charles Edison, the Democratic candidate, effectively established his political independence from Hague, however, and thus negated any potency the issue may have had. Even though Republicans swept senatorial, congressional, and state assembly races, Edison garnered enough split tickets to win the governorship by nearly 57,000 votes. Based on contemporary newspaper accounts and secondary sources; 5 illus., 4 tables, 36 notes.
                    E. R. McKinstry

797. Stickle, Warren E. THE REPUBLICAN CAMPAIGN OF 1940. *New Jersey Hist. 1975 93(1-2): 43-57.* In 1940 Jerseymen voted nationally for a president and elected their governor. Discusses the discord and disunity of Wendell Willkie's primary and general election campaigns symbolized by the many statewide Willkie Clubs, reviews the heated G.O.P. gubernatorial primary battle between former governor Harold G. Hoffman and state senator Robert Hendrickson, the eventual winner; and summarizes the contest between Henrickson and Charles Edison, the Democratic standard bearer. Republican Party losses in both elections are blamed on extensive party factionalism. Based on primary and secondary sources; 6 illus., 27 notes.   E. R. McKinstry

798. Sweeney, James R. THE GOLDEN SILENCE: THE VIRGINIA DEMOCRATIC PARTY AND THE PRESIDENTIAL ELECTION OF 1948. *Virginia Mag. of Hist. and Biog. 1974 82(3): 351-371.* Disturbed by President Harry S. Truman's stand on civil rights, the Democratic Party leadership in Virginia, headed by Senator Harry Flood Byrd, determined to fight Truman's election in 1948. The Byrd organization's strategy was to keep Truman from winning Virginia's electoral votes by releasing the state's electors from the obligation to vote for the national party nominee, but Byrd's opposition managed to

mount a last minute pro-Truman movement which carried the state for the President. Based on primary and secondary sources; 2 cartoons, 52 notes.

R. F. Oaks

799. Sweeney, James R. REVOLT IN VIRGINIA: HARRY BYRD AND THE 1952 PRESIDENTIAL ELECTION. *Virginia Mag. of Hist. and Biog. 1978 86(2): 180-195.* When Senator Harry F. Byrd, longtime opponent of the policies of Presidents Roosevelt and Truman, decided to support Republican candidate Dwight D. Eisenhower for the Presidency in 1952, he weakened the Democratic Party in Virginia and set off a political revolt in that state that lasted for a quarter century. Based on newspaper accounts and on primary material in the University of Virginia; 40 notes.

R. F. Oaks

800. Syrett, John. ROOSEVELT VS. FARLEY: THE NEW YORK GUBERNATORIAL ELECTION OF 1942. *New York Hist. 1975 56(1): 51-81.* Examines the 1942 gubernatorial election that marked the end of Democratic Party solidarity in New York state politics. Anti-Roosevelt forces, led by James A. Farley, split the state party and guaranteed the election of Republican Thomas E. Dewey. President Franklin D. Roosevelt, although concerned about the New York election, failed to provide adequate leadership for pro-Roosevelt forces desiring a stronger Democratic candidate for governor than Farley-backed John J. Bennett, Jr. 5 illus., 59 notes.

R. N. Lokken

801. Tarter, Brent. A FLIER ON THE NATIONAL SCENE, HARRY F. BYRD'S FAVORITE-SON PRESIDENTIAL CANDIDACY OF 1932. *Virginia Mag. of Hist. and Biog. 1974 82(3): 282-305.* Former Virginia Governor Harry F. Byrd ran as a favorite-son candidate for President in 1932, primarily to consolidate his control over the Democratic political machinery in his state and to prevent national issues, such as prohibition, from splitting his supporters. Byrd's candidacy also reflected his suspicion of front runner Franklin D. Roosevelt, and his participation in an anti-Roosevelt movement nearly succeeded. Based on primary and secondary sources; cartoon, 44 notes.

R. F. Oaks

802. Terekhov, V. I. RAZVITIE VZGLIADOV RESPUBLIKANTSEV NA ROL' GOSUDARSTVA V EKONOMICHESKOI I SOTSIALNOI ZHIZNI OBSHCHESTVA V PERIOD PREZIDENTSTVA D. EIZENKHAUERA [The development of Republican views on the role of the state in the economic and social life of society in the period of the Presidency of D. Eisenhower]. *Vestnik Moskovskogo U. Seriia 8 Istoriia [USSR] 1976 (5): 35-54.* "Rugged individualism" was still strong in the Republican Party before 1952. Eisenhower preserved the system of state regulation and accepted the state's role in the economy in case of need. The new conservatism formed a consensus with neoliberalism. Some Democrats argued for a more pro-business attitude in the party. Programs in education and space represented the principle of state intervention as expressed in the work of Larson. The right wing remained important in the party. Still, Eisenhower's administration strengthened the position of the Republican Party in the two-party system. 67 notes.

D. Balmuth

803. Voight, Barton R. JOSEPH C. O'MAHONEY AND THE 1952 SENATE ELECTION IN WYOMING. *Ann. of Wyoming 1973 45(2): 177-226.* Considered a national statesman by 1952, Joseph C. O'Mahoney was targeted as

vulnerable by Republicans. The New Dealer was accused of ineffectually using his seniority and of absenteeism from Wyoming. The Korean War, communism, and the pull of Eisenhower hurt O'Mahoney as did the weak Democratic party organization, resulting in his defeat. Based on the O'Mahoney and other manuscript collections; illus., 4 tables, 122 notes, biblio.   S. S. Sprague

804.   Wallace, Lew.   ALBEN BARKLEY AND THE DEMOCRATIC CONVENTION OF 1948.   *Filson Club Hist. Q. 1981 55(3): 231-252.* Narrates the events at the 1948 Democratic convention, briefly discussing Alben Barkley's nomination as vice-president of the United States. Based on contemporary newspapers and published autobiographies; photo, 68 notes.   G. B. McKinney

805.   Wallace, Lew.   THE TRUMAN-DEWEY UPSET.   *Am. Hist. Illus. 1976 11(6): 20-30.* Examines the presidential election of 1948 in which Harry S. Truman upset Thomas E. Dewey in an unexpected victory.

806.   Weiss, Stuart.   KENT KELLER, THE LIBERAL BLOC, AND THE NEW DEAL.   *J. of the Illinois State Hist. Soc. 1975 68(2): 143-158.* Keller was a stalwart member of the unofficial "liberal bloc" of Democrats, progressive Republicans and independents in Congress during 1930-40. Representing "Egypt," the 25th District in southern Illinois, he supported almost every item of New Deal legislation that would benefit his coal-miner and small-farmer constituents. Believing that public works projects would alleviate the mass unemployment in his area, he supported a scheme to provide cheap electric power for his district through the construction by the federal government of a "little TVA" on Crab Orchard Creek. By 1938 the liberal bloc had largely been dismantled in Congress and the defeat of Keller and other Congressmen in 1940 and 1942 marked the ascendancy of a conservative Congress hostile to the New Deal.
    N. Lederer

807.   Whitehead, Ralph, Jr.   THE ORGANIZATION MAN.   *Am. Scholar 1977 46(3): 351-357.* Studies Richard J. Daley as big-city Democratic Party machine boss; investigates his methods and his values. The Chicago Democratic machine, under his leadership, became a powerful instrument not only in politics, but also in the economic development of the city. All of this came, not by promoting his own self-image, but by unflagging attention to the organization, its personnel, patronage, and loyalty at every level. Although this was sometimes at the price of moral values, there was a grass roots immediacy about his presence.
    R. V. Ritter

808.   Wildgen, John K.   THE DETECTION OF CRITICAL ELECTIONS IN THE ABSENCE OF TWO-PARTY COMPETITION.   *J. of Pol. 1974 36(2): 465-479.* Applies V. O. Key's concept of critical elections to single-party politics. Uses "geographical shifts in voting patterns" to describe variations in Louisiana Democratic primaries, 1952-64. Demonstrates the possibility of bringing the South "into the mainstream of analysis." 3 tables, 14 notes.
    A. R. Stoesen

809.   Wolf, T. Phillip.   BRONSON CUTTING AND FRANKLIN ROOSEVELT: FACTORS IN PRESIDENTIAL ENDORSEMENT.   *New Mexico Hist. Rev. 1977 52(4): 317-334.* Roosevelt did not endorse the reelection of New Mexico's Bronson M. Cutting to the US Senate in 1934. Such liberal senators as

Hiram W. Johnson (California), George W. Norris (Nebraska), and Robert Marion La Follette, Jr. (Wisconsin), were endorsed by the President. Roosevelt did not endorse Cutting because Cutting did not endorse F. D. R. until two weeks before the election. Roosevelt and Cutting did not agree on veterans' benefits. The chief reason for Roosevelt's unwillingness to endorse Cutting was the weakness of the Democratic Party in New Mexico. 51 notes.

J. H. Krenkel

810. Wright, Peter M. WYOMING AND THE O.P.A.: THE POSTWAR POLITICS OF DECONTROL. *Ann. of Wyoming 1980 52(1): 25-33.* Immediately after World War II, President Harry S. Truman initiated action through the Office of Price Administration (OPA) to offset projected economic problems. He hoped to establish a spirit of cooperation among labor, management, and consumers so that postwar efforts to boost wages, prices, and purchasing would not produce uncontrolled inflation. A conservative coalition of Republicans and Southern Democrats, led by Senators Robert A. Taft and Kenneth Wherry, opposed any government controls and called for a return to free enterprise. As Truman's spokesman in Wyoming, Senator Joseph C. O'Mahoney worked hard on the state and national level for passage of enabling legislation, which became a reality on 25 July 1946. Unfortunately, a spectacular rise in inflation continued, partly due to exceptions in price and wage controls allowed by Truman. Archival sources; 3 photos, 45 notes.

M. L. Tate

5

REDEFINITIONS AND REALIGNMENTS
(1960-1982)

811. Abbott, Philip. UNDERSTANDING THE "NEW CONSERVA-TIVES." *Polity 1977 10(2): 261-273.* Discusses new books by Alexander Bickel, Daniel Bell, and Robert Nisbet, and a collection of essays edited by Irving Kristol and Nathan Glazer (with an introduction by Daniel Moynihan). These men speak for the "new conservatism" of the 1970's. This trend is the latest outgrowth of the American Whig tradition, one which Bickel sees as pragmatic and relativist, as opposed to the more absolutist liberal tradition. Bell notes that a "revolution of rising entitlements" is making ever-increasing demands upon, while sapping, the nation's productivity, and calls for a return to "some conception of religion." This moral sense of the new Whigs, which urges moderation in the demands made by the proliferating factions in American society, may alienate them from society. 7 notes.   L. W. Van Wyk

812. Abramowitz, Alan; McGlennon, John; and Rapoport, Ronald. A NOTE ON STRATEGIC VOTING IN A PRIMARY ELECTION. *J. of Pol. 1981 43(3): 899-904.* There is little evidence of strategic voting in the 1977 Virginia Democratic gubernatorial primary between Andrew Miller and Henry Howell. Approximately 20% of those voting in the primary were Republican, and 10% of the surveyed voters indicated their support for Republican John Dalton over either Democratic candidate. The more conservative Miller received 80% of the votes of Dalton supporters. The foremost concern of the crossover voters was candidate preference rather than the comparative strength of the Democratic candidates. 10 notes.   A. W. Novitsky

813. Abramowitz, Alan I. IS THE REVOLT FADING? A NOTE ON PARTY LOYALTY AMONG SOUTHERN DEMOCRATIC CONGRESS-MEN. *J. of Pol. 1980 42(2): 568-572.* Since the New Deal, and especially since the end of World War II, the Democratic Party's national commitment to civil rights and economic liberalism strained the loyalty of the South. During the 1960's, a congressional conservative coalition of southern Democrats and Republicans became a powerful obstacle to liberal social and economic legislation. From 1965 through 1978, there has been no increase in party loyalty among southern Democrats and a decline in party loyalty among nonsouthern Democratic representatives. Southern party loyalty reached a low point with the 1972 presidential election and rebounded to more normal levels with the Watergate investigation. Illus., 8 notes.   A. W. Novitsky

814. Abrams, Elliott. THE DEMOCRATS' DILEMMA. *Commentary 1975 59(2): 51-56.* Discusses the failure of the Democratic Party to appeal to voters in 1972, and indicates ideological changes necessary if the party is to win in 1976.
                                                                                                                S

815. Abramson, Paul R. CLASS VOTING IN THE 1976 PRESIDENTIAL ELECTION. *J. of Pol. 1978 40(4): 1066-1072.* In 1972 there was virtually no relationship between social class and party choice among white voters. The percentage of working-class white major-party voters who supported the Democratic party minus the percentage of middle class white major-party voters supporting the Democrats was 44 in 1948, fell to 20 in 1952, 8 in 1956, rose to 12 in 1960, 19 in 1964, and fell to 10 in 1968 and 2 in 1976 [sic]. Economic, social, and political forces contributed to an increase in class voting in 1976, with the youngest voters manifesting the highest level. Democrats won three of the four elections in which class voting was above the median and lost three of the four in which it was below. Primary and secondary sources; fig., 8 notes.
                                                                                                                A. W. Novitsky

816. Aiesi, Margaret and Rosenbaum, Walter A. NOT QUITE LIKE YANKEES: THE DIFFUSION OF PARTISAN COMPETITION IN TWO SOUTHERN CITIES. Steed, Robert P.; Moreland, Laurence W.; and Baker, Tod A., ed. *Party Politics in the South* (New York: Praeger, 1980): 152-174. Examines partisan diffusion in Richmond, Virginia, and Greenville, South Carolina, from 1972 to 1974. The diffusion of Republican voting in the two cities from the presidential to state and local levels is determined, and the significance of this diffusion is evaluated in terms of three theories of party realignment: a New Deal realignment, ideological realignment, and transient confusion. Based on election data from Greenville County Elections Commission, and Chesterfield County election commissions; 7 tables, 21 notes.
                                                                                                                J. Powell

817. Annunziata, Frank. THE REVOLT AGAINST THE WELFARE STATE: GOLDWATER CONSERVATISM AND THE ELECTION OF 1964. *Presidential Studies Q. 1980 10(2): 254-265.* Barry M. Goldwater's nomination for president by the Republican Party in 1964 contravened the idea that neither party could nominate an intense ideologue and abandon electoral pragmatism. He represented a repudiation of Dwight D. Eisenhower's and Robert Taft's liberal Republicanism. Instead of deciding just who would govern, Goldwater focused on just what government should or should not do. Goldwater was a man who would rather be right than win, and one who wanted to offer a clear choice to the voters. 57 notes.
                                                                                                                D. H. Cline

818. Arterton, F. Christopher. STRATEGIES AND TACTICS OF CANDIDATE ORGANIZATIONS. *Pol. Sci. Q. 1977-78 92(4): 663-671.* Discusses the strategies and tactics of the Gerald R. Ford and Ronald Reagan candidate organizations. One of five articles on "Exploring the 1976 Republican Convention."
                                                                                                                J

819. Beatty, Kathleen Murphy. COLORADO: INCREASINGLY UNPREDICTABLE. *Social Sci. J. 1981 18(3): 31-40.* The 1980 elections showed state politics to be business as usual as voters split tickets, electing candidates who showed a mixture of conservative and liberal views and continuing to fragment the party system, while Ronald Reagan won decisively.

820.   Beck, Kent M.   THE KENNEDY IMAGE: POLITICS, CAMELOT, AND VIETNAM.   *Wisconsin Mag. of Hist. 1974 58(1): 45-55.* The "*way* that Americans have honored and remembered the thirty-fifth President can tell us much about John F. Kennedy and convey even more about the American experience before and since his passing." The author traces the changing attitude of political analysts, historians, and journalists toward the Kennedy administration over the past ten years. Immediate reaction to the slain President's policies was favorable when court histories and first-hand accounts published by his entourage held center stage. As the Vietnam War escalated, revisionists began to see Kennedy's foreign policy as one of the most strikingly negative aspects of his administration. More recently, however, a counter-reaction has set in, emphasizing a more balanced picture of his administration. 5 illus., 52 notes.   N. C. Burckel

821.   Beck, Paul Allen.   ENVIRONMENT AND PARTY: THE IMPACT OF POLITICAL AND DEMOGRAPHIC COUNTY CHARACTERISTICS ON PARTY BEHAVIOR.   *Am. Pol. Sci. Rev. 1974 68(3): 1229-1244.* While many scholars have recognized that decentralization encourages American party organizations to tailor activities to the local environment, few have studied systematically the relationships between that environment and party behavior. This study examines the impact of certain political and demographic county characteristics on the activities of a national sample of county party organizations in 1964. Three dimensions of party behavior—organization, mobilization, and persuasion—are utilized as dependent variables. The relationships between the environment and these dimensions of party behavior in the North support a revised "machine theory" of environment and party: organizational effort does not vary with environmental conditions, while mobilization and persuasion activities are opposites in their relationships with the concentration of parochially-oriented voters. Additionally, the division of partisan strength influences party activity: parties perform their "natural" activities well where they have strong support and the other party's "natural" activities well under competitive conditions. Few significant relationships are found in the South, but their similarity in direction to those in the North suggests that the normal relationships may have been attenuated by circumstances unique to that region, particularly one-partyism and decades of "whites only" politics.   J

822.   Beck, Paul Allen.   REALIGNMENT BEGINS? THE REPUBLICAN SURGE IN FLORIDA.   *Am. Pol. Q. 1982 10(4): 421-438.* Results from statewide surveys contain signs of an emerging partisan realignment in Florida since early 1980. After a period of stability in the relative sizes of the mass party coalitions, a surge in Republican Party identifiers and a parallel decline in the Democratic Party appeared after the 1980 presidential election. Partisan changes during this period were pronounced among conservatives and the young, where they also have a distinct ideological flavor. Aggregate partisan shifts appear among older voters as well, but they are smaller and can be accounted for largely by the acquisition of partisanship by nonpartisans.   J/S

823.   Bell, Charles G.   CALIFORNIA: THE START OF A NEW ERA? *Social Sci. J. 1981 18(3): 15-30.* Analyzes the results of the 1980 state and national elections with emphasis on the growing conservative electorate, the increased expenditure of seeking state office in California, and the effects of redistricting on future candidates.

824. Bennett, Roy and Greer, Colin. CONGRESS VERSUS THE PRESI-DENT. *Social Policy 1976 7(1): 12-18.* The disillusioned political attitudes of the 1970's could be remedied by the election of a Democratic Party president in 1976 who could work with the liberal Democratic Congress in solving problems of inflation, unemployment, and detente.

825. Bernstein, Robert A. and Horn, Stephen R. EXPLAINING HOUSE VOTING ON ENERGY POLICY: IDEOLOGY AND THE CONDITIONAL EFFECTS OF PARTY AND DISTRICT ECONOMIC INTERESTS. *Western Pol. Q. 1981 34(2): 235-245.* This analysis of House votes on energy issues in the 94th Congress shows much stronger empirical support for an explanation based on the ideology of the congressman than for one based on the congressman's party or on the economic benefits which might accrue to the congressional district. Party was found to have a significant conditional effect on the relationship between ideology and opposition. Democrats tended to show more opposition than did Republicans, and were significantly more responsive to variation in ideology than were Republicans. When congressmen's district interests ran counter to their party interests, their responsiveness to ideological variation increased greatly.   J/S

826. Bibby, John F. THE GOLDWATER MOVEMENT: ITS INFLUENCE ON THE REPUBLICAN PARTY IN THE 1970'S. *Am. Behavioral Scientist 1973 17(2): 249-271.*

827. Bibby, John F. POLITICAL PARTIES AND FEDERALISM: THE REPUBLICAN NATIONAL COMMITTEE INVOLVEMENT IN GUBER-NATORIAL AND LEGISLATIVE ELECTIONS. *Publius 1979 9(1): 229-236.* The Republican National Committee (RNC) has been getting more actively involved in state and local politics. There was a gain of six governorships in 1978. Additional attention to state legislative elections also resulted in gains. There is a clear need for revision of the conventional wisdom that the RNC is of slight significance at state and local levels. Table, 12 notes.   R. V. Ritter

828. Black, Merle. REGIONAL AND PARTISAN BASES OF CONGRES-SIONAL SUPPORT FOR THE CHANGING AGENDA OF CIVIL RIGHTS LEGISLATION. *J. of Pol. 1979 41(2): 665-679.* In each Congress from the 88th through the 92nd (1963-72), regional (North-South) cleavages were stronger on civil rights legislation than were partisan (Democratic-Republican) differences. Since the 89th Congress, Democrats have consistently provided more support for all civil rights legislation. Extreme regional polarization last occurred in the 88th Congress, remained stable from the 89th through the 91st Congress, and substantially declined in the 92nd, as national school desegregation and busing monopolized the agenda. 2 illus., 2 tables, 24 notes.   A. W. Novitsky

829. Black, Merle and Black, Earl. REPUBLICAN PARTY DEVELOP-MENT IN THE SOUTH: THE RISE OF THE CONTESTED PRIMARY. *Social Sci. Q. 1976 57(3): 566-578.* Notes that the contested Republican primary commonly follows a demonstration of Republican competitiveness in general elections. The size of the minority party's primary electorate is associated with interparty and intraparty competition.   J

830.   Born, Richard.   CHANGES IN THE COMPETITIVENESS OF HOUSE PRIMARY ELECTIONS, 1956-1976.   *Am. Pol. Q. 1980 8(4): 495-506.* This study examines trends in US House primary election competition from 1956-76. While primaries generally have become more contested, the degree of change varies with the partisanship of the primary and the opportunities for winning the seat in the fall. Democratic races have increased in competitiveness more than have Republican contests, thus making even greater the normal party difference. Furthermore, stronger trends toward competitiveness exist within the primaries of more marginal incumbents in both parties. In primaries not involving an incumbent, however, there is an important difference between the parties; here, Democratic candidates to a greater extent have been drawn to contests in districts where they stand a better chance in November, while exactly the opposite obtains for Republicans. This suggests, therefore, that close primaries increasingly signify real candidate interest in obtaining a House seat among Democrats, but internecine ideological or factional struggles for the opposition.   J

831.   Bouzas, Roberto and Maira, Luis.   ALGUNAS CLAVES ECONÓMICAS Y POLÍTICAS PARA EL EXAMEN DE LA ADMINSTRACIÓN REAGAN   [Some economic and political keys for an examination of the Reagan administration]. *Investigación Econ. [Mexico] 1981 40(156): 307-337.* To understand the essentials of the Reagan administration and, therefore, its state of opposition to the interests of the developing nations, three things are necessary: to understand the cause of the conservative turn in US politics; to decipher the ideological rhetoric which enabled the Republican Party to defeat the liberal faction in control since the postwar period; and to examine the rationale behind Reagan's political plans, their limits, and the conflicts they may cause. Presented at the 2d Congress of the Association of Third World Economists, Havana 1981; 2 charts, 32 notes. Spanish.   J. V. Coutinho

832.   Bremner, John Evan.   THE WINNING CANDIDATE.   *Washington Monthly 1976 8(3): 58-61.* Discusses issues in the political campaigns of presidential candidates Jimmy Carter and Jerry Brown in the Democratic Party in 1976.

833.   Brown, Roger G.   PARTY AND BUREAUCRACY: FROM KENNEDY TO REAGAN.   *Pol. Sci. Q. 1982 97(2): 279-294.* Attempts to determine patterns of party affiliation among top-level presidential appointees, 1961-80. Distribution of prestigious positions is less a matter of patronage than of politics, of bargaining chips to further legislative goals and to insure support for executive policy. Staffs in the Executive Branch are less influenced by national parties than in former years. 3 tables, 51 notes.   J. Powell

834.   Bullock, Charles S., III.   CONGRESSIONAL VOTING AND THE MOBILIZATION OF A BLACK ELECTORATE IN THE SOUTH.   *J. of Pol. 1981 43(3): 662-682.* Since 1956, Southern black voter registration has increased by over two million, and the percentages of Negroes registered to vote rose from 25% to 60%. Legislators from districts with large black populations have become notably more responsive to their concerns. Generational replacement is a major factor as freshmen Democrats in the last three congresses have been most responsive, while freshmen Republicans have been more conservative than their predecessors. Subregional differences have decreased. While legislators from the deep South have responded to black political activity, rim state representatives with fewer black constituents have remained more consistent. 8 tables, 44 notes.
A. W. Novitsky

835. Burstein, Paul and Freudenburg, William. ENDING THE VIETNAM WAR: COMPONENTS OF CHANGE IN SENATE VOTING ON VIETNAM WAR BILLS. *Am. J. of Sociol. 1977 82(5): 991-1006.* Very little quantitative academic work has dealt with the politics of American involvement in and withdrawal from Indochina. This article is a preliminary examination of how the U.S. Senate moved from a strong pro-involvement stance to a strong anti-involvement one. The main findings are: (1) the aggregate change in Senate voting came about disproportionately through replacement of supporters of the war by opponents, as opposed to changes of mind by incumbents; (2) nevertheless, dovish bills adopted toward the end of the conflict would have passed even without the support of replacements, because incumbents were converting fairly rapidly; (3) doves were disproportionately Democrats, relatively young, low in seniority, and from the northeast and north central states; (4) elections were important in the Senate change of mind, but often not in the way expected; rather than doves defeating hawks toward the end of the war, hawks tended disproportionately to die or retire and may have been replaced by doves because most candidates running by the end of the war were doves. Theoretical implications and research proposals are discussed.
J

836. Bushnell, Eleanore and Driggs, Don W. NEVADA: BUSINESS AS USUAL. *Social Sci. J. 1981 18(3): 65-74.* In Nevada state politics the political tradition of electing conservative Democrats to the state legislature and Republicans to national office continued in the general election with the Ronald Reagan landslide victory of 1980.

837. Calvert, Jerry W. THE SOCIAL AND IDEOLOGICAL BASES OF SUPPORT FOR ENVIRONMENTAL LEGISLATION: AN EXAMINATION OF PUBLIC ATTITUDES AND LEGISLATIVE ACTION. *Western Pol. Q. 1979 32(3): 327-337.* The immense pressures to develop the natural resources of the West require that assessments of public preferences concerning energy and environmental policy be made in the states affected. The degree to which public sentiments are reflected in legislative choice should also be examined. In Montana surveys of public preferences were conducted in 1975 and 1977 immediately after the state legislature had adjourned. There was often a considerable gap between constituent sentiment, generally supporting environmental protection, and the choices made by their elected representatives, especially Republican lawmakers whose hostility to state intervention to protect environmental resources often put them at a considerable distance from their constituents. The study confirms the partisan affiliation of legislators is the prime determinant of policy choice in the environmental area. While there were differences between constituents the differences were small by comparison to the differences between legislators. Further, the differences between constituents were overshadowed by the broad consensus among constituents, cutting across partisan and class lines, in support of the value of environmental protection and regulated resource development. Based on legislative records and secondary sources; 3 tables, 22 notes, appendix.
J

838. Campbell, Bruce A. PATTERNS OF CHANGE IN THE PARTISAN LOYALTIES OF NATIVE SOUTHERNERS: 1952-1972. *J. of Pol. 1977 39(3): 730-761.* Southern loyalty to the Democratic Party declined 10 percent during 1952-72. This trend reversed itself only in 1964. Neither in-migration nor

out-migration adequately explains the change. During the 1950's, native southern blacks moved toward the Republican Party to support President Eisenhower's integration policies; during the 1960's, they overwhelmingly supported the civil rights positions of Democratic presidents John F. Kennedy and Lyndon B. Johnson. Southern whites, in contrast, moved toward the Republican Party because that party more accurately reflected their attitudes on integration and the expanding power of the federal government. Based on six national presidential election studies by the staff of the Center for Political Studies and other primary and secondary sources; 3 tables, 10 graphs, 31 notes.   A. W. Novitsky

839. Carlson, James M. and Hamilton, Howard. DEMOCRATIC ELECTORAL COALITIONS. *Polity 1978 11(2): 290-297.* Examines the composition of Democratic Party electoral coalitions in three states for levels of president, governor, and senators, and their implications. From data in the Comparative State Election Project (1968), Illinois, North Carolina, and South Dakota were selected as representative of major regions. Analyzes the contributions of the poor, blacks and nonwhites, Catholics, union members and their families, and people under 30. Union members account for 40% of the Democratic vote in Illinois, but they are not part of the Democratic coalition in North Carolina; in South Dakota they exhibit greater loyalty than in Ilinois and the nation as a whole but the small size of the group reduces its impact. Catholics' attachment to the Democratic Party is not uniform across the nation. In North Carolina blacks are the only dependable base of the party. Table, 11 notes.   E. P. Stickney

840. Carmines, Edward G. and Gopoian, J. David. ISSUE COALITIONS, ISSUELESS CAMPAIGNS: THE PARADOX OF RATIONALITY IN AMERICAN PRESIDENTIAL ELECTIONS. *J. of Pol. 1981 43(4): 1170-1189.* Between 1956 and 1976, Democratic presidential candidates received strong support from voters who took liberal positions on federal aid to education, government provision of health care, and government guarantees of full employment. Republican candidates received support from conservatives on these issues. Since 1964, attitudes toward fair employment and school integration have served as similar predictors of voting behavior. However, candidates continue to avoid substantive campaigns in favor of consensus-building, recognizing the politically harmful effects of issue-oriented appeals. While the existence of issue-oriented electoral coalitions indicates that party cleavage is a long-term and stable element of American politics, popular response to specific presidential candidates may cut across such partisan coalitions. 4 illus., 6 tables, 18 notes.   A. W. Novitsky

841. Carmines, Edward G. and Stimson, James A. RACIAL ISSUES AND THE STRUCTURE OF MASS BELIEF SYSTEMS. *J. of Pol. 1982 44(1): 2-20.* Through the early 1960's, New Deal social welfare issues and racial issues remained distinct, permitting the latter to maintain a separate ideological axis. With the 1964 presidential election and the Johnson administration, the Democratic Party appropriated racial liberalism and assumed federal responsibility for ending racial discrimination. Partisan racial attitudes led to increased ideological constraint as responses to such issues were aligned with other political questions. The growing importance of racial issues was a major factor in the restructuring of political attitudes as the unconstrained electorate of the 1950's was replaced by a more contemporary electorate displaying coherent, integrated political belief systems. 6 tables, 32 notes.   A. W. Novitsky

842. Carton, Paul. A BLACK MAN RUNS FOR MAYOR: THE EX-TRAORDINARY CAMPAIGN OF ARTHUR O. EVE. *Afro-Americans in New York Life and Hist. 1980 4(2): 7-54.* Failure of Buffalo, New York, media polls to canvass black voters adequately in 1977 led to underestimated popularity statistics for black Democratic Party mayoral primary candidate Arthur O. Eve, who won the primary even though the opposition tried to capitalize on the incorrect statistics.

843. Cassel, Carol A. COHORT ANALYSIS OF PARTY IDENTIFICA-TION AMONG SOUTHERN WHITES, 1952-1972. *Public Opinion Q. 1977 41(1): 28-33.* Cohort studies generally find that different generations retain the same pattern of partisanship throughout their lifecycles. In contrast, this study finds that changes *within* generations contribute greatly to the decline in tradi-tional Democratic affilation among southern whites.   J

844. Center, Judith A. 1972 DEMOCRATIC CONVENTION REFORMS AND PARTY DEMOCRACY. *Pol. Sci. Q. 1974 89(2): 325-350.* "Analyzes the origins and content of the Democratic party's delegate selection 'reforms' for the 1972 convention. In a sharp attack on the new procedures, Center argues that a convention constituted under the 1972 rules was incapable of choosing a presi-dential nominee with maximum chance of winning the November general elec-tion."   J

845. Claggett, William. PARTISAN ACQUISITION VERSUS PARTISAN INTENSITY: LIFE-CYCLE, GENERATION, AND PERIOD EFFECTS, 1952-1976. *Am. J. of Pol. Sci. 1981 25(2): 193-214.* Partisan strength is recon-ceptualized as a product of acquisition processes and intensity processes. The dynamic properties of these processes differ. In particular, while a life-cycle effect characterizes both processes in both the pre- and post-1964 periods, its magnitude differs for each. Furthermore, generational effects are substantially larger for acquisition than intensity, and the pattern differs for these two components of partisan strength.   J

846. Clancy, Paul R. ALL THE PRESIDENTIAL MEN. *Washington Monthly 1975 7(1): 23-30.* Assesses congressional leaders who, despite their non-candidacy, would make excellent Democratic presidential candidates be-cause of their high ideals, intelligence, character, and understanding of the politi-cal process.   S

847. Clark, Cal and Clark, Janet. NEW MEXICO: MOVING IN THE DI-RECTION OF A REPUBLICAN REALIGNMENT. *Social Sci. J. 1981 18(3): 75-85.* Analyzes the results of the 1980 general election in New Mexico that led to the election of Ronald Reagan and Republican incumbent victories in general; the most interest was generated by the election of Republican Joe Skeen to the House of Representatives, which marked only the third time that a write-in candidate for Congress won.

848. Clark, Cal and Walter, B. Oliver. RISING REPUBLICANISM IN THE WEST: A REGIONAL TIDE OR HARMONIC STATE WAVES? *Social Sci. J. 1981 18(3): 1-6.* Examines the general trends evident in the 1980 Republican Party election victories in the western states.

849.   Clark, Jack.   THE DEMOCRATS: FEUDS & FACTIONS.   *Dissent 1974 21(4): 518-525.* Analyzes problems between George Meany and the reformers in the Democratic Party in terms of the 1976 presidential election.   S

850.   Conway, M. Margaret and Feigert, Frank B.   INCENTIVES AND TASK PERFORMANCE AMONG PARTY PRECINCT WORKERS. *Western Pol. Q. 1974 27(4): 693-709.* Analyzes data gathered during 1966-67 from personal interviews in Montgomery County, Maryland, and Knox County, Illinois.   S

851.   Costantini, Edmond and King, Joel.   CHECKBOOK DEMOCRATS AND THEIR COPARTISANS: CAMPAIGN CONTRIBUTORS AND CALIFORNIA POLITICAL LEADERS, 1964-1976.   *Am. Pol. Q. 1982 10(1): 65-92.* This study tests the notion that those who contribute substantial sums of money to their party and its candidates are distinctive in ways above and beyond the extent of their largess when compared to other party leaders and that they have had declining importance in their party's elite over the past two decades. Data analyzed from questionnaires submitted to California Democratic Party leaders at four year intervals since 1964 demonstrate that regulatory changes in the 1970's have substantially achieved the goal of removing big contributors from places of political prominence. Further, they demonstrate support for certain popular images of big contributors, that is, the "socioeconomic elite" image, the "self-serving" image, and the "ideological conservative" image. A fourth image —the "sporadic interventionist" image—is not supported by the present data.   J

852.   DaCosta Nunes, Ralph.   PUBLIC OPINION, CRIME AND RACE: A CONGRESSIONAL RESPONSE TO LAW AND ORDER IN AMERICA. *Pol. Studies [Great Britain] 1980 28(3): 420-430.* Examines congressional party voting on law and order issues, 1965-73, when the problem was very important for the electorate and associated in the public mind with race. Republicans generally supported hard anticrime legislation, while Democrats favored softer approaches. The influence of black constituents was more complex: it had no effect on Republicans, while Democrats were softer in nonblack districts, and harder as the percentage of blacks increased. In predominantly black districts, however, Democratic support for hard measures was weakest. Congressional voting figures and public opinion polls; 2 tables, 3 fig., 13 notes.   D. J. Nicholls

853.   David, Paul T.   PARTY STRENGTH IN THE UNITED STATES: CHANGES IN 1972.   *J. of Pol. 1974 36(3): 785-796.* Comprehensive biennial index numbers of party strength published in 1972 indicate the "country was somewhat more Republican in 1972 than in 1968," that party competition is rising in the South, and that the Congressional strength of the parties remains unchanged. Cautions users of index numbers as to their artificiality, and suggests they will be used "for many purposes that were not at all foreseen when they were first constructed." 4 tables, fig., 5 notes.   A. R. Stoesen

854.   David, Paul T.   PARTY STRENGTH IN THE UNITED STATES. *J. of Pol. 1975 37(2): 641-642; 1978 40(3): 770-780.* Continued from an earlier article (see abstract 853). Part II. SOME CORRECTIONS. Corrects errors in

figures for party strength in 1972. 2 tables. Part III. (see abstract 855). Part IV. CHANGES IN 1976. Updates previous studies on political parties. Democrats improved their voting results in comparison with 1976 but not as strongly as in 1974. Republicans recovered in the Middle and Far West but not in the South or Northeast. 4 tables, fig., note.   A. W. Novitsky/D. L. Schermerhorn

855.   David, Paul T.   PARTY STRENGTH IN THE UNITED STATES: CHANGE IN 1974.   *J. of Pol. 1976 38(2): 416-425.* Updates the author's index numbers of party strength previously published in *Party Strength in the United States, 1872-1970* (Charlottesville: U. Pr. of Virginia, 1972); "Party Strength in the United States: Changes in 1972," *Journal of Politics* 36 (August 1974), 785-796 (see abstract 853); "Party Strength in the United States: Some Corrections," *Journal of Politics* 37 (May 1975), 641-642 (see abstract 854). 4 tables, 3 notes.
R. V. Ritter

856.   David, Paul T.   POLITICAL PARTIES CONTINUE STRUGGLE FOR REFORM.   *Natl. Civic R. 1973 62(3): 118-124.* There were a number of innovations in political party reform in 1972. Work of Democratic reform commissions came to fruition at the Democratic national convention. Less extensive changes were experienced on the Republican side. New precedents were established which will have their effect at future conventions.
J

857.   Deckard, Barbara.   POLITICAL UPHEAVAL AND CONGRESSIONAL VOTING: THE EFFECTS OF THE 1960'S ON VOTING PATTERNS IN THE HOUSE OF REPRESENTATIVES.   *J. of Pol. 1976 38(2): 326-345.* Studies changes in the House of Representatives' voting patterns during 1959-70. Finds that a change in political issues occurred and that southern Democrats and eastern Republicans increasingly voted in line with their districts' characteristics rather than the majority segments of their parties. 8 tables, 15 notes.
R. V. Ritter

858.   DelaIsla, José.   THE POLITICS OF REELECTION: SE HABLA ESPAÑOL.   *Aztlán 1976 7(3): 427-451.* Traces the growing power of Hispanic Americans in elections and the appeal of Richard M. Nixon's administration for their support; the policy of revenue sharing meant that federal funds would no longer flow directly to Hispanic groups, so to reduce opposition the administration channeled grants to key Spanish-speaking groups and Republican sympathizers in time to influence the election of 1972.

859.   Dellums, Ronald V.   BLACK LEADERSHIP: FOR CHANGE OR FOR STATUS QUO?   *Black Scholar 1977 8(4): 2-5.* Discusses the possibilities of change of moral stance in the national character with leaders of another color.

860.   DeNardo, James.   TURNOUT AND THE VOTE: THE JOKE'S ON THE DEMOCRATS.   *Am. Pol. Sci. Rev. 1980 74(2): 406-420.* A heavy turnout is commonly believed to favor the Democrats. This study presents theoretical reasoning and empirical evidence that challenge the conventional view. Reasonable assumptions about the behavior of core and peripheral voters lead to the conclusion that the majority party is most likely to suffer when turnout increases, common sense notwithstanding. It also appears that the recent decay of partisan loyalties among voters has eroded the relationship between turnout and the vote.
J

861.   Denhardt, Robert B. and Hakes, Jay E.   DELEGATE SELECTION IN NON-PRIMARY STATES.   *Natl. Civic R. 1974 63(10): 521-525.* "As political parties at the state and local level prepare for the Democratic party's mini-convention the issue of delegate selection is being raised. In 1972, roughly 60 percent of the states used some sort of open meetings other than primaries for this purpose yet the role of state convention and caucus systems has been virtually ignored."   J

862.   Denhardt, Robert B. and Jakes, Jay E.   THE IMPACT OF DEMO-CRATIC PARTY REFORM ON THE SOUTH.   *J. of Pol. Sci. 1976 4(1): 36-51.* Guidelines for delegate selection for the 1972 Democratic Party convention adopted the McGovern-Fraser reforms which were committed to nondiscrimination. Adherence to the guidelines was mandatory for seating at the convention. Louisiana's resistance to guidelines became an issue. Southern states complied; the representation was achieved by normative, utilitarian compliance, and by the dynamics of political bargaining and negotiations. Based on participant-observer method by authors working in the McGovern campaign, and on questionnaires; 5 tables, 24 notes.   T. P. Richardson

863.   Dennis, James R.   ROLL-CALL VOTES AND NATIONAL SECURITY: FOCUSING IN ON THE FRESHMEN.   *Orbis 1978 22(3): 713-735.* Analysis of the roll-call voting of freshmen in the 92d, 93d, and 94th Congresses indicates that 1) Democrats gave mixed support to primary-strategic issues, while Republicans gave moderate to high support, 2) secondary-strategic issues were in extreme disfavor with Democrats, though strongly supported by Republicans, and 3) freshmen of both parties supported military research and development. These voting patterns were related to four variables: party affiliation, degree of labor support, level of electorate urbanization, and the amount of Department of Defense money received by a freshman's state. Secondary published sources; 17 notes.   J. D. Moore

864.   Dierenfield , Bruce J.   CONSERVATIVE OUTRAGE: THE DEFEAT IN 1966 OF REPRESENTATIVE HOWARD W. SMITH OF VIRGINIA.   *Virginia Mag. of Hist. and Biog. 1981 89(2): 181-205.* Analyzes the fall of Smith, conservative Democrat, by a liberal opponent, and his defeat in turn in the general election by a conservative Republican, the first Republican victory in the district in the 20th century. Smith had authored the 1940 anti-Communist act and by 1955 chaired the House Rules Committee. In 1966 Smith, who traditionally merely stood for office, felt moved to campaign vigorously against Delegate George Rawlings, who was helped when redistricting put more blacks in his area and was supported by party liberals and loyalists who disliked Smith's opposition to the Lyndon Johnson domestic program. Smith stressed his seniority and opened the pork barrel a bit. Rawlings attacked Smith's conservatism and alleged conflicts of interest, and won a very narrow victory in a primary that Smith had approved, instead of the previous convention system. Attorney William Scott beat Rawlings decisively in the general election, adding disgruntled conservative Democrats to his Republican minority. Scott went on to the Senate, but Rawlings lost his Assembly seat after one more term. Based on the Smith papers, newspapers, and secondary sources; 37 notes.   P. J. Woehrmann

865. Dodd, Lawrence C. THE EXPANDED ROLES OF THE HOUSE DEMOCRATIC WHIP SYSTEM: THE 93RD AND 94TH CONGRESSES. *Congressional Studies 1979 7(1): 27-56.* Discusses the changes that have occurred in the whip system, an important area of party leadership, and describes its functions in the Democratic Party in the House of Representatives, 1975-77.

866. Dunlap, Riley E. and Gale, Richard P. PARTY MEMBERSHIP AND ENVIRONMENTAL POLITICS: A LEGISLATIVE ROLL-CALL ANALYSIS. *Social Sci. Q. 1974 55(3): 670-690.* Examines the partisan nature of current environmental issues in Oregon.   S

867. Echols, Margaret Thompson and Ranney, Austin. THE IMPACT OF INTERPARTY COMPETITION RECONSIDERED: THE CASE OF FLORIDA. *J. of Pol. 1976 38(1): 142-152.* Challenges V. O. Key's theory about interparty competition and intraparty factionalism. Key used Florida as a classical example of single-party multifactionalism and published his ideas in 1947. Since then Republican Party power has increased steadily and dependably amasses over 40 percent of the vote. By all measures, multifactionalism within the Democratic Party has not decreased. 3 tables, fig., 15 notes.

V. L. Human

868. Ehrenhalt, Alan. LAST HURRAHS FOR THE NEW DEAL. *Washington Monthly 1976 7(11): 56-60* Discusses the National Democratic Issues Convention held at Louisville, Kentucky, in 1975 and the emerging skepticism about New Deal policies within the Democratic Party demonstrated there.

869. Ehrenhalt, Alan. POLITICAL NUMBERS: NO WATERGATE LANDSLIDE. *Washington Monthly 1974 5(12): 43-47.* Predicts the outcome of the 1974 congressional elections for the Republican Party.   S

870. Einsiedel, Edna F. TELEVISION NETWORK NEWS COVERAGE OF THE EAGLETON AFFAIR: A CASE STUDY. *Journalism Q. 1975 52(1): 56-60.* Media performance during the controversy which resulted in the resignation of Senator Thomas Eagleton as Democratic vice-presidential candidate has been criticized. Television network news, however, was not disproportionately negative toward Eagleton. Commentary by the National Broadcasting Company (NCB) was unfavorable, the American Broadcasting Company (ABC) was favorable, and the Columbia Broadcasting System (CBS) was nearly neutral. The Eagleton story was the most important political news story of the time. Based on transcripts of television newscasts; 2 tables, 9 notes.   K. J. Puffer

871. Ellwood, John W. and Spitzer, Robert J. THE DEMOCRATIC NATIONAL TELETHONS: THEIR SUCCESSES AND FAILURES. *J. of Pol. 1979 41(3): 828-864.* The Democratic National Committee conducted a telethon each year from 1972 through 1975. Attempting to broaden the party's financial base, they were an extension of the participatory democracy stressed in the 1960's and early 1970's. Those who contributed to the telecasts were even less representative of the party's rank and file than were the elite group of traditional donors. While the first three telethons were broadcast at key moments in the political career of President Nixon, the 1975 telethon was less successful due to decreased interest in politics, use of the ABC Television Network, especially pleasant summer weather and a close baseball pennant race of interest to the northeast. 5 illus., 9 tables, 42 notes.   A. W. Novitsky

872.   Epstein, Leon D.   WHO VOTED FOR MC GOVERN: THE WISCON-SIN CASE.   *Am. Pol. Q. 1973 1(4): 465-478.* Discusses voting patterns and support within the Democratic Party for candidate George McGovern in the 1972 presidential election in Wisconsin.

873.   Fairlie, Henry.   LETTER FROM WASHINGTON.   *Encounter [Great Britain] 1973 40(1): 11-18.* Discusses the campaign of George S. McGovern in the presidential election of 1972, demonstrating that McGovern failed to capture the Democratic Party because "he was paying almost no attention to the variety and generosity of its impulses over the years which have caused it to do so many great things." Refers in particular to basic attitudes toward foreign policy since 1948 and their role in this election.   D. H. Murdoch

874.   Frantzich, Stephen E.   TECHNOLOGICAL INNOVATION AMONG MEMBERS OF THE HOUSE OF REPRESENTATIVES.   *Polity 1979 12(2): 333-348.* Examines variation in the use of government-supplied computer services by members of the House in relation to a cluster of independent variables chosen as reflecting 1) electoral insecurity, and 2) social marginality. Electorally marginal congressmen used computer services more than those electorally secure (57% v. 39%). New arrivals from the business community seemed to bring with them a proclivity for using computers, and junior and younger members were high users, as were those entering Congress after age 50. The tendency of Republicans to use computer services more than Democrats (62% v. 39%) remains statistically significant when controlled for electoral marginality and obvious background factors. Based on Congressional publications, an interview with Neal Gregory of the House Policy Group on Information and Computers, and data on computer usage (covering January-July 1976) supplied by the clerk of the House.   L. W. Van Wyk

875.   Gelb, Leslie H. and Lake, Anthony.   THE AGE OF JACKSON? *Foreign Policy 1974 (14): 178-188.* Examines the political future of Senator Henry M. Jackson and foreign policy of the Democratic Party.   S

876.   Goldstein, Joel H.   THE INFLUENCE OF MONEY ON THE PRE-NOMINATION STAGE OF THE PRESIDENTIAL SELECTION PROCESS: THE CASE OF THE 1976 ELECTION.   *Presidential Studies Q. 1978 8(2): 164-179.* Explores the relationship between campaign expenditures and electoral success using the 1976 prenomination campaigns for the Republican and Democratic presidential candidacies. For the first time, federal matching funds from the Presidential Election Campaign Fund were available to qualified candidates in the prenomination period. Compares primary votes won or raw votes received in caucus with reported campaign spending by each candidate in each state. Evaluates significant unreported resources such as volunteer workers, candidate's time, independent group spending, media coverage, staff talent, and campaign timing. Heavy spending does not necessarily lead to electoral success or bring proportionate returns, but it is more effective in early primaries when candidates' images are still fluid. 5 tables, 29 notes.   S. C. Strom

877.   Goodin, Robert E.   CONVENTION QUOTAS AND COMMUNAL REPRESENTATION.   *British J. of Pol. Sci. [Great Britain] 1977 7(2): 225-261.* The 1972 reforms of the Democratic Party Convention did little to change the

party opinion voiced by delegates stressing the benefits of more democratic representation.

878. Graebner, Norman A. PRESIDENTIAL POLITICS IN A DIVIDED AMERICA: 1972. *Australian J. of Pol. and Hist. 1973 19(1): 28-47.* Analysis of the 1972 presidential election suggests that George S. McGovern lost to Richard M. Nixon because the electorate looked to stability and not radical reform. McGovern was nominated at the Democratic Convention because constitutional changes in the party gave exponents of the "New Politics" a larger voice in the Convention than their grass roots support warranted. America's discontents were those of upper middle class intellectuals who were vocal in the media—at most 10% of the population. Workingmen went over to the Republicans, who "offered a defence against unwanted changes and the assurance of social stability."

W. D. McIntyre

879. Greeley, Andrew M. A SCRAPYARD FOR THE DALEY ORGANIZATION? *Sci. and Public Affairs 1973 29(2): 9-14.* Election "setbacks" to Chicago mayor Richard J. Daley's Democratic political organization in 1972 were overrated by liberals.

880. Hadley, Charles D. and Howell, Susan E. THE SOUTHERN SPLIT TICKET VOTER 1952-76: REPUBLICAN CONVERSION OR DEMOCRATIC DECLINE? Steed, Robert P.; Moreland, Laurence W.; and Baker, Tod A., ed. *Party Politics in the South* (New York: Praeger, 1980): 127-151. Attempts to discover the long-term significance of split ticket voting in the South, especially the question whether split ticket voting for presidential and congressional candidates indicates a halfway house between former Democratic identification and future Republican affiliation, or whether split ticket voting is simply an index of party dealignment. Party identification and attachment tend to be stable, changing more slowly than voting behavior. Based on 1952-76 election data from the University of Michigan Survey Research Center/Center for Political Studies; 7 tables, 33 notes.

J. Powell

881. Haeberle, Steven H. THE INSTITUTIONALIZATION OF THE SUBCOMMITTEE IN THE UNITED STATES HOUSE OF REPRESENTATIVES. *J. of Pol. 1978 40(4): 1054-1065.* The institutionalization of the congressional subcommittee has produced a new unit capable of reshaping the present distribution of power and altering legislative results. Reform began in 1971 when the Democratic caucus barred its members from chairing more than one subcommittee and continued when subcommittees gained autonomy from committee chairmen in 1973. Expansion of subcommittee power has not been continuous over the past several decades: the last dramatic increase had occurred in 1955-58. Primary and secondary sources; 3 fig., 15 notes.

A. W. Novitsky

882. Hagner, Paul and Mullen, William F. WASHINGTON: MORE REPUBLICAN, YES; MORE CONSERVATIVE, NO. *Social Sci. J. 1981 18(3): 115-129.* The 1980 general election led to the defeat of Democratic incumbent Senator Warren Magnusen and the election of Republican politicians to many state offices as Ronald Reagan received the state's electoral votes.

883.   Haines, Richard L.   MONTANA: A MODEST COUNTERREVOLU-TION.   *Social Sci. J. 1981 18(3): 51-63.* The 1980 general election victory of Ronald Reagan led to a Republican sweep in the Montana state legislature.

884.   Hajda, Joseph.   CHOOSING THE 1960 DEMOCRATIC PRESIDEN-TIAL CANDIDATE: THE CASE OF THE UNBOSSED DELEGATION. *Kansas Q. 1976 8(2): 71-87.* A Kansas delegate's perspective on the 1960 Democratic National Convention in Los Angeles, and the contest over delegate selection in the race among John F. Kennedy, Stuart Symington, Lyndon B. Johnson, and Adlai E. Stevenson, with a distribution of Kansas votes.

885.   Hamilton, Charles V.   BLACKS AND THE CRISIS OF POLITICAL PARTICIPATION.   *Public Interest 1974 (34): 188-210.* Traces the efforts of increasingly politicized Negroes in the 1960's working for voter participation in the South, access to the delegation selection process in the Democratic Party, and participation in the administration of local poverty programs.

886.   Hammond, Thomas H.   ANOTHER LOOK AT THE ROLE OF "THE RULES" IN THE 1972 DEMOCRATIC PRESIDENTIAL PRIMARIES. *Western Pol. Q. 1980 33(1): 50-72.* Lengle and Shafer argue in "Primary Rules, Political Power and Social Change" [see abstract 924] that the rules of the 1972 Democratic presidential primaries had a major effect on who the nominee was. Had the rules in force been Winner-Take-All, they suggest, Hubert Humphrey might have been the nominee. They also project their 1972-based conclusions into the future and suggest that different rules apportion power among the states in different ways, and with different consequences for the party. Unfortunately, their arguments are unsupported by their own evidence. Biases in their data lead to misleading conclusions. When the biases are corrected, we find that candidates like Humphrey were aided by Proportional rules. Lengle and Shafer also neglect two other variables crucial to understanding presidential primaries: the sequence of primaries and the extent of "ideological crowding" among the candidates. Correction of these and other errors leads to very different predictions about the effects of the rules on the party's future. 5 tables, 4 fig., 33 notes.   J

887.   Hart, John.   KENNEDY, CONGRESS AND CIVIL RIGHTS.   *J. of Am. Studies [Great Britain] 1979 13(2): 165-178.* President John F. Kennedy took into account the roadblocks to implementing the broad civil rights plank in the Democratic Party platform of 1960. He campaigned in 1960 not for sweeping civil rights legislation but expanded employment and educational opportunities for minorities. After the election, Kennedy cajoled and bargained with an unreceptive Congress until his "moderate and pragmatic" civil rights proposals were headed for Congressional approval when Kennedy was assassinated in 1963. Archival materials and secondary sources; 39 notes.   H. T. Lovin

888.   Havard, William C.   THE PRESIDENCY: THE OFFICE, THE MAN, AND THE CONSTITUENCIES.   *Virginia Q. R. 1974 50(4): 497-514.* Analyzes the post-Watergate demands for changes in the Constitution by arguing that the real problem is political rather than structural. Discusses four major presidential constituencies: the body politic, party organization, Congress and the administrative bureaucracy. Describes the constituency relations of each president from Franklin D. Roosevelt through Nixon. Fears paralysis of the presidency and

argues that the present structure is viable if constituency relations do "not break down completely." O. H. Zabel

889. Havick, John J. AMATEURS AND PROFESSIONALS AT THE 1972 DEMOCRATIC CONVENTION. *Polity 1978 10(3): 448-457.* Focuses on party loyalty of delegates supporting winning and losing candidates at the 1972 Democratic Party convention. There was a significant relationship between delegates and changes in their intention to campaign for the ticket. Those supporting losers reduced their commitment, while those favoring winners kept it constant or increased it. Delegates without positions in the party supporting losers lowered commitment more than those holding party positions. Party regulars supported the party; delegates without party ties reduced their commitment. J. Tull

890. Havic, John J. and Heffron, Florence. THE IOWA CAUCUSES: CARTER'S EARLY CAMPAIGN FOR THE PRESIDENTIAL NOMINATION. *Midwest Q. 1978 20(1): 32-48.* Examines Jimmy Carter's early campaign strategy for the 1976 presidential election, focusing on his efforts to achieve success in the Iowa Democratic Party caucuses; covers 1975-76.

891. Henderson, Lenneal J., Jr. IMPACT OF MILITARY BASE SHUTDOWNS. *Black Scholar 1974 5(2): 9-15.* Documents the impact on black workers of Defense budget cutbacks as announced by Secretary of Defense Elliot Richardson 17 April 1973, and asserts that the decision has obvious political motives; the hardest-hit cities have Democratic Party mayors, legislators, and voting majorities, and a substantial nonwhite population; voted overwhelmingly for Humphrey; and have many black elected officials. M. T. Wilson

892. Hertz, Edwin. IDEOLOGICAL LIBERALS IN REFORM POLITICS: A NOTE ON THE BACKGROUND AND MOVEMENT OF POLITICAL OUTSIDERS INTO MAJOR PARTY POLITICS. *Int. J. of Contemporary Sociol. 1974 11(1): 1-11.* Discusses the political participation of working class Jews, Negroes, and Puerto Rican Americans as pressure groups in social reform and civil rights issues in New York City, 1963-70's.

893. Hibbs, Douglas A., Jr. POLITICAL PARTIES AND MACROECONOMIC POLICY. *Am. Pol. Sci. Rev. 1977 71(4): 1467-1487.* This study examines postwar patterns in macroeconomic policies and outcomes associated with left- and right-wing governments in capitalist democracies. It argues that the objective economic interests as well as the subjective preferences of lower income and occupational status groups are best served by a relatively low unemployment-high inflation macroeconomic configuration, whereas a comparatively high unemployment-low inflation configuration is compatible with the interests and preferences of upper income and occupational status groups. Highly aggregated data on unemployment and inflation outcomes in relation to the political orientation of governments in 12 West European and North American nations are analyzed revealing a low unemployment-high inflation configuration in nations regularly governed by the Left and a high unemployment-low inflation pattern in political systems dominated by center and rightist parties. Finally, time-series analyses of quarterly postwar unemployment data for the United States and Great Britain suggests that the unemployment rate has been driven downward by Democratic and Labour administrations and upward by Republican and Conser-

vative governments. The general conclusion is that governments pursue macro-economic policies broadly in accordance with the objective economic interests and subjective preferences of their class-defined core political constituencies.
                                                                                                J

894.   Himmelfarb, Milton.   ARE JEWS BECOMING REPUBLICANS? *Commentary 1981 72(2): 27-31.* Statistics for 1972-80 clearly demonstrate that Jewish political attitudes are shifting to the right; in 1980, for the first time in a national election, the Democratic candidate received less than half of the Jewish vote.

895.   Hitchcock, James.   PROPHECY AND POLITICS: ABORTION IN THE ELECTION OF 1976.   *Worldview 1977 20(3): 25-26, 35-37.* Discusses the intrusion of politics into religion, as in the 1976 Presidential election, where pressure was put on Catholics to disregard abortion as a key moral issue, in the interests of Democratic Party loyalty.

896.   Hitlin, Robert A. and Jackson, John S., III.   CHANGE & REFORM IN THE DEMOCRATIC PARTY.   *Polity 1979 11(4): 617-633.* A study of changes in how the US party system functions, especially the response of the Democratic Party. To evaluate the direction and extent of change, one may note the tendencies toward centralization (not local control) in rules changes, candidate selection processes, party finance, ideological coherence, and the potential for discipline. It is expected that the 1974 approval of the Charter will induce the party to "move further along the ideological and discipline dimensions." There has already been major change in the direction of a previously uncharted model for an American political party. 19 notes.   R. V. Ritter

897.   Hitlin, Robert A.   SUPPORT FOR CHANGES IN THE CONVENTION SYSTEM: 1968.   *Western Pol. Q. 1973 26(4): 686-701.* The 1972 national convention reforms had their roots in the attitudes of delegates to the 1968 conventions, especially among the Democratic Party.

898.   Hrebenar, Ron.   UTAH: THE MOST REPUBLICAN STATE IN THE UNION.   *Social Sci. J. 1981 18(3): 103-114.* With the exception of the election of Democratic candidate for governor Scott Matheson, the Republican Party swept into office throughout Utah with the 1980 election victory of Ronald Reagan.

899.   Jackson, John E.   ISSUES, PARTY CHOICES, AND PRESIDENTIAL VOTES.   *Am. J. of Pol. Sci. 1975 19(2): 161-185.* Discusses the role of issues, and the electorate's evaluation of the political parties' stance on issues, in the US electoral process. Produces a statistical model drawn from data of the 1964 presidential election study of the Survey Research Center. Concludes that the most important influences on the evaluation of parties are the effects of peoples' stance upon issues. Fig., 3 tables.   S. P. Carr

900.   Jackson, John S., III; Brown, Barbara Leavitt; and Bositis, David. HERBERT MCCLOSKY AND FRIENDS REVISITED: 1980 DEMOCRATIC AND REPUBLICAN PARTY ELITES COMPARED TO THE MASS PUBLIC.   *Am. Pol. Q. 1982 10(2): 158-180.* Herbert McClosky's classic study of party leaders and followers is replicated and extended using 1980 data

on party elites, party followers, and the mass public. Dramatic interparty differences emerge in terms of liberalism-conservatism and views on public policy issues. As in the McClosky study, party elites tend to take relatively extreme issue positions, while the mass public continues to occupy a centrist position. J

901. Jackson, John S., III and Hitlin, Robert A. THE NATIONALIZATION OF THE DEMOCRATIC PARTY. *Western Pol. Q. 1981 34(2): 270-276.* Examines the attitudes of delegates to the Democratic Party's 1974 Mid-Term Conference and the 1976 National Convention toward recent changes in the party, and develops a Party Nationalization Scale. The data strongly suggest that several recent changes are now widely accepted and that acceptance actually increased between 1974 and 1976. However, proposals for new and additional changes are not uniformly supported, and a state of some equilibrium may have been reached. Increased centralization of national party authority and activities has taken place within the Democratic Party since 1970, as has elite support for those changes. J/S

902. Jackson, John S., III; Brown, Jesse C.; and Brown, Barbara L. RECRUITMENT, REPRESENTATION, AND POLITICAL VALUES: THE 1976 DEMOCRATIC NATIONAL CONVENTION DELEGATES. *Am. Pol. Q. 1978 6(2): 187-212.* Makes comparisons with other recent conventions, all in the context of recent changes in the delegates selection rules. Discusses how the delegate selection rules and/or the group characteristics of the delegates systematically affect the delegates' candidate preferences. Examines other more "political" variables for their relationship to candidates' fortunes. Analyzes why Jimmy Carter was nominated and elected in 1976. 7 tables, fig., 14 notes. R. V. Ritter

903. Jackson, John S., III and Hitlin, Robert A. THE SANFORD COMMISSION AND THE DELEGATES TO THE DEMOCRATIC MID-TERM CONFERENCE. *Am. Pol. Q. 1976 4(4): 441-482.* Analyzes descriptive data on some important personal characteristics, political preferences, and party policy preferences of the Sanford Commission members who drafted the national charter of the Democratic Party and the Democratic Party Mid-Term Conference delegates in Kansas City (1974) who ratified that charter. Makes comparisons to 1968 and 1972 Democratic Convention delegates. P. Travis

904. Jackson, John S., III. SOME CORRELATES OF MINORITY REPRESENTATION IN THE NATIONAL CONVENTIONS, 1964-1972. *Am. Pol. Q. 1975 3(2): 171-188.* Discusses the extent of minority representation in state delegations to the national Democratic Party conventions, 1964-72, emphasizing the representation of Negroes, women, and youths.

905. Jacobson, Gary C. PRESIDENTIAL COATTAILS IN 1972. *Public Opinion Q. 1976 40(2): 194-200.* Because Richard Nixon's overwhelming victory in the 1972 presidential election was not accompanied by any significant increase in Republican representation in Congress, it has been assumed that his coattails were exceedingly short. However, analysis of several kinds of evidence suggests that such an assumption is premature and that Nixon's pulling power has been underestimated. An explanation of the failure of Republican gains to materialize as congressional seats may be found in the competitive disadvantages suffered by Republicans in a period of increasingly safe seats. J

906. James, Judson Lehman and James, Dorothy Buckton. LESSONS OF WATERGATE: THE NIXON CAMPAIGNS. *Current Hist. 1974 67(395): 30-33, 38.* Discusses the impact of the Watergate scandal on political parties and analyzes Nixon's campaigns of 1968 and 1972. One of seven articles in this issue on the two-party system.   S

907. Jewell, Malcolm E. PARTICIPATION IN SOUTHERN PRIMARIES. Steed, Robert P.; Moreland, Laurence W.; and Baker, Tod A., ed. *Party Politics in the South* (New York: Praeger, 1980): 8-32. Focuses on the development of Republican primaries for statewide offices during 1960-77, a topic virtually ignored by past researchers. Using data from all southern states, seeks to determine such matters as which states have experienced the growth of contested Republican primaries, what the implications of such growth are for the Democratic Party's primary and for the general electoral system, and where the voters in these Republican primaries come from. Also, identifies some aspects of primary politics of both regional and national significance, especially the changing status of the Democratic Party primary in the face of significant levels of participation in the Republican Party primary and increased two-party competition in the region. Based on voting turnout data in state gubernatorial primaries; 7 tables, 10 notes.
J. Powell

908. Jewell, Malcolm E. THE 1978 ELECTIONS AND AMERICAN STATE PARTY SYSTEMS. *Publius 1979 9(1): 191-196.* Searches for meaningful developments in the 1978 elections pertinent to the relationships between national and state politics. There is a closer balance between parties due to Republican gains; the state legislative campaign by the national party was more impressive than usual; the increasing independence of voters was in conflict with state party organization trying to regain control, and the Republican Party in most southern states has yet to achieve a good competitive status.
R. V. Ritter

909. Jones, Charles O. BETWEEN PARTY BATTALIONS AND COMMITTEE SUZERAINTY. *Ann. of the Am. Acad. of Pol. and Social Sci. 1974 (411): 158-168.* "President Nixon's challenge to congressional authority in the early months of 1973 stimulated critical review of how Congress does its work. As Lord Bryce observed long ago, of the three methods to facilitate the operation of large assemblies, the United States has emphasized development of a strong committee system. While providing many advantages, Bryce noted that the system also tends to lessen cohesion, reduce responsibility and lower public interest in legislative proceedings. Questions whether the committee system accommodates the new political realities of frequently split party control between Congress and the White House, and argues that changes should be made to increase the authority and visibility of party leaders so that presidential programs might be challenged more coherently in Congress. Specific changes are suggested to that end—changes which seek to maintain the advantages of the committee system, while reducing its disadvantages."   J

910. Jones, Ruth S. STATE PUBLIC CAMPAIGN FINANCE: IMPLICATIONS FOR PARTISAN POLITICS. *Am. J. of Pol. Sci. 1981 25(2): 342-361.* During 1972-80 17 states enacted legislation to provide public funding of state-level election campaigns. These public campaign funding programs vary on four

key policy dimensions. States are treated as "laboratories of reform" in which variations on a common policy are examined systematically. Assessment of the partisan impact of public campaign policies reveals that the majority party is generally advantaged in absolute dollar amounts regardless of policy variations. However, depending on the procedures of collecting and allocating funds, minority parties may gain more from public funding programs than their numerical strength in the electorate would warrant. J

911. Kemble, Penn. A NEW DIRECTION FOR THE DEMOCRATS? *Commentary 1982 74(4): 31-38.* The mid-term Democratic Convention met in Philadelphia, Pennsylvania, to determine its goals and principles for 1982, and decided among other things that the United States must stop pursuing a military solution in El Salvador and must seek a freeze on the use of nuclear weapons; the convention also felt pressure from the feminist coalition over the defeat of the ERA.

912. Kenski, Henry C. and Kenski, Margaret C. PARTNERSHIP, IDEOLOGY, AND CONSTITUENCY DIFFERENCES IN ENVIRONMENTAL ISSUES IN THE U.S. HOUSE OF REPRESENTATIVES; 1973-1978. *Policy Studies J. 1980 9(3): 325-335.* Establishes, through analysis of data sets for the US House of Representatives from 1973 to 1978, that political support for environmental legislation has remained stable drawing its primary strength from eastern, Democratic, urban constituencies.

913. Kilson, Martin. FROM CIVIL RIGHTS TO PARTY POLITICS: THE BLACK POLITICAL TRANSITION. *Current Hist. 1974 67(399): 193-199.* From an issue on "Changing Black America." S

914. Klonoski, James and Aiken, Ann. OREGON: STILL LIBERAL BUT SLIPPING. *Social Sci. J. 1981 18(3): 87-101.* In the 1980 general election, Ronald Reagan carried the Republican Party to victory in key races throughout the state, especially the defeat of long-term Congressman Al Ullman by a conservative Republican.

915. Knoke, David. RELIGION, STRATIFICATION, AND POLITICS: AMERICA IN THE 1960'S. *Am. J. of Pol. Sci. 1974 18(2): 331-345.* "The party identifications of the American electorate in the presidential elections of the 1960s are analyzed in an additive model of effects due to occupation, education, income, and religious preference. Religion is seen to have the largest net effect, although the eight-year trend shows education increasing in importance as religion declines slightly. Great variation in party identification between Protestant denominations is noted, indicating that the traditional Protestant-Catholic-Jew trichotomy does not fully reflect the political cleavages between religious groups." J

916. Kritzer, Herbert M. and Eubank, Robert B. PRESIDENTIAL COATTAILS REVISITED: PARTISANSHIP AND INCUMBENCY EFFECTS. *Am. J. of Pol. Sci. 1979 23(3): 615-626.* One question raised by recent presidential elections is the failure of the winner to carry into office any sizable number of congressional candidates. This paper suggests that explanations based upon previous theories are inadequate and describes and tests an alternate explanation using SRC-CPS data for five elections. The results show that the proposed alternative

fails to account for the results of the elections examined. This failure seems to result from the inability of the Republican Party to capture or hold a large number of voters at the congressional level. Additional analyses indicate that much, though not all, of this apparent asymmetry is a result of incumbency effects in congressional elections.   J

917.   Land, Guy Paul.   MISSISSIPPI REPUBLICANISM AND THE 1960 PRESIDENTIAL ELECTION.   *J. of Mississippi Hist. 1978 40(1): 33-48.* Investigates the 1960 presidential campaign between Richard Nixon and John Kennedy in Mississippi. Describes the actions of state party leaders at both conventions and during the race. The split in the Democratic Party between the Loyalists led by Senator James O. Eastland and the forces led by Ross R. Barnett calling for independent electors, inspired Republican Party leaders such as Wirt Yerger, Jr., to launch the first serious Republican campaign in the state since Reconstruction. Mississippians, primarily concerned with the racial issue, gave the unpledged elector slate a plurality, but the Republican party emerged from the campaign with stronger urban support which provided a foundation for later expansion.   M. S. Legan

918.   Larew, James C.   A PARTY REBORN: HAROLD HUGHES AND THE IOWA DEMOCRATS.   *Palimpsest 1978 59(5): 148-161.* This excerpt from the author's forthcoming book, *A Party Reborn,* chronicles Harold Hughes's rise to governorship, and the change in the 1960's of Iowa's political power structure symbolized by that inauguration. Hughes's success was due to his issue-oriented, aggressive political style, his keen political advisors, and a personality enabling him to reestablish a sense of community in a state fractured by recent, rapid changes. Due largely to Hughes, a new generation of Democratic Party leaders had arrived by the 1968 and 1972 conventions to restructure party organization of liberal and traditional elements into a powerful, rejuvenated party. 3 photos, editor's notes.   N. Cahill

919.   Latimer, Margaret K.   "NO-PARTY" POLITICS AT THE END OF THE WALLACE ERA.   *Publius 1979 9(1): 215-228.* Lack of party loyalties has characterized Alabama state politics for some time. George Wallace consistently operated outside his party. The Republicans, in order to vitalize their hold on the state, renewed efforts with the aid of the national organization, but with little headway. There is a growing emphasis on political campaign ethics, and some indication that a strengthening of the party system is on the way. 22 notes.   R. V. Ritter

920.   LeBlanc, Hugh L. and Merrin, Mary Beth.   PARTIES, ISSUES, AND CANDIDATES: ANOTHER LOOK AT RESPONSIBLE PARTIES.   *Western Pol. Q. 1978 31(4): 523-534.* Previous research has indicated that our political parties have been unable to organize the electorate on the basis of meaningful issue cleavages in the manner envisaged by the responsible party doctrine . . . It has been suggested that voters are now more issue conscious in their presidential choices . . . Based on an analysis of the American electorate from 1960 through 1972, we are led to conclude that the nation is moving away from rather than closer to a responsible party system.   J

921. Lee, Robert D., Jr. DIFFERENCES BETWEEN SUBURBAN RE-PUBLICANS AND DEMOCRATS. *Policy and Pol. [Great Britain] 1974 3(1): 51-59.* Analyzes the political attitudes of whites (particularly those living in suburbs) belonging to the Republican and Democratic Parties in 1972 in Bucks County, Pennsylvania.

922. Leitel, Erich. MACHTKAMPF IN DER HOCHBURG DES IMPERI-ALISMUS: PRÄSIDENTENWAHLEN IN DEN USA [Power struggle in the center of imperialism: presidential elections in the United States]. *Wissenschaftliche Zeitschrift der Friedrich-Schiller-U. Jena. Gesellschafts- und Sprachwissenschaftliche Reihe [East Germany] 1969 18(4): 149-158.* Reviews the development of the Republican and Democratic Parties since the elections of 1964, the primaries for the 1968 campaign, the programs of the candidates, and the results of the elections.

923. Lenchner, Paul. CONGRESSIONAL PARTY UNITY AND EXECU-TIVE-LEGISLATIVE RELATIONS. *Social Sci. Q. 1976 57(3): 589-596.* Uses factor analysis to examine senate voting patterns in five years. Concludes that control of the presidency promotes legislative party unity and that majority status in Congress may make an additional contribution to party unity.   J

924. Lengle, James I. and Shafer, Byron. PRIMARY RULES, POLITICAL POWER, AND SOCIAL CHANGE. *Am. Pol. Sci. Rev. 1976 70(1): 25-40.* Examines the relationship between the kinds of delegate allocation rules used in Democratic presidential primaries (Winner-Take-All, Districted, and Proportional) and the power of various states within the national Democratic Party. It demonstrates that these rules are often, in the short run, more important than a state's voters in determining the fate of particular candidates. It shows, in the middle run, that different types of states are clearly favored by different sets of primary regulations. It closes with some speculation about the long-run impact of these tendencies.   J

925. Levantroser, William F. FINANCING PRESIDENTIAL CAM-PAIGNS: THE IMPACT OF REFORM FINANCE LAWS ON THE DEMO-CRATIC PRESIDENTIAL NOMINATION OF 1976. *Presidential Studies Q. 1981 11(2): 280-288.* The Campaign Finance Act (US, 1974) and its 1976 amendments were important factors in the nomination of Jimmy Carter as Democratic Party candidate in the 1976 campaign. As the primaries started, all candidates relied on matching funds. For the two-month period that payments were suspended while Congress revised the law, only Carter's financial picture was maintained, giving him a definite advantage. Primary sources, 4 tables, 11 notes.
                                                                    A. Drysdale

926. Linnik, V. A. S'EZD V CHIKAGO [Convention in Chicago]. *Voprosy Istorii [USSR] 1978 (6): 113-123.* Describes the government's social and political oppression of and violence against dissidents and innocent but accidentally involved people in the United States. Considers McCarthy's "witch-hunt," and focuses on the aggressive participation of the police in Chicago in 1968 and the Democratic National Convention and riots which took place there, quoting detailed British and American journalists' accounts of particular acts of violence. Outlines the importance of Chicago in American history and politics, and its

place in contemporary American society. Discusses the attitude of American students and their attempts to combat government repression. Based on British and American newspaper articles 1968-69, and secondary works; 27 notes.

L. Smith

927.   Lipset, Seymour Martin and Raab, Earl.   THE ELECTION AND THE NATIONAL MOOD.   *Commentary 1973 55(1): 43-50.* Explains the defeat of Democratic Senator George S. McGovern in the 1972 presidential elections, and analyzes the American electorate at that time.

928.   Lugato, Giuseppe.   LA CRISI AMERICANA DOPO LE ELEZIONI DI NOVEMBRE   [The American crisis after the November elections]. *Civitas [Italy] 1974 25(12): 33-44.* "The November elections, a fundamental test for US politics, have confirmed the forecasts: a Democratic triumph and a Republican collapse. After the Nixon resignation, and Ford's unhappy start, this result was not completely unexpected. With 'stagflation' and the obscure prospects of American economy, one should not be surprised if the vote was also a protest vote for the inability of politicians to annihilate the crisis. Nonetheless, the author analyzing the situation still senses some serious problems at the level of working political institutions, of organizing the consensus and trust of citizens. Could the American political system face today's problems? This is the fundamental question on which the debate has already started."   J

929.   Manykin, A. S.   THE REPUBLICAN PARTY OF THE UNITED STATES IN SEARCH FOR AN ALTERNATIVE TO THE "NEW DEAL." *Soviet Studies in Hist. 1980 19(1): 87-112.* English translation of an article that first appeared in *Novaia i Noveishaia Istoriia* 1978 (see abstract 757). 66 notes.

S

930.   Margolis, Diane R.   THE INVISIBLE HANDS: SEX ROLES AND THE DIVISION OF LABOR IN TWO LOCAL POLITICAL PARTIES. *Social Problems 1979 26(3): 314-324.* Describes the male and female members of the Republican and Democratic committees of a small New England town in 1974, showing that the men played the customary leading role as chairmen of both committees, while the women handled many unofficial tasks, recasting their roles as housewives, a role whose menial status men despised but whose effects they required and praised.

931.   Marshall, Thomas R.   PARTY RESPONSIBILITY REVISITED: A CASE OF POLICY DISCUSSION AT THE GRASS ROOTS.   *Western Pol. Q. 1979 32(1): 70-78.* Advocates of party responsibility often suggest that a greater role for amateur party activists would result in clearer policy differences between political parties in the U.S. So far, however, little empirical evidence exists to test this hypothesis. The caucus-convention system is one institution through which amateur party activists may introduce and discuss policies. An analysis of policy discussion and resolutions from a sample of one state's precinct caucuses from 1972 and 1974 for both the Democratic and Republican parties suggest that party activists will not hesitate to introduce and debate policies. However, high levels of party discussion apparently do not lead to policy consensus *within* parties and policy differences *between* parties (the "responsible party" outcome) . . .   J

932. McAnaw, Richard L. MICHIGAN'S PRESIDENTIAL PRIMARY. *Michigan Academician 1979 12(1): 3-14.* Features of Michigan's presidential primary system (1972, 1976), notably the open primary, indirect primary, parties on ballot, candidates, and delegate selection and apportionment features, largely resulted from Democratic Party reform, 1970-72.

933. McAnaw, Richard L. THOSE WHO NOMINATE: THE MICHIGAN DELEGATION TO THE DEMOCRATIC NATIONAL CONVENTION— 1972. *Michigan Academician 1974 7(2): 227-252.*

934. McElvaine, Robert S. OLD TIMES THERE ARE NOT FORGOT-TEN: A PERSONAL VIEW OF THE "NEW SOUTH." *Midwest Q. 1978 19(3): 238-250.* Conditions have been improving in Georgia and Mississippi since 1969, especially among the younger generation. Huey Long's elections proved that Southerners were Populists rather than conservatives. Recently both Cliff Finch's and Jimmy Carter's campaigns successfully appealed to the populist alliance of blacks, poor rural whites, and urban workers, and Mississippi has a united biracial Democratic party for the first time. This progress has been partly the result of the Civil Rights Act (US, 1964) which integrated public facilities and the Voting Rights Act (US, 1965) which gave blacks political importance through the vote. S. J. Quinlan

935. McFeeley, Neil D. and Blank, Robert H. IDAHO: A CONSERVATIVE REPUBLICAN LANDSLIDE. *Social Sci. J. 1981 18(3): 41-50.* The 1980 presidential election of Ronald Reagan carried over onto Idaho state politics and led to the defeat of incumbent Democratic Senator Frank Church and the election of an entirely Republican congressional delegation thanks largely to the efforts of the National Conservative Political Action Committee and the Sagebrush Rebellion movement.

936. McGrath, Wilma E. and Soule, John W. ROCKING THE CRADLE OR ROCKING THE BOAT: WOMEN AT THE 1972 DEMOCRATIC NA-TIONAL CONVENTION. *Social Sci. Q. 1974 55(1): 141-150.* " . . . Find that women delegates were deeply influenced by the women's liberation movement, were keenly aware of sex discrimination in politics and that they were more liberal on questions of public policy than their male counterparts." J

937. McKay, David H. and Wilson, Graham K. THE U.S. MID-TERM ELECTIONS. *Parliamentary Affairs [Great Britain] 1975 28(2): 216-224.* Reviews the causes and consequences of the Democratic victory in the 1974 elections. The Watergate influence is difficult to assess, but a flagging economy was probably the main cause of the Republican defeat. Liberal Democrats now hold an overwhelming numerical edge in Congress and in the state houses, but agreement may still be difficult. Southern states are losing power, though the trend to Republicanism may have been halted. With so many Democratic congressmen coming from increasingly safe seats, traditional Democratic reforms, such as elimination of the seniority system, might be abandoned. 4 tables, 17 notes. V. L. Human

938. Meadow, Robert G. and Jackson-Beeck, Marilyn. CANDIDATE PO-LITICAL PHILOSOPHY: REVELATIONS IN THE 1960 AND 1976 DE-BATES. *Presidential Studies Q. 1980 10(2): 234-243.* By topically analyzing the

1960 and 1976 debates, the two Democratic candidates are seen to have had greater concern for the lessons of history, social change, and national diversity than the Republican candidates, who expressed concern for smaller government and power, and the increase in influence of the private sector. Through this analysis, we can not only better understand the views of each candidate, but also the person. 9 tables, fig., 7 ref.   D. H. Cline

939.   Merrill, Bruce D.   ARIZONA: GROWTH, POLITICS, AND SELF INTEREST.   *Social Sci. J. 1981 18(3): 7-13.* In the 1980 election, Arizona state politics and politicians were deeply influenced by the victory of Ronald Reagan, and, in a period of economic crisis and scarce resources, the electorate seemed to be more informed about the political issues.

940.   Miller, Abraham H.   ETHNICITY AND PARTY IDENTIFICATION: CONTINUATION OF A THEORETICAL DIALOGUE.   *Western Pol. Q. 1974 27(3): 479-490.* "In terms of party identification in the national political universe, ethnic-based political loyalties have converged under the umbrella of religion."   S

941.   Miller, Arthur H.   PARTISANSHIP REINSTATED? A COMPARISON OF THE 1972 AND 1976 US PRESIDENTIAL ELECTIONS.   *British J. of Pol. Sci. [Great Britain] 1978 8(2): 129-152.* Reemergence of party identification is the significant difference between the two elections.

942.   Miroff, Bruce.   PRESIDENTIAL LEVERAGE OVER SOCIAL MOVEMENTS: THE JOHNSON WHITE HOUSE AND CIVIL RIGHTS. *J. of Pol. 1981 43(1): 2-23.* While no other administration achieved as much in the field of civil rights as did that of Lyndon Baines Johnson, when activists defined black emancipation in terms alien to the administration's, the confident exercise of presidential leadership was frustrated. Fearing mass activism and defining the racial issue in terms of consensus politics, the Johnson White House sought a shift in black activity from civil rights to party politics. A black Democratic network was to serve as a means of both riot prevention and electoral gains. The administration lost control over the issue by mid-1966 as the movement turned militant and both the Vietnam War and resistance to it preoccupied Washington. 35 notes.   A. W. Novitsky

943.   Molnar, Thomas.   WATERGATE UND DIE FOLGEN   [Watergate and the consequences]. *Schweizer Monatshefte [Switzerland] 1974 53(10): 672-675.* Richard M. Nixon's deeds have led to growing cynicism among the American people and could lead to disaster for the Republican Party; he should resign by next summer.

944.   Montjoy, Robert S.; Shaffer, William R.; and Weber, Ronald E.   POLICY PREFERENCES OF PARTY ELITES AND MASSES: CONFLICT OR CONSENSUS?   *Am. Pol. Q. 1980 8(3): 319-343.* This study examines the sharing of public policy preferences between American state political party elites and party followers in the mass public on ten matters of state policy. Employing responses from about 1600 county political party chairmen in the 50 states and responses of party followers in several nationai-level surveys, we find meaningful differences between Democratic and Republican party elites, with the Democratic chairmen consistently more liberal on the ten matters of state policy than the Republican

chairmen. Smaller differences in policy preferences, generally, are reported between the Democratic and Republican followers in the mass public. Spatially, the Democratic elite, the Democratic mass, and the Republican mass are grouped together near a centrist position on the policy questions, while the Republican elite is positioned at a distance in the conservative direction on most of the ten matters of state policy.
J

945. Moon, John S. and Saunders, Nancy Bowen. THE IDEOLOGICAL CHARACTERISTICS OF PARTY LEADERS: A CASE OF TEXAS. *Western Pol. Q. 1979 32(2): 209-214.* Examines the ideological characteristics of the Democratic and Republican leaders of Texas in terms of ideological content and consensus. Further, their ideological characteristics are compared with those of their counterparts at the national level and in other states. Texas Democratic and Republican leaders are two distinct groups of co-believers, and the ideological concepts of these leaders are similar, with some variations, to those of the national party leaders and California groups. With regard to the ideological consensus, varied characteristics are discovered as the Texas, California, and national party leaders are compared. The variations found in the ideological characteristics of these party leader groups suggest impacts of regionalism on idelogical groupings and a need for further research.
J

946. Moore, David W. and Hofstetter, C. Richard. THE REPRESENTATIVENESS OF PRIMARY ELECTIONS: OHIO, 1968. *Polity 1973 6(2): 197-222.* Moore and Hofstetter carry further the discussion of the representativeness of direct primary voters, commenting on the Wisconsin studies and the Amsterdam studies published in *Polity* in 1972. Are those who vote in primary elections of a higher social stratum than those who do not? Are primary voters considerably more involved in politics than nonvoters? Do candidate and issue preferences differ among the two groups? Are the results parallel for the two parties? In this Columbus, Ohio study some significant differences between the primary voters and nonvoters were found in the Democratic party, a result that differs somewhat from earlier studies and from the Republican findings, leading to questions of the conditions in which such "misrepresentation" is likely to occur. The livelier the election, the more likely misrepresentation may be, the authors suggest. Interestingly, by checking actual voting records it was determined that thirty percent of those who claimed to have voted (in interviews) actually had not voted, reclassifying the voters on the basis of these records increased the misrepresentation found in the primary.
J

947. Morehouse, Sarah McCally. THE POLITICS OF GUBERNATORIAL NOMINATIONS. *State Government 1980 53(3): 125-128.* Examines the recruiting of gubernatorial candidates in different states during 1956-78, and the impact of the direct primary and preprimary forms of nomination on state political parties and party competition.

948. Murphy, James T. POLITICAL PARTIES AND THE PORKBARREL: PARTY CONFLICT AND COOPERATION IN HOUSE PUBLIC WORKS COMMITTEE DECISION-MAKING. *Am. Pol. Sci. Rev. 1974 68(1): 169-185.* This study of the House Public Works committee examines the relationship between membership goals and the degree of party conflict, identifies conditions of party conflict and cooperation, and links party conflict and cooper-

ation to policies adopted by the House. Party conflict is the Public Works committee's most striking behavioral characteristic. This party conflict stems from (a) the issues processed by the committee and (b) the partisan program orientations of committee members. Beyond these initial sources of party conflict on Public Works, there is a norm of partisanship adopted by each of the parties on the committee in order to achieve an extra measure of party cohesion. Public Works committee party conflict is, to be sure, often modified by shared interests cutting across party lines. Committee party cooperation stems, however, not from widespread shared interests but, instead, from a fundamental distrust between the parties respecting the allocation of federal largesse. To preclude porkbarreling, Congress has adopted fixed allocation formulas for distributing the boodle on programs likely to involve a majority in each party, thereby constraining the parties on the committee to cooperate on such proposals.   J

949. Nakamura, Robert T. BEYOND PURISM AND PROFES-SIONALISM: STYLES OF CONVENTION DELEGATE FOLLOWERSHIP. *Am. J. of Pol. Sci. 1980 24(2): 207-232.* Research on presidential nominating conventions has explored the relationship between two competing delegate political styles, purism and professionalism, and their impact on follower and candidate behavior. This article proposes a more elaborate theoretical framework, based on the work of Erving Goffman, that seeks to enrich the study of delegate styles by distinguishing, as separate determinants of style, the effect of candidates' self-presentations from their followers' acceptances of that presentation. Style is treated as a consequence of individual rational calculations about how supporting a candidate will help the person to achieve his or her goals. Styles are differentiated by the distinctive rationales characteristic of particular delegate goals and decisions. Each style or rationale, in turn, influences the delegate's perception and behavior with respect to other convention decisions: such as attitudes toward the platform and the decision to legitimate (accept) a party nominee who was not the person's first choice. This framework is then applied to interviews conducted at the 1976 Republican and Democratic national conventions. Diagram, biblio.
J

950. Nakamura, Robert T. IMPRESSIONS OF FORD AND REAGAN. *Pol. Sci. Q. 1977-78 92(4): 647-654.* Examines the images of Gerald Ford and Ronald Reagan that were held by delegates and how these images contributed to, or inhibited, the losing delegates' adjustment to the convention outcome. One of five articles on "Exploring the 1976 Republican Convention."   J

951. Nelson, Michael C. PARTISAN BIAS IN THE ELECTORAL COLLEGE. *J. of Pol. 1974 36(4): 1033-1048.* The biases of electoral systems have long been objects of concern to political scientists and political reformers. "Partisan Bias in the Electoral College" develops a method for simulating presidential elections to measure the presence and extent of partisan bias in the electoral college. Such a bias, which Michael C. Nelson found to be based in the different distributions of party support among states, would determine the victor when the major-party presidential candidates divided the national popular vote almost evenly between them, as in 1960. Since 1956 the bias has been consistently pro-Democratic and will probably result in a Democratic victory if the 1976 presidential election is as close as that of 1960.   J

952. Norpoth, Helmut. EXPLAINING PARTY COHESION IN CONGRESS: THE CASE OF SHARED POLICY ATTITUDES. *Am. Pol. Sci. Rev. 1976 70(4): 1156-1171.* Partisanship has often been noted as one of the most conspicuous factors in legislative voting in the U.S. Congress. This paper attempts to trace party voting to shared policy goals. After the mean attitudes of congressmen belonging to the same party were ascertained for a number of policy domains, the effect of mean party attitudes on roll-call voting was estimated by regression analysis, taking into account the deviation of individual congressmen from their respective mean party attitudes. The results demonstrate that in all three policy domains examined, i.e., social welfare, civil rights, and foreign policy, shared party attitudes leave a strong imprint on individual roll-call decisions. The voting decisions of congressmen, in fact, are found to owe more to the shared party attitudes than to their own individual attitudes. The paper also explores the communication process through which shared policy attitudes are translated within Congress into partisan roll-call votes and points to a way of reconciling the "predispositional" and the "interactional" approach to legislative decision making. J

953. Nyitray, Joseph P. AMATEUR AND PROFESSIONAL DEMOCRATS AT THE 1972 TEXAS STATE CONVENTION. *Western Pol. Q. 1975 28(4): 685-699.* This study examines the political style or orientation toward politics of delegates to the 1972 Texas State Democratic Convention by focusing on some of the same questions Soule and Clarke considered in their study of 1968 Democratic National Convention delegates. Texas delegates are classified as amateurs, semi-professionals, and professionals on the basis of their responses to interview questions. The article considers whether social characteristics, political socialization experiences, and political background characteristics differentiate amateurs from professionals. It also considers the relative influence of political style and ideology on delegates' leadership preferences. While confirming to some extent Soule and Clarke's picture of the amateur and professional, the Texas data question the adequacy of their socialization explanation of political style, and indicate that ideology, alone, is a better prediction of 1972 leadership preferences than either political style or a factor combining political style and ideology. J

954. Ostlund, Lyman E. INTERPERSONAL COMMUNICATION FOLLOWING MCGOVERN'S EAGLETON DECISION. *Public Opinion Q. 1973/74 37(4): 601-610.* Based on a questionnaire given to pedestrians in midtown Manhattan following Senator McGovern's decision to drop Senator Eagleton from the 1972 Democratic ticket following the disclosure of Eagleton's past mental illness. Shows that interpersonal communication played little role in establishing awareness, but that it did occur extensively in reaction to the event. Nearly half of the voters questioned made some attempt to persuade others on some aspect of the controversy. The most important criteria for judging presidential candidates were found to be issues, images, and party. 6 tables, 17 notes. E. P. Stickney

955. Pace, David. LENOIR CHAMBERS OPPOSES MASSIVE RESISTANCE: AN EDITOR AGAINST VIRGINIA'S DEMOCRATIC ORGANIZATION, 1955-1959. *Virginia Mag. of Hist. and Biog. 1974 82(4): 415-429.* The Supreme Court's 1954 decision outlawing racial segregation in public schools

led to a campaign in Virginia to prevent implementation of the decision. Lenoir Chambers, editor of the *Norfolk Virginian-Pilot*, waged an editorial struggle against the plan backed by Senator Harry F. Byrd to close schools before accepting integration. Chambers' position resulted not from racial liberalism but from a traditional respect for law and order. Based on primary sources; photo, 34 notes.

R. F. Oaks

956. Perkins, Jerry. BASES OF PARTISAN CLEAVAGE IN A SOUTHERN URBAN COUNTY. *J. of Pol. 1974 36(1): 208-214.* Confirms the view that high status and conservatism lead to loyalty to the Republican Party among urban white southerners. In making this identity, the southerners are following a national trend. Based on data from DeKalb County, Georgia, in 1970; 5 tables, 12 notes.

A. R. Stoesen

957. Perkins, Jerry and Guynes, Randall. FEDERALISM AND PARTISANSHIP. *Publius 1979 9(3): 51-74.* Examines variations in the strength of partisanship identification between state and national parties in Georgia by analyzing questionnaires on party preference administered to 476 persons in Dekalb County in 1970, and 500 persons statewide in 1974. Using a standard series of partisan questions developed by the Michigan Center for Political Studies, and a two-question format focusing on perceptions of whether state or national parties would behave more positively on particular issues, the data base represents respondent recall of the presidential elections of 1968 and 1972. Partisanship in both studies was predominantly consistent at state and national levels; those who perceived inconsistencies were those who identified inconsistently. Strong national Democrats were more liberal on race issues than strong state Democrats. Based on 2 questionnaires; 6 tables.

C. B. Schulz

958. Pilegge, Joseph C., Jr. TWO-PARTY ENDORSEMENTS IN A ONE-PARTY STATE. *Journalism Q. 1981 58(3): 449-453.* A study of editorial endorsements by the daily press in Alabama, 1962-78, showed that newspapers were, on the whole, evenly divided between Democratic and Republican candidates. This was somewhat surprising in light of the fact that Democrats greatly out-numbered Republicans in the state. Endorsements for Republicans tended to be limited to candidates for the presidency and for the House of Representatives. Urban papers were more likely to endorse Republicans than were their rural counterparts. The newspapers in the study had a very high rate of success in backing winning candidates. 4 tables, 14 notes.

J. S. Coleman

959. Plekhanov, S. M. DVISHENIE DZHORDZHA UOLLESA [The George Wallace Movement]. *Novaia i Noveishaia Istoriia [USSR] 1974 (1): 164-174.* Examines the development and interaction of American right-wing politics in the 1960's and early 1970's and the role of George C. Wallace in unifying such diverse groups as neo-Nazis and some trade unions into the American Independent Party. Wallace's popularity could not resolve inherent contradictions in his policies and most AIP supporters eventually returned to the Republican camp. Primary and secondary sources; 31 notes.

L. Smith

960. Podhoretz, Norman. THE NEW AMERICAN MAJORITY. *Commentary 1981 71(1): 19-28.* Analysts could have predicted Ronald Reagan's landslide victory in the 1980 presidential campaign had they been more conscious

of the connection with 1972: in 1980, Reagan overcame his ultraconservative image to reconstitute Richard M. Nixon's "new Republican majority"; whereas, like George McGovern in 1972, President Jimmy Carter split the Democrats into new and old liberals, disaffecting the latter, many of whom voted for Reagan, who, ironically, "represented the values of growth and strength which the Democratic party had once believed in."

961. Polsby, Nelson W. PRESIDENTIAL CABINET MAKING: LESSONS FOR THE POLITICAL SYSTEM. *Pol. Sci. Q. 1978 93(1): 15-25.* Suggests that the pattern of appointments in the Carter cabinet shows the persistence of a type of presidential leadership that the Nixon presidency did not put out of style. The causes of President Carter's brand of leadership are traced to the Democratic nomination process, however, rather than to attitudes about presidential authority that Carter evidently does not share with former president Nixon.   J

962. Pressman, Jeffrey L. and Sullivan, Denis G.   CONVENTIONAL RE-FORM AND CONVENTIONAL WISDOM: AN EMPIRICAL ASSESS-MENT OF DEMOCRATIC PARTY REFORMS. *Pol. Sci. Q. 1974 89(3): 539-562.* "Present empirical data which challenge widely expressed assertions that recent Democratic party convention reforms were crucial in the 1972 nomination of George McGovern, that they radically changed convention behavior, and that they were a major factor in the Democratic defeat of that year."   J

963. Pressman, Jeffrey L. GROUPS AND GROUP CAUCUSES. *Pol. Sci. Q. 1977-78 92(4): 673-682.* Examines the behavior of delegates as participants in organized social groupings, or what the Democrats have come to call "group caucuses" or "affinity caucuses." One of five articles on "Exploring the 1976 Republican Convention."   J

964. Randolph, Eleanor. THE "WHIP-HIS-ASS" STORY, OR THE GANG THAT COULDN'T LEAK STRAIGHT. *Washington Monthly 1979 11(7): 50-51.* Recounts President Jimmy Carter's awkward attempts to leak to the press his statement that he would beat Senator Edward M. Kennedy in the 1980 Democratic presidential campaign.

965. Reiter, Howard L. DEMOCRATIC RESURGENCE AND PARTY DECLINE IN CONNECTICUT. *Publius 1979 9(1): 205-214.* Analyzes change in Connecticut state politics despite ostensible Democratic victories there in 1978. Signs of change were appearing by 1955, and can be traced through succeeding years, including the lieutenant governor's challenge of the governor for her office, the decline of party organization, and a new "knuckling under" to national party rules even with little actual help from the top. Table, 7 notes.
R. V. Ritter

966. Reiter, Howard L. INTRA-PARTY CLEAVAGES IN THE UNITED STATES TODAY. *Western Pol. Q. 1981 34(2): 287-300.* In the 1960's, as realignment seemed imminent, the dominant ideological group within each major American political party split into two groups, one favoring a realignment around newly salient issues, the other wishing to continue traditional strategies. The coexistence of these groups with the minority ideologues within each party—Democratic conservatives and Republican liberals—presents a tripartite cleavage structure, in which the fundamental intraparty conflict is over strategy and

agenda much more than over ideological differences, as the McGovern-Jackson and Ford-Reagan nominating battles make clear. This scheme methodologically implies that the most efficient taxonomic scheme must include measures of receptivity to realignment, attitudes toward different agendas, and the role of issues in campaigns.   J/S

967. Ripley, Randall B. CONGRESSIONAL PARTY LEADERS AND STANDING COMMITTEES. *R. of Pol. 1974 36(3): 394-409.*

968. Roback, Thomas H. AMATEURS AND PROFESSIONALS: DELEGATES TO THE 1972 REPUBLICAN NATIONAL CONVENTION. *J. of Pol. 1975 37(2): 436-468.* Uses Wilson's seminal conception as a guide to develop meaningful interpretation of activist style among activists in a party of the right. An attitudinal index based on Soule and Clarke's 1968 study of Democratic delegates is used to measure amateurism-professionalism in relation to socio-economic characteristics, political socialization and recruitment experiences, incentives for party activism, liberal-conservative ideology, and attitudes toward the attributes of the 1972 nominee. The dangers of amoral party professionalism are discussed in evaluating the role of Republican activist style at the 1972 Convention.   J

969. Roback, Thomas H. MOTIVATING FOR ACTIVISM AMONG REPUBLICAN NATIONAL CONVENTION DELEGATES: CONTINUITY AND CHANGE 1972-1976. *J. of Pol. 1980 42(1): 181-201.* Delegates to the 1972 and 1976 Republican Party conventions were surveyed to determine the motivation of their political activism. The 1972 convention was a programmed ritual to renominate Richard M. Nixon with as much unanimity and as little conflict as possible, but the 1976 convention saw a party deeply wounded by Watergate and facing a bitter contest for the nomination between Gerald R. Ford and Ronald Reagan. Supporters of Nixon and later Ford were traditional Republicans who considered political careers important; in contrast Reagan supporters were self-recruited ideological converts, often from traditionally Democratic regions, who placed little emphasis on personal political careers. 4 tables, 17 notes.
                                                                                A. W. Novitsky

970. Roeder, Edward. POPULIST ELECTRONICS. *Working Papers Mag. 1981 8(4): 40-45.* Traces changes in American electoral politics during the 1970's: loss of the Democratic Party's ideological identity, money raising power of the Republicans, the high cost of political campaigns that are funded by out-of-state interest groups, a drop in popular participation through voting or working in elections; discusses how sophisticated technology and political action committees (PACs) can effectively mobilize popular support and participation.

971. Scarrow, Howard. THE IMPACT OF REAPPORTIONMENT ON PARTY REPRESENTATION IN THE STATE OF NEW YORK. *Policy Studies J. 1980-81 9(6): 937-946.* Focuses on the impact of reapportionment on political parties, especially patterns of representation before and after reapportionment in 1966.

972. Schier, Steven E. NEW RULES, NEW GAMES: NATIONAL PARTY GUIDELINES AND DEMOCRATIC NATIONAL CONVENTION DELEGATE SELECTION IN IOWA AND WISCONSIN, 1968-1976. *Publius 1980*

10(3): 101-127. The procedures for nomination in the Democratic Party have undergone numerous changes since 1968. This article analyzes the impact of such procedural changes in Iowa and Wisconsin during the 1968-76 period of national party rules reform. The guidelines with the greatest impact were those that introduced proportionality into the process of delegate selection. Instituted in 1972 and 1976, the proportional selection of delegates made the influence of participants more equal. Primary sources; 5 tables, 54 notes.   J. Powell

973. Schlesinger, Stephen. PARTIES TO REFORM. *Working Papers for a New Soc. 1975 3(3): 22-28.* Discusses the political representation reform movement in the Democratic Party during 1968-75.

974. Shaffer, William R. A DISCRIMINANT FUNCTION ANALYSIS OF POSITION-TAKING: CARTER VS. KENNEDY. *Presidential Studies Q. 1980 10(3): 451-468.* Studies the political positions of John F. Kennedy and Jimmy Carter since Carter took office in 1977, to test the recent theory that Carter is more a Republican than a Democrat. Although Kennedy was more liberal than Carter in 1978, Carter was every bit as Democratic as Kennedy when compared to Republican positions. Also, like Kennedy, Carter's positions were similar to those of a northern Democrat, and not a southern Democrat (or quasi-Republican.) Ideologically, then, the two men have not been far apart. The differences between them appear to be more personal and stylistic than political and ideological. Uses the roll-call voting record of the Americans for Democratic Action; 12 tables, 6 graphs, 13 notes, 21 ref., 3 appendixes.   D. H. Cline

975. Shaffer, William R. PARTY AND IDEOLOGY IN THE U.S. HOUSE OF REPRESENTATIVES. *Western Pol. Q. 1982 35(1): 92-106.* Analyzes the relationship between partisan affiliation and ideology for the House of Representatives. Explores the impact of region upon the linkage between party and ideological orientation. Cross-sectional analyses reveal a decided ideological split between Democratic and Republican congressmen, with Democrats generally left-of-center and Republicans far to the right. The overall degree of liberalism for all representatives was largely a function of the proportion of seats held by Democrats. Region is found to have an important impact upon the relationship between party and ideology, with unusually large partisan differences emerging in the Northeast, Midwest, Rocky Mountain, and Far West sections. Ironically, Democratic and Republican House members were least divided in the South, the very region which spawned the Wallace movement.   J/S

976. Shapiro, Walter. GAYLORD NELSON AND THE MYTH OF THE WHITE KNIGHT. *Washington Monthly 1975 7(5/6): 22-36.* Examines the career of Democratic Senator Gaylord Nelson of Wisconsin, 1962-74.

977. Shapiro, Walter. THE TWO PARTY PORK BARREL. *Washington Monthly 1975 7(9): 24-29.* Explains the current tendency in the federal government toward Republican presidents and Democratic Congresses as a result of their respective support for military and social programs.   S

978. Simpson, William. THE BIRTH OF THE MISSISSIPPI "LOYALIST DEMOCRATS" (1965-1968). *J. of Mississippi Hist. 1982 44(1): 27-45.* Discusses the events leading to the establishment of a Loyalist Democratic faction in 1968 after a predominantly black group from Mississippi, the Freedom Demo-

crats, challenged the seating of the state's regular delegation at the 1964 national convention. Describes the disputes between the state NAACP, led by Aaron Henry, and the Freedom Democratic faction. Moderate black leaders, including Charles Evers, white liberals, including Hodding Carter, III, and state labor leaders, including Claude Ramsey, sought to establish a biracial coalition to either capture or reform the state Democratic machinery. The Loyalist Democrats, composed of the Young Democrats, the Freedom Democrats, the NAACP, the state AFL-CIO, the Prince Hall Masons, and the Mississippi Teachers Association, were able to win recognition and be seated over the state regulars at both the 1968 and the 1972 Democratic national conventions. Based on personal interviews, newspaper accounts, monographs, and dissertations; 49 notes.

M. S. Legan

979. Skidmore, Max J. THE TUMULTUOUS DECADE: THE AMERI-CAN OF THE 1960S. *Indian J. of Am. Studies [India] 1979 9(2): 38-50.* Describes America from the nomination of John F. Kennedy in 1960 to the inauguration of Richard M. Nixon in 1969. In this period of ferment, old ideas mixed with new ideas derived from them. The New Left itself had many anteced-ents. Consumerism, the civil rights movement, participatory democracy, the peace movement, and the women's movement all had long histories in the intellec-tual and cultural life of the nation. Nixon's presidency introduced great changes in tone and feeling as much as substance, but the America of the Eisenhower years was irreversibly gone; technology, popular culture, political administrations, and social movements had brought about social change. 6 notes.   L. V. Eid

980. Smith, Craig R. THE REPUBLICAN KEYNOTE ADDRESS OF 1968: ADAPTIVE RHETORIC FOR THE MULTIPLE AUDIENCE. *Western Speech 1975 39(1): 32-39.* The 1968 Republican Party Convention keynote address by Daniel J. Evans illustrated an over-adaptation of rhetoric that appealed to neither conservative nor liberal public opinion.   S

981. Smith, Matthew J. RHODE ISLAND POLITICS, 1956-1964: PARTY REALIGNMENT. *Rhode Island Hist. 1976 35(2): 49-61.* Examines the col-lapse of the Democratic Party's hegemony in 1956 when the Republican Party used the politics of personality to leapfrog the organizational politics practiced by the Democrats. Based on oral interviews, papers in the Providence College archives, published documents, newspapers, and secondary sources.

P. J. Coleman

982. Soule, John W. and McGrath, Wilma E. A COMPARATIVE STUDY OF PRESIDENTIAL NOMINATION CONVENTIONS: THE DEMO-CRATS 1968 AND 1972. *Am. J. of Pol. Sci. 1975 19(3): 501-517.* This is intended to be a longitudinal study of politics at the 1968 and 1972 National Democratic Conventions. Although the casts of delegates, candidates, and issues were different at the two conventions, more generic political variables were available for observation and analysis at both conventions. Selected for compari-son were (1) the socioeconomic representativeness of delegates, (2) the ideological positions of delegates, and (3) the stylistic preferences (amateur-professional) of delegates. Data used are based upon sample surveys at the two conventions. Results indicate noticeable changes in delegate characteristics which were accom-panied by predictable shifts in ideological and stylistic commitments of delegates.

J

983.   Spencer, Martin E.   POLITICAL CULTURES IN AMERICA.   *Midwest Q. 1979 21(1): 7-20.* First published in *Midwest Quarterly* in 1974. Analyzes the split in the Democratic Party that became evident in the conventions of 1968 and 1972. It rests on fundamentally different views of the nature of politics and the political process. There has been a weakening of the balance of political cultures. No longer do the liberals and old professionals balance each other off. Instead there has come to be a cluster of extremist and essentially antiliberal, political cultures. The crusaders, adventurers, and ideologues have come to the fore at the expense of the older groups. The prospect therefore becomes unpromising.

R. V. Ritter

984.   Spinrad, William.   THE CONTINUING DEMOCRATIC MAJORITY. *Dissent 1976 23(2): 127-130.* Comments on the political constituency since 1948 and speculates on the strength of the Democratic Party and the presidential election of 1976.

985.   Stevens, Arthur G., Jr.; Miller, Arthur H.; and Mann, Thomas E. MOBILIZATION OF LIBERAL STRENGTH IN THE HOUSE, 1955-1970: THE DEMOCRATIC STUDY GROUP.   *Am. Pol. Sci. Rev. 1974 68(2): 667-681.* In 1959 a number of progressive Democratic congressmen organized the Democratic Study Group (DSG) as a vehicle for countering certain conservative biases then present in the decision-making process in the House of Representatives. This paper presents brief descriptions of the difficulties faced by these congressmen in their efforts to pass more "liberal" legislation and of the organization and activities of the DSG. The analytical focus is on an assessment of DSG success in developing an effective communication network as a means of achieving its policy goals. The central hypothesis is that this communication network has had an impact on the voting behavior of DSG members. Roll-call data from the 84th through the 91st Congress are examined to ascertain whether longitudinal patterns in the voting of DSG members, non-southern non-DSG Democrats, southern Democrats, and Republicans tend to confirm or deny this hypothesis.

J

986.   Strafford, Peter.   THE US MID-TERM ELECTIONS.   *World Today [Great Britain] 1974 30(12): 487-496.* Discusses problems of the political parties in the 1974 elections.

S

987.   Sullivan, Denis G.   PARTY UNITY: APPEARANCE AND REALITY.   *Pol. Sci. Q. 1977-78 92(4): 635-645.* Explores the ways in which convention behavior contributed to the legitimation of the convention's nominees. One of five articles on "Exploring the 1976 Republican Convention."

J

988.   Uhlman, Thomas M. and Kritzer, Herbert M.   THE PRESIDENTIAL AMBITION OF DEMOCRATIC SENATORS: ITS TIMING AND IMPACT. *Presidental Studies Q. 1979 9(3): 316-329.* Discusses the presidential ambition of 17 Democratic senators from 1952 to 1976 based primarily on a 1966 analysis of presidential seekers by Joseph Schlesinger.

989.   VanDerSlik, Jack R.; Pernacciaro, Samuel J.; and Kenney, David. PATTERNS OF PARTISANSHIP IN A NONPARTISAN REPRESENTATIONAL SETTING: THE ILLINOIS CONSTITUTIONAL CONVENTION. *Am. J. of Pol. Sci. 1974 18(1): 95-116.* "Roll call voting in the convention [The

Sixth Illinois Constitutional Convention, 1969-70] was highly structured. Using MacRae's clustering and scaling techniques, 78 per cent of the roll calls with disagreement fitted into 13 substantive dimensions. Although members were elected on a nonpartisan ballot, and did not organize the convention in a partisan fashion, partisan identification of the members was the best of several political, social, career, and constituency variables in accounting for roll call voting variance on most dimensions. Multiple regression analysis reveals that the other independent variables account for little roll call voting variance on dimensions not explained by partisanship."   J

990.   VanDerSlik, Jack R. and Pernacciaro, Samuel J.   OFFICE AMBITIONS AND VOTING BEHAVIOR IN THE U.S. SENATE: A LONGITUDINAL STUDY.   *Am. Pol. Q. 1979 7(2): 198-224.* Joseph Schlesinger's ambition theory of political behavior argues that differing opportunities and the aspirations of politicians for them cause politicians to make political choices today in terms of the office or status they aspire to gain in the future. We have looked at the behavior of continuing members of the Senate from 1967-1972 to establish norms of roll call behavior among southern and nonsouthern Democrats and Republicans on major dimensions of policy. We have looked specifically at the behavior of several subsets of senators: aspirants for party leadership positions and nominations to the U.S. presidency and the committee leaders of each party for the prestigious committees. The data rather clearly show that behavior conforms to hypotheses based upon ambition theory. The theory has applied significance for possible legislative reforms.   J

991.   VanWingen, John R. and Parker, Joseph B.   MEASURING FRIENDS-AND-NEIGHBORS VOTING.   *Am. Pol. Q. 1979 7(3): 367-383.* Although the friends-and-neighbors factor helps explain the results of Democratic primaries in several Southern states, an adequate measure of the phenomenon is conspicuously missing. A procedure for measuring the hometown support, the concentration of that support, and the importance of friends-and-neighbors is developed herein. The 1947 special general election and the 1978 Democratic primaries for the Mississippi U.S. Senate seat are analyzed to show how the measure is better than a previous one, how the importance of friends-and-neighbors in determining election outcomes can be calculated, and how one can detect if the importance is spurious. The analysis demonstrates that friends-and-neighbors was as important in the 1978 first primary as it was in the 1947 special general election. The high importance in the 1978 runoff is partially explained, however, by the emerging North-South cleavage in Mississippi politics. 6 tables, fig., 15 notes, biblio.
                                                         J

992.   Walter, B. Oliver.   WYOMING: CONSERVATIVE AND REPUBLICAN BUT NOT ALWAYS SO.   *Social Sci. J. 1981 18(3): 131-142.* Wyoming is a conservative state in which the 1980 general election generated little enthusiasm.

993.   Ware, Alan.   THE 1978 U.S. MID-TERM ELECTIONS IN HISTORICAL PERSPECTIVE.   *Parliamentary Affairs [Great Britain] 1979 32(2): 207-221.* Examines the 1978 mid-term elections as reflecting the president's strength in his party, and relative strengths of the Republican and Democratic parties; compares 1978 to other mid-term elections, 1958-78.

994.   Wattenberg, Martin P.   THE DECLINE OF POLITICAL PARTISAN-SHIP IN THE UNITED STATES: NEGATIVITY OR NEUTRALITY? *Am. Pol. Sci. Rev. 1981 75(4): 941-950.* Examines attitudes toward the two major political parties in the United States from 1952 to 1980, using national election study data from open-ended likes/dislikes questions. The major trend which is found is a shift toward neutral evaluations of the parties. A reinterpretation of party decline in the electorate is offered, in which the much-discussed alienation from parties is largely rejected as an explanation. Rather, the link between parties and candidates has been substantially weakened over the years and hence political parties have become increasingly meaningless to the electorate.   J

995.   Weinberg, Martha Wagner.   WRITING THE REPUBLICAN PLAT-FORM. *Pol. Sci. Q. 1977-78 92(4): 655-662.* Traces the writing of the Republican platform and explains how that process differed from Democratic party platform writing and reflected the particular ideological and structural composition of the Republican Party. One of five articles on "Exploring the 1976 Republican Convention."   J

996.   Welch, Susan and Brown, Buster J.   CORRELATES OF SOUTHERN REPUBLICAN SUCCESS AT THE CONGRESSIONAL DISTRICT LEVEL. *Social Sci. Q. 1979 59(4): 732-742.* A study of the bases of support for the resurgence of Republicanism in the southern states on the congressional level. Despite Republican strength on the presidential level, successes have been much more moderate on the congressional. Republicans have failed to penetrate Democratic strongholds in urban areas, black counties, and rural areas. Republican strength, though slowly growing, remains confined to the middle classes, much as it does elsewhere in the nation. Thus speculation concerning pending Republican dominance in the southland seems premature. 3 tables, 8 notes, ref.
V. L. Human

997.   White, John K.   ALL IN THE FAMILY: THE 1978 MASSACHU-SETTS DEMOCRATIC GUBERNATORIAL PRIMARY. *Polity 1982 14(4): 641-656.* Analyzes the 1978 Democratic primary in Massachusetts from the perspective of troublesome issues, such as abortion and the death penalty.
J/S

998.   Williams, Philip and Wilson, Graham.   THE AMERICAN MID-TERM ELECTIONS. *Pol. Studies [Great Britain] 1979 27(4): 603-609.* Considers the congressional elections in terms of advantages won and lost by the Republican and Democratic parties in 1978.

999.   Williams, Philip and Wilson, Graham K.   THE 1976 ELECTION AND THE AMERICAN POLITICAL SYSTEM. *Pol. Studies [Great Britain] 1977 25(2): 182-200.* Analyzes the 1976 elections in the United States with a view to their impact on general theories about American elections. Stresses the Democratic Party's selection of a moderate around whom they could unite, while the Republicans engaged in bitter factional struggle. The popular vote was not as close as in other postwar elections, while regional variations were less pronounced and party more important than had been supposed. The discrepancy between Republican Party performance in presidential elections and at other levels is reviewed, with the conclusion that no theory satisfactorily explains the phenomenon. 13 tables, 22 notes.
R. Howell

1000.   Windhauser, John W.   REPORTING OF OHIO MUNICIPAL ELEC-
TIONS BY THE OHIO METROPOLITAN DAILY PRESS.   *Journalism Q.
1977 54(3): 552-565.* Data received from Ohio metropolitan daily newspapers
during 28 September-1 November 1971 indicate that while coverage slightly
favored Democrats, no one party or political candidate was consistently favored.

1001.   Wittmer, Lawrence S.   PRINCIPLES AND OPPORTUNITIES IN
AMERICAN POLITICS.   *Rev. in Am. Hist. 1976 4(4): 594-600.* Review article
prompted by Herbert S. Parmet's *The Democrats: The Years after FDR* (New
York: Macmillan, 1976); chronicles the evolution in political ideology in the
Democratic Party, 1945-68.

1002.   Wolfe, Alan.   BEYOND REAGAN.   *Working Papers Mag. 1981 8(6):
38-41.* Discusses the contradictions in the Republican Party's philosophies on
such issues as human rights, foreign policy, social services, and the environment;
rather than focusing on "growth politics" the conservatives must help revamp the
whole political system.

1003.   Zolotukhin, Iu.   START PREZIDENTSKOI KAMPANII V SSHA
[The start of the presidential campaign in the USA].   *Mirovaia Ekonomika i
Mezhdunarodnye Otnosheniia [USSR] 1976 (3): 92-98.* Discusses the standing of
the Republican and Democratic Parties in the 1976 presidential campaign and
the political, social, and economic problems facing the candidates.

1004.   —.   [DEMOCRATIC DELEGATE SELECTION REFORM].   *Am.
Pol. Sci. Rev. 1974 68(1): 27-44.*
Cavala, William.   CHANGING THE RULES CHANGES THE GAME:
PARTY REFORM AND THE 1972 CALIFORNIA DELEGATION TO
THE DEMOCRATIC NATIONAL CONVENTION,   *pp. 27-42.* During
1968-72 the Democratic Party developed new rules governing the selection
of delegates to their National Convention. In California the result was a
delegation dominated by women, youth, and minorities, but with few party
leaders. This produced a change in the strategic environment and hindered
George McGovern's efforts to wage an effective electoral campaign. To
avoid another electoral loss in 1976, the rules are being revised "to drop the
demographic quotas and include more party notables" in delegate selection.
55 notes.
Ranney, Austin.   COMMENT,   *pp. 43-44.*   T. Simmerman

1005.   —.   JIMMY CARTER: KENNEDY OR KEFAUVER?   *Washington
Monthly 1976 7(12): 17-21.* Reports on the 1976 political campaign work of
Jimmy Carter for the Democratic Party nomination in New Hampshire, Iowa,
Florida, and Oregon.

1006.   —.   [VOTING BEHAVIOR AND THE 1972 ELECTION].   *Am. Pol.
Sci. Rev. 1976 70(3): 753-849.*
Miller, Arthur H.; Miller, Warren E.; Raine, Alden S.; and Brown, Thad A.
A MAJORITY PARTY IN DISARRAY: POLICY POLARIZATION IN
THE 1972 ELECTION,   *pp. 753-778.* Theories of voting behavior attribute
varying importance to candidates, parties, and issues in presidential elec-
tions. The voting public was better informed on issues in 1972 than ever
before, and the Democratic Party's loss "was the result of the ideological

polarization within the Democratic ranks." Based on a study of the Center for Political Studies; 4 tables, 41 notes.

Popkin, Samuel; Gorman, John W.; Phillips, Charles; and Smith, Jeffrey. COMMENT: WHAT HAVE YOU DONE FOR ME LATELY? TOWARD AN INVESTMENT THEORY OF VOTING, *pp. 779-805.* Offers an economic approach to voting behavior in which a voter uses his vote as an investment and is concerned "with what the candidate can be expected to 'deliver' and, thus, the voter looks for signs of competence." In 1972 voters perceived incompetence in the George McGovern campaign's handling of the Thomas Eagleton affair and its approaches to the Vietnam and welfare problems, and withdrew their support. 9 tables, 69 notes.

Steeper, Frederick T. and Teeter, Robert M. COMMENT ON "A MAJORITY PARTY IN DISARRAY," *pp. 806-813.* To separate issues from candidate preferences is often an oversimplification. Voters generally select a candidate based on the candidate's projected ability to solve a problem. 3 tables, note.

RePass, David E. COMMENT: POLITICAL METHODOLOGIES IN DISARRAY: SOME ALTERNATIVE INTERPRETATIONS OF THE 1972 ELECTION, *pp. 814-831.* Candidate identification has been the leading factor in voting behavior in the 1952-72 presidential elections. Problems in the use of new methodology and research methods for measuring candidate proximity and ideology led the Center for Political Studies to identify ideology as the key voting factor in the 1972 election. 3 tables, 43 notes.

Miller, Arthur and Miller, Warren E. IDEOLOGY IN THE 1972 ELECTION: MYTH OR REALITY—A REJOINDER, *pp. 832-849.* Challenges the above comments and reaffirms that "issue awareness and policy preferences interacted with the clearly articulated candidate differences to produce a vote heavily laden with ideology and policy concerns . . . 1972 was an ideological election." 4 tables, 53 notes.   T. Simmerman

SUBJECT INDEX

Subject Profile Index (ABC-SPIndex) carries both generic and specific index terms. Begin a search at the general term but also look under more specific or related terms.

Each string of index descriptors is intended to present a profile of a given article; however, no particular relationship between any two terms in the profile is implied. Terms within the profile are listed alphabetically after the leading term. The variety of punctuation and capitalization reflects production methods and has no intrinsic meaning; e.g., there is no difference in meaning between "History, study of" and "History (study of)."

Cities, towns, and counties are listed following their respective states or provinces; e.g., "Ohio (Columbus)." Terms beginning with an arabic numeral are listed after the letter Z. The chronology of the bibliographic entry follows the subject index descriptors. In the chronology, "c" stands for "century"; e.g., "19c" means "19th century."

Note that "United States" is not used as a leading index term; if no country is mentioned, the index entry refers to the United States alone. When an entry refers to both Canada and the United States, both "Canada" and "USA" appear in the string of index descriptors, but "USA" is not a leading term. When an entry refers to any other country and the United States, only the other country is indexed.

The last number in the index string, in italics, refers to the bibliographic entry number.

A

Abolition Movement *See also* Antislavery sentiments.
—. Brown, John. Harpers Ferry raid. North Carolina. Sectionalism. State Politics. 1840-60. *220*
—. Constitutional Union Party. Political Campaigns. Republican Party. 1860. *559*
—. Democratic Party. New York (Utica). Proslavery Sentiments. Riots. 1835. *282*
—. Fessenden, Samuel. Free Soil movement. Liberty Party. Maine. State Politics. Willey, Austin. 1830's-48. *234*
—. *Green Mountain Freeman* (newspaper). Liberty Party. Poland, Joseph. State politics. Vermont. 1840-48. *232*
—. Liberty Party. New York. 1840-48. *241*
—. Political Participation. Rantoul, Robert, Jr. 1820's-56. *157*
Abortion. Catholic Church. Democratic Party. Elections (presidential). 1976. *895*
Actors and Actresses. Douglas, Melvyn. Political Activism. 1936-42. *700*
Adams, John Quincy. Democratic Party. Elections (presidential). Jackson, Andrew. Slavery. Whig Party. 1828-44. *297*
Adams party. Clayton, John M. Delaware. Elections (presidential). State Politics. 1824-28. *335*
Administrative polarity, principle of. Federalism, representational. *Federalist*. Political theory. 1787-20c. *183*
Age. Converse, Philip E. 1952-76. *112*
Agrarianism. Rhode Island. State Politics. 1800-60. *262*
Agricultural Policy. Congress. Democratic Party. Federal Programs. Presidents. South. 1933-61. *776*
Agriculture. Alabama. Elections (gubernatorial). Industry. Jones, Thomas G. Kolb, Reuben F. 1892. *608*
Aiken, George D. Flood control. Governors. Political Campaigns (presidential). Republican Party. Vermont. 1937-39. *774*

Alabama. Agriculture. Elections (gubernatorial). Industry. Jones, Thomas G. Kolb, Reuben F. 1892. *608*
—. Boyd, Alexander (murder of). Elections. Ku Klux Klan. 1870. *610*
—. Clayton, Henry D. Democratic Party. House of Representatives. 1897-1914. *605*
—. Congressional District (7th). Denson, William H. Howard, Milford W. Political Campaigns. Populism. 1894. *476*
—. Dead Shoes senatorial primary (1906). Direct primary system. Political reform. 1890-1915. *500*
—. Democratic Party. Elections, gubernatorial. Folsom, James E. Graves, Bibb. Sparks, Chauncey. 1926-50. *701*
—. Democratic Party. Farmers' Alliance. Jones, Thomas G. Kolb, Reuben F. Political Campaigns (gubernatorial). 1889-90. *609*
—. Democratic Party. Federal Elections Bill (1890). Political Campaigns. South. Stevenson, Adlai E. (1835-1914). 1889-93. *621*
—. Democratic Party. Manning, Joseph C. Populism. State Politics. 1892-96. *596*
—. Democratic Party. Reconstruction. Republican Party. 1868-76. *682*
—. Editorials. Political endorsements. 1962-78. *958*
—. Elections. Senate. 1819-61. *329*
—. Haralson, J. Negro Suffrage. Reconstruction. Republican Party. 1867-82. *638*
—. House of Representatives. Political Attitudes. 1849-61. *274*
—. Legislation. Reconstruction. 1867. *637*
—. Political Ostracism. Reconstruction. Republican Party. 1865-80. *683*
—. State politics. ca 1970-78. *919*
Alabama (Dothan). Civil Service. Clayton, Henry D. Patronage. Postal Service. Taft, William H. (administration). Wilson, Woodrow (administration). 1900-13. *606*
—. Democratic Party. Local Politics. Political Factions. Postmasters. 1912. *607*
Alabama (Eufaula County). Democratic Party. Politics and the Military. Reconstruction. Republican Party. Riots. 1874. *483*

"Appeal of the Independent Democrats" (manifesto). Antislavery Sentiments. Chase, Salmon P. Civil War (antecedents). Democratic Party. Douglas, Stephen A. Historiography. Kansas-Nebraska Act (US, 1854). 1892-1967. *230*

Appointments to Office. Bureaucracies. Executive Branch. 1961-80. *833*

Apportionment. 1954-78. *971*

—. Brayton, Charles R. Connecticut. Political machines. Rhode Island. Roraback, J. Henry. 1818-1937. *393*

Argentina. Alberdi, Juan Bautista. Hamilton, Alexander. Political thought. USA. 1787-1860. *160*

Argersinger, Peter H. Goodwyn, Lawrence. Parson, Stanley. Populism (review article). Youngdale, James M. 1890's. 1970's. *582*

Arizona. Campbell, Thomas E. Elections (gubernatorial, dispute). Hunt, George. 1859-1917. *514*

—. Campbell, Tom. Republican Party. State Politics. 1875-1944. *399*

—. Congressional Union for Woman Suffrage. Democratic Party. Political Campaigns. Women. 1914. 1916. *654*

—. Elections. Republican Party. 1980. *939*

Arizona (Globe). Elections (gubernatorial). Hunt, George. Newspapers. Political Commentary. Republican Party. 1911. *564*

Arizona (Pima County). Constitutional conventions, state (delegate election). Politics (territorial, local issues). 1910. *585*

Arkansas. Brough, Charles Hillman (biography). Democratic Party. State Politics. Wilson, Woodrow. 1903-35. *681*

—. Clayton, Powell. Federal Government. Ku Klux Klan. Martial law. Militia. Republican Party. Violence. 1868. *679*

—. Compromise of 1850. Democratic Party. Elections. Whigs. 1848-52. *328*

—. Constitutional conventions, state. Negroes. Reconstruction. Whites, southern. 1868. *495*

—. Democratic Party. Historiography (revisionist). Social Classes. Whigs. 1836-50. *145*

—. Democratic Party. Jones, Daniel. Jones, James K. Political Conventions. Populism. 1890-1900. *576*

—. Elections (presidential). Know-Nothing Party. 1855-56. *315*

—. Garland, Rufus King. Greenback Party. State politics. Tobey, Charles E. 1876-82. *363*

—. Negroes. Racial conflict. Republican Party. 1867-1928. *418*

—. Pike, Albert. ca 1850-61. *155*

—. Political Leadership. Remmel, Harmon L. Republican Party. 1880-1913. *612*

—. Race Relations. Republican Party. 1890's-1924. *419*

Arkansas (Pope County). Hays, Brooks (reminiscence). Political Conventions. 1908. *480*

Arkansas State Penitentiary. Convict-lease. Democratic administrations. Prisoners, abuse of. 1874-96. *368*

Armies. Jefferson, Thomas. Military Peace Establishment Act (US, 1802). 1793-1802. *170*

Arvey, Jacob M. Democratic Party (Convention). Illinois (Chicago). Nominations for office. Stevenson, Adlai E., II. 1932-52. *706*

Ashley, James M. Chase, Salmon P. Elections, presidential. 1854-56. *219*

Attitudes. Delegates. Political Conventions. 1968. *897*

—. Impeachment. Johnson, Andrew. Letters. Republican Party. Ross, Edmund. 1867-68. *374*

Authority. History. New England. Political Attitudes. Whig Party. 1840's-50's. *263*

B

Bailey, Gamaliel. Antislavery Sentiments. Chase, Salmon P. Liberty Party. Ohio. Republican Party. 1836-60. *209*

Baker, Edward D. California. Political Campaigns (presidential). Republican Party. 1855-56. *116*

Ballot. Elections. Legislation, antifusion. Political Reform. Republican Party. 1880-1902. *355*

Bamberger, Simon. Governors. Jews. Utah. 1916. *427*

Bank, national. Political Commentary. Whigs. Wise, Henry A. Yell, Archibald (letters). 1841. *144*

Bank of America. California. Elections, gubernatorial. Giannini, Amadeo P. Merriam, Frank. Roosevelt, Franklin D. Sinclair, Upton. ca 1923-34. *698*

Bank of the United States, 2d. Dallas, George M. Democratic Party. Elections. Jackson, Andrew. Pennsylvania. 1832. *117*

Bank wars. Ohio. Two-party system. Voting and Voting Behavior. 1818-40. *189*

Banking services. Fletcher, Calvin. Indiana (Indianapolis). Junto. Whig businessmen. ca 1820-50. *259*

Bannan, Benjamin. Anti-Catholicism. Antislavery Sentiments. Nativism. Pennsylvania (Schuylkill County). Temperance Movements. Whig Party. 1852-54. *200*

Banning, Lance. Federalists. Ideology. Jeffersonians. Political Parties (review articles). Zvesper, John. 1790's. 1977-78. *268*

Barkley, Alben W. Democratic Party. Judges. Kentucky (McCracken County). Political corruption. State Politics. 1897-1909. *466*

—. Democratic Party. Political Conventions. Vice Presidency. 1948. *804*

—. Democratic Party. Roosevelt, Franklin D. Senate. Taxation. 1944. *715*

—. Democratic Party (convention). Kentucky. Partisanship. Rhetoric. State Politics. 1919. *465*

Barlow, Joel (essays). Federalism. History. Jefferson, Thomas. Political Systems. 1790-1815. *257*

Barnard, Daniel Dewey. New York. Weed, Thurlow. Whig Party. 1834-55. *286*

Barnes, Cassius McDonald. Governors. Oklahoma Territory. Public welfare. Republican Party. 1897-1901. *685*

Barnes, William, Jr. Bossism. Lawsuits. New York. Republican Party. Roosevelt, Theodore. 1915. *382*

Bartley, Numan V. Graham, Hugh D. Political Parties (review article). Seagull, Louis M. South. 1944-70's. *83*

Bass, Robert P. Boston and Maine Railroad. Churchill, Winston (1871-1947). New Hampshire. Progressivism. Republican Party. 1890-1912. *344*

Battle, John Stewart. Byrd, Harry F. Edwards, Horace. Elections (gubernatorial). Miller, Francis P. Virginia. 1949. *739*

Beamish, Frank A. City Politics. Knights of Labor. Pennsylvania (Scranton). Powderly, Terence V. 1878-84. *428*

Bedinger, Henry. Democratic Party. Denmark. Diplomacy. House of Representatives. Law. Virginia. 1854-58. *253*

Behavior. Republican Party (convention). 1976. *987*

Bell, Rudolph M. House of Representatives. McDonald, Forrest. Presidency. 1789-1801. 1973-74. *198*

Bellamy, Edward *(Looking Backward 2000-1887)*. Economic Theory. North Central States. Populism. 1880's-90's. *551*

Belz, Herman. Linden, Glenn M. Mohr, James C. North. Reconstruction (review article). State politics. 1850's-69. *371*

Belz, Herman (review article). Civil War. Freedmen. Law. Republican Party. 1861-66. 1976. *409*

Benson, Lee. Historiography. Massachusetts. Mugwumps. Republican Party. Voting and Voting Behavior. 1880's. *367*

Berk, Stephen E. Dwight, Timothy. Federalism (review article). Higher Education. McCaughey, Robert A. Quincy, Josiah. 1795-1864. 1974. *279*

Berrien, John M. (letter). Federalists. Georgia. State Politics. 1808. *272*

—. Georgia. Know-Nothing Party. Political Attitudes. 1854-56. *271*

Bias. Political activism. Public Policy. 1952-76. *92*

Bibliographies. Elections (congressional). New Jersey. 1838-40. *135*

Bilbo, Theodore G. Mississippi. Political Leadership. State Government. Whites. 1908-32. *457*

Bill of Rights. American Revolution. Constitutional Convention. Declaration of Independence. Hamilton, Alexander (policies). Inflation. Liberty, ordered. Washington, George (administrations). 1607-1800. *163*

Bimetallism. Democrats, silver. Tennessee (Memphis). 1895-96. *424*

Bisbee, Horatio, Jr. Florida. Lee, Joseph E. Letters. Negroes. Republican Party. 1880. *507*

Black Capitalism. Alabama (Mobile). Editors and Editing. Johnson, Andrew N. Republican Party. Tennessee (Nashville). 1890-1920. *349*

Black power. Bryant, John Emory. Georgia. Pledger, William A. Republican Party. 1876-84. *549*

Blaine, James G. Hayes, Rutherford B. Ohio (Cincinnati). Republican Party Convention. 1876. *404*

Blaine, John J. Progressivism. Republican Party. Senate. Wisconsin. 1927-33. *578*

Blair, Francis. Jacksonian era. Jeffersonian heritage. Kendall, Amos. 1819-37. *249*

Bland, Richard Parks. Democratic Party. Free Silver movement. Missouri. Political Campaigns. 1878-96. *647*

Blumberg, Barbara. Andersen, Kristi. Fine, Sidney. Jeffries, John W. New Deal (review article). Roosevelt, Franklin D. Swain, Martha H. 1933-39. *708*

Boernstein, Heinrich. *Anzeiger des Westens* (newspaper). German Americans. Missouri (St. Louis). Republican Party. Voting and Voting behavior. 1848-60. *238*

Bond, Hugh Lennox. Ideology. Maryland. Racism. Radical Republicans. ca 1861-68. *440*

Border States. Congress. Legislation. Loyalty oath. Republican Party. Republican Party. 1861-67. *356*

Bossism. Barnes, William, Jr. Lawsuits. New York. Republican Party. Roosevelt, Theodore. 1915. *382*

—. Buckley, Christopher. California (San Francisco). Elections, municipal. Spreckels, John D. ca 1896. *395*

—. City Politics. Democratic Party. Maryland (Baltimore). 1919-47. *699*

—. Illinois (Chicago). Kelly, Edward J. Mayors. Negroes. Voting and Voting Behavior. 1933-50. *705*

Boston and Maine Railroad. Bass, Robert P. Churchill, Winston (1871-1947). New Hampshire. Progressivism. Republican Party. 1890-1912. *344*

Boston Finance Commission. Democratic Party. Massachusetts. Matthews, Nathan. Mayors. Political Reform. 1890-1910. *650*

Boyd, Alexander (murder of). Alabama. Elections. Ku Klux Klan. 1870. *610*

Boyd, Julian. Hamilton, Alexander (character). Political scandal. Reynolds, Maria Lewis. 1791-97. 1971. *115*

Boyd, Steven R. Antifederalism (review article). Constitutions. O'Connor, John E. Paterson, William. 1787-99. *156*

Brayton, Charles R. Apportionment. Connecticut. Political machines. Rhode Island. Roraback, J. Henry. 1818-1937. *393*

Breckinridge, John. Elections (presidential). Georgia. Newspapers. 1860. *591*

Bristow, Benjamin Helm. Hayes, Rutherford B. Kentucky. Political Campaigns (presidential). Republican Party. 1876. *678*

Broadsides. Canada. Democratic-Republican Party. Embargoes. Federalists. Great Britain. Vermont. 1809-16. *180*

Brock, Richard. Negroes. Republican Party. Voting and Voting Behavior. 1937-80. *86*

Brookhart, Smith Wildman. Iowa (Washington County). Prohibition. 1890-94. *548*

Brooks, Preston S. Civil War (antecedents). Congress. Republican Party. Sumner, Charles. Violence. 1856. *193*

Brough, Charles Hillman (biography). Arkansas. Democratic Party. State Politics. Wilson, Woodrow. 1903-35. *681*

Broussard, James H. (review article). Federalists. South. 1800-16. 1978. *311*

Brown, Albert Gallatin. Democratic Party. Mississippi. Political Campaigns (congressional). Winans, William. 1849. *217*

Brown, Edmund G. (Pat). California. Feather River Project. State Legislatures. Water Supply. 1955-60. *733*

Brown, Jerry. Carter, Jimmy. Democratic Party. Political campaigns. Presidential candidates. 1976. *832*

Brown, John. Abolition Movement. Harpers Ferry raid. North Carolina. Sectionalism. State Politics. 1840-60. *220*

Brown, John Y. Democratic Party. Goebel, William. Kentucky. L and N Railroad. State Politics. 1890-1900. *499*

Browning, Gordon. Elections (gubernatorial). Political machines. Tennessee. 1936. *696*

Brownlow, W. G. "Parson". Elections, gubernatorial. Reconstruction. Tennessee. 1865-80. *695*

Bryan, William Jennings. Cleveland, Grover. Democratic Party. Free silver movement. North Carolina. Political Campaigns. Populism. Republican Party. 1892-96. *430*

—. Delaware. Foreign Policy. Political Campaigns (presidential). Stevenson, Adlai E. (1835-1914). 1900. *618*

—. Democratic Party. Imperialism. Philippines. Political Campaigns (presidential). Stevenson, Adlai E. (1835-1914). 1900. *631*

—. Democratic Party. Maine (Bath). Political Campaigns (vice-presidential). Sewall, Arthur. 1896. *624*

—. Democratic Party. Political Campaigns (presidential). Stevenson, Adlai E. (1835-1914). 1892-1900. *622*

Constitutional conventions, state (delegate election). Arizona (Pima County). Politics (territorial, local issues). 1910. *585*

Constitutional law. Conservatism. Kansas. New Deal. Newspapers. Supreme Court. 1934-35. *718*

Constitutional Union Party. Abolition Movement. Political Campaigns. Republican Party. 1860. *559*

—. Elections. Texas. 1860-61. *124*

Constitutions. Antifederalism (review article). Boyd, Steven R. O'Connor, John E. Paterson, William. 1787-99. *156*

—. Antifederalists. Foreign policy. 1787-88. *261*

—. Church and state. Connecticut (Windham). Democratic-Republican Party. Federalists. Local Politics. Toleration Party. 1790-1818. *334*

—. Debates. Federalism. Government, forms of. New York State Ratifying Convention. 1788. *171*

Constitutions (ratification). Antifederalists. Collins, John. Hazard, Jonathan J. Rhode Island. 1786-90. *237*

—. Antifederalists. Federal government. Pennsylvania. 1787-92. *143*

—. Antifederalists. Republican ideology. 1789-93. *129*

Constitutions, state. American Revolution. Pennsylvania. 1750-89. *341*

—. Colorado. Democratic Party. Eight-hour day. Republican Party. State Legislatures. Working Conditions. 1902-05. *527*

—. Elections. New York. Political Reform. Republican Party. 1907-16. *556*

—. Know-Nothing Party. Massachusetts (western). Republican Party. State Politics. Voting and Voting Behavior. 1854-58. *284*

Converse, Philip E. Age. 1952-76. *112*

Convict-lease. Arkansas State Penitentiary. Democratic administrations. Prisoners, abuse of. 1874-96. *368*

Coolidge, Calvin. Income tax. Inheritance tax. Mellon, Andrew W. Republican Party. 1925-28. *504*

Cooper, Edward E. *Colored American* (newspaper). Editors and Editing. Imperialism. Negroes. 1898-1901. *446*

Copperheads. Civil War. Democratic Party. Illinois. Lincoln, Abraham. 1861-65. *506*

Corwin, Thomas. Mexican War. Political Speeches. Whig Party. 1847. *140*

County chairmen. Political attitudes. Texas. 1968-69. *32*

County characteristics. Demography. Political Parties (behavior). 1964. *821*

Court of Visitation. Kansas. Populism. Railroads. Republican Party. State Legislatures. 1890-1900. *595*

Courts. Montana. Murphy, John L. Potts, Benjamin Franklin. Republican Party. 1870-72. *656*

Courts (lower federal). Civil War. Reconstruction. ca 1861-69. *469*

—. Democratic process. Judges (recruitment). Social backgrounds. 1829-61. *206*

Crawford, Coe Isaac. Progressivism. Republican Party. Roosevelt, Theodore. South Dakota. State Politics. 1912-14. *626*

Creel, Cecil. Democratic Party. Nevada. New Deal. Pittman, Key. Political Factions. Public Welfare. 1933-34. *786*

Creel, George. Conservatism. New Deal. Progressivism. Works Progress Administration. 1900-53. *697*

Crime, organized. Illinois (Chicago). Political Corruption. Primaries. Republican Party. 1928. *516*

Crittenden, Thomas T. Democratic Party. Elections (presidential). Free Silver Movement. Missouri. 1873-98. *593*

Croker, Richard. New York City. Political Corruption. Tammany Hall. 1886-1901. *511*

Crossfiling. California. 1914-56. *49*

Crump, Edward. Democratic Party. Elections (gubernatorial). Tennessee (Shelby County). 1932. *521*

Cuba. Dallas, George M. Diplomacy (assignments). Elections (presidential). Pierce, Franklin. USA. 1852-56. *118*

—. Florida (Monroe County). Reconstruction. Revolutionary Movements. 1868-76. *594*

Cuba (proposed acquisition). Buchanan, James. Democratic Party. Douglas, Stephen A. Slidell, John. 1857-60. *240*

Curley, James Michael. Democratic Party. Elections (senatorial). Irish Americans. Massachusetts. State Politics. 1936. *743*

Cushing, Caleb. Elections (congressional). Massachusetts (Essex County). Political Campaigns. 1830-32. *126*

Customs officials. New Jersey. Patronage. Ports. 1798-1803. *290*

Cutting, Bronson M. Democratic Party. New Mexico. Political Campaigns. Roosevelt, Franklin D. Senate. 1934. *809*

D

Dakota Territory. Democratic Party. Land. Lobbying. North Dakota. South Dakota. Speculation. 1857-61. *120*

Daley, Richard J. Democratic Party. Elections. Illinois (Chicago). Local Politics. 1972. *879*

—. Democratic Party. Illinois (Chicago). Political Leadership. 1950-76. *807*

Dallas, George M. Bank of the United States, 2d. Democratic Party. Elections. Jackson, Andrew. Pennsylvania. 1832. *117*

—. Cuba. Diplomacy (assignments). Elections (presidential). Pierce, Franklin. USA. 1852-56. *118*

—. Democratic Party. Pennsylvania. Political Campaigns. 1844. *136*

Davis, James John. Labor, Secretaries of. Pennsylvania. Political Leadership. Republican Party. 1873-1947. *692*

Dawes, Charles Gates. Democratic Party. LaFollette, Robert Marion, Sr. Political Campaigns (presidential). Republican Party. South Dakota (Sioux Falls). 1924. *668*

Dawes, Henry L. Johnson, Andrew. Reconstruction. Republican Party. 1865-75. *354*

Dayton, William L. Elections (presidential). Frémont, John C. Republican Party (convention). 1854-56. *280*

Dead Shoes senatorial primary (1906). Alabama. Direct primary system. Political reform. 1890-1915. *500*

Debates. Congress. Decisionmaking. Models. Rhetoric. Roll-call voting. War of 1812. 1798-1812. *210*

—. Constitutions. Federalism. Government, forms of. New York State Ratifying Convention. 1788. *171*

—. Democratic Party. Political Attitudes. Political candidates, presidential. Republican Party. 1960-76. *938*

Decentralization. Government. Reform. 1970's. *113*

—. Boston Finance Commission. Massachusetts.
Matthews, Nathan. Mayors. Political Reform.
1890-1910. *650*
—. Brown, Albert Gallatin. Mississippi. Political
Campaigns (congressional). Winans, William.
1849. *217*
—. Brown, Jerry. Carter, Jimmy. Political
campaigns. Presidential candidates. 1976.
832
—. Brown, John Y. Goebel, William. Kentucky.
L and N Railroad. State Politics. 1890-1900.
499
—. Bryan, William Jennings. Cleveland, Grover.
Free silver movement. North Carolina. Political
Campaigns. Populism. Republican Party.
1892-96. *430*
—. Bryan, William Jennings. Imperialism.
Philippines. Political Campaigns (presidential).
Stevenson, Adlai E. (1835-1914). 1900. *631*
—. Bryan, William Jennings. Maine (Bath).
Political Campaigns (vice-presidential). Sewall,
Arthur. 1896. *624*
—. Bryan, William Jennings. Political Campaigns
(presidential). Stevenson, Adlai E. (1835-1914).
1892-1900. *622*
—. Buchanan, James. Cuba (proposed acquisition).
Douglas, Stephen A. Slidell, John. 1857-60.
240
—. Buchanan, James. Douglas, Stephen A.
Elections. Kansas. Lecompton Constitution.
Slavery. 1854-60. *168*
—. Buchanan, James (administration). Patronage.
1857-61. *277*
—. Buckley, Christopher. California. Political
Reform. White, Stephen M. 1886-98. *461*
—. Business. Campbell, Thomas M. Progressivism.
State Government. Texas. 1907-11. *634*
—. Byrd, Harry F. Eisenhower, Dwight D.
Elections (presidential). Virginia. 1952. *799*
—. Byrd, Harry F. Elections (presidential).
Roosevelt, Franklin D. State Politics. Virginia.
1932. *801*
—. Byrd, Harry F. Elections, presidential. Truman,
Harry S. Virginia. 1948. *798*
—. Byrd, Harry F. Glass, Carter. Roosevelt,
Franklin D. Senate. Virginia. 1938. *734*
—. Byrd, Harry F. Patronage. Senate. Virginia.
1935-39. *745*
—. Byrd, Harry F. Political Reform. State
government. Virginia. 1926-30. *479*
—. Byrd, Harry F., Sr. Elections (congressional).
Peery, George. Slemp, C. Bascom. Virginia
(southwest). 1922. *438*
—. Byrd, Harry F., Sr. Liberalism. State Politics.
Virginia. 1950-53. *738*
—. Byrd, Harry F., Sr. Reed, William Thomas.
State Politics. Virginia. 1925-35. *439*
—. Byrnes, James F. Nominations for office.
Political Factions. Roosevelt, Franklin D.
Truman, Harry S. Vice Presidency. Wallace,
Henry A. 1944. *763*
—. Calhoun, John C. Congress. Mexican War
(opposition to). Polk, James K. Whigs.
1846-48. *308*
—. Calhoun, John C. Economic policy. Slavery.
South. VanBuren, Martin (administration).
1837-41. *178*
—. California. Campaign Finance. Elites. Political
Leadership. 1964-76. *851*
—. California. Civil War (antecedents). Political
Conventions. 1860. *684*
—. California. Delegate selection. Political
Conventions (national). 1968-76. *1004*
—. California. End Poverty In California program.
Political Campaigns (gubernatorial). Sinclair,
Upton. ca 1933-34. *785*

—. California. Gould, Lewis L. Political Factions
(review article). Progressivism. Texas.
Williams, R. Hal. 1880-1919. 1973. *590*
—. California. Political Campaigns (gubernatorial).
Sinclair, Upton. Socialist Party. 1933-34.
749
—. California (Los Angeles). Civil War. Kewen,
Edward J. C. Political Speeches. South.
1825-79. *604*
—. Callahan, Patrick Henry. Catholic Church.
Kentucky (Louisville). 1866-1940. *426*
—. Campaign Finance Act (US, 1974; amended,
1976). Carter, Jimmy. Nominations for office.
Primaries. 1974-76. *925*
—. Carter, Jimmy. Kennedy, Edward M. Political
Campaigns. Press. 1979. *964*
—. Carter, Jimmy. Kennedy, John F. 1961-63.
1977-80. *974*
—. Catholic Church. 1972-73. *34*
—. Cattlemen. Mercer, Asa S. *(The Banditti of the
Plains)*. Wyoming. 1890's. *468*
—. Centralization. Political Attitudes. 1974-76.
901
—. Charter revision. City Government. New York
City. Political Reform. Whig Party. 1845-49.
251
—. Choctaw Club. Fitzpatrick, John. Louisiana
(New Orleans). 1896-99. *467*
—. City Politics. Ethnic Groups. Illinois (Chicago).
1890-1936. *392*
—. City Politics. Eve, Arthur O. Negroes. New
York (Buffalo). Political Surveys. Primaries
(mayoral). 1977. *842*
—. Civil rights. Congress. Kennedy, John F.
1960-63. *887*
—. Civil rights. Congress. Legislation.
Partisanship. Regionalism. Republican Party.
1963-72. *828*
—. Civil rights. Elections (presidential). South
Carolina. 1948-72. *62*
—. Civil War. Congress. North. Roll-call voting.
1861-63. *361*
—. Civil War. Copperheads. Illinois. Lincoln,
Abraham. 1861-65. *506*
—. Civil War. Lincoln, Abraham. Phelps, Richard
Harvey. Political Protest. 1861-64. *373*
—. Clark, Bennett Champ. Committee of One.
Missouri. Political Campaigns (presidential).
1936. *793*
—. Clement, Frank Goad. Elections (gubernatorial).
Tennessee. 1950's. *716*
—. Cleveland, Grover. 1884-97. *423*
—. Cleveland, Grover. Political Campaigns
(presidential). Stevenson, Adlai E. (1835-1914).
1888-92. *628*
—. Clingman, Thomas Lanier. North Carolina.
Political reform. State Politics. States' rights.
Whig Party. 1840-60. *228*
—. Colorado. Constitutions, State. Eight-hour day.
Republican Party. State Legislatures. Working
Conditions. 1902-05. *527*
—. Compromise of 1877. Elections (presidential).
Reconstruction, Civil War (historiography).
Republican Party. Woodward, C. Vann.
1876-77. *693*
—. Cone, Fred P. Elections (presidential). Florida
(Hamilton County). Morrison, C. L. (shooting).
Postal Service. 1888-92. *646*
—. Conflict and Conflict Resolution. Partisanship.
Realignment. Republican Party. Roll-call
voting. Senate. 1925-73. *63*
—. Congress. Elections. 1974. *937*
—. Congress. Elections (presidential). Political
attitudes. 1970's. *824*
—. Congress. Hunter, Robert M. T. States' rights.
Whig Party. 1837-41. *185*

—. Elections (presidential). Voting and Voting Behavior. 1948-76. *984*
—. Elections (presidential). Voting and Voting Behavior. 1956-79. *81*
—. Elections, presidential. Voting and Voting Behavior. 1972. *1006*
—. Elections (senatorial). Missouri. New Deal. Primaries. Truman, Harry S. 1934. *724*
—. Elections (senatorial). States' Rights. Texas. Wigfall, Louis T. 1859. *519*
—. Elections (state). Iowa. Republican Party. 1950-56. *773*
—. Equal opportunity. Jacksonianism. Social theory. Wealth. 1836-46. *121*
—. Erickson, John E. Montana. State Politics. Walsh, Thomas J. 1932-33. *756*
—. Erie Canal Ring. Governmental Investigations. New York. Political Reform. Tilden, Samuel J. 1868-76. *353*
—. Ethnicity. Nebraska. Prohibition. Republican Party. 1907-20. *437*
—. Expansionism. Free Soil Movement. Slavery. Southern strategy. 1847-60. *264*
—. Expansionism. North. Slavery. 1845-60. *167*
—. Farmers' Alliance. North Carolina. State Politics. Subtreasury, planned. Vance, Zebulon B. 1880-90. *388*
—. Filibuster. House of Representatives. Race Relations. Reconstruction. Roll-call voting. 1876-77. *372*
—. Foreign policy. Jackson, Henry M. 1972-74. *875*
—. Free Soil Party. Massachusetts. Reform. 1849-53. *323*
—. Friends-and-neighbors factor. Mississippi. Primaries. State Government. 1947-78. *991*
—. Garner, John Nance. State Politics. Texas. Wells, Jim. 1896-1923. *365*
—. Garson, Robert A. (review article). South. 1941-48. 1974. *737*
—. Georgia. New Deal. Roosevelt, Franklin D. Talmadge, Eugene. 1926-38. *713*
—. Georgia. Political Campaigns (presidential nomination). Press. Russell, Richard B. 1952. *723*
—. Gerrish, Benjamin, Jr. (journal). New Hampshire (Dover). Republican Party. 1859. *127*
—. Hague, Frank. New Deal. New Jersey. Roosevelt, Franklin D. 1932-40. *717*
—. Hampton, Wade. Racism. South Carolina. State politics. 1876-78. *450*
—. Higgins, Andrew J. Political Campaigns (presidential). Roosevelt, Franklin D. 1944. *758*
—. Historians. Progressivism. Republican Party (Insurgents; image). 1908-12. *615*
—. Historiography. Massachusetts. Republican Party. 1880's. 1964-74. *474*
—. Historiography. Redeemers. South. 1870-1900. 1920's-50's. *566*
—. House of Representatives. Ideology. Regions. Republican Party. 1965-77. *975*
—. House of Representatives. Political Leadership. Whip system. 1975-77. *865*
—. Hughes, Harold. Iowa. State Politics. 1940-74. *918*
—. Ideology. Parmet, Herbert S. (review article). 1945-68. 1976. *1001*
—. Ideology. Political Campaigns (presidential). 1972-76. *814*
—. Ideology. Political Leadership. Republican Party. Texas. 1972-74. *945*
—. Illinois. Lucas, Scott W. Senate (majority leader). 1938-50. *777*

—. Illinois. Political Campaigns (presidential). Progressives. Stringer, Lawrence Beaumont. 1910-12. *526*
—. Illinois. Republican Party. Slavery. Trumbull, Lyman. 1855-72. *176*
—. Illinois (Chicago). Law Enforcement. Political Conventions. Political Protest. Students. 1856-1978. *926*
—. Internal improvements. North Carolina. Sectionalism. State Legislatures. Whig Party. 1836-60. *227*
—. Intervention. Republican Party. War. 19c-20c. *5*
—. Jackson, Andrew. VanBuren, Martin (administration). 1823-40. *172*
—. Kentucky (Louisville). National Democratic Issues Convention. New Deal policies. 1975. *868*
—. Lea, Luke. Peay, Austin. Political Factions. Republican Party. State Government. Tennessee, Eastern. 1922-32. *520*
—. Letters. Mennonites. Risser, Johannes. Slavery. 1856-57. *338*
—. Liberty Party. Negro suffrage. New York. Referendum. Whig Party. 1840-47. *242*
—. Martin-Rosier affair. Political Factions. Senators. West Virginia. 1941. *755*
—. Massachusetts. Primaries (gubernatorial). 1978. *997*
—. McClosky, Herbert. Political Leadership. Public Opinion. Republican Party. 1980. *900*
—. McGovern, George S. Political Conventions (reforms). 1972. *962*
—. Michigan. Political Reform. Primaries (presidential). 1970-76. *932*
—. Military bases. Negroes. Politics and the Military. 1962-73. *891*
—. Mississippi. Political Factions. 1965-68. *978*
—. Missouri. Pendergast, Thomas J. Political Conventions. Roosevelt, Franklin D. State Politics. 1932. *778*
—. Missouri. Political coalitions. Republican Party. Roosevelt, Franklin D. 1936-52. *788*
—. NAACP. Negro Suffrage. Primaries. *Smith* v. *Allwright* (US, 1944). South. Supreme Court. 1890's-1944. *740*
—. NAACP. Negro Suffrage. Primaries. Supreme Court. Texas. 1927-45. *741*
—. Nebraska. Political Parties (fusion). Populists. 1890's. *670*
—. Negroes. Political participation. Poverty programs, local. South. 1960's. *885*
—. Nelson, Gaylord. Senate. Wisconsin. 1962-74. *976*
—. New Deal. Ohio. Political Campaigns (presidential). 1936. *792*
—. New Deal. Pennsylvania (Pittsburgh). Political Theory. Quantitative Methods. Voting and Voting Behavior. Wisconsin. 1912-40. *84*
—. New Deal. Primaries (senatorial). Russell, Richard B. Talmadge, Eugene. 1936. *759*
—. New England. Republican Party. Sex roles. 1974. *930*
—. New York. Republican Party. State politics. Voting and Voting behavior. 1945-73. *8*
—. North Carolina. Primaries (senatorial). 1932. *589*
—. Oklahoma. Political Attitudes. Social attitudes. Socialist party. Williams, Robert Lee. 1907-20. *396*
—. Palmer, A. Mitchell. Pennsylvania. 1910-12. *403*
—. Parker, Alton Brooks. Political Campaigns (presidential). 1904. *623*
—. Parr, Archer. Political machines. Texas (Duval County). 1907-18. *351*

E

G

Inter-party competition. Indiana. Political participation. Voter turnout. 1876-1968. *48*
Interpersonal communication. Eagleton, Thomas F. McGovern, George S. Political Surveys. Presidential candidates. 1972. *954*
Intervention. Democratic Party. Republican Party. War. 19c-20c. *5*
Iowa. Carter, Jimmy. Democratic Party caucuses. Political Campaigns (presidential). 1975-76. *890*
—. Delegate selection. Democratic Party. Political Conventions. Reform. Wisconsin. 1968-76. *972*
—. Democratic Party. Elections (presidential). Roosevelt, Franklin D. 1932. *721*
—. Democratic Party. Elections (state). Republican Party. 1950-56. *773*
—. Democratic Party. Hughes, Harold. State Politics. 1940-74. *918*
—. Documents. Harding, William Lloyd. Sioux City Public Museum (William Lloyd Harding Papers). State Government. 1905-34. *655*
—. Elections (congressional). Greenback Party. Weaver, James B. 1878. *406*
—. Kirkwood, Samuel J. (career). 1855-94. *204*
Iowa (Washington County). Brookhart, Smith Wildman. Prohibition. 1890-94. *548*
Irish Americans. Chile. Diplomacy. Egan, Patrick. Republican Party. Revolution. 1880's-93. *458*
—. Clan na Gael. Illinois (Chicago). Nationalism. 1880's. *441*
—. Curley, James Michael. Democratic Party. Elections (senatorial). Massachusetts. State Politics. 1936. *743*
—. Massachusetts. State Politics. Voting and Voting Behavior. 1860-76. *366*
Irving, Washington. Cartoons and Caricatures. Federalists. New York. *Salmagundi* (periodical). 1807. *142*
Isolationism. Alliances. France. Jefferson, Thomas. 1778-1801. *239*

J

Jackson, Andrew. Adams, John Quincy. Democratic Party. Elections (presidential). Slavery. Whig Party. 1828-44. *297*
—. Antipartyism. District of Columbia. Gales, Joseph, Jr. *National Intelligencer*. Political Commentary. Republicanism. Seaton, William Winston. 1827-35. *265*
—. Bank of the United States, 2d. Dallas, George M. Democratic Party. Elections. Pennsylvania. 1832. *117*
—. Calhoun, John C. Clay, Henry. Tariff of 1832. 1828-32. *281*
—. Clayton, John M. Domestic Policy. Foreign policy. Senate. Whig Party. 1833-36. *336*
—. Democratic Party. Eaton, Margaret (Peggy) O'Neale. Ely, Ezra Stiles. 1829-30. *173*
—. Democratic Party. VanBuren, Martin (administration). 1823-40. *172*
—. Judiciary, territorial. Michigan. 1828-32. *205*
Jackson, Henry M. Democratic Party. Foreign policy. 1972-74. *875*
"Jacksonian Democracy", term. Historians. 1820's-30's. 1890's-1970's. *283*
Jacksonian era. Blair, Francis. Jeffersonian heritage. Kendall, Amos. 1819-37. *249*
—. Morality. Slavery. 1828-36. *273*
Jacksonianism. Democratic Party. Economic Conditions. Ohio. Social Change. State Politics. 1820-50. *291*
—. Democratic Party. Equal opportunity. Social theory. Wealth. 1836-46. *121*

Jacksonians. Maryland. Patronage. State Politics. 1823-36. *299*
James, Arthur H. Elections (gubernatorial). Pennsylvania. 1938. *762*
James, Green *(Grass-Roots Socialism)*. Democracy. Goodwyn, Lawrence *(Democratic Promise)*. Populism. Radicals and Radicalism. Socialism. 1890-1980. *462*
Jay, John. *Federalist.* Hamilton, Alexander. Liberty. Madison, James. Political Theory. 1787-88. *123*
Jefferson, Thomas. Alliances. France. Isolationism. 1778-1801. *239*
—. American Revolution. Mazzei, Philip. Republicanism. 1730-92. *296*
—. Armies. Military Peace Establishment Act (US, 1802). 1793-1802. *170*
—. Barlow, Joel (essays). Federalism. History. Political Systems. 1790-1815. *257*
—. Hemings, Madison. Newspapers. Ohio (Waverly). 1873. *536*
Jeffersonian heritage. Blair, Francis. Jacksonian era. Kendall, Amos. 1819-37. *249*
Jeffersonianism. Federalism. Republican utopia. Rush, Benjamin (political thought). 1776-1800. *248*
Jeffersonians. Banning, Lance. Federalists. Ideology. Political Parties (review articles). Zvesper, John. 1790's. 1977-78. *268*
Jeffries, John W. Andersen, Kristi. Blumberg, Barbara. Fine, Sidney. New Deal (review article). Roosevelt, Franklin D. Swain, Martha H. 1933-39. *708*
Jensen, Merrill. Antifederalists. Historiography. Kenyon, Cecelia M. Turner, Frederick Jackson. 1776-1800. 1893-1974. *222*
Jews. Bamberger, Simon. Governors. Utah. 1916. *427*
—. California (Los Angeles). Grant, Ulysses S. Political Campaigns (presidential). Seymour, Horatio. 1868. *661*
—. Democratic Party. Elections (presidential). Political attitudes. Voting and Voting Behavior. 1972-80. *894*
Johnson, Andrew. Attitudes. Impeachment. Letters. Republican Party. Ross, Edmund. 1867-68. *374*
—. Civil War. Florida (Amelia Island; Fernandina). Land Tenure. Military Occupation. Property Tax. Unionists. 1860's-90's. *643*
—. Colorado. Newspapers. Reconstruction. Republican Party. 1865-67. *375*
—. Dawes, Henry L. Reconstruction. Republican Party. 1865-75. *354*
—. Dixon, James. Doolittle, James R. Impeachment trial. Norton, Daniel S. Republican Party. 1860-70. *346*
—. Elections (congressional). Illinois. Reconstruction. 1866. *579*
—. Michigan, southern. Political Speeches. Reconstruction. 1866. *505*
Johnson, Andrew N. Alabama (Mobile). Black Capitalism. Editors and Editing. Republican Party. Tennessee (Nashville). 1890-1920. *349*
Johnson, Benton. Political preference. Protestant ethic. 1960's-70's. *87*
Johnson, Henry Lincoln. Georgia. Harding, Warren G. Philips, John Louis. Republican Party. 1920-24. *478*
Johnson, Joseph. Commutation powers. Governors. Hatcher, Jordan (slave). State Politics. Virginia. 1852. *182*
Johnson, Lyndon B. Kennedy, John F. New Deal. Truman, Harry S. 1933-68. *65*
Johnson, Lyndon B. (administration). Civil rights. 1963-69. *942*

Know-Nothing Party. Anti-Catholicism. California (San Francisco). City Politics. People's Party. Vigilance Committee. 1854-56. *310*
—. Anti-Catholicism. Fillmore, Millard. Nativism. Political Campaigns (presidential). Whig Party. 1850-56. *305*
—. Anti-Catholicism. Maine. Morrill, Anson P. Nativism. Working class. 1854-55. *332*
—. Anti-Catholicism. Political Leadership. Thompson, Richard W. 1850's. *285*
—. Antislavery Sentiments. Massachusetts. Nativism. Republican Party. Voting and Voting Behavior. 1850's. *132*
—. Arkansas. Elections (presidential). 1855-56. *315*
—. Berrien, John M. (letter). Georgia. Political Attitudes. 1854-56. *271*
—. Constitutions (state). Massachusetts (western). Republican Party. State Politics. Voting and Voting Behavior. 1854-58. *284*
—. Democratic Party. Elections. Local Politics. Missouri (St. Louis). Riots. 1844-56. *307*
—. German Americans. Illinois (Chicago). Local Politics. Riots. Temperance law. 1855. *294*
—. Louisiana. Political leadership. Social Classes. 1845-60. *162*
Know-Nothing Party (origins). 1853-56. *218*
Kolb, Reuben F. Agriculture. Alabama. Elections (gubernatorial). Industry. Jones, Thomas G. 1892. *608*
—. Alabama. Democratic Party. Farmers' Alliance. Jones, Thomas G. Political Campaigns (gubernatorial). 1889-90. *609*
Koreshan Unity (community). *American Eagle* (newspaper). Elections. Florida (Lee County). Progressive Liberty Party. Teed, Cyrus R. 1894-1908. *534*
Ku Klux Klan. Alabama. Boyd, Alexander (murder of). Elections. 1870. *610*
—. Arkansas. Clayton, Powell. Federal Government. Martial law. Militia. Republican Party. Violence. 1868. *679*
—. Democratic Party. Elections (gubernatorial). Johnston, Henry S. Oklahoma. 1926. *386*
—. Lusk, Virgil. North Carolina (Asheville). Reconstruction. Republican Party. Shotwell, Randolph. Violence. 1869. *552*
Ku Klux Klan bill (1871). States' Rights. Trumbull, Lyman. 1854-94. *417*

L

L and N Railroad. Brown, John Y. Democratic Party. Goebel, William. Kentucky. State Politics. 1890-1900. *499*
La Follette, Philip F. MacArthur, Douglas. Political Campaigns. Primaries (presidential). Republican Party. Wisconsin. 1948. *779*
Labor. American Revolution (effects). New York City. Political participation. 1797-1813. *301*
—. California (San Francisco). Hughes, Charles Evans. Political Campaigns (presidential). Republican Party. 1916. *525*
—. Farmers. Ohio. Political Campaigns (presidential). 1892-96. *689*
Labor Reform Party. Greenback Party. New Hampshire. 1870-78. *554*
Labor, Secretaries of. Davis, James John. Pennsylvania. Political Leadership. Republican Party. 1873-1947. *692*
LaFollette, Robert Marion, Sr. Dawes, Charles Gates. Democratic Party. Political Campaigns (presidential). Republican Party. South Dakota (Sioux Falls). 1924. *668*
—. Farmers. Income tax. Industry. Progressivism. Wisconsin. 1890-1930. *391*

—. Presidential nomination. Republican Party. Roosevelt, Theodore. 1910-12. *537*
Laissez-faire economics. Populism. 1880-1900. *377*
Land. Dakota Territory. Democratic Party. Lobbying. North Dakota. South Dakota. Speculation. 1857-61. *120*
Land Tenure. Civil War. Florida (Amelia Island; Fernandina). Johnson, Andrew. Military Occupation. Property Tax. Unionists. 1860's-90's. *643*
Land tenure reform. Political Reform. Populism. Rogers, John R. State Politics. Washington. 1890-1900. *378*
Landon, Alfred M. Hoover, Herbert C. Political Leadership. Republican Party (conference; proposed). 1937-38. *703*
Lane, James Henry. Civil War. Free State Party. Kansas. State politics. 1850's-1866. *164*
Law. Bedinger, Henry. Democratic Party. Denmark. Diplomacy. House of Representatives. Virginia. 1854-58. *253*
—. Belz, Herman (review article). Civil War. Freedmen. Republican Party. 1861-66. 1976. *409*
Law and order. Congress. Public opinion. Race. 1965-73. *852*
Law Enforcement. Democratic Party. Illinois (Chicago). Political Conventions. Political Protest. Students. 1856-1978. *926*
Lawsuits. Barnes, William, Jr. Bossism. New York. Republican Party. Roosevelt, Theodore. 1915. *382*
Lea, Luke. Democratic Party. Peay, Austin. Political Factions. Republican Party. State Government. Tennessee, Eastern. 1922-32. *520*
Leadership. Massachusetts (Boston). Press. 1828-39. *125*
Leadership, black. Federal Government. Moral stance, change of. National character. Negroes. 1970's. *859*
Leake, Walter. Letters. Mississippi Territory. 1807. *236*
Lecompton Constitution. Buchanan, James. Democratic Party. Douglas, Stephen A. Elections. Kansas. Slavery. 1854-60. *168*
Lee, Joseph E. Bisbee, Horatio, Jr. Florida. Letters. Negroes. Republican Party. 1880. *507*
Leftism. Andersen, Kristi (review article). Democratic Party. 1928-36. 1979. *732*
Legaré, Hugh Swinton. Congress. Presidency. Republicanism. Tyler, John (administration). 1841-43. *159*
Legislation. Alabama. Reconstruction. 1867. *637*
—. Border States. Congress. Loyalty oath. Republican Party. Republican Party. 1861-67. *356*
—. Civil rights. Congress. Democratic Party. Partisanship. Regionalism. Republican Party. 1963-72. *828*
—. Civil rights. Population. Race Relations. Riots. Tennessee (Memphis). 1865-66. *529*
—. Environmentalism. Montana. Public Opinion. State Legislatures. 1973-77. *837*
—. House of Representatives. Illinois (Chicago). Sabath, Adolph Joachim (biography). 1920-52. *707*
—. Political Parties (realignment). Public Welfare. 1933-54. *784*
Legislation, antifusion. Ballot. Elections. Political Reform. Republican Party. 1880-1902. *355*
Legislative parties. New Jersey. State government. 1829-44. *255*

Philips, John Louis. Georgia. Harding, Warren G. Johnson, Henry Lincoln. Republican Party. 1920-24. *478*

Philips, Waite (letters). Depressions. New Deal (criticism of). Political philosophy. 1940. *767*

Pierce, Franklin. Cuba. Dallas, George M. Diplomacy (assignments). Elections (presidential). USA. 1852-56. *118*

Pike, Albert. Arkansas. ca 1850-61. *155*

Pillsbury, Rosecrans W. Churchill, Winston (1871-1947). Floyd, Charles M. Greenleaf, Charles H. New Hampshire. Political Conventions (gubernatorial). Reform. Republican Party. 1906. *348*

Pinchot, Gifford. Elections (gubernatorial). Pennsylvania. Prohibition. Public utilities. Republican Party. 1930. *463*

Pinckney, Thomas. Elections (presidential). Federalists. Republican Party. South Carolina. 1796. *306*

Pingree, Hazen S. Elections (gubernatorial). Michigan. Republican Party. 1889-96. *487*

Pittman, Key. Creel, Cecil. Democratic Party. Nevada. New Deal. Political Factions. Public Welfare. 1933-34. *786*

Plantations. Ideology. Luraghi, Raimondo. South (review article). Thornton, J. Miller, III. 1607-1860. 1970's. *337*

Platt, Thomas C. New York. Progressivism. Public policy. Republican Party. State politics. 1890-1910. *546*

Platt, Thomas Collier (papers). New York. Political change. Republican Party. Yale University. 1896-1902. *547*

Pledger, William A. Black power. Bryant, John Emory. Georgia. Republican Party. 1876-84. *549*

Pluralist analysis. *Federalist* No. 10. Madison, James. Political Theory. 1787-20c. *141*

Poetry. *Alabama State Journal* (newspaper). Reconstruction. Satire. 1868. *611*

Poland (issue). Elections (presidential). Polish Americans. Roosevelt, Franklin D. 1942-44. *735*

Poland, Joseph. Abolition Movement. *Green Mountain Freeman* (newspaper). Liberty Party. State politics. Vermont. 1840-48. *232*

Polish Americans. Elections (presidential). Poland (issue). Roosevelt, Franklin D. 1942-44. *735*

Political Activism. Actors and Actresses. Douglas, Melvyn. 1936-42. *700*

—. Bias. Public Policy. 1952-76. *92*

Political ambition. Careers. State Legislatures. 1957-70. *45*

—. Democratic Party. Presidency. Roll-call voting. Senate. 1969-70. *80*

—. Democratic Party. Presidency. Schlesinger, Joseph. Senate. 1952-76. *988*

—. Roll-call voting. Senate. 1967-72. *990*

Political Attitudes. Alabama. House of Representatives. 1849-61. *274*

—. Authority. History. New England. Whig Party. 1840's-50's. *263*

—. Berrien, John M. (letter). Georgia. Know-Nothing Party. 1854-56. *271*

—. Carter, Jimmy. Delegate selection. Democratic Party (convention). 1976. *902*

—. Centralization. Democratic Party. 1974-76. *901*

—. Class consciousness. 1956-68. *42*

—. Congress. Democratic Party. Elections (presidential). 1970's. *824*

—. County chairmen. Texas. 1968-69. *32*

—. Debates. Democratic Party. Political candidates, presidential. Republican Party. 1960-76. *938*

—. Democratic Party. Elections (presidential). Jews. Voting and Voting Behavior. 1972-80. *894*

—. Democratic Party. Oklahoma. Social attitudes. Socialist party. Williams, Robert Lee. 1907-20. *396*

—. Democratic Party. Republican Party. 1952-80. *994*

—. Developing nations. Economic Policy. Reagan, Ronald (administration). 1980. *831*

—. Domestic policy. North Carolina. Truman, Harry S. 1944-48. *729*

—. Elites. Public policy. 1960-78. *944*

—. Elites. Social Classes. Tennessee (Davidson County). 1835-61. *187*

—. Federal Government. Federalists. Publicity, importance of. Secrecy. 1800-12. *175*

—. Federal Policy. Racism. Voting and Voting Behavior. 1964-81. *841*

—. Florida. Negroes. Reconstruction. Republican Party. Walls, Josiah T. 1867-85. *508*

—. Georgia. Negroes. Progressive Party. Roosevelt, Theodore. Wilson, Woodrow. 1912. *568*

—. Hawkins, Benjamin. North Carolina. Senate. 1790-95. *199*

—. Idaho. Mormons. Voting and Voting Behavior. 1880's. *533*

—. Industrialization. Populism. Slavery. South. 1860-96. *584*

—. McFarland, Gerald W. (review article). Mugwumps. New York City. 1884-1920. 1975. *432*

Political Attitudes (congruence). Intergenerational continuity. 1960's-70's. *94*

Political Campaigns. Abolition Movement. Constitutional Union Party. Republican Party. 1860. *559*

—. Alabama. Congressional District (7th). Denson, William H. Howard, Milford W. Populism. 1894. *476*

—. Alabama. Democratic Party. Federal Elections Bill (1890). South. Stevenson, Adlai E. (1835-1914). 1889-93. *621*

—. Arizona. Congressional Union for Woman Suffrage. Democratic Party. Women. 1914. 1916. *654*

—. Bland, Richard Parks. Democratic Party. Free Silver movement. Missouri. 1878-96. *647*

—. Brown, Jerry. Carter, Jimmy. Democratic Party. Presidential candidates. 1976. *832*

—. Bryan, William Jennings. Cleveland, Grover. Democratic Party. Free silver movement. North Carolina. Populism. Republican Party. 1892-96. *430*

—. Byrd, Harry F. Democratic Party convention. Presidential nomination. Roosevelt, Franklin D. 1932. *481*

—. California. Congress. Nixon, Richard M. Voorhis, Jerry. 1946. *710*

—. Carter, Jimmy. Democratic Party. Kennedy, Edward M. Press. 1979. *964*

—. Cushing, Caleb. Elections (congressional). Massachusetts (Essex County). 1830-32. *126*

—. Cutting, Bronson M. Democratic Party. New Mexico. Roosevelt, Franklin D. Senate. 1934. *809*

—. Dallas, George M. Democratic Party. Pennsylvania. 1844. *136*

—. Democratic Party. Domestic Policy. Internationalism. New Deal. Roosevelt, Franklin D. 1938-40. *719*

—. Democratic Party. Primaries. Smith, Al. South Dakota. 1928. *587*

—. Incumbency. Senators (reelection; terms). 1920-70. *60*

—. Eagleton, Thomas F. Interpersonal communication. McGovern, George S. Presidential candidates. 1972. *954*

Political Systems. Anti-Catholicism. Ohio. Republican Party. Slavery. Whig Party. 1850's. *243*

—. Barlow, Joel (essays). Federalism. History. Jefferson, Thomas. 1790-1815. *257*

—. Bryce, James. Ostrogorski, Moisei Y. Tocqueville, Alexis de. 1832-1902. *98*

—. Democratic Party. Elections. Republican Party. 1976. *999*

—. Interest groups. 1960's-80. *9*

—. New Deal. Voting and Voting Behavior. 1894-1975. *662*

Political theory. Administrative polarity, principle of. Federalism, representational. *Federalist.* 1787-20c. *183*

—. Clinton, DeWitt. Hammond, Jabez. New York. 1800-22. 1842. *247*

—. Delegate allocation rules. Democratic Party. Lengle, James. Primaries, presidential. Shafer, Byron. 1972. *886*

—. Democratic Party. New Deal. Pennsylvania (Pittsburgh). Quantitative Methods. Voting and Voting Behavior. Wisconsin. 1912-40. *84*

—. *Federalist.* Hamilton, Alexander. Jay, John. Liberty. Madison, James. 1787-88. *123*

—. *Federalist.* Madison, James. Public Welfare. 1787-92. *181*

—. *Federalist* No. 10. Madison, James. Pluralist analysis. 1787-20c. *141*

Political thought. Alberdi, Juan Bautista. Argentina. Hamilton, Alexander. USA. 1787-1860. *160*

Politicians. Appalachia. Civil War. Identity, regional. 1860-99. *553*

—. Duels. 1770's-1850's. *10*

Politics and Media. Eagleton, Thomas F. News coverage. Television networks. 1972. *870*

Politics and the Military. Alabama (Eufaula County). Democratic Party. Reconstruction. Republican Party. Riots. 1874. *483*

—. Democratic Party. Military bases. Negroes. 1962-73. *891*

Politics (conventions, speeches). Evans, Daniel S. (address). Republican Party. Rhetoric, adaptive. 1968. *980*

Politics (cyclical periodicity). Conservatism. Democracy. Liberalism. 1939-74. *110*

Politics, deferential-participant. Political culture. 1789-1840. *188*

Politics (territorial, local issues). Arizona (Pima County). Constitutional conventions, state (delegate election). 1910. *585*

Polk, James K. Antiwar Sentiment. Mexican War. Tennessee. Whig Party. 1846-48. *194*

—. Calhoun, John C. Congress. Democratic Party. Mexican War (opposition to). Whigs. 1846-48. *308*

Poor. Antifederalists. Federalists. Pennsylvania (Crawford County). Social Classes. Wealth. 1800-40. *224*

—. Elections. Elites. Louisiana. Political Reform. Progressive Party. 1894-1921. *635*

Popular culture. Kennedy, John F. New Left. Nixon, Richard M. Social change. 1960-69. *979*

Population. Civil rights. Legislation. Race Relations. Riots. Tennessee (Memphis). 1865-66. *529*

Populism. Alabama. Congressional District (7th). Denson, William H. Howard, Milford W. Political Campaigns. 1894. *476*

—. Alabama. Democratic Party. Manning, Joseph C. State Politics. 1892-96. *596*

—. American Tobacco Company. Elections (congressional). Kentucky. 1886-92. *383*

—. Arkansas. Democratic Party. Jones, Daniel. Jones, James K. Political Conventions. 1890-1900. *576*

—. Bellamy, Edward *(Looking Backward 2000-1887).* Economic Theory. North Central States. 1880's-90's. *551*

—. Bryan, William Jennings. Cleveland, Grover. Democratic Party. Free silver movement. North Carolina. Political Campaigns. Republican Party. 1892-96. *430*

—. Civil Rights Act (US, 1964). Georgia. Mississippi. Voting Rights Act (US, 1965). 20c. *934*

—. Court of Visitation. Kansas. Railroads. Republican Party. State Legislatures. 1890-1900. *595*

—. Democracy. Goodwyn, Lawrence *(Democratic Promise).* James, Green *(Grass-Roots Socialism).* Radicals and Radicalism. Socialism. 1890-1980. *462*

—. Democratic Party. Political Campaigns (vice-presidential). South. Stevenson, Adlai E. (1835-1914). 1892. *617*

—. Ideology. Walsh, Thomas J. ca 1890-1900. *364*

—. Industrialization. Political Attitudes. Slavery. South. 1860-96. *584*

—. Laissez-faire economics. 1880-1900. *377*

—. Land tenure reform. Political Reform. Rogers, John R. State Politics. Washington. 1890-1900. *378*

—. Negroes. Press. Republican Party. 1890-96. *420*

—. Reformers, marginal. State Legislatures. West and Western States. 1890's. *379*

—. Southern history. 1850's-90's. *583*

Populism (review article). Argersinger, Peter H. Goodwyn, Lawrence. Parson, Stanley. Youngdale, James M. 1890's. 1970's. *582*

Populist Party. American Independent Party. Progressive Party. Realignment. Third parties. 1884-1976. *39*

—. Colorado. Hofstadter, Richard. Progressive movement. 1890-1910. 1950's. *542*

—. North Carolina. Republican Party. Roll-call voting. State Legislatures. 1895-97. *673*

Populists. Democratic Party. Nebraska. Political Parties (fusion). 1890's. *670*

Porkbarreling. Decisionmaking. House Public Works Committee. Political Factions. 1950's-70's. *948*

Porter, James M. Democratic Party. Pennsylvania. Political Change. Tyler, John. 1824-43. *191*

Ports. Customs officials. New Jersey. Patronage. 1798-1803. *290*

Postal Service. Alabama (Dothan). Civil Service. Clayton, Henry D. Patronage. Taft, William H. (administration). Wilson, Woodrow (administration). 1900-13. *606*

—. Cone, Fred P. Democratic Party. Elections (presidential). Florida (Hamilton County). Morrison, C. L. (shooting). 1888-92. *646*

Posters. Lincoln, Abraham. Lloyd, H. H. and Company. New York City (lower Manhattan). Political Campaigns. 1860. *489*

Postmasters. Alabama (Dothan). Democratic Party. Local Politics. Political Factions. 1912. *607*

Potts, Benjamin Franklin. Courts. Montana. Murphy, John L. Republican Party. 1870-72. *656*

Poverty programs, local. Democratic Party. Negroes. Political participation. South. 1960's. *885*

Powderly, Terence V. Beamish, Frank A. City Politics. Knights of Labor. Pennsylvania (Scranton). 1878-84. *428*

Pragmatism. Democracy. Government, role of. Public Opinion. 18c-20c. *47*

Religious liberty. Elections (presidential). Illuminati controversy. Ogden, John C. Philadelphia *Aurora* (newspaper). 1798-1800. *148*
Remmel, Harmon L. Arkansas. Political Leadership. Republican Party. 1880-1913. *612*
Renfrow, William Cary. Governors. Indian Territory. Indians (land transfers). Oklahoma Territory. 1893-97. *567*
Reporters and Reporting. Elections, municipal. Newspapers. Ohio. 1971. *1000*
Republican ideology. Antifederalists. Constitutions (ratification). 1789-93. *129*
Republican National Committee. Elections. Federalism. ca 1964-78. *827*
Republican National Convention. Lincoln, Abraham. New Hampshire delegation. Presidential nomination. 1860. *530*
Republican Party. Abolition Movement. Constitutional Union Party. Political Campaigns. 1860. *559*
—. Aiken, George D. Flood control. Governors. Political Campaigns (presidential). Vermont. 1937-39. *774*
—. Alabama. Democratic Party. Reconstruction. 1868-76. *682*
—. Alabama. Haralson, J. Negro Suffrage. Reconstruction. 1867-82. *638*
—. Alabama. Political Ostracism. Reconstruction. 1865-80. *683*
—. Alabama (Eufaula County). Democratic Party. Politics and the Military. Reconstruction. Riots. 1874. *483*
—. Alabama (Mobile). Black Capitalism. Editors and Editing. Johnson, Andrew N. Tennessee (Nashville). 1890-1920. *349*
—. American Abolition Society. 1855-58. *287*
—. Andersen, Kristi. Democratic Party. Partisanship. Voting and Voting Behavior. 1920-32. *771*
—. Anderson, Lucien. Congress. Kentucky. Randall, William Harrison. Smith, Green Clay. 1863-65. *490*
—. Anti-Catholicism. Ohio. Political Systems. Slavery. Whig Party. 1850's. *243*
—. Antislavery Sentiments. Bailey, Gamaliel. Chase, Salmon P. Liberty Party. Ohio. 1836-60. *209*
—. Antislavery Sentiments. Democratic Party. Elections. New York. 1850's. *195*
—. Antislavery Sentiments. Free Soil Party. Illinois. Racism. 1848-60. *303*
—. Antislavery Sentiments. Know-Nothing Party. Massachusetts. Nativism. Voting and Voting Behavior. 1850's. *132*
—. Antislavery Sentiments. Michigan. 1846-54. *309*
—. *Anzeiger des Westens* (newspaper). Boernstein, Heinrich. German Americans. Missouri (St. Louis). Voting and Voting behavior. 1848-60. *238*
—. Appalachia. Negroes. Reconstruction. State Politics. 1865-1900. *555*
—. Arizona. Campbell, Tom. State Politics. 1875-1944. *399*
—. Arizona. Elections. 1980. *939*
—. Arizona (Globe). Elections (gubernatorial). Hunt, George. Newspapers. Political Commentary. 1911. *564*
—. Arkansas. Clayton, Powell. Federal Government. Ku Klux Klan. Martial law. Militia. Violence. 1868. *679*
—. Arkansas. Negroes. Racial conflict. 1867-1928. *418*
—. Arkansas. Political Leadership. Remmel, Harmon L. 1880-1913. *612*
—. Arkansas. Race Relations. 1890's-1924. *419*

—. Attitudes. Impeachment. Johnson, Andrew. Letters. Ross, Edmund. 1867-68. *374*
—. Baker, Edward D. California. Political Campaigns (presidential). 1855-56. *116*
—. Ballot. Elections. Legislation, antifusion. Political Reform. 1880-1902. *355*
—. Barnes, Cassius McDonald. Governors. Oklahoma Territory. Public welfare. 1897-1901. *685*
—. Barnes, William, Jr. Bossism. Lawsuits. New York. Roosevelt, Theodore. 1915. *382*
—. Bass, Robert P. Boston and Maine Railroad. Churchill, Winston (1871-1947). New Hampshire. Progressivism. 1890-1912. *344*
—. Belz, Herman (review article). Civil War. Freedmen. Law. 1861-66. 1976. *409*
—. Benson, Lee. Historiography. Massachusetts. Mugwumps. Voting and Voting Behavior. 1880's. *367*
—. Bisbee, Horatio, Jr. Florida. Lee, Joseph E. Letters. Negroes. 1880. *507*
—. Black power. Bryant, John Emory. Georgia. Pledger, William A. 1876-84. *549*
—. Blaine, John J. Progressivism. Senate. Wisconsin. 1927-33. *578*
—. Border States. Congress. Legislation. Loyalty oath. Republican Party. 1861-67. *356*
—. Border States. Congress. Legislation. Loyalty oath. Republican Party. 1861-67. *356*
—. Bristow, Benjamin Helm. Hayes, Rutherford B. Kentucky. Political Campaigns (presidential). 1876. *678*
—. Brock, Richard. Negroes. Voting and Voting Behavior. 1937-80. *86*
—. Brooks, Preston S. Civil War (antecedents). Congress. Sumner, Charles. Violence. 1856. *193*
—. Bryan, William Jennings. Cleveland, Grover. Democratic Party. Free silver movement. North Carolina. Political Campaigns. Populism. 1892-96. *430*
—. Bryan, William Jennings. Newspapers. Red River of the North (valley). 1890-96. *415*
—. Burlingame, Anson. China. Diplomacy. House of Representatives. 1854-69. *119*
—. Butler, Hugh. Foreign policy. Griswold, Dwight. Nebraska. Primaries. Public opinion. 1946. *766*
—. Butler, Hugh. Griswold, Dwight. Nebraska. Wherry, Kenneth. 1940-46. *765*
—. California. Civil War. Indian-White Relations. Reform. 1860-70. *400*
—. California. Civil War. Slavery. 1860-67. *658*
—. California. Elections (presidential). Racism. Slavery. 1860. *659*
—. California. Elections, presidential. Slavery, extension of. 1856. *317*
—. California. One-party era. Political Factions. 1920's-30's. *491*
—. California. Slavery issue. 1852-56. *318*
—. California (San Diego). City Government. Lincoln-Roosevelt Republican League. Political reform. Progressivism. 1905-10. *563*
—. California (San Francisco). Hughes, Charles Evans. Labor. Political Campaigns (presidential). 1916. *525*
—. Carpetbaggers. House of Representatives. Negroes. Reconstruction. Scalawags. South. 1868-72. *510*
—. Carpetbaggers. Louisiana. Negroes. State Politics. 1868. *381*
—. Carse, George B. Florida (Leon County). Freedmen's Bureau. Reconstruction. 1867-70. *645*
—. Chase, Salmon P. Ohio. 1855-56. *231*
—. Chase, Salmon P. Ohio. State Government. 1850-73. *138*

—. Depressions. Hoover, Herbert C. New Deal. Political Commentary. 1933-35. *704*
—. Dixon, James. Doolittle, James R. Impeachment trial. Johnson, Andrew. Norton, Daniel S. 1860-70. *346*
—. Donnell, Forrest C. Elections (gubernatorial). McDaniel, Lawrence. Missouri. 1940. *789*
—. Economic Conditions. Elections, presidential. Mississippi. Social Status. 1940-76. *97*
—. Eisenhower, Dwight D. Minnesota. Political Campaigns (write-in). Primaries. 1952. *728*
—. Elections. Idaho. 1980. *935*
—. Elections. McKinley, William. Ohio. Working class. 1891-93. *677*
—. Elections. Montana. 1980. *883*
—. Elections. New Mexico. 1980. *847*
—. Elections. Oregon. 1980. *914*
—. Elections. Utah. 1980. *898*
—. Elections. Washington. 1980. *882*
—. Elections. Western states. 1980. *848*
—. Elections (congressional). Middle classes. South. 1972-76. *996*
—. Elections, congressional. New Deal. Roosevelt, Franklin D. 1937-38. *768*
—. Elections, congressional. Voting and Voting behavior. 1974. *869*
—. Elections (gubernatorial). Michigan. Pingree, Hazen S. 1889-96. *487*
—. Elections (gubernatorial). Negroes. North Carolina. Russell, Daniel L. 1896. *412*
—. Elections (gubernatorial). Pennsylvania. Pinchot, Gifford. Prohibition. Public utilities. 1930. *463*
—. Elections (mayoral). Illinois (Chicago). Merriam, Charles E. Political machines. Progressivism. 1911. *544*
—. Elections (presidential). Ethnic Groups. Nativism. Ohio (Cleveland). 1860. *513*
—. Elections (presidential). Federalists. Pinckney, Thomas. South Carolina. 1796. *306*
—. Elections (presidential). Foraker, Joseph B. Negroes. Taft, William H. 1908. *471*
—. Elections (presidential). Hoover, Herbert C. Progressivism. Senate. 1930-32. *431*
—. Elections (senatorial). Glasscock, William E. Political Factions. Scott, Nathan B. West Virginia. 1910. *675*
—. Elkins, Stephen B. Reform. State Politics. West Virginia. White, Albert B. 1901-05. *397*
—. Emancipation Proclamation. Freedmen. Lincoln, Abraham (administration). Personal liberty, protection of. 1862. *370*
—. Emancipation Proclamation. Lincoln Abraham. 1863-64. *515*
—. Ethnic Groups. Pennsylvania (Schuylkill County). Voting and Voting Behavior. 1844-1972. *58*
—. Evans, Daniel S. (address). Politics (conventions, speeches). Rhetoric, adaptive. 1968. *980*
—. Feinman, Ronald L. (review article). New Deal. Progressivism. Senate. Western States. 1929-41. *750*
—. Ferguson, Thompson Benton. Governors. Oklahoma Territory. 1901-06. *454*
—. Florida. Hoover, Herbert C. (administration). Patronage. State Politics. 1928-33. *456*
—. Florida. Negroes. Political attitudes. Reconstruction. Walls, Josiah T. 1867-85. *508*
—. Florida. Reconstruction. 1868-77. *644*
—. Foreign policy. Mexico. Political Leadership. Revolution. Wilson, Woodrow (administration). 1913-16. *557*
—. Foreign policy. Mexico. Wilson, Henry Lane. Wilson, Woodrow. 1913-20. *642*

—. Freedmen. Hartzell, Joseph C. Methodists, Northern. Missionaries. South. 1870-73. *528*
—. Freedmen. House of Representatives. Murray, George Washington. South Carolina. Suffrage. 1893-97. *443*
—. Frémont, John C. Lincoln, Abraham. Material culture. Political Campaigns (presidential). 1856. 1860. *184*
—. Georgia. Harding, Warren G. Johnson, Henry Lincoln. Philips, John Louis. 1920-24. *478*
—. Georgia. Hoover, Herbert C. (administration). Patronage. Political factions. Race Relations. 1928-32. *455*
—. Georgia Equal Rights Association. Negroes. Reconstruction. Union League. 1865-80. *538*
—. Government regulation. Neoconservatism. New Deal. Political Leadership. Social security. 1936-40. *757*
—. Governors. Grimes, William C. Oklahoma Territory. 1889-1906. *390*
—. Hansbrough, Henry Clay. North Dakota. Progressivism. Senate. 1907-12. *630*
—. Hatch, Ozias M. Illinois. Knapp, Nathan (letter). Lincoln, Abraham. 1859. *694*
—. Hoover, Herbert C. (administration). Negroes. 1928-32. *444*
—. Hoover, Herbert C. (party politics). 1920-32. *574*
—. House of Representatives. Montana. Political Campaigns (congressional). Rankin, Jeannette. Woman suffrage. 1900-16. *473*
—. House of Representatives. Oregon. Statehood (opposition to). 1850's. *250*
—. House of Representatives. Pennsylvania. Reconstruction. 1871-73. *436*
—. Howard, Perry W. Mississippi. Negroes. 1924-60. *70*
—. Ideology. 1946-80. *1002*
—. Industrialism. Political order. Progressivism, Midwestern. Urbanization. 1900-12. *581*
—. Ku Klux Klan. Lusk, Virgil. North Carolina (Asheville). Reconstruction. Shotwell, Randolph. Violence. 1869. *552*
—. La Follette, Philip F. MacArthur, Douglas. Political Campaigns. Primaries (presidential). Wisconsin. 1948. *779*
—. LaFollette, Robert Marion, Sr. Presidential nomination. Roosevelt, Theodore. 1910-12. *537*
—. Liberia. Negroes. Turner, James Milton. 1865-77. *512*
—. Lincoln, Abraham. Political Conventions. Political Speeches (rhetorical analysis). Presidential nomination. 1860. *523*
—. Lincoln, Abraham. Political Factions. Rhode Island. Travel. 1860. *472*
—. Louisiana. Negroes. *New Orleans Tribune.* Newspapers. Reconstruction. 1864-68. *408*
—. Louisiana. Negroes. Ray, John. Scalawags. ca 1836-88. *108*
—. Louisiana. Political Parties, evolution of. Whig Party. 1832-34. *114*
—. Louisiana (St. Landry). Race Relations. Reconstruction. Riots. 1868. *416*
—. Madison, James. Political malcontents. War of 1812 (causes). 1800-15. *316*
—. McClure, Alexander K. (thesis). Pennsylvania. Political Conventions. Seward, William H. 1860. 1892. *414*
—. McKinley, William. Myers, George A. Negroes. 1859-96. *498*
—. Mellon family. Pennsylvania (Pittsburgh). Political organizations. 1920-30. *570*
—. Midwest. Political Parties (realignment). 1850's. *313*
—. Minorities in Politics. Missouri (St. Louis). Negroes. Wheeler, John W. 1870-1915. *401*

Roosevelt, Franklin D. (administration). Dewey, Thomas E. Elections (presidential). Pearl Harbor, attack on (issue). 1944. *760*

Roosevelt, Theodore. Barnes, William, Jr. Bossism. Lawsuits. New York. Republican Party. 1915. *382*

—. Clarkson, James S. New York City. Political Campaigns (presidential). Progressivism. Republican Party. 1901-04. *411*

—. Crawford, Coe Isaac. Progressivism. Republican Party. South Dakota. State Politics. 1912-14. *626*

—. Delegates, disputed. Republican Party (convention). Taft, William H. Texas. 1912. *459*

—. Elections (presidential). Illinois. Progressive Party. 1912-16. *545*

—. Georgia. Negroes. Political Attitudes. Progressive Party. Wilson, Woodrow. 1912. *568*

—. Grigsby, Melvin. Rough Riders. Spanish-American War. Torrey, Jay L. Wood, Leonard. 1898. *539*

—. LaFollette, Robert Marion, Sr. Presidential nomination. Republican Party. 1910-12. *537*

—. Oklahoma. Progressive Party. Statehood. 1900-12. *651*

Roraback, J. Henry. Apportionment. Brayton, Charles R. Connecticut. Political machines. Rhode Island. 1818-1937. *393*

Ross, Edmund. Attitudes. Impeachment. Johnson, Andrew. Letters. Republican Party. 1867-68. *374*

Rough Riders. Grigsby, Melvin. Roosevelt, Theodore. Spanish-American War. Torrey, Jay L. Wood, Leonard. 1898. *539*

Rousseau, Jean Jacques. *Federalist* No. 10. General will (concept), obsolescence of. Interests, balance of. Madison, James. 1787. *169*

Rural-urban alliance. Democratic Party (Bourbons). Francis, David R. Missouri. 1894-96. *597*

Rush, Benjamin (political thought). Federalism. Jeffersonianism. Republican utopia. 1776-1800. *248*

Russell, Daniel L. Elections (gubernatorial). Negroes. North Carolina. Republican Party. 1896. *412*

Russell, Richard B. Democratic Party. Georgia. Political Campaigns (presidential nomination). Press. 1952. *723*

—. Democratic Party. New Deal. Primaries (senatorial). Talmadge, Eugene. 1936. *759*

S

Sabath, Adolph Joachim (biography). House of Representatives. Illinois (Chicago). Legislation. 1920-52. *707*

Sacramento Union (newspaper). California. Chinese Americans. Immigration (restrictions). 1850-82. *25*

Sage, Ebenezer. Democratic-Republican Party. New York (Long Island). 1812-34. *207*

Salmagundi (periodical). Cartoons and Caricatures. Federalists. Irving, Washington. New York. 1807. *142*

Sanders, George. Democratic Party. Douglas, Stephen A. Political Factions. Young America. 1850's. *174*

Sanford Commission. Democratic Party Mid-Term Conference. 1968-74. *903*

Satire. *Alabama State Journal* (newspaper). Poetry. Reconstruction. 1868. *611*

Scalawags. Carpetbaggers. House of Representatives. Negroes. Reconstruction. Republican Party. South. 1868-72. *510*

—. Louisiana. Negroes. Ray, John. Republican Party. ca 1836-88. *108*

—. Louisiana. Ostracism. Reconstruction. State Politics. Terrorism. 1866-78. *680*

—. North Carolina. Reconstruction. Republican Party. State legislatures. 1868-70. *674*

Schlesinger, Joseph. Democratic Party. Political ambition. Presidency. Senate. 1952-76. *988*

School integration. Anti-Communist Movements. Elections (gubernatorial). Shivers, Allan. Texas. Yarborough, Ralph. 1954. *730*

—. Byrd, Harry F. Chambers, Lenoir. Editors and Editing. Virginia. 1955-59. *955*

Scott, Nathan B. Elections (senatorial). Glasscock, William E. Political Factions. Republican Party. West Virginia. 1910. *675*

Scott, William. Elections (congressional). Rawlings, George. Smith, Howard W. Virginia. 1966. *864*

Seagull, Louis M. Bartley, Numan V. Graham, Hugh D. Political Parties (review article). South. 1944-70's. *83*

Seaton, William Winston. Antipartyism. District of Columbia. Gales, Joseph, Jr. Jackson, Andrew. *National Intelligencer.* Political Commentary. Republicanism. 1827-35. *265*

Secession. Civil War (antecedents). Elections. South. 1859-61. *560*

—. Civil War (antecedents). Fort Sumter (issue). Lincoln, Abraham. South. Union Party. 1860-61. *410*

Secrecy. Federal Government. Federalists. Political Attitudes. Publicity, importance of. 1800-12. *175*

Sectionalism. Abolition Movement. Brown, John. Harpers Ferry raid. North Carolina. State Politics. 1840-60. *220*

—. Democratic Party. Internal improvements. North Carolina. State Legislatures. Whig Party. 1836-60. *227*

—. House of Representatives (constituencies). Industrialization. Voting and Voting Behavior. 1890-1910. *15*

—. Negroes. South. 1830-1976. *130*

Senate *See also* Congress, House of Representatives.

—. Alabama. Elections. 1819-61. *329*

—. Antislavery Sentiments. Connecticut. Dixon, James. Episcopal Church, Protestant. Political Leadership. 1830-73. *158*

—. Barkley, Alben W. Democratic Party. Roosevelt, Franklin D. Taxation. 1944. *715*

—. Blaine, John J. Progressivism. Republican Party. Wisconsin. 1927-33. *578*

—. Byrd, Harry F. Democratic Party. Glass, Carter. Roosevelt, Franklin D. Virginia. 1938. *734*

—. Byrd, Harry F. Democratic Party. Patronage. Virginia. 1935-39. *745*

—. Cherry, U. S. G. Elections (senatorial). Factionalism. McMaster, William Henry. South Dakota. 1923-24. *667*

—. Civil War. Methodology. Radicals and non-Radicals, definition of. 1861-66. 1973. *385*

—. Clayton, John M. Domestic Policy. Foreign policy. Jackson, Andrew. Whig Party. 1833-36. *336*

—. Conflict and Conflict Resolution. Democratic Party. Partisanship. Realignment. Republican Party. Roll-call voting. 1925-73. *63*

—. Conservatism. Martin, Thomas S. Wilson, Woodrow. 1912-19. *488*

—. Cutting, Bronson M. Democratic Party. New Mexico. Political Campaigns. Roosevelt, Franklin D. 1934. *809*

—. Democratic Party. Elections. Indiana. Kern, John W. Political Leadership. Wilson, Woodrow. 1916. *601*

—. New York. Platt, Thomas C. Progressivism. Public policy. Republican Party. 1890-1910. 546

—. New York. Whig Party (Silver Grays). 1834-56. 331

—. North Carolina. Reconstruction. Republican Party. 1865-78. 580

—. Political factions. Texas. 1944-72. 99

—. Primaries, gubernatorial. Republican Party. South. 1960-77. 907

Statehood. Colorado. Mining. 1858-76. 652

—. Oklahoma. Progressive Party. Roosevelt, Theodore. 1900-12. 651

Statehood (opposition to). House of Representatives. Oregon. Republican Party. 1850's. 250

States. Delegate allocation rules. Democratic Party. Primaries, presidential. 1968-72. 924

States' rights. Clingman, Thomas Lanier. Democratic Party. North Carolina. Political reform. State Politics. Whig Party. 1840-60. 228

—. Congress. Democratic Party. Hunter, Robert M. T. Whig Party. 1837-41. 185

—. Democratic Party. Elections (senatorial). Texas. Wigfall, Louis T. 1859. 519

—. Ku Klux Klan bill (1871). Trumbull, Lyman. 1854-94. 417

Statistics. Index numbers. Political Parties (relative strength). 1968-72. 853

Status, high. Conservatism. Georgia (DeKalb County). Political Stratification. Republican Party. 1970. 956

Stephens, Alexander H. Democratic Party. Douglas, Stephen A. Political Conventions. South Carolina (Charleston). Vallandigham, Clement L. (letter). 1860. 447

Stevens, Thaddeus. Local politics. Pennsylvania (Lancaster). 1842-68. 216

Stevenson, Adlai E., II. Arvey, Jacob M. Democratic Party (Convention). Illinois (Chicago). Nominations for office. 1932-52. 706

Stevenson, Adlai E., II (letters). Elections (presidential). Lewis, Mort R. (reminiscences). 1952-63. 752

Stevenson, Adlai E. (1835-1914). Alabama. Democratic Party. Federal Elections Bill (1890). Political Campaigns. South. 1889-93. 621

—. Bryan, William Jennings. Delaware. Foreign Policy. Political Campaigns (presidential). 1900. 618

—. Bryan, William Jennings. Democratic Party. Imperialism. Philippines. Political Campaigns (presidential). 1900. 631

—. Bryan, William Jennings. Democratic Party. Political Campaigns (presidential). 1892-1900. 622

—. Cleveland, Grover. Democratic Party. Political Campaigns (presidential). 1888-92. 628

—. Cleveland, Grover (administrations). Political career. Vilas, William Freeman. 1884-92. 636

—. Democratic Party. 1876-1908. 627

—. Democratic Party. 1893-97. 632

—. Democratic Party. Political Campaigns (vice-presidential). Populism. South. 1892. 617

—. Democratic Party. Political Campaigns (vice-presidential). Virginia. 1892. 619

—. Democratic Party (unification of). Elections (presidential). 1896. 620

Stoddert, Benjamin. Navy, Secretary of. ca 1783-1812. 304

Stringer, Lawrence Beaumont. Democratic Party. Illinois. Political Campaigns (presidential). Progressives. 1910-12. 526

Students. Democratic Party. Illinois (Chicago). Law Enforcement. Political Conventions. Political Protest. 1856-1978. 926

Subtreasury, planned. Democratic Party. Farmers' Alliance. North Carolina. State Politics. Vance, Zebulon B. 1880-90. 388

Suburbs. Democratic Party. Pennsylvania (Bucks County). Republican Party. Whites. 1972. 921

Suffrage. California. Chinese. Elections. Reconstruction. 1867. 660

—. City Government. Missouri (St. Louis). Political Change. 1833-38. 293

—. Democratic Party. Elections. North Carolina. Reform. State Legislatures. Whig Party. 1848-54. 226

—. Freedmen. House of Representatives. Murray, George Washington. Republican Party. South Carolina. 1893-97. 443

—. Republican Party. Senter, DeWitt Clinton. Tennessee. 1869-70. 380

Sugar production. Elections (presidential, gubernatorial). Ethnicity. Louisiana. Slavery. Voting and Voting behavior. 1828-44. 201

Sumner, Charles. Brooks, Preston S. Civil War (antecedents). Congress. Republican Party. Violence. 1856. 193

Supreme Court. Congress. Political Reform. 1970's. 44

—. Conservatism. Constitutional law. Kansas. New Deal. Newspapers. 1934-35. 718

—. Democratic Party. NAACP. Negro Suffrage. Primaries. Smith v. Allwright (US, 1944). South. 1890's-1944. 740

—. Democratic Party. NAACP. Negro Suffrage. Primaries. Texas. 1927-45. 741

Swain, Martha H. Andersen, Kristi. Blumberg, Barbara. Fine, Sidney. Jeffries, John W. New Deal (review article). Roosevelt, Franklin D. 1933-39. 708

Swanwick, John. Democratic-Republicanism. Pennsylvania (Philadelphia). 1790-98. 133

Swedish Americans. Farmer-Labor Party. Minnesota. State politics. 1922-44. 518

T

Taft, Robert A. Primaries (presidential). Republican Party. South Dakota. 1952. 722

Taft, William H. Delegates, disputed. Republican Party (convention). Roosevelt, Theodore. Texas. 1912. 459

—. Elections (presidential). Foraker, Joseph B. Negroes. Republican Party. 1908. 471

Taft, William H. (administration). Alabama (Dothan). Civil Service. Clayton, Henry D. Patronage. Postal Service. Wilson, Woodrow (administration). 1900-13. 606

Talmadge, Eugene. Democratic Party. Georgia. New Deal. Roosevelt, Franklin D. 1926-38. 713

—. Democratic Party. New Deal. Primaries (senatorial). Russell, Richard B. 1936. 759

Tammany Hall. Croker, Richard. New York City. Political Corruption. 1886-1901. 511

Tariff of 1832. Calhoun, John C. Clay, Henry. Jackson, Andrew. 1828-32. 281

Taxation. Barkley, Alben W. Democratic Party. Roosevelt, Franklin D. Senate. 1944. 715

—. Bureaucracies. Economic Policy. Mellon, Andrew W. Treasury Department. 1918-32. 569

Taylor, John (of Caroline). McCoy, Drew. Political Economy. Shalhope, Robert E. 1790-1824. 1980. 221

Y

Z

AUTHOR INDEX